TRIUMPH AMIDST BLOODSHED

Civil War Soldiers' Spiritual Victories

A Topically Indexed Edition of

Incidents of the U.S. Christian Commission

Originally Published 1869

Craig L. Claybrook
&
John W. Reed, Editors

DEDICATION

TO THE CHRISTIAN
SOLDIERS AND SAILORS OF THE UNION

Entered according to Act of Congress,
in the year 1868, by
HORATIO GATES JONES,

Secretary of the Trustees of the U. S. Christian Commission,
In the Clerk's Office of the District Court of the United States,
for the Eastern District of Pennsylvania.

WHO, BY TOIL AND PIETY UNDER ARMS, IN
LOYALTY TO COUNTRY AND TO CHRIST, ENDING
OFTEN IN CHEERFUL DEATH, HAVE FURNISHED
THE INCIDENTS

WHICH ARE HERE GROUPED TOGETHER—IN JUST
PRAISE OF THE SURVIVING AND IN LOVING
MEMORY OF THE DEAD, THIS BOOK

Is
GRATEFULLY INSCRIBED.

LIPPINCOTT'S PRESS,
PHILADELPHIA.

FORWARD

During the early days of the American Civil War, an organization came into existence to minister to the needs of soldiers after the onslaught of battle. This group was an outgrowth of the Young Men's Christian Association (YMCA) and their leaders—primarily in Boston, New York, Baltimore, Philadelphia, and Chicago. The YMCA had been founded by George Williams in London, England on June 8, 1844 to provide healthy activities for young men in major cities. By 1851, YMCAs had been formed across Europe and North America. Many of the chapters were organized and managed by older men. As a result of the spiritual awakening in North America during the revivals of 1857 and 1858, a significant number of young and progressive business leaders dedicated themselves to the service of Jesus Christ. They revitalized the YMCAs.

The organization they formed to help the soldiers was named the United States Christian Commission. Its purpose was to render aid and comfort to the wounded and dying by ministering to their mental, emotional, physical, and spiritual needs. From 1862 to 1865, the U. S. Christian Commission raised money to send some five thousand ministers, Christian laymen and women to the various battlefields to serve the soldiers. They often arrived at the battlefields while the engagements were still in progress, thereby, taking shot and shell with the soldiers. They were usually called "delegates" rather than chaplains since the army had regularly commissioned chaplains. Some three hundred Christian Commission delegates were in attendance at the Gettysburg Battle.

Through the untiring efforts of the YMCA members, money was also raised to distribute food and purchase items that were not normally provided by the army, such as, articles of clothing and assorted comforts, Bibles and New Testaments, hymnals and books, periodicals and letter writing materials. The delegates often wrote letters for dying soldiers and made sure they were delivered to their families. They rented space in many cities for "Soldier's Rest" facilities. These were like the United Service Organization (USO) accommodations made available to soldiers of modern wars.

Some twelve members of the United States Christian Commission Women's Auxiliary were on board the ill-fated riverboat the *Sultana* when its boilers exploded at two o'clock in the morning of April 27, 1865. The *Sultana* was carrying Union soldiers to their homes. The women were ministering to the more than two thousand survivors of Confederate Prisons at Andersonville, Georgia and Cahaba, Alabama. The overloaded riverboat was in the middle of the flooded Mississippi River headed to Cairo, Illinois from Memphis, Tennessee. After the explosion, the wooden vessel immediately burst into flames. Many of the soldiers leaped into the river to escape the flames. A large number could not swim and were pulling each other underwater. A Christian Commission lady standing on the deck called down, urging them to cease struggling and to hold onto the ropes and chains hanging from the boat. The men calmed down. When they saw that the flames were about to engulf the lady, they begged her to leap into the water. She refused, saying, "I might lose my presence of mind and be the means of the death of some of you." With these words, she became a voluntary martyr to the men she had helped and remains a lasting symbol of the sacrificial spirit of the United States Christian Commission. (Source: Chester D. Berry, *Loss of the Sultana*, 10)

At the end of the Civil War, these five thousand delegates were asked to send specific incidents of their experiences to Reverend Edward P. Smith, Field Secretary of the U.S. Christian Commission. Some ten thousand handwritten accounts were received. These were reduced down to those in the original book and republished here with a topical index of the stories. Inasmuch as possible, the accounts are presented in their historical context throughout the progression of the war.

In 1869, the book *Incidents of the Christian Commission* was published to provide a representative record of the U.S. Christian Commission's work among soldiers during the Civil War. These eyewitness stories breathe the charged air of the battles and their aftermaths. In this revision, we have sought to provide a topical index of these accounts to make them accessible to writers, public speakers, preachers and all those who wish to experience the pathos and spiritual triumphs of those who fought and died to preserve the Union.

Since many of the soldiers in the accounts died, some may question our choice of the revision's title *TRIUMPH AMIDST BLOODSHED: Civil War Soldiers' Spiritual Victories*. But these Christian soldiers firmly believed they would go straight to Heaven and often urged others to join them there. They considered eternal life with God as the highest form of triumph. This was a reality to them and made dying easier and some even longed for it.

This thought is captured in the concluding account of this book from an address by Reverend Herrick Johnson, Pastor of the (N. S.) Presbyterian Church, in Pittsburg, Pennsylvania. He was a U.S. Christian Commission delegate about the time of the Wilderness Battle and his eloquence captures the heart of the

Christian soldier's hope of victory over death. He used a metaphor related to his experience of standing on the summit of a mountain in the Swiss Alps at sunset where he saw ". . . the bridge of golden sheen that stretched over hills and valleys, the lakes and dells from the far distant horizon to our very feet."

In the pastoral oratorical flourishes of the day, he continued, ". . . I have stood beside the dying soldier when it seemed as if a bridge of golden sheen were let down from heaven, a highway for the ransomed of the Lord. And that way, cast up of God, has glowed with the steps of the angels, which come to bear the soldier—who has made his last charge and fought his last battle—*home*. And up that shining path with angel convoy, the spirit has gone—away from the clang of arms and the din of strife and the groans of the wounded—away, away to the very gates of pearl, to the Peace like a river and to the Eternal Rest of God.

"*There* are the undying tokens and proof of the success of the United States Christian Commission. The Nation may point to its States won back from treason! The army may point to its battle flags wrung from the foe by vigor and valor and victory! Generals may point to their starred shoulders as proofs of undaunted heroism! Sanitary Agencies may roll up their peerless record of sublime beneficence!

"But *there*, up *there*, are the souls that are marching on—marching on! *There* are the trophies immortal that have been snatched from death! *There* are the unfading stars that have been set in Christ's diadem through the agency of this United States Christian Commission."

Craig L. Claybrook & John W. Reed, Editors
CivilWarStories.org

PREFACE OF THE ORIGINAL EDITION

This volume came into existence not because of the military forces arrayed against each other, the movements these armies executed, or the victories won. Rather, this book was created to memorialize the forces of Christianity, which developed and were exemplified amidst the carnage of battle and the more perilous tests of hospital and camp.

These religious forces were not brought about by the formation of the United States Christian Commission. They came into the army from the Christian homes of its citizen soldiery. The Commission was borne out of these homes. The soldiers' need for help caused the formation of this group and it immediately became their helper in life-threatening circumstances and a recorder of events.

The officers of the Commission numbered five thousand, the majority of whom were ministers of the Gospel of various denominations. They traveled to the mission field, laden with good cheer and tokens of love for the soldiers. This spirit of compassion enabled them to demonstrate the deepest sympathy for the soldiers in times of extreme pain and suffering. They returned home to their firesides with fresh truthful stories of camp life, having witnessed scenes of faith and heroism, conversion to new life, and renewed dedication to Christ. These incidents occurred in chapel tents, hospital wards, and on bloody battlefields.

These delegates heard hundreds of manly testimonies for truth. They took many messages from the lips of dying men and recorded them, so as not to be lost to the nation, the Christian church, or to history. They removed the possibility of oral tradition diluting the import of what these soldiers did and said. Accordingly, incidents were placed in a permanent record by Home Secretary, Reverend Lemuel Moss in his *Annuls of the United States Christian Commission.* He also instructed Field Secretary, Reverend Edward P. Smith "to prepare a volume of such Incidents as may be regarded by him as fully authentic and the most valuable of those, which have occurred during the work of the Commission."

Having received these instructions, Reverend Smith found himself completely absorbed in another labor growing out of the war. Unexpected difficulties in gathering and authenticating so many incidents caused delay in the preparation of the original volume. In most of these incidents, the names of the authors are given, unless the person mentioned belonged to some other relief organization or served in the army for some other purpose. All others are delegates of the Christian Commission. When an incident is credited to a delegate who is not named, the name of the person receiving it from the delegate is given.

A few incidents were taken from the religious press and generally bear the names of their authors. A few exceptions to this rule do occur but the periodical in which they originally appeared is offered as evidence of their authenticity.

Out of the 10,000-plus incidents that were submitted, more than 500-plus incidents were selected. They were chosen because they represented the widest variety of character in their subjects and the time and place of their occurrence.

Every attempt has been made to avoid the peril of sameness but, it seems, the more perfect each sketch may be in and of itself, the greater the peril. We have attempted to group the incidents along the lines of army operations in both time and place. If a story takes place on a given day, it becomes a part of army history for that day, serving as an illustration in this one man of what may have transpired with hundreds of others. It also lends to the historical and topographical interest of certain readers.

The briefest sketch of army movements and the results of great battles provide a historical timeline for the reader. We have borrowed freely from Mr. Horace Greeley and his *American Conflict* in this regard.

When an author has furnished a story out of his own personal experience, it seemed best that he should speak in third person to secure authenticity. In this way, he could speak of himself in the same way he could speak of others.

If this book possesses excellence, it can be attributed as follows: To the delegates and members of the Commission who have responded so kindly and generously to requests for incidents they personally observed; to the watchful care of the Committee of Publication who poured over every chapter; to Charles Demond, Esquire, of Boston, who has patiently and skillfully proofread all these pages; and to Reverend John Irving Forbes, especially, who by his long and intimate work with the Christian Commission at the Philadelphia office was eminently qualified to help with this project. In personal interviews with many delegates throughout the country, he has taken from their lips many of the gems included in this collection. By his skill, patience, and diligence, amid other duties, he has performed most of the mechanical and intellectual labor in bringing this volume to press.

When strong men are stirred to action or if youth are to be incited to deeds of valor and virtue, one thing is sure. No portion of human history is more frequently quoted than the words borne out of the smoke of battle from the lips of men who were willing to die for strongly-held principles. Most of the incidents gathered here relate to memorable scenes in which men say and do that which is worthy of mention and imitation. Our fond hope is that the words of this book may not be void of inspiration to all who read them and that these incidents may be of special service to those who teach and help others to be truly noble.

EDWARD P. SMITH
Rooms of the American Missionary Association,
New York, October 1868

CONTENTS

ILLUSTRATIONS

ALPHABETIZED INDEX OF THE ACCOUNTS

CHAPTER I
THE EASTERN ARMIES

UNTIL THE RETREAT FROM THE PENINSULA
April 1861–July 1862

Profound Effects of Simple Faith

The Fulton Street Prayer Meeting in New York City became the center of a deep spiritual interest for the soldiers. This meeting, along with the numerous meetings like it throughout the land, had a noticeable influence in causing the men to feel the need for a Christian ministry such as the Commission. The *Sunday School Times*, of June 29, 1861 gives the report of a story told at the Fulton Street meeting a few days before. A speaker rose and told this story:

A drummer-boy traveled by ship from Brooklyn to Fortress Monroe, Virginia. He was a Sunday school scholar. One evening, having been overcome with fatigue, he had lain down upon the deck and fallen asleep. The dew was falling. The Colonel came along, shook him by the shoulder and told him he would take cold if he did not go below. As he was getting up, his Bible fell out of his pocket. He picked it up, replaced it, and went below to prepare himself for bed. When all ready, he knelt down beside his bed—with many loud-talking men standing around. Putting his hands together in the attitude of prayer, he poured out his heart silently to God. He never heeded the noise around him. In a moment, all the noise was hushed. The company, awed by the conduct of a boy, reverently stood silent until he had finished.

After this moving account had been given, another attendee stated that this praying drummer-boy had been killed in a late battle and that the news had just reached his father. A mood of tearful sympathy instantly passed through the meeting. A few days later at the meeting, someone stated that the little boy had prayed every day up to the time that he was killed. He was also constantly reading his Bible, as he could snatch the opportunity. So anxious was he to read his Bible, that he was known to rise occasionally in the night to do so.

Cries for Mercy

General McDowell's army began its advance into Virginia on Tuesday, July 16, 1861. On Sunday, July 21st, the first battle of "Bull Run" was fought and the Union forces then retreated to Washington. *The Sunday School Times* of August 24, 1861, gives this account of a scene in that battle, which was related in the Fulton Street Prayer Meeting:

A clergyman stated that a soldier told him that, immediately after the first fire, many Union soldiers were killed and wounded. He heard a cry, which could only come from a man on the borders of eternity: "God, have mercy on my soul." The cry soon became contagious and he himself, though fighting with all his might, joined in repeating the words, "God, have mercy on my soul." The soldier stated that he was not a pious man yet the impression received from that cry on the battlefield had never left him. For several nights after his return to New York City, he had not been able to sleep. Through all the silent hours, he would hear that continual cry, made as none but the dying could make it: "God, have mercy on my soul."

The Effects of Wife's Prayer for Soldier Husband

Ms. E. N. Harris, of Philadelphia, visited the hospitals in Washington, Georgetown, and Alexandria, immediately after the first battle of Bull Run, Virginia, July 21, 1861. She wrote a letter to Reverend Dr. Taylor, Pastor of a Reformed Protestant (Dutch) Church in Philadelphia. Her letter, now contained in *Annals, U. S. Christian Commission*, 90-92, describes this incident:

One soldier's placid expression told of great peace. I remarked, "You have been shielded in the day of battle—perhaps in answer to a mother's prayers."

He replied, "Yes, to those prayers of a sainted mother but especially to those of a praying wife. I just received a letter in which she wrote, 'I spent all day Sunday in prayer for you,' not knowing I was in battle. But her Heavenly Father and my Heavenly Father knew it and that was enough. I went into the battle with prayer and returned with thanksgiving for a spared life."

I was about to move on to my next needy soldier when the awkward position of his arm caught my attention. "Are you wounded in the arm?" I asked.

"Yes."

"I hope not seriously."

"Yes, it was amputated at the elbow before I left the field."

Wholly unprepared for such an announcement, my feelings overpowered me. He soothingly said,

"It is only my left arm. That is not much to give my country. It might have been my life."

Memory of Home at Time of Death

One handsome youth, whose bright, restless eye and flushed cheek told of great suffering, grasped my hand and gently pulled me toward him. I knelt beside him and said, "My dear boy, what can I do for you? Shall I talk to you of Jesus?"

"Oh yes," he said, "I am used to that. I have loved Him for two years, but not near enough, and now He is going to take me home."

"You are very young. Do you have a mother?"

"Oh, yes," he replied, as tears filled his eyes.

"It must have been a great trial to give you to your country."

"Yes, it was. When I first mentioned it, she would not listen to me but we both prayed over it and, at last, she consented. She said, 'My country deserves this sacrifice. I gave you to God at your birth and this is His cause.'"

As I fanned the dear boy, brushing back the hair from his forehead, he fell asleep. When I withdrew my hand, it startled him and he exclaimed, "Oh, I dreamed that was Annie's hand. Won't you put it on my head again?"

"Who is Annie?"

"My twin sister. We have both turned seventeen since I left home."

This dear youth is now with the Savior. He died from his wounds the next day. (Ms. E. N. Harris)

Mother's Appeal Convicts Son

General McClellan was called from Western Virginia to Washington immediately following the first battle of Bull Run, July 21, 1861, to replace General McDowell. McClellan's previous command devolved to General Rosecrans. In September, severe skirmishes took place at Cheat Mountain, Virginia (now West Virginia). *The New York Advocate and Journal* related an incident from that battle:

The night before the battle, a soldier received a letter from his mother, which he opened and began to read. He had read but a few lines when a flood of tears baptized the letter and prevented him from reading further. He handed it to a friend and requested that he read it for him, which he did. The friend had his own heart melted by the tender appeals of that mother to her boy—to come to Christ. The last words of the letter were, "O my son! My son! Will you not take your mother's Savior for your Savior?"

He went into the battle and was killed. In the morning, as they gathered the dead, he was found with one hand firmly grasping the letter now baptized in his own heart's blood and his tears.

Soldiers' Unique Prayer Meeting Room

Shortly after its organization in November 1861, members of the Christian Commission visited Washington D.C. to survey the yet scarcely attempted work. Passing near Fort Albany, which was located about a mile from Long Bridge in Virginia, one of the delegates asked a soldier of the 14th Massachusetts Regiment, "Do you have any praying men in the regiment?"

"Oh, yes, a great many," he answered.

And do you ever meet for prayer?"

"Every day."

"Where do you meet?"

"Just come here."

The party went inside the new and beautiful fort, which the regiment had been building.

"I can see no place for prayer," said one.

"Look down there," said the soldier, raising a trap door as he spoke.

"What is down there?" for it was like looking into darkness itself.

"That's the bomb-proof shelter and, down there, is the place where we hold our daily prayer meetings."

"That's going down to get up, isn't it?" replied the questioner.

Finding Credibility

The army defending Washington remained inactive during the autumn and winter of 1861. However, in April 1862, it began the advance upon Richmond by the way of the Peninsula. A month's delay before moving on Yorktown provided the opportunity for several skirmishes but then sickness set in. By the time the army moved from Yorktown, a call for Christian benevolence and patriotism sounded forth throughout the North—a call that could no longer be refused. Shortly afterward, the long-delayed messengers of the Christian Commission entered the scene. Because the organization was yet unknown, the delegates were met, at first, with a less than enthusiastic reception. Reverend George J. Mingins, Pastor of (O. S.) Presbyterian Church, Huntington Valley, Pennsylvania, was one of the first seven delegates sent out from Philadelphia to Fortress Monroe and Yorktown in May 1862. In a public address, he gave a graphic account of the advent at Old Point Comfort:

I remember my introduction to the Medical Director at Fortress Monroe. At the time, we had no documents of authorization. In Baltimore, we had worked hard to obtain a pass to the Fortress but, the moment we set foot on land, we were marched like a file of Indians to the Provost-Marshal's office. Before they would permit us to open our mouths, they made us take the oath of allegiance. After we had taken the oath, we found we could not go anywhere but what were bumping up against a sentry at almost every corner. Every hundred or thousand yards, we were asked for our passes. So we went back to the Provost-Marshal and told him, "We can't go anywhere."

He replied, "I know it."

We said, "We wanted to see the Medical Director and tried to get into the Fortress and couldn't."

"I know it."

"But, sir, can't you give us a pass by which we may obtain an interview with the Director?"

"Who are you?" he asked.

"We are delegates of the United States Christian Commission."

He asked, "What's that?"

As the war progressed, I doubt whether you could find a squad of soldiers who would have needed to ask that question but, at last, he gave us a pass and we went into the Fortress. We felt very strange but finally attained an interview with the Director. As we stood in his office, he looked up and, in a brusque manner, said, "Well, gentlemen, what can I do for you?"

One of us became spokesman. I did not. I was afraid. I had had enough of their intimidation tactics already. From that day to this, I have had a healthy fear of a military man, sitting in an office with a quill behind his ear instead of a sword in his hand. I can face him with a sword but I cannot bear him with a quill. So an Episcopalian minister stepped forward and began to tell him that we were delegates of the Christian Commission. I do not know whether he thought that he would astonish the Director but, I can safely say, he did not.

"What's that?" he asked.

We told him what it was and he replied, "Gentlemen! Gentlemen! What do you want down here?"

Then this gentleman gave him a pretty good idea of what we wanted. He rose, put down his pen, and said, "So, gentlemen, you have come down here to see what you can do for the sick and wounded?"

"Precisely so," I ventured to remark.

He said, "Aye. Well, who are you in the first place?"

We told him that we were four clergymen and three laymen. When we talked of "clergymen," I noticed a smile lurking round the corners of his mouth when he said, "And you want to do something?

We said, "Yes."

"Then I will give you work in ten minutes. There are three hundred sick and wounded men lying on board one of the transports at the wharf. I want three men to accompany them to New York, Philadelphia or Baltimore—I don't know where they are going. You will get your orders when you are on board. Will you go?"

Three of us volunteered at once. He said, "Gentlemen, do you know what you are going to do? You are not going to preach, I remind you. I tell you what—I want you as nurses."

He looked into their eyes but they never flinched. Two of them were "clergymen." When they were gone, he gave us work also.

"But, mark me, gentlemen," he said, "I want men who will wash wounds, who will scrub floors, if necessary—in fact, who will perform the duties of a hired nurse. Then, after that, I have no objections if you put into practice any higher mission you may have."

We separated and went to our work. A few days later, the same Director sent for us but, this time deference was his manner, a kinder tone in his voice. He sent us to the three thousand wounded and sick at Yorktown. When we met him two or three weeks afterward, we again found that the young Christian Commission had conquered a way to his heart.

Breaking through Opposition

In spite of obstacles, the work of the Christian Commission began and prospered. The following story comes from Reverend Mr. George J. Mingins, Pastor of (O. S.) Presbyterian Church, Huntington Valley, Pennsylvania. This incident is taken from an address at the Washington Anniversary of the Christian Commission, February 2, 1864. It will show that the Commission gained favor with the men in the ranks, for whom it was especially intended.

The scene is at Yorktown, the site of the siege from April 5th to May 4, 1962, and the subject is an Irishman:

Well, this was a one very tough Irishman, I assure you. It was at a time when a great many were sick at Yorktown. These men had marched and dug until they were completely broken down. A great many of them had no clean shirts. I had received a large supply of shirts and was going through the tent, giving them to the poor fellows when I came to this Irishman.

"My dear friend," I said, "how are you? You seem to be an old man."

In a thick Irish brogue, he replied, "Sure—and I am an old man, sir."

"Well, how come you are here in the army, as old as you are?"

"Oh, sir, I'm not only an old man but an old soldier, too, I'd have you to know." He had been twenty years in the British service in the East Indies and had fought America's foes in Mexico.

"Yes, sir," he continued, "I'm old and I know it. But I'm not too old to shoulder a musket and hit a rap for the old flag yet."

"You're a brave fellow," I said, as I held out a shirt and a pair of drawers, "and I've brought these things to make you comfortable." He looked at me and said, "Is them things for…"

"Yes, I want to give them to you to wear."

"Well, I don't want them."

"But you do want them."

"Well, I don't," he said, as I urged him again. He looked at me and then at the goods and said somewhat sharply, "Never mind, sir. I don't want them and, I tell you, I won't have them."

"Why?"

"Sure," he said, "do you take me for an object of charity?"

This presented a kind of dilemma for me. I looked squarely at him and said, "No, sir. I do not take you for an object of charity and I don't want you to look on me as a dispenser of charity, for I am not."

"Well, what are you then?"

"I am a delegate of the United States Christian Commission, bearing the thank offerings of mothers and wives and sisters to you brave defenders of the Stars and Stripes." And I thought, surely, after such a speech as that, I would get hold of the old fellow's heart.

But he looked at me and said, *"Anyhow, I won't have them."*

I felt really hurt. I did not like it at all but I have told you, he was an Irishman and I happened to be a Scotchman. I was determined not to be conquered. I meant to try further and, when a Scotchman means to try something, he will come very near to doing it.

I didn't talk any further at the time but determined to prove, by my acts, that I had come down to do good to this old man. So day after day, I went about my work, nursing, giving medicines, cleaning up the tent—doing anything and everything I could.

Ministry of Helps

One day, as I went in, a soldier said, "There's good news today, Chaplain," as the soldiers almost uniformly called the Christian Commission delegates, "Chaplains."

"Ah, good, what is it?"

"Paymaster's come."

"Well, that is good news."

"Yes, but not to me, Chaplain."

"How is that?"

"I've not got my descriptive list and, if a fellow's not got that, the Paymaster may come and go and he's none the better off for it."

"Well, why don't you get it?"

"I can't write, Chaplain. I've got chronic rheumatism."

"Shall I write for you?"

"If only you would, Chaplain."

I hauled out paper and pencil, asked the number of his regiment, name of his captain, company, etc. I then sent a simple request that the descriptive list might be remitted to that point. When I had done this, I found a good many who wanted their lists written up and I went on writing lists until I came to the cot next to the old Irishman's. It was occupied by another Irishman and I asked him if he had his descriptive list.

"No."

"Shall I write to your captain for it?"

"As you please," he said and I began to write.

I noticed the old Irishman stretching over to hear. Now and then, I spoke a word intended for him, though I pretended not to notice him. After I had written the request, I asked the young man if I should read it to him aloud. "As you please, sir" and I read him the simple note.

When I had finished, the old Irishman exclaimed, "Upon my soul, sir, you wrote the nicest letter for a descriptive list that I ever heard in my life for sure and a man would think you'd been a soldier all your days, you do write so nice a letter."

I turned round and asked, "Have you got yours?"

"And I haven't, sir."

"Do you want it?"

"And to be sure, I do," he said, flaring up, "And that's a fair question to ask a man—if he wants his descriptive list, if he wants his pay to buy some delicacies to send home to the old woman and the children. I do want it and, if you'll lend us the stroke of your pen, Chaplain, you'll oblige us."

I sat down and wrote the letter and, when I had finished, I said, "Now, boys, give me your letters and I'll have them postpaid and sent for you."
(George J. Mingins)

Dying Thoughts of Mother

When I returned, sad work awaited me. One of Massachusetts' sons lay in the tent, dying. I spoke to the dying boy of his mother, of Jesus, of home, of heaven. I believe it to be a great characteristic of the American heart to cling to home and mother. I remember passing over a battlefield and seeing a man in the throes of dying. His mind was wandering. His spirit was no longer on that bloody field. It was at his home far away. A smile passed over his face—a smile, oh, of such sweetness, and looking up he said, "O mother! Mother! I'm so glad you have come."

And it seemed as if she were there at his side. A little later, he said again, "Mother, it's cold, it's so cold. Won't you pull the blanket over me?"

I stooped down and pulled the poor fellow's ragged blanket closer to his shivering form. And he smiled again and said, "That will do, mother, that will do."

And turning over, he passed sweetly into rest and was borne up to the presence of God on the wings of a pious mother's prayers.
(George J. Mingins)

Humility Conquers Pride

Back to the case in the tent: After I had done all I could for the dying man, I shook his hand in farewell. As I turned to leave the tent, who should meet me at the door but the old Irishman for whom I had written the description list! He looked very strange. Something was the matter with him. He was scratching his head, pulling at his beard, and acting very strangely but I did not take much notice of him, as I had been so solemnly engaged.

He came up to me and, clasping my hands, said, "By my soul, sir, you're no humbug, anyhow."

"What do you mean?" I asked.

"Oh," he said, "haven't I watched you every day as you've been going through the tents, caring for the boys? And you've been like a mother to every one of them. Thanks to you, Chaplain, thanks to you, and may God bless you," he repeated, as he again wrung my hand. "And," he said," you do all this for nothing. The boys have been telling me about you."

"Oh," I said, "that's a mistake."

"Well, now, how's that? They've been telling me you were a Presbyterian minister and that you came away from your home down here for the love you had for the boys. But you don't do it for nothing, eh? Who then pays you—the Government?"

"No. If it had to pay me, it would take a great deal more money than it can spare."

"Well, does the Christian Commission pay you?"

"No."

"Well, then, if the Government doesn't pay you, nor the Commission, then who does pay you?"

I looked the man straight in the eyes and said, "That honest, hearty grasp of the hand, and that hearty 'God bless you,' are ample reward for all that I have done for you. My brave fellow, remember that you have suffered and sacrificed for me and I couldn't do less for you now."

He was broken down. He bowed his head and wept and then taking me by the hand again, he said, "Sure, and if that's the pay you take, why then, *God bless you! God bless you!* You'll be rich of the coin of my heart all your days." And then, after pausing a few minutes, he added, *"And now, Chaplain, if you'll just give me the shirt and the drawers, I'll wear them till there's not a thread of them left."*

(George J. Mingins)

Soldier's Thoughts of Mother

Reverend E. P. Goodwin, Pastor of the Congregational Church, Columbus, Ohio, narrates a story related to him by Inspector Reed of the U. S. Sanitary Commission in the Western Department. This incident beautifully illustrates the law or characteristic of "love for mother" previously described by Reverend Mr. Mingins:

At Elizabeth, Kentucky, a number of wounded, literally, were lying in the mud and utterly without care. The Sanitary Commission sent an agent with beds, clothing, and other needed items. Among the neglected men, a sick youth was entirely unconscious of the care being given him. The next morning, when the surgeon made his rounds, he found the sufferer very much brightened up. He spoke to him pleasantly. The little fellow was entirely bewildered. He had looked around and found clean sheets and bedding, as well as something to read at the head of his cot. A little later, after rubbing his eyes and getting the mist away, he faintly spoke, "Oh, yes. I guess I'm better. Somehow it seems as if mother had been here."

Finding Christ through the Hymn Rock of Ages

Reverend George Bringhurst, Rector of All Saints' Protestant Episcopal Church, Moyamensing, of Philadelphia, still retains a precious memorial of the war, the simple papers which designate him the first delegate of the Christian Commission. He narrates this incident, which tells of his first trip to the army:

In so many instances, the precious Gospel was brought to the soldiers through the strains of music set to Psalms and Hymns? In camp and hospital, on the march and in the field, the sweet songs of Zion wooed many a prodigal back to the Father's loving embrace. None could have possibly been more effective than that familiar hymn, "Rock of Ages." We heard it sung for the first time in the army on the beach at Fortress Monroe by some Delegates of the Christian Commission, just beneath the "Lincoln Gun." Its grateful truth, borne by the winds, fell upon the ear of a soldier on the parapet. Not only this but it touched his heart and, in time, led him to build on the "Rock of Ages."

Again, we heard the same hymn at Yorktown, sung by some of the same delegates. After its singing, as we were returning to our quarters, one of the delegates was overtaken by a soldier, who belonged to the "Lost Children," the name of a New York Regiment— *"Enfans Perdus."* He asked, "Won't you please tell me how I may be built on the 'Rock' you sang about? I was thinking of it while on guard the other day."

He briefly told us his story: "I am from New York City and I received my mother's dying blessing. Before she breathed her last, she sang this hymn, and said, 'George, my son, I would not feel so badly about your enlisting if you were only built upon that 'Rock.'"

These sacred memories were revived by the singing of the hymn and, as the delegate and soldier knelt on the dusty roadside beneath the stars, the wanderer lost his weariness and his thirst for sin in the shadow of the "Rock of Ages."

The story continues eighteen months later. Going to Fortress Monroe, Reverend Bringhurst traveled on a boat that had, as part of her passengers, a happy company of the Signal Corps. This delegate conversed and sang and prayed together with them. The name of a New York Regiment was *"Enfans Perdus."* He related to them the story of one of their comrades who was converted to Christ through hearing the singing of "Rock of Ages," while stationed on the parapet at Fortress Monroe. The delegate later retired to his state room.

Soon thereafter, a gentle tap called him to the door where he found a tall lieutenant, full of grace, who, with tears streaming down his face, said, "O sir, I could not let you go to bed tonight until I had told you what you have done. As I sat, with my head leaning against a spar, I listened to your words and to that hymn. You brought back memories of my dead mother with all her prayers and love. I have been a wanderer until this night and now, by God's grace, I want to hide myself in that 'Rock of Ages.'"

Companionship Found through the New Testament

Reverend Mr. Bringhurst visited the Mill Creek Hospital, near Fortress Monroe, where this incident occurred:

Because of the awful nature of his disease, a dying soldier was placed in a tent far away from his comrades. When I asked if he was lonely, he placed his hand upon his New Testament and replied, "My companion is here. How can I be lonely?" The same night, he passed away into the country wherein there shall be neither sickness nor loneliness anymore."

Reverend Dr. Neale's translation of Bernard's *Celestial Country* reads:

> "I know not, oh, I know not
>   What social joys are there;
> What pure, unfading glory;
>   What light beyond compare.
> O Garden free from sorrow!
>   O Plains that fear no strife!

O princely Bowers, all blooming!
O Realm and Home of life!"

(George Bringhurst)

Identifying with the Prodigal Son

This incident occurred when Reverend Mr. George Bringhurst visited the Mill Creek Hospital, near Fortress Monroe:

One Sunday afternoon, I was reading the fifteenth chapter of St. Luke's Gospel in a ward of the hospital. When I came to the words, "I will arise and go to my father," a soldier near me suddenly cried out, "That's me. That's me."

Going to his side, I found him very anxious. I pointed him to the Father and very soon he gave his heart to Jesus.

Two years later, he laid down his life at Fredericksburg. His path, meanwhile, had been like that of the just, "shining more and more unto the perfect day." (George Bringhurst)

Historical Context:

The pursuit of Confederate forces, retreating from the Siege of Yorktown, which began on April 5, 1862, was prompt and energetic. On May 4th, the place was evacuated. On the next day, Hooker, Kearny, and Hancock fought the battle of Williamsburg. The Union loss was nearly 2,000 in killed and wounded, while nearly 800 severely wounded Confederates were left in the hastily evacuated defenses of Fort Magruder. The work of death had begun in earnest.

Ever Mindful of Mother

Several days after the battle, a soldier hurriedly came to a chaplain's tent with an urgent message. He said, "Chaplain, one of our boys is badly wounded and wants to see you right away."

The Chaplain followed the soldier and later wrote that he was taken to a cot on which lay a noble young man. He was pale and blood-stained from a terrible wound above the temple. He saw in a glance that the soldier had but a short time to live. Taking his hand, he said, "Well, my brother, what can I do for you?"

The poor, dying soldier looked up in the chaplain's face and, placing his finger where his hair was stained with blood, said, "Chaplain, cut a big lock from here for mother—mind, Chaplain, for mother!"

The chaplain hesitated to do it. So the soldier said, "Chaplain, don't be afraid to disfigure my hair. It's for mother and nobody will come to see me in the dead-house tomorrow." I did as he requested me.

"Now, Chaplain," said the dying man, "I want you to kneel down by me and *return thanks* to God."

"For what?" I asked.

"For giving me such a mother. O Chaplain, she is a good mother. And thank God that, by His grace, I am a Christian. Oh, what would I do now if I wasn't a Christian? 'I know that my Redeemer liveth.' I know that His finished work has saved me. And, Chaplain, thank God for giving me dying grace. He has made this dying bed 'feel soft as downy pillows are.' Thank Him for the promised home in glory. I'll soon be there—where there is no war, nor sorrow, nor desolation, nor death—where I'll see Jesus and be 'forever with the Lord.'"

I knelt by the dying man and thanked God for the blessings He had bestowed upon him—the blessings of a good mother, a Christian hope, and dying grace. Shortly after the prayer, he said,

"Good-bye, Chaplain. If you ever see mother, tell her it was all well."

Acknowledging Life-saving Kindness

In an address to a graduating class of Berkshire Medical College, Pittsfield, Massachusetts, Dr. Greene told this story:

Let me relate one incident that occurred while I was on the Peninsula during the bloody campaign of last summer. At the Battle of Williamsburg in Virginia, May 4, 1862, a soldier lay in the edge of the forest that surrounded the field. He had been struck by a bit of shell, which severed the brachial artery. He fell just as a surgeon was riding rapidly toward the front to get orders for establishing a hospital at a certain point. Faint from the profuse hemorrhage, the poor fellow had just enough strength to raise his bleeding arm and say, "Doctor, please." The surgeon dismounted, rapidly ligated the vessel, applied a compress and bandage, and administered a cordial. As he turned to go away the man asked, "Doctor, what is your name?"

"No matter," said the surgeon, and leaping on his horse, dashed away.

"But, Doctor," said the wounded man, "I want to tell my wife and children *who saved me.*"

Historical Context:

The march to Richmond was a slow one. Rain fell frequently and the roads were horrible. As a result, General McClellan's headquarters did not reach

White House Landing, Virginia until May 16, 1862, nor did they reach Cold Harbor until the 22nd. The first collision between the hostile armies occurred May 24th, near New Bridge. On the 27th, the battle of Hanover Court House was fought by Fitz John Porter and, on the last day of the month, the battle at Fair Oaks or Seven Pines occurred.

General Lee had now succeeded to the chief command of the Confederate forces in Virginia. The month of June had almost passed and very little seemed to have been done. The sluggish Chickahominy, with its miry swamp bottom, was sending pestilence through the Union ranks. The Confederate commander determined to strike a decisive blow. The battles of Mechanicsville and Gaines' Mills followed each other in quick succession on June 26th and 27th. General McClellan decided to retreat. Battles at White Oak Swamp and Glendale closed the month. The struggle of Malvern Hills on July 1, 1862 brought about the complete routing of the Confederates but the Union Army then retreated to Harrison's Bar.

Washing Feet

The delegates of the Christian Commission were as busy as possible with the limited means at their disposal throughout these terrible scenes. Mr. Charles Demond, of Boston and one of the original members of the Commission, paid attention to its extensive and varied interests in New England. The following story is an extract from his Williams College Alumni Address, 24, 25:

A delegate found sixty-five men, sick and wounded, lying on the second floor of a barn, just under the roof. The Virginia sun was pouring July heat upon the building, a few feet above their heads. They were suffering badly. The delegate gave them some delicacies and then asked the soldier-nurse to wash their hands and feet.

"I did not enlist to wash men's feet," came the reply.

"Then bring me the water and I will do it." The nurse brought the water and the gentleman proceeded to wash the heads and hands and feet of the sixty-five suffering men.

Remembering Loved Ones in Death

Ms. E. N. Harris received the freely-given supplies from the Christian Commission stores during the summer campaign of 1862. Writing from near Savage's Station on June 22nd, she offers the following story:

Passing a forlorn-looking house, we were told by a sentinel that a young officer from a Maine regiment, Lieutenant Colonel William S. Heath, lay within and was very sick. In a corner, we found him lying on a stretcher. This handsome young man was still struggling with the last Confederate soldier he had fought. His mind wandered and, as we approached him, he exclaimed, "Is it not cruel to keep me here, when my mother and sister whom I have not seen for a year, are in the next room? They might let me go in."

Once for only a moment, he seemed to have a glimpse of his real condition. From his finger, he drew two rings, placed there by a loving mother and sister. He handed them to an attendant, saying, "Carry them home." A moment later, he was amid battle scenes, calling out, "Deploy to the left." "Keep out of that ambuscade." "Now, go, my braves, double quick, and strike for your flag." "On, on," and he threw up his arms as if cheering them on. "You'll win the day," he said.

His very last words were about his men. A graduate of Waterville College, some twenty of his company were from the same institution. This, in some measure, accounted for his deep interest in his soldiers. He was an only son and the very thought almost choked us as we whispered a few sentences of God's Word into his ear. He looked up, smiling thankfully but his manner gave no indication of understanding the sacred words.

Brothers Comforting Each Other in Death

The battle at Gaines' Mills was the third in a series known as the Seven Days Battles or the Peninsula Campaign. This battle, which took place on June 27, 1862, is recognized as what saved Richmond for the Confederacy from McClellan. Here is a memorial of Gaines' Mills:

Two wounded brothers were brought to Savage's Station and laid at the foot of a tree. When found by a friend, their arms were entwined about each other and, having been severely wounded, they were trying to comfort the other. They talked of loved ones at home, of longing to see their mother, of the service in which they had been engaged, and their love of country. They prayed for each other, for their friends far away, and especially that mother might be comforted. After a little while, the younger went up home. The survivor, blind from a shot in the face, did not know but continued to speak encouraging words to him. After receiving no response, in a pleased, gentle way, he said, "Poor little Rob's asleep."

After a few minutes more, he too slept—and awoke with his brother.
(Ms. E. N. Harris)

Gratitude Shown even in Death

During the Seven Days Battles or the Peninsula Campaign of late June 1862, the wounded were conveyed to White House Landing, Virginia until that place was evacuated. Reverend Charles H. Corey, Pastor of Baptist Church, Seabrook, New Hampshire, served as a delegate here and relates this story:

I assisted in taking a young man on board one of the hospital steamers at White House Landing. He was scarcely nineteen years old. I saw that he was dying and watched him breathing his last. As I bathed his hands, the soldier reached up, threw his arms round my neck, and drew my face down close to his own. This simple act conveyed more gratitude and affection than any words could ever have told. All that could be known of him was that his name was Watkins. Afterward, amid the din, a low murmur of talk was heard from his dying lips but the only intelligible words were something about "drill." The poor fellow, his drilling on earth was done. The next morning, I saw him lying in the dead-house. As unconscious as he may have been when he said it, the soldier's words contained a strangely true meaning if the "upper country" is, indeed, the place of blessed growth and toil.

Divine Intervention

During the Seven Days Battles or Peninsula Campaign of late June 1862, the wounded were conveyed to White House Landing, Virginia until it was evacuated. The soldier himself gives the following account to the German Agent of the Christian Commission in the Army of the Potomac some time after the event:

George Greedy, of Company C, 3rd Pennsylvania Reserves, had received a pocket New Testament from the ladies of Bucks County when he departed from home. It had two inscriptions: "He shall give His angels charge over thee to keep thee in all thy ways (Psalm 91:11)" and "Fight the good fight (1 Timothy 6:12)." He always carried this New Testament in his shirt pocket. In the battle of White Oak Swamp, a minie ball passed through his left arm, shattering the bone severely, traveled through his coat into the Testament, splitting it from Revelation to Chapter 11 of St. John's Gospel. It ended up slightly wounding him in the stomach. Had it not been for his New Testament, he would have been killed on the spot. I asked him to give me the book to show to the committee of the Christian Commission. He willingly assented but added, "I would never sell it for it saved my life."

Theodore Roosevelt's
50-page speech 1912

Ministering in the Camp

Mr. John Patterson, of Philadelphia, gives a graphic account of the White House Landing "Station" of the Christian Commission in June 1862, just before the army retired from the Peninsula Campaign. This gentleman was an earnest and indefatigable delegate of the Christian Commission from the beginning to the close of its work. This extract is from "Hospital Recollections," a series of papers published in the *Presbyterian*, a Philadelphia publication:

We had two tents and a cook shed. One tent was used for sleeping, the other for storage. We were three delegates of the Christian Commission. We were assisted by a young convalescent soldier and a Black boy and woman who cooked for us. Her hoe-cakes were our great solace three times a day. We worked in pairs—two at the hospital, two at the store-tent, and two at the cook-shed. We tolerated no drones in our beehive. When the Black boy was not employed in chopping wood or carrying water for Dinah, he was regaling himself and a circle of select admirers with a genuine Virginia "breakdown" or country dance. When Dinah had fixed up all the odds and ends around the tents, she began manufacturing cornstarch in huge cauldrons, five or six times a day.

The two storekeepers were kept busy from morning to night by a hungry-looking crowd, which we called the "staff brigade," who begged for themselves and their comrades who were incapable of walking. The supplies dispensed here included shirts and drawers, handkerchiefs and books, papers and combs, soap and pickles. It included sugar and tea, bread and nearly everything eatable, wearable, or usable to be found in a regular "Yankee-notion" country store.

But the two itinerants had the most exacting and delicate duties. Their duty was to visit the sick and dying, to bear them little comforts, and to cheer the despondent. They also soothed the agony of some and ministered during the last moments of others. As the occasion required, they played the role nurse, physician, and clergyman. Evening brought them no rest. The semi-secular activities of the day gave way to the religious labors of the night. So pleasant and blessed were these that we longed for the evening when we could meet the eager congregations.

We began early, and ended late—so much so that, more than once, we paid the penalty of our protracted devotion by being arrested by the night guards, whose duty required them to stop all stragglers. But the young delegates were well-known and easily recognized and no authority would jail them. The attendees enjoyed our meetings so much that, sometimes, they would repay someone for an occasional arrest and for the dark and muddy walks by which they were reached.

After a short sermon, prepared while walking between our tent and the church, we held a prayer and inquiry meeting—open to all. One after another would lead in prayer, testify to a newly-found faith, or make an exhortation to his comrades. Some were hoary-headed sinners while others were mere boys. Some would flounder painfully as they tried to express their feelings, frequently bursting into tears. Others would charm with the simplicity and power of their inherent eloquence. From such men, we had no difficulty in securing an effective corps of tract distributors. Every morning, a number of bronzed faces would look in at our tent door and we supplied them with loads of tracts, papers, and hymnbooks. They would head in various directions for the different houses, tents, and to the camp of the "Lost Children," a regiment from New York.

One day, the quiet was disturbed by the thunder of distant cannon. Soon afterward, stragglers from the front came in, followed by a battery of field artillery, which had annihilated the path of the advancing Confederate Army. Then the order came to break up the hospital 'as soon as possible,' which, being interpreted, meant twelve hours. That evening, all who could walk or hobble to our tents were there. We distributed our entire remaining stock. Two of us delivered farewell addresses, which were answered by the hearty cheers of our audience. Then we concluded with a hymn.

In the middle of July, we began the retreat from Harrison's Landing. The points of embarkation were Newport News, Fortress Monroe, and Yorktown. General McClellan reached Acquia Creek on the 24th. This brought an end to the unfortunate campaign of the Peninsula.

CHAPTER II

THE EASTERN ARMIES

FROM POPE'S BATTLES UNTIL HOOKER TAKES COMMAND

July 1862–January 1863

When McClellan failed to take Richmond, Virginia, Major General Pope was assigned to command the three corps of McDowell, Banks, and Sigel. The original plan had been to advance upon Richmond while, at the same time, covering Washington and protecting Maryland. But the outcome of the Seven Days' Battles frustrated these intentions. To meld the two armies of McClellan and Pope into a cohesive fighting force, Major General Halleck was called to Washington and placed as commander-in-chief.

General Pope's objective then turned to creating a diversion so the army could retire from the Peninsula. After some cavalry movements severed communication between Richmond and the Shenandoah, General Banks occupied Culpepper in early August 1862. Pushing forward, he was met at Slaughter's or Cedar Mountain on August 9th by vastly superior Confederate forces under Jackson. After a desperate battle, Banks was compelled to retreat with severe losses.

On the 18th, Pope withdrew to the north side of the Rappahannock River. Soon afterward, Jackson moved into the Shenandoah Valley and then through Thoroughfare Gap into Pope's rear.

In an attempt to cut off Pope's retreat, Jackson engaged in some blind maneuvering, which brought on the Second Battle of Bull Run on August 29th. Battles at Gainesville and Chantilly were fought immediately afterward. Pope's retreat to Centreville began on September 1st. As soon as Pope's army had been drawn back within the Washington entrenchments, he resigned. The command again devolved on General McClellan.

Christ's Model for Service

Reverend Charles H. Corey, Pastor of the Baptist Church in Seabrook, New Hampshire, joined the Christian Commission and traveled to Virginia. After the evacuation of White House Landing, he and others were hastening to Warrenton to meet the wounded from the battle at Cedar Mountain on August 9, 1862 during their final retreat. Suddenly, they came upon four box-cars, loaded with wounded. These men would have fallen into Confederate hands had he not taken fast action. His small band of men and the walking wounded rolled the four cars, with their living cargo of mangled men, more than four miles. They finally reached a point where locomotives could take them. In the process, Reverend Corey's shoes were ripped apart and he came into Fairfax Court House barefooted.

Caring for the Wounded

The scene at Fairfax Station was tragic. Literally, "acres" of wounded men covered the area. They had arrived after the Second Battle of Bull Run of August 29, 1862. Many had tasted neither food nor drink for one or two days. A small "army" of Christian Commission workers distributed coffee with soft crackers to all the wounded until, by the morning dawn, all had been served. About seven hundred were lifted aboard boxcars. The helpless were carried carefully and laid on the floor, covered with hay. Those who could walk were arranged on the car roofs. In this makeshift way, the wounded were then transported to Washington. (Charles H. Corey)

Highest Order of Gratitude

Mr. James Grant from Philadelphia labored among the wounded at Fairfax Station, Virginia, following the Second Battle of Bull Run on August 29, 1862. He tells this story:

I was busy removing bloody garments from a wounded Union soldier when I found a small book in his pocket. Taking it out to find his name, I discovered that it was a New Testament. To my surprise, I also found the name of a North Carolina soldier inside. I asked how he came to have it and he explained that he had fallen on the battlefield near a severely wounded Confederate soldier. The man was crying out piteously for water. Wanting to relieve the poor man's thirst, he had crawled to a stream and filled his canteen. Upon returning, he held it to the lips of the dying man who drank every drop.

In return, the North Carolinian took out his New Testament and handed it to the Union soldier and said, "I have no way to thank you for this but to give you the thing I love most of all—my precious New Testament." Within the hour, the grateful sufferer was silent and without thirst in death. The "precious New Testament" will be an heirloom in the family of the Union soldier—a sacred memento of Christian love in scenes of intense hatred and brutal carnage.

Devotion to Serving

Union Army Colonel, James C. Rice of New York, tells of meeting a sergeant in a Washington hospital about ten days after the Second Battle of Bull Run, which occurred on August 29, 1862 in Virginia:

While passing through the wards, I was approached by two weeping ladies—the sister and aunt of one of the wounded. They asked for my help with surgery. When I met the man, he was suffering intensely but saluted anyway. He told me that he served as a sergeant in the 5th New York Volunteer Infantry, which I knew as one of the most famous and highly regarded regiments of the war. He was wounded late in the action and remained where he fell from Saturday until the following Wednesday. He said he survived on "a few hard crackers left in my haversack and with the water God gave me from heaven—in rain and dew—which I caught in my blanket." A surgeon found him on the Virginia battlefield, sent him to Washington, and amputated his leg on Thursday. Now he needed re-amputation to save his life but the surgeon could see that he was severely exhausted, failing fast, and would probably not survive the hour. My job was to inform the grieving sister and aunt.

They sobbed bitterly but their grief was borne as only Christian women can bear. They heard the voice of Jesus, the "Elder Brother," speaking to them as unto Martha: "I am the Resurrection and the Life; he that believeth in Me, though he were dead, yet shall he live."

My duty also called for me to inform the sergeant himself. I said, "Sergeant, we are going to halt soon. We shall not march much further today."

"Are we going to halt, Colonel, so early in the day? Are we going into bivouac before night?"

"Yes, Sergeant," I replied. "The march is nearly over. The bugle call will soon sound 'the halt.'"

His mind wandered. "Ah, Colonel," he said, "do you mean that I am to die so soon?"

"Yes, Sergeant," I said. "You are soon to die."

"Well, Colonel, I am glad I am going to die. I want to rest. I am weary—very weary. I want to halt. I want to be with Christ. I want to be with my Savior."

NOT ENEMIES

He added, "Colonel, tell my comrades of the noble Army of the Potomac, that I died bravely, that I died for the good old flag."

Moments after he had comforted his sister and aunt, his pulse beat more and more feebly and, at last, he rested. The sergeant halted. His bivouac is now in heaven.

Joy in Severe Trials

Chaplain Brown, of Douglas Hospital, Washington, gives an illustration of the power of Christ's presence to make the soldier joyful in the midst of pain. The experience took place following the Battle at Cedar Mountain in Virginia on August 9, 1862:

"Chaplain," said Sergeant McCoy, "are you the chaplain of this hospital?"

"Yes, sir," I said, "and I shall be glad to serve you."

"Oh, I'm so glad we have a chaplain here. I'm the happiest man you ever saw!" His whole countenance was radiant with joy.

"How is that?" I replied. "You have lost a leg, and..."

"No matter about my leg," he quickly replied. "I shall have both legs in heaven. I tell you I'm the happiest man you ever saw." His very heart seemed to leap with gladness.

"Well, what makes you so happy?" I inquired.

He said. "As we were going into the battle, I said to myself: 'this is serious work.' I prayed for God to spare my life and pardon my sins or, if I should be killed, to take me to heaven. Presently, a shell struck my leg below the knee and I just lay still and prayed. I was left on the battlefield all that night but I lay still and prayed. Oh, Chaplain, that was the happiest night of my life!" Again his countenance was lit up with inexpressible joy.

"How could you be happy under such circumstances?" I asked again.

"Oh, I just prayed and Christ seemed to come and stand by my side all night and He comforted me. I felt sure that all my sins were pardoned and washed away in His blood and I do tell you, Chaplain, I forgot all about my wounds for the moment. It was the happiest night of my life."

This conversation occurred twelve days after the battle. I asked, "And do you feel as happy still?"

"Oh, yes. I'm the happiest man you ever saw."

And, indeed, it seemed so. He lingered several days, happy all the while—then sweetly fell asleep in Jesus.

Historical Context:

Having chased the Union troops all the way back to Washington in late summer of 1862, General Lee wisely chose to not follow McClellan into the entrenchments that surrounded the city. In September, it became Lee and Jackson versus McClellan in battles at Prince Frederick, South Mountain, and Harper's Ferry. General D. H. Hill's fresh division from Richmond joined Lee and became part of his vanguard at Leesburg. The Confederate

Army crossed the Potomac and then moved to Frederick, which they occupied on September 6th. McClellan quickly brought his army to the north of Washington and, after a brief skirmish, entered Frederick on the 12th. However, the main body of the Confederates had moved west two days before.

On the 14th, the battle of South Mountain took place for possession of Turner's Gap, where Confederate General Longstreet was defeated. Meanwhile, Jackson re-crossed the Potomac and hastened to Harper's Ferry, where Union Forces surrendered to Jackson and 12,000 Union troops were taken prisoner. In other action, Lee took up a strong position along Antietam Creek in front of the village of Sharpsburg.

On September 17th, the famous battle of Antietam occurred near Sharpsburg, Maryland. McClellan was credited with a strategic victory for the North. Considered one of the bloodiest days of the war, official reports placed the casualties at between 11,000 and 12,000 on each side. The next day, the shattered armies watched each other from afar. In the evening, Lee quietly re-crossed the Potomac for safer territory. This victory served as the impetus for Lincoln's *Emancipation Proclamation*, which he wrote, in part, to prevent European countries from recognizing the Confederacy.

Immediately after the battle at South Mountain, Virginia, several Christian Commission delegates left Washington with four horse-drawn ambulances, loaded with supplies. They reached the Antietam Battlefield in advance of the other supply wagons. Other delegates from Philadelphia and Baltimore, via Hagerstown and Frederick, arrived the next day. Soon, more than seventy were at work in the hospitals and on the field, where several delegates placed themselves in range of enemy fire.

Seeking Jesus

Reverend Archibald Beatty, Rector of Cranmer Protestant Episcopal Chapel, Philadelphia, placed himself in harm's way at the "Stone Bridge," near McClellan's headquarters at the Battle of Antietam in Maryland on September 17, 1862. He was one of several Christian Commission delegates who were exposed throughout the day to fire from the enemy's artillery. Beatty would later become a chaplain to Union troops. He wrote of the following incident:

In the midst of the roar of cannons and with shells above and around us, I labored all day among the wounded until eleven that night. Being completely exhausted, I laid down on the ground next to the wounded to rest. I had just fallen asleep when I was awakened by a request to visit a dying soldier who desired to see me. I found him lying in a wagon. He was obviously near the end and anxiously said, "I want to know the way to Christ." As briefly as I could, I spoke of Jesus, His death, and of His love of sinners.

I then raised my voice in prayer. As soon as that sound permeated the night air, every moan and groan of those within hearing distance was hushed. Thousands of wounded men may have heard this prayer in the solemn stillness. I prayed for him who, so very soon, would meet the Judge. I also prayed for his comrades who surrounded us. After the prayer, Mrs. Harris, a lady delegate sang most sweetly. When finished, she stooped down and gently kissed the soldier's forehead. We then left him. When we returned early the next morning, we found one of his kind friends just closing his eyes—his spirit having gone away to be with Him to whom the last, grand song of the redeemed shall be raised.

Tears of Gratitude

Mr. James Grant was one of several Christian Commission delegates who placed himself in harm's way. After the battle at South Mountain in Virginia on September 14, 1862, he rushed to the battle of Antietam near Sharpsburg, Maryland on September 17th. He gives the following account of a life saved:

On the night after Antietam, I labored among the wounded of General Sedgwick's Division. A disabled officer informed me that a friend of his was badly wounded in the face and lying somewhere in the darkness with no blanket. After following his directions, I shined the light of my lantern toward the foot of a wooden fence and soon discovered the soldier.

He was a lieutenant with a Pennsylvania regiment. The bullet had entered one cheek and passed through the other cheek. It had grazed his tongue and blew away several teeth. His face was horribly swollen and he was unable to speak. When I asked if he was Lieutenant Mabry of Philadelphia, he assented with a nod of his head.

Unfortunately, the rain was heavy and he was soaked. We made him as comfortable as possible before leaving for the night. During the next two days, all the surgeons were so busy that this man's wound, though hurriedly dressed on the field, had remained untouched. Yet, he showed no signs of impatience. Because of the inflamed condition of his mouth, he could not swallow. On the third day, the surgeons still had more than they could handle, so we assisted them in washing and redressing wounds, most of which had remained untouched since the battle.

With hesitation, I took the Lieutenant's case and, after laboring for two hours, succeeded in cutting away his whiskers and washing the wound thoroughly, both inside and outside the mouth. Having cleared away all the clotted blood and matter, the swelling subsided and he was able to utter some words. A day or so later, he could swallow liquids. We carefully washed his wound daily and, in less than a week, he was able to travel back to Philadelphia.

The next time I saw him was at his home where tears of gratitude filled his eyes and those of his wife. Those tears amply repaid me. The gallant soldier even introduced me as "the man who picked me up at midnight and dressed my wound when I had given myself up to die."

Unselfishness Toward Enemies

Delegate James Grant, of the Christian Commission, remembered the unselfish spirit of the Union soldiers after the famous battle of Antietam, which took place on September 17, 1862. They often extended this spirit of unselfishness to Confederate wounded, as reflected in this incident:

No one who walked the Antietam battleground in Maryland, while the dead lay unburied, can ever forget the long, deep road or cut which ran along the edge of a cornfield. It formed a natural rifle pit for the Confederates during the fight. The Irish Brigade from New York, with their impetuous bravery, finally managed to overtake them—but not without suffering very severe losses. For half a mile, the road was literally covered with dead and wounded.

Most of the disabled from this vicinity were carried to a farm house that overlooked this bloody ground. We found them suffering and destitute. Our own supplies were exhausted almost immediately. Our stock of clothing was reduced to a single shirt. Looking around to find the neediest man, I observed a soldier with the New York regiment, an elderly man who was leaning against the barn door. He had endured a severe chest wound and appeared weak from the loss of blood. He had no shirt but had pieced together a few blood-soaked, weather-hardened fragments of an outer coat to wear.

"You are the very man I am looking for," I said enthusiastically. "Nobody could need this 'last shirt' more than you."

His reply thrilled me. In a thick Irish brogue, he muttered, "I'm much obliged to you, sir, but…" and he pointed to a spot on the hillside nearby. "Down yonder, there's a poor Confederate soldier far worse off than I am and, if you'll please give it to me, I'll put it on him by-and-bye." I handed him the shirt and this man's benevolent errand was soon accomplished.

No Greater Joy

Reverend Robert J. Parvin, Rector of St. Paul's Episcopal Church, Cheltenham, Pennsylvania, took charge of an important part of the Christian

Commission's operations at Antietam in Maryland. The following incident occurred in his work:

Three or four days after the famous battle of Antietam on September 17, 1862, Mr. Parvin sent out Reverend S. W. Thomas and another delegate to search for wounded men who might have been overlooked on the battle-field. After walking a long distance over bloody ground, thirst led them to a deserted farmhouse. While drinking at the pump, they noticed something that looked like bundles of rags near the barn. It turned out to be the bodies of two dead soldiers. Behind the barn, they discovered thirteen Confederate soldiers—all badly wounded.

Assurance of Salvation

Help was summoned from Sharpsburg and, not long afterwards, Mr. Parvin, other delegates, and needed supplies arrived in a horse-drawn ambulance. The delegates carried out the dead. One of the living, whose legs were gone, kept moaning for water. We made tea in the barnyard and performed every possible ministry of mercy for these poor men, nearly all whom were Confederates. A nearby Union regiment helped us move them to a Field Hospital, only three-quarters of a mile away. One more unattended night would have been fatal for all.

Help from this regiment came about when a captain, who happened to be riding by, saw the ambulance near the barn. Just as he rode up, Mr. Parvin was kneeling in the cow pen, praying with a dying soldier from Alabama. The captain reined in, uncovered his head, and listened reverently to the petition. Then I asked, "Young man, are you prepared to die?" The dying soldier replied, "Yes, yes, my trust is in the Lord Jesus. I'm as 'happy as a prince.'"

The Captain, moved by the scene, volunteered all the help that was needed, along with the ambulances. Afterward, he rode over again and saw that the soldier had died. In a conversation with Mr. Parvin, he confessed, "What that soldier said meant more to me than any sermon I ever heard."
(Robert J. Parvin)

Expressions of Servanthood

A man named Mr. Demond delivered an Alumni Address at Williams College that contains this incident that followed the battle of Antietam in Maryland, on September 17, 1862:

Reverend George J. Mingins, Pastor of (O.S.) Presbyterian Church, Huntingdon Valley, Pennsylvania and a Christian Commission delegate, was passing over the field of blood when he saw a man washing at a brook. As he came near, he recognized the man, a Doctor of Divinity and Pastor of one of the largest

Churches in Philadelphia, who was also a Christian Commission deleg said, "Doctor, what are you doing?"

The Doctor straightened up and, pointing with his finger, said, "Over yonder are six hundred wounded men, most of them lying in the bloody shirts in which they were wounded. We have no fresh shirts and we shall have none until tomorrow morning. So I thought I would take a few of the worst out here and wash and dry them in the sun. Do you think there is any harm in it?"

The gentleman said, "Doctor, I know God has blessed you abundantly in your work in Philadelphia but I do not think the Master ever looked upon any act of your life with more pleasure than this."

"I believe it," said the Doctor as he turned back to his washing.

Nonbeliever Sees Divine Intervention

After the battle at Antietam in Maryland on September 17, 1862, Reverend George J. Mingins, Pastor of (O.S.) Presbyterian Church from Huntingdon Valley, Pennsylvania, spoke of the solemnity some soldiers experience in battle:

One day we were burying some poor fellows who had fallen in the battle and a soldier was helping us. He told us how he had passed through the fierce conflict unharmed, "For which," he said, "I thank God."

A man near us sarcastically said, "Thank the 'Rebels' for being such bad marksmen."

The soldier looked squarely into the soldier's face and replied, "I ain't no Christian, God knows. But after what we passed through, I ought to be a better man. You may think as you like but I think God saved me, not the Rebels' bad shooting."

Christian Love for Enemies

Hospitals for the wounded from the Battle of Antietam were scattered throughout western Maryland, with the main one located at Sharpsburg. Christian Commission delegates visited these hospitals for as long as they remained in operation. Members of the Baltimore Committee were extremely dedicated and the impression they made on Confederate soldiers was deep and lasting. One delegate shared this incident:

Members of the Christian Committee were standing nearby as a Southern sympathizer approached a wounded Confederate who was lying between two Union soldiers. One leg of each of the three men had been amputated. The lady said: "Here, soldier, I have brought you some baked goods and I want you to have them. But don't let these Yankee men have any of them."

The suffering man replied, "Madam, these men share everything they get with me and if I cannot share what you give me with them, I cannot take it."

Assurance of Salvation

Following the September 17, 1862 battle at Antietam in Maryland, many of the wounded were taken to Baltimore. Reverend R. Spencer Vinton, Chaplain of McKim's Hospital in that city, relates the following incident:

Sylvester McKinley, of Clarion County, Pennsylvania, was a handsome, muscular, and intelligent young man. After losing his left arm in the battle, he was overcome by his sufferings. When brought to the hospital, he had neither coat, vest, nor hat. The Ladies of the North Pillow Baltimore Union Relief Association took his case and spared neither means nor labors in his behalf.

His condition was critical and I lost no time in pointing him to Jesus Christ. I learned that he had been a Sunday school scholar and was quite familiar with the Bible. He joyfully responded, "I am assured that Christ has intense interest in my well-being and it greatly encourages me to know I will soon find rest in heaven." I visited him daily and always found him with his New Testament in hand or by his side. I prayed with him and had the strongest assurance of his confidence in God. A faithful nurse was ever by his side.

Near the last, weakened by his sufferings and exhaustion, he asked the nurse to hand him his New Testament. He read a brief passage and, upon closing it, feebly said, "Now, nurse, put it under my head." She placed his "pillow" as he desired and, in a moment, he was asleep in Jesus.

Christ's Presence Found on Battlefield

One of the most effective delegates of the Christian Commission was Reverend Isaac Oliver Sloan, connected with the Fourth (N. S.) Presbytery of Philadelphia. He was part of the original party, which went to Fortress Monroe in May, 1862, and he remained on the Peninsula until McClellan's army had withdrawn. Among the first to reach the September 17, 1862 battle at Antietam, he continued his work in the Maryland hospitals for several months. He wrote about the following incident:

General Burnside was preparing to move on Fredericksburg and all who could possibly go to the front were ordered out of the hospitals. I had become very much interested in a very ill soldier named Monroe, of Company H, 12th Massachusetts Regiment, who had been left behind when the army moved out against General Lee.

Before the order came for all who were well enough to go to the front, the surgeon had permitted Monroe, who was sufficiently recovered, to assist me in my hospital work. He was only nineteen but I found him a ready helper—a faithful Christian in all his conduct. I was sorry to lose him this time and I was especially concerned that he would soon join his regiment for duty as an able-bodied man. To many of the poor, half-recovered fellows who had been left behind after the battle, this order to the front was a death sentence. I was concerned about how Monroe himself might receive the news.

His answer was very calm: "Why should I be away from my regiment when the other boys are still fighting? My life is no more valuable than theirs and, besides, God will be with me and I have no need to fear. I shall try to live close to Christ. He will give me courage."

Soon after joining his regiment, he wrote to tell me how glad he was to return to duty. The following summer, he lost an arm at Gettysburg.

Historical Context:

A long "quiet" followed Antietam. Not until October 26th did the army cross the Potomac. On November 7, 1862, General McClellan was relieved of duty and General A. E. Burnside assumed command. By this time, the army had reached Warrenton. General Burnside promptly moved his forces down the Rappahannock River Valley to Fredericksburg on the north bank and General Lee kept parallel to him on the south bank.

The Union Army crossed on pontoons and then, on December 13, 1862, they assaulted the Confederate entrenchments behind Fredericksburg. The attack by Union forces was decisive and the slaughter was terrible. However, the battle was not renewed and, on the night of December 15, the entire army was withdrawn north of the river. About January 20, 1863, General Burnside considered another battle but a storm prevented it. On January 28th, Burnside was relieved of command and Major General Joseph Hooker assumed command.

A large party of Christian Commission delegates known as "Minutemen" went to the front after the December battle. They served under the direction of Reverend Alexander Reed, Pastor of South Presbyterian Church of Parkesburg, Pennsylvania. (What distinguished the Minutemen from the regular delegates was their willingness to serve in emergency situations on very short notice and for briefer periods of time.) Scenes of distress met them on every hand. The wounded were carried in horse-drawn ambulances to Falmouth Station where they waited for transport to Washington via Acquia Creek. The delays at these transfer points were wearisome and painful. However, this served as an opportunity for the Christian Commission to be used of God in a most profound way.

Dying Soldier Receives Comfort

The March 19, 1863 edition of *The New York Observer* gives the following account of the Battle of Fredericksburg, in Virginia, as told at the Fulton Street Prayer Meeting:

A speaker held up a New Testament, stating that it was from the battlefield. On one of the flyleaves, someone had written, "Found on the battlefield of Fredericksburg, December 16th, at 2 A.M., while covering the evacuation of that place, by P. H. B. Taken from beside a dead body."

Since the New Testament was found lying open, it gave every appearance that the book had been read after its owner had been wounded. An inscription on the front flyleaf stated, "A present to William Glover, from his sister Maggy. Read this often." It was a beautiful, gilt-edged Testament, clasped, and bearing the imprint of the American Bible Society in 1860.

Of this New Testament, the speaker said, "I find that the Gospels show signs of much reading. I find two pages turned down, evidently intended to mark these passages: 'And as Moses lifted up the serpent in the wilderness, even so must the Son of Man be lifted up, that whosoever believeth in Him should not perish, but have eternal life. For God so loved the world that He gave His Only Begotten Son, that whosoever believeth in Him should not perish, but have everlasting life (John 3:14-16).'

"Then I find another leaf turned to point to this passage in St. Luke: 'Ought not Christ to have suffered these things, and to enter into His glory (Luke 24:26)?'

"The speaker then asked, 'Who can estimate the value of this Testament to such a dying man?' Surely no earthly arithmetic can calculate it."

Angels Rejoicing

A narrative from *The Bible Society Record* tells of this incident about the December 13, 1862 battle: Among the articles returned from the battlefield at Fredericksburg, Virginia with the body of a young Connecticut soldier was a New Testament, given to him by a praying mother. Upon examining it, a single leaf was found turned down and pointing to the following verse: "There is joy in the presence of the angels of God over one sinner that repenteth (Luke 15:10)."

Historical Context:

Among those who took care of the wounded in Washington as they arrived from Fredericksburg, were Reverends Christopher Cushing and F. N. Peloubet, of Congregational Churches in North Brookfield and Oakham,

Massachusetts respectively. (Reverend Francis Nathan Peloubet was in the vanguard of the Sunday school movement.) They found that government officials faced more than they could handle and the weather was bitterly cold. They encountered a staggering number of disabled men, most of whom were incredibly destitute. They tell of the following incidents:

Gesture of Brotherly Love

After the Battle of Fredericksburg, December 13, 1862, Reverend Christopher Cushing, Pastor of the Congregational Church in North Brookfield, Massachusetts wrote: I found a man taking a worn out shoe from his bosom and then placing it on a comrade's foot. When I inquired about this, he said. "I have no way of warming my friend's cold foot unless I heat his shoe in my bosom and then put it back on his foot." To relieve such suffering was, indeed, a blessed ministry.

Resisting the Urge to Complain

After the December 13, 1862 battle at Fredericksburg, I asked one poor fellow, who had just been removed from the boat, why he did not complain. There was a rare fortitude in his answer: "Where we've been, sir, it did no good to complain!" And I thought, "He's right. Complaining never did me any good." (Christopher Cushing)

Ministry of Touching

The wounded from the battle at Fredericksburg, December 13, 1862, were transported upriver to Washington. In removing men from the boats, we sometimes found that their wounds did not to require a stretcher but it helped them immensely to put their arms around us or for us to place our arms around them. These wounded men periodically told us that we were "the best kind of crutches."
(Christopher Cushing)

Affliction Produces Joy

Reverend Peloubet, Pastor of the Congregational Church in Oakham, Massachussetts, writes of ministering to the wounded from Fredericksburg, Virginia, after the December 13, 1862 battle: The hospitalized soldiers thought we expected payment for the little delicacies we gave them. I responded, "No, you don't pay. These things are as free as the Gospel."

Taken aback by our baked goods, the men said, "Soldiers don't have these kinds of delicacies."

I responded, "Well, I hope you will like the Gospel as well as these little things."

"Yes," said some in a doubting voice, "the Gospel's good too." But others responded enthusiastically at the very mention of the "Gospel," as if they had felt it deeply on that terrible day.

Finding Joy

As I was giving some soft white bread to these hungry men, one of them started laughing. I asked, "What are you laughing at, sir?"

He replied, "Who wouldn't laugh just to see bread again!"
(F. N. Peloubet)

Using Humor During Trials

After the December 13, 1862 battle at Fredericksburg, two Congregational ministers from Brookfield and Oakham, Massachusetts respectively wanted to serve the wounded. Reverend Christopher Cushing and Reverend F. N. Peloubet greatly desired to go down the river to help transport the wounded back to Washington. But because of changes on the front at Fredericksburg, they were not able to obtain passes for several days. Mr. Peloubet tells how they finally boarded a boat and what happened next:

After dealing with "red tape" to the point of exhaustion, we were frustrated all the more because the boat was returning that very day to Acquia Creek to pick up more wounded. However, the captain, who had seen us working on the wharves with the wounded men, invited us on board. Without a moment's hesitation, we were on our way.

Once on board, we noticed that the boat was carrying a large company of unskilled laborers who worked for the government and that the boat had no accommodations for us. The men on board passed their time by telling stories and jokes. We noticed a placard, "Beware of pickpockets," which brought out some amusing comments from the laborers.

"It'll take two to pick my pockets," remarked one.

"What will the second man do?" asked another.

"Put something in to be picked," he replied.

We had brought along bread and applesauce, eating only the bread while saving the applesauce for the soldiers. We had two bags of bread, which required constant vigilance to keep it from this hungry bunch. As the night wore on, we took turns sleeping and watching our supplies.

Prayer Produces Peace

We had lost track of where we were on the river and of the time but about 2:30 that morning, the men began to wake up—hungry and noisy. Because the raucous chaos was spiraling out of control, I finally proposed some singing. So we began with "Shining Shore," and kept on with "Will you go?" the "Star Spangled Banner," and others. I then read 2 Corinthians 4 and Reverend Cushing prayed and made some excellent remarks.

To our joy and astonishment, we noticed that, during the prayer, nearly all rose and uncovered their heads. The crew foreman came to us afterwards and announced, "So you will know, I am the 'head devil' among the men."

I suggested, "It would be better if you were the 'head angel.'"

He responded, "I'll try to be. And, uh, if you can spare them, I'd like to have some singing books for special use on Sundays for the men."

In addition, nine men wanted to buy New Testaments. After we sang a few more songs, we reached Acquia Creek. Amazingly, we had no difficulty at the Provost Marshal's office in procuring passes to travel the government road to the front.

(F. N. Peloubet)

Reaching the Lost

Toward the close of the year, the distinguished Chairman of the Christian Commission, George H. Stuart, came to Washington for one of his frequent army visits. On February 2, 1864, he gave a public address to commemorate the Washington Anniversary of the Christian Commission and related this incident about his work near the Capitol:

I have visited many hospitals and camps and have distributed many of our books. I can testify that, from the beginning until now, I have never met a man who refused them, except one, and he was from my own city—Philadelphia. This man said, "You can call me an 'infidel.' I do not believe in your books, nor do I have any need for them."

He also said, "I am from Philadelphia. I live at such and such number on Callowhill Street. If you go there, you will hear about my character and discover that I am as good a man as you are."

"I trust a great deal better," I said.

Several days later, I approached him again and he asked, "What was the book you wanted to give me the other day?"

I told him it was a selection from the Scriptures called *Cromwell's Bible.*

"Oh," he said, "I don't want your Bible. I have no need of it. I'm a good enough man without it," and with an air of supreme indifference, he turned his head away.

"My friend," I said, "I'm from Philadelphia too. I know where you live and can find the exact house. On next Sunday evening, if God spares my life, I plan to speak for the Christian Commission in the Church of the Epiphany."

He looked at me inquisitively. "And what are you going to say?" he asked.

"I am going to tell the people that I had been distributing tracts all day through the hospitals and camps and that I found but one man who refused to take them and he was from Philadelphia."

"Well, what more are you going to say?" the man asked with a steady, seemingly defiant gaze.

"I'll tell them that I began my distribution in the morning at the White House and then I am going to tell them that the first gentleman to whom I offered one of the little books was Abraham Lincoln. I will explain that he rose from his chair, read the title, and expressed great pleasure in receiving it. He also promised to read it. But then I will tell them that I came to one of his cooks who thought of himself as so exceedingly good that he didn't need a copy of God's Word and refused to have one."

"Well," said the man, reaching out his hand, "if the President can take one, I suppose I can too."

Defiant Resistance Turns to Repentance

Reverend H. C. Henries, Chaplain of the U. S. General Hospital at Annapolis, had acted as the Christian Commission's Agent in Annapolis. He also served at the nearby Prisoner of War Camp from the time its active relief work began. His only compensation was the assistance given him by delegates who occasionally labored, under his direction, throughout his immense parish of disabled men. The tangible presence of the Holy Spirit was near and blessed the work that took place. Reverend R. J. Parvin, Rector of St. Paul's Episcopal Church, Cheltenham, Pennsylvania, labored with Chaplain Henries at one time. Reverend Parvin communicated this incident:

One morning, toward the close of July 1862, Chaplain Henries was passing through the rooms of the General Hospital at the Navy Yard. On the vacant bed of a soldier, he placed the single-paged tract, entitled, "Will you go?" It was a copy of the hymn bearing the same name. Its first lines contained the words:

> "We're traveling home to heaven above.
>
> Will you go?
>
> To sing the Savior's dying love.
>
> Will you go?
>
> Millions have reached that blessed shore,
> Their trials and labors all are o'er,
> But still there's room for millions more.
>
> Will you go?"

Other lines of it read:

> "The way to heaven is straight and plain.
>
> Will you go?
>
> Repent, believe, be born again.
>
> Will you go?
>
> The Savior cries aloud to thee,
> 'Take up thy cross and follow Me.
> And thou shalt My salvation see.'
>
> Will you go?"

The soldier returned, sat down on his bed, and picked up the hymn. He looked at the title, read a few lines of the invitation, and threw it down. He then picked it up a second time, read a little, and threw it upon the floor again. But the invitation that he was so unwilling to hear had pierced his volition through this silent messenger of the Lord. Playing with the tract for a while with his foot, the soldier picked it up for a third time. He then read it carefully, without throwing it down. The soldier read and re-read it. While holding it thoughtfully, he listened to the solemn voice speaking to him, "Will you go?" He took a pencil from his pocket and wrote in the margin of the tract these words: "By the grace of God, I will try to go. John Waugh, Company G, 10th Regiment. P. R. V. C."

A soldiers' prayer meeting was held that night in the Hospital. John Waugh attended with his wounded arm in a sling and tract in hand. When given the opportunity, he told his comrades of his conflict with that little piece of paper. He read what he had written in the margin and asked for all to pray that he might keep his promise and never to be ashamed of his Savior. He added, "I'm not ashamed of Christ now but I am ashamed of myself for having been so long time ashamed of Him."

Some months passed and upon opening my morning paper, I read a brief account of "A Skirmish Yesterday in Virginia. Ten Persons Killed." Glancing over the list of names, I stopped at this one: "John Waugh, Company G, 10th Regiment. P. R." It comforted me to lay down my paper, take up the little tract that he had given to me as a gift, and read once more the penciled pledge in its margin, "By the grace of God, I will try to go."

Reverend Parvin adds this epilogue: Since then, the faithful Chaplain, who laid the printed page upon the soldier's cot, has been called from earth. And now, we have good reason to believe that both Chaplain H. C. Henries and Private John Waugh know, much better than we do, the full import of these other lines of that beloved hymn:

> "We're going to walk the plains of light.
>
> Will you go?
>
> Far, far from death, and curse, and night.
>
> Will you go?
>
> The crown of life we then shall wear.
> The conqueror's palm we then shall bear.
> And all the joys of heaven share.
>
> Will you go?"

Power of the Cross

Writing from Annapolis on October 27, 1862, Reverend George Bringhurst, Rector of All Saints' Episcopal Church, Moyamensing, Philadelphia, gives an incident which illustrates the power of the Cross to quell even the worst of human passions:

Arriving at the Prisoner of War Camp, I found a scene of fearful insubordination caused by the recklessness of a few inebriated prisoners of war. Already, several buildings had been burned while others were about to be torched. Fiendish yells and bitter swearing filled the air. Six companies of the 131st New York Regiment, along with three companies of a Maryland Cavalry Regiment were desperately striving to restore order.

In the midst of this mass confusion, I assembled about fifty men around me and we began to sing, "Say, brothers, will you meet us?" Hundreds responded positively and soon I was surrounded by a large audience. After singing, we united in prayer. This formerly riotous audience then listened with earnestness to my brief address—the simple story of Jesus. In this way, order was restored—not by the sword but by the Cross. The power of God had descended upon us.

Later, the Colonel in command told me that, after order was restored, he had never experienced a quieter night in the camp. At the time of this incident, the POW Camp confined an astonishing 7,662 Confederate soldiers.

CHAPTER III
THE WESTERN ARMIES

UNTIL AFTER THE STONE RIVER BATTLES
April 1861–January 1863

The first Delegation to the West was sent from the central office of the Christian Commission to meet up with the Cumberland Army. This took place immediately following the Stone River battles on December 31, 1862. Earlier in the war, various "Army Committees" had engaged in fruitful labors in the Western armies on every major battlefield. These "Committees" were appointed by the Young Men's Christian Associations of such places as Chicago, Peoria, and St. Louis—to name a few.

The war in Missouri was an endless succession of forced marches, toilsome retreats, and desperate battles between comparatively small armies. Generals Fremont and Hunter were successively dismissed from the chief command and General Halleck assumed the role of commander-in-chief of the Department of War in November 1861.

Finding Christ Through a Hymn

Among the troops waging war in Missouri was the famous "Normal School" regiment, known as the 33rd Illinois. The faithful and devoted Secretary of the Chicago Army Committee, Mr. B. F. Jacobs, also served in connection with the Northwestern Branch of the Christian Commission until the close of the war. He writes about an incident, which occurred in autumn of 1861 at a Friday evening prayer meeting, held at the First Baptist Church of Chicago:

Toward the close of the meeting, a Union Army officer rose and said, "I am a stranger to you and am visiting Chicago. My reason for speaking is to carry out a sacred trust. I serve with the 33rd Illinois. In the early part of our campaigns in Missouri, we received a box containing a few hymnbooks and New Testaments, some papers and sewing kits, and other soldier comforts. A note inside the box told us that it came from a lady of the First Baptist Church, Chicago. The men were so excited to receive the hymnbooks that they shared these precious books with each other because of the short supply. More than one hundred men committed the principal hymns to memory so they could sing at the meetings. These books even circulated at the hospital. One of my men sent for me to visit a dying soldier, whose words were few but rich in substance.

"'Captain, I am dying. I long to see my wife and children but I know I shall die without ever seeing them again. I've been trying to think of what I could send my wife. I have nothing except these books.' And taking one of the New Testaments and hymnbooks from under his head, he added, 'Please send these to them. And Captain, if you are ever in Chicago, I want you to go to the First Baptist Church and tell the lady who sent those hymnbooks that the 27th hymn has led me to Jesus. I am going home to wait for her.'"

Conviction of Spiritual Truth

The story of the stranger Captain deeply impressed the audience. He paused for a moment, then continued.

"One of the captains in our regiment paid a young lad to take care of his horse. The men nicknamed him, 'Little Piety,' because of his sincere religious convictions. The Christian soldiers of the regiment had organized a prayer meeting and, one evening, they were holding it in a tent near the quarters of the officer of the day. He was a very profane man who, upon hearing the singing, started toward the tent. He exclaimed with profanity, 'I'll stop that noise.' As he approached the tent, the fly door was up and 'Little Piety' was speaking. He was standing near the cracker box that served as a desk and it held a candle—the only candle in the tent. Light from this candle lit up his face.

"He said 'When I was preparing to leave home, my mother said, 'My son, a great many men don't love Christ and they will tempt you to swerve from your dedication and purpose. You may be subjected to trials on account of your faith but, my son, I want you to promise you will not forget your mother's Savior.' With tears in his eyes, the little fellow said, 'I always want to remember Jesus.'

The sight of the boy and the tone of his voice stopped the Captain. He listened until the meeting closed.

The leader then asked, 'Where shall we hold our next meeting?'

Stepping forward out of the darkness, the Captain responded, 'In my tent.'

"Soon afterwards, that Captain put his faith in Christ and, since then, has been one of the most committed Christians in the regiment."
(B. F. Jacobs)

Prepared for Eternity

During the aimless operations in Missouri, General Grant was in command at Cairo. He moved down the Mississippi and, on November 7, 1862, fought the battle of Belmont, opposite Columbus, the headquarters of Confederate General Polk. The Chicago Army Committee sent a delegate, D. L. Moody of Chicago, to Cairo to care for the wounded on the battlefield. Reverend G. S. F. Savage, District Secretary of the American Tract Society in Chicago, was also on a similar mission at Cairo. He wrote the following:

A Lieutenant in an Iowa regiment, wounded by a bullet in the shoulder, was brought to the hospital. At first, the doctors thought he would recover but, after a few days, he declined rapidly. Just before his death, a lady nurse said, "Lieutenant, you have but a few moments to live. If you have any word to send to your wife and little one in Iowa, you must speak it very quickly."

With his face shining like an angel's, he looked up and said, "Tell my wife that there is not a cloud between me and Jesus."

Historical Context:

In Tennessee, a few miles south of the Kentucky line, the Confederates had constructed two fortified and extensive structures, Forts Henry and Donelson. Within eleven miles of each other, these forts controlled passage up the Tennessee and Cumberland rivers. General Grant, with the aid of Commodore Foote's powerful flotilla of gunboats, undertook the task of reducing them to matchsticks. On February 6, 1862, Fort Henry fell. Ten days later, Fort Donelson also fell after a brilliant siege and some hard fighting.

Compassion for Others

A correspondent of the *Boston Journal*, Mr. C. C. Coffin who was better recognized by his *nom de plume* "Carlton," was covering the battle of Fort Henry in Tennessee. Of Commodore Foote, a devoted Christian, he said, "He is not afraid to have all men know that he recognizes his obligation to his Divine Maker. On the day after the capture of Fort Henry on February 6, 1862, a gentleman remarked that Foote was getting nervous, that he probably did not sleep well."

The Commodore replied, "I never slept better in my life than the night before the battle and I never prayed more fervently than on yesterday morning. But last night, I couldn't sleep for thinking of those poor fellows on the Essex."

The Essex was the gunboat that took a shell in a vulnerable spot during the bombardment of Fort Henry. The shell penetrated the boiler and the vessel instantly exploded with burning steam. Captain Porter and forty of his crew were severely scalded! Several died instantly while others jumped overboard and drowned.

Remember the Lord's Day

Preceding the battle at Fort Henry in Tennessee on February 6, 1862, Commodore Foote issued order, "Number Six," to his fleet and carefully enforced it while he commanded:

Cairo, Dec. 17, 1861

A strict recognition of Sunday, so far as abstaining from all unnecessary work and giving officers and men the opportunity of attending public worship on board, will be observed by all persons connected with the flotilla.

It is the wish of the commander-in-chief that, on Sunday, the public worship of Almighty God may be observed on board all vessels composing the flotilla and that the respective commanders will either pronounce prayers publicly or delegate such a task to others. This observance shall take place when as many of the officers and men as possible can be spared from duty so they may attend the public worship of Almighty God.

Profane swearing is forbidden by the laws of better government of the navy. All officers and men will strictly observe this law. Every officer who uses profane language towards the men, in carrying out their duty, will be held accountable for such gross violation of law and order.

Discipline, to be permanent, must be based on moral grounds. Officers must, in themselves, show a good example in morals, order, and patriotism, in order to secure these qualities in the men.

Andrew H. Foote, Flag Officer,

Commanding Officer, U. S. Naval Forces on the Western waters ("Carlton")

Hymn Brings Comfort

A beautiful little story connected with the siege of Fort Donelson in Tennessee on February 16, 1862 was related at a Western Sunday school convention in 1863:

A young man was wounded and left behind by his comrades, who pressed on in battle. When they returned, they found him resting against a tree, dead, with his hand in a book opened to this hymn:

"Nearer, my God, to Thee,
Nearer to Thee;
E'en though it be a cross
That raiseth me;
Still all my song shall be,
Nearer, my God, to Thee,
Nearer to Thee."

("Carlton")

Almost Persuaded

Mr. B. F. Jacobs was one of the Chicago Army Committee delegates to the wounded after the surrender of Fort Donelson in Tennessee on February 16, 1862. From him, we gather the following incident: A week after the surrender, our own men had all been cared for. That Sabbath evening, we were about to start down the river with the last of the wounded. Mr. D. L. Moody went with me to visit the Confederate soldiers who crowded the twenty-three log house hospitals at Dover. In one of them, we found almost every square inch of room covered with the wounded. In a kitchen corner, an old, gray-haired man was lying on some hay. I went up to him, knelt down by his side, and asked if I could do anything for him.

"No," he said, "you can't."

"Don't you want anything? Is there nothing that might comfort you?"

"Oh, yes." he replied. "I want to go home. I have a wife and six children in Tennessee and, oh, how I want to go home and see them."

"Well," I said, "maybe you'll be exchanged."

He looked up at me with an expression of astonishment.

"Why," he said "I'll never go home. I'm dying. Don't you know?"

"No, I didn't know. But, my friend, if you are dying, are you not going home? Don't you know how Christ said He had gone to prepare a home for those who loved Him? Have you never thought of that home in heaven?"

He gazed at me with an expression of perfect despair.

"My wife has talked to me about this for thirty-five years. And God knows how I have treated her. I've rejected every invitation and I'm dying here without Christ—without Christ."

For a long time, he kept groaning out, "I can't die. I can't die." And with no light to show him the heavenly way, he went alone into the darkness of death.

Gratitude in Hardships

In one of the huts, housing the wounded from the battle at Fort Donelson in Tennessee on February 16, 1862, I found a man lying on the floor. As I went up to minister to him, I realized he was unable to speak. We carried him down to the hospital-boat that was going out and nursed him during the trip. He had been shot through the lower jaw, and was too weak to stand. Wounded in the first day's fight, he had lain on the field for forty-eight hours before he was picked up. In the storm, his back froze fast to the ground where he lay, and both his feet were frozen also. After we had him on the boat a while, I learned that his name was Burgess and that I had previously known him in Chicago.

At Cairo we put him into a hospital. A nurse promised that she would see to it that he received special care. Six months later, the man walked into my supply store. He was on his way back to the army. He stopped to tell us that he owed his life to the care he had received on the boat. He also said, "In gratitude to God for sparing my life, I promised to serve Him forevermore."

Cleansing through Spiritual Refreshment

Mr. B.F. Jacobs of Chicago tells this story about transporting the wounded from Fort Donelson in Tennessee after the February 16, 1862 battle: As we steamed down the river that night, I had charge of the patients after ten o'clock. In a state room, I found a young fellow who had been shot through the lungs. I asked him if there was anything he wanted.

"I want a drink," he answered.

I went to get him some water out of the Cumberland River. For a minute, he looked at it—so muddy and impure—with an expression of intense longing and desire. "Oh, for one cupful of water out of my father's well," he uttered.

I asked him if he had ever heard of "Living water."

With a face filled with joy, he turned toward me and answered, "Yes, this is the inner fountain that brings refreshment and cleansing."
(B. F. Jacobs)

Power of Scripture

I made good use of the time by distributing books in the hospitals. I gave one young soldier, whose distraught appearance caught my attention, a little volume containing Scripture texts for each day of the year. A week later, as I was returning again from Fort Donelson by the same route, I sought out my young friend. With a countenance all aglow with joy, he answered my inquiries as to his health, by pulling out the little book I had given him. He opened it and pointed to a verse near the middle and said, "That little verse has led me to the Savior and I have enjoyed Him, oh, so much!"

Our conversation was brief, as I had to return to the boat. Over time, the verse has faded from my memory but that soldier's face, filled with transfiguration and peace, can never fade away.
(B. F. Jacobs)

Power in the Word

Reverend Dr. Robert Patterson, Pastor of the Reformed Church, Chicago, was returning from his work at Fort Donelson after the February 16, 1862 battle in Tennessee when the boat stopped at Paducah. He relates an incident about one of the little books distributed by delegates of the Christian Commission: I visited the Campbell House, which served as a hospital for Confederate soldiers. In the corner of a room, lay a young boy, John Posey, who was looking very weak and sick.

"How old are you, John?"

"Fourteen, sir."

"I hear you have been very ill. How did you feel when you thought you might die?"

"I knew the Lord would take care of me."

"How so? Do you love the Lord Jesus?"

"Yes, sir. Indeed I do."

"How long has it been since you became a Christian?"

"About two years."

"John, how did you manage to maintain your love for Christ in the camp?"

He drew from under his pillow a diminutive book, slightly more than an inch square, called *Dew Drops*, a book rich in Scripture, issued by the American Tract Society.

"Sir," he said, "I lived on that."

Living with a Vision

A correspondent with the *Boston Journal*, named C. C. Coffin, who was better known by his *nom de plume* "Carlton," covered the February 16, 1862 battle of Fort Donelson in Tennessee. He tells the story of Frankie Bragg, who died in a Paducah hospital:[1]

Frankie was a brave and honorable boy. Several kind ladies took care of the sick and their very presence was like sunshine. Wherever they walked, the eyes of the wounded followed them. One of these ladies recalled little Frankie Bragg, saying, "Many will remember him, the fifteen-year old boy who fought valiantly at Donelson—one of the bravest of Colonel John W. Birge's sharpshooters. His answer to my questioning about why he joined the Union Army at such a young age was so worthy of recording.

"He said, 'I joined because I was so young and strong and because life would be worth nothing to me unless I offered it for my country.'[2]

Need for Love

"I saw him die. I can never forget the pleading gaze of his violet eyes, the brow from which ringlets of light brown hair were swept by strange fingers bathed in the death dew, and the desire for someone to love him in his last hours.

"'Oh, I am going to die and there is no one here to love me,' he said. 'I didn't think I was going to die until now—but it can't last long. If only my sisters were here. I have no friends near me now and it is so hard!'

"Frankie, I know it is hard to be away from your relatives but you are not friendless. I am your friend. Mrs. Sharp and the kind Doctor are your friends and we will take care of you. More than this, God is your friend. He is nearer to you now than any of us can get. Trust Him, my boy. He will help you.

"A faint smile passed over his face.

"'Oh, do you think He will?' he asked.

"Then, as he held my hands closer, he turned his face toward me and said, 'My mother taught me to pray when I was a very little boy and I never forgot it. I have always said my prayers every day and tried not to be bad. Do you think God always heard me?'

"'Yes, most assuredly. Did He not promise in His good book, from which your mother taught you, that He would always hear the prayers of His children? "Ask, and ye shall receive." Don't you remember this? One of the worst

[1]Days and Nights on the Battlefield, 277-280
[2]Hospital Incidents, New York Post, Oct. 22, 1863

things we can do is to doubt God's truth. He has promised us and He will fulfill His promises. Don't you feel this is so, Frankie?'

"He hesitated for a moment and then slowly answered, 'Yes, I do believe it. I am not afraid to die but I want somebody to love me.'

"The old cry for love, the strong yearning for the sympathy of kindred hearts would not be put down. I said, 'Frankie, I love you. Poor boy, you shall not be left alone. Does this bring some comfort to you?'

"'Do you love me? Will you stay with me and not leave me?'

"'I will not leave you. Be comforted. I will stay as long as you wish.'

"I kissed the pale forehead as if it had been that of my own child. A glad light flashed across his face.

"'Oh, kiss me again. That was given like my sister. Mrs. Sharp, won't you kiss me too? I don't think it will be so hard to die if you will both love me.'

"His suffering did not last long. With his face nestled against mine and his large blue eyes fixed in perfect composure upon me to the last, he breathed out his life."
("Carlton")

Crying Out for Mercy

Camp Douglas, near Chicago, became the prison camp for captured Confederate soldiers taken after the battle at Fort Donelson, Tennessee of February 16, 1862. Reverend Dr. Robert Patterson of Reformed Church in Chicago worked with the Army Committee among the Confederates and others at this camp. He relates the following story:

Upon arrival, I observed the hospital flag flying over a cavalry horse stable at Camp Douglas. I directed my steps toward it and was met at the door by one of our Chicago city physicians. I asked him if the building was used as a hospital and he assured me it was. He mentioned that he was the physician in charge and that he had volunteered for the duty. He said that a number of the men were in a dangerous condition, some of them dying, and that no minister had yet called to see them.

The long building was filled with cots, most of which were occupied. In the furthest corner lay a man in the agonies of death. His voice was unimpaired, though the contracted lips, the pale bloodless face, and the glazing eye plainly told me that his hours were almost over. He was conscious of his situation but utterly indifferent to the friends who stood around him and to anything they might have said. Only one prayer issued from his lips: "God, have mercy on my soul," which he uttered with all his dying energy. The cry became fainter and fainter, until his voice ceased in death.

Learning to Pray

This solemn phrase and the sad departure of the man's spirit made a profound impression upon all in the hospital. As I turned my face toward the other end of the room, a soldier raised his hand from a cot down the row. I approached him and sat on the empty cot next to his to listen to his request.

"Stranger," said the man, an East Tennessee Confederate, with feverish energy, "the man that lay on that cot was taken out this morning and I have got the same sickness. I don't know how soon my turn may come but I want you to tell me what I ought to do."

I explained to him the way of salvation and thought I had done so with great simplicity. He looked at me with an earnestness, which I can never forget, and said, "Stranger, couldn't you make it very plain to a poor feller that never got no schoolin'?"

His words, spoken haltingly due to the fever sapping his strength, had a strange intensity in them. I tried again, this time simplifying and illustrating my points, hoping to succeed in helping him understand how Christ died for our sins. I concluded by saying, "You must pray to God to forgive you of your sins for Christ's sake."

"Preacher," he said, "I can't pray. Nobody never taught me nothing."

I asked, "Have you never prayed?"

His manner grew almost fierce as he shouted out, "I tell you I never got no schoolin'." Then, as if recollecting himself, he raised his head and added, "Stranger, couldn't you teach me a prayer? And, if I said it, then maybe the Lord would hear me."

I replied, "I will teach you a prayer and the Lord will hear you if you mean it sincerely." I

began to recite Psalm 51: "Have mercy upon me, O God, according to Thy lovingkindness: according unto the multitude of Thy tender mercies blot out my transgressions. Wash me thoroughly from mine iniquity, and cleanse me from my sin. For I acknowledge my transgressions: and my sin is ever before me."

"Yes," he said, raising his finger, "that's it, that's it exactly. But, stranger," rubbing his hand across his fevered brow and looking at me more piteously than ever through pain-filled eyes, "stranger, my head's full of the fever and I can't remember it. If it was writ down now, and I was to read it, don't you think the Lord would hear me? I could spell it out, preacher, if you think He'd hear me."

"It is written down, my poor brother, and, if there's a Bible in this hospital, I'll get it for you—and God will hear you."

I set out to find a Bible and discovered that, in a camp containing hundreds of sick and dying men and thousands of Confederate prisoners, there was not an accessible copy of the Word of God! I returned and told him, "There is not a Bible I can lay my hands on in camp but I will bring you one tomorrow, if God spares me."

Wistfully, he said, "But, stranger, what's to become of a poor feller if I should die tonight?"

I thought, "This is a most serious question."
(Robert Patterson)

Moving from Darkness into Light

After our regular meetings in the Chapel at Camp Douglas were dismissed, a little group of Christians would usually gather on the platform and have a season of prayer. The lights in the hall were extinguished at such times—only one or two were left burning near the speaker's stand. These candles cast little or no light into the large room, which then looked more like a great, dark, and forsaken cavern.

One night, as this meeting was about to conclude, a tall, muscular sergeant walked from the darkness into the light near us. In a voice trembling with emotion, he said, "Friends, there is something in this religion after all. I wish I had it. Will you pray for me that I may become a Christian?" Tears filled his eyes as we all knelt down with him and prayed.
(Robert Patterson)

Transforming Power

On one occasion, a number of delegates visited Camp Douglas and found a number of boys dancing around a fiddler. The visitors proposed a prayer meeting, very much to the disgust of a burly corporal who led the entertainment. However, after putting the matter to a vote in true democratic fashion, a large majority agreed that we should have a meeting for a while.

We asked the fiddler to assist us with the hymns. He replied, "I know nothing serious but 'John Brown's body lies a-mould'ring in the grave.'" But, after tasking his memory a bit, he recalled some other tunes and led the music quite acceptably.
(Robert Patterson)

Trading Sin for Righteousness

At its conclusion, the corporal, who had opposed us, mounted a box and alluded to some remarks we had made about gambling. He began a little speech, which concluded, "Now all of you fellers that want to give up this gambling "bidness," just do as I do and "shy up" your cards."

He pulled out a pack of cards from his pocket and, right there, "shied" them up into the air as high as he could. From all sides, a shower of cards went up and came down, fluttering into the mud where they were trampled under the feet of man.

Postscript: At one time, the offices at the Chicago Army Committee contained a peach basket, filled with playing cards that had been traded for books.
(Robert Patterson)

Heathen's Christian Worldview

On another occasion, an artillery officer said, "I am with you in everything to promote instruction and good morals among the soldiers."

For a moment, we thought that he himself was a Christian but, when asked, he replied, "No, I am a 'Tom Paine' infidel and I don't believe in the divine origin of religion but, if your tracts and preaching keep the men from gambling and drinking, I will help you." In this effort, he rendered a most effective service.
(Robert Patterson)

Historical Context:

The victory at Fort Donelson was followed up by impressive successes throughout Kentucky and Tennessee. At the same time the fighting was taking place at Fort Donelson, General Mitchell, leading the vanguard of the Army of the Ohio, now under General Buell, entered Bowling Green, Kentucky. This forced Sidney Johnston, the Confederate commander, to retreat toward Nashville. On February 24, 1862, Nashville surrendered. General Buell's army then quartered around it. In addition, operations were undertaken to open up the Mississippi. Columbus, Kentucky, Island "Number Ten," Forts Pillow and Randolph, and the city of Memphis fell in succession—the last one on June 5, 1862.

Meanwhile, in March, General Grant's army began a movement up the Tennessee River, which met its first resistance from Johnston's forces at Pittsburg Landing. A desperate battle followed on Sunday, April 6, 1862, which forced Grant back into a dangerous position. However, a part of Buell's army arrived

GIVING UP THE BUSINESS

at nightfall and, the next day, helped turn the tide against the Confederate Army. Union troops then followed Johnston's army to Corinth, Mississippi, which was evacuated on the April 29, 1862.

Mortally Wounded and Heaven Bound

The history of the April 6-7, 1862 battle at Pittsburg Landing, also known as Shiloh, is especially rich in incidents. Afterward, Mr. D. L. Moody, as was his custom, went from the Chicago Branch to serve the wounded. He recalls these two stories of his service there:

A surgeon, going over the field to bandage wounds, came upon a soldier lying in his blood with his face to the ground. Seeing the horrible wound in his side and the death pallor on his face, he was passing on to attend to others, when the dying man called him with a moan to come for just a moment—he wanted to be turned over. The doctor gently lifted his mangled body and laid the poor fellow on his back. A few moments later, while dressing wounds nearby, the surgeon heard him say, "This is glory. This is glory!"

Supposing it was the regret of a dying soldier, correcting his former view of the "pomp and circumstances of war" to one of carnage, the surgeon put his lips to the man's ear and asked, "What is glory, my dear fellow?"

"Oh, doctor, it's glory to die with my face upward!" And lifting his hand feebly to point his forefinger heavenward, he made his last earthly sign.

Conversion Experience

A man on one of the boatloads of wounded from the field was very low and in a kind of stupor. He was entirely unknown by anyone. A little stimulant was poured down his throat and Mr. Moody called him by different names but could get no response. Finally, upon hearing the name "William," the man opened his eyes and looked up. When revived, he was given more cordial and Mr. Moody asked if he was a Christian. With great anxiety, the man replied, "No, but I am so great a sinner that I can't be a Christian."

Mr. Moody told him he would read what Christ said about that. So turning to John 3, he started reading at the 14th verse:

"And as Moses lifted up the serpent in the wilderness, even so must the Son of Man be lifted up: that whosoever believeth in Him should not perish, but have everlasting life. For God so loved the world, that He gave His Only Begotten Son, that whosoever believeth in Him should not perish, but have everlasting life."

"Stop," said the dying man, "read that over again, will you?"

After Mr. Moody read it again, the man asked "Is that in there?"

"Yes," said Mr. Moody; "it's there just as I read it to you."

"And did Christ say that?"

"Yes."

Settling back on his pillow, the man began repeating the words with a strange, solemn look of peace in his face. He became oblivious to what was going on around him and continued murmuring the blessed words until Mr. Moody left him.

When Mr. Moody visited the next morning, he found the soldier's place empty. When he asked if anyone knew what happened to him, a nurse who had spent the hours with him replied,

"All the time I was with him, he was repeating something about Moses lifting up a serpent in the wilderness. When I asked him if there was anything I could do for him, he kept muttering what he had been muttering all along. Just before he died around midnight, his lips were still moving, though no sound escaped. I asked him if he might have some dying message for home but he only whispered the words: 'As Moses lifted up the serpent in the wilderness, even so must the Son of Man be lifted up: that whosoever believeth in Him…' until his voice died away and his lips moved no longer."
(D. L. Moody)

Impact of Magnificent Hymns

Of the aftermath of the battle at Pittsburg Landing (Shiloh), Tennessee on April 6-7, 1862, Reverend Dr. Robert Patterson, of the Reformed Church, Chicago, writes of this incident:

A brave and godly captain in one of our Western regiments told us his story as we were moving him to the hospital. He was shot through both thighs—a wound from which he could not recover. While lying on the field, he suffered intense agony because of thirst. While rain from heaven fell around him, he supported his head with his hand.

A pool of water quickly filled the hole made by his elbow. If he could only get to that puddle, he could quench his thirst. As hard as he tried, he was unable to reach it. He said, "I never felt such disappointment before—so needy, so near, and yet so helpless. After night fell and the stars sparkled clear and beautiful over the dark field, I began to think of the great God who had given His Son to die a death of agony for me. He was up there looking down—up above the scene of suffering and up above those glorious stars. I felt that I was going home to meet Him and praise Him there when I realized I ought to praise Him now in the midst of my wounds and in the rain. So with parched lips, I began to sing:

> "'When I can read my title clear
> To mansions in the skies,
> I bid farewell to every fear,
> And wipe my weeping eyes.'

"A Christian brother was in the brush near me. I could not see him but I could hear him. He took up the strain—and beyond him, another and another and another—until all across the battlefield of Shiloh, hymns of praise to God rang out far into the night."

Maintaining Endurance

The battle at Chickamauga, on September 19-20, 1863, brought great defeat and the second highest losses of the War for Union forces. Immediately after the Chickamauga battle, a delegate made this observation:

"When our men are stricken upon the field of battle, if anyone thinks they fill the air with cries and groans of agony, he greatly errs. An arm is shattered, a leg carried away, a bullet pierces the chest, and the soldier sinks down *silently* upon the ground or creeps away, if he can, without a murmur or complaint. The dying horse gives out his fearful utterance of suffering but the mangled rider remains quiet. The crash of musketry and the crack of rifles, the roar of guns and the shriek of shells, the Confederate whoop and the Federal cheer— all with an indescribable undertone of grinding, rumbling and splintering— make up the fearful noise of the battlefield. But our soldiers fall as the sparrow falls, speechlessly, and not without the Father's care."

Conviction of Sin

Pittsburg Landing (or Shiloh) was a solemn place during that interval on Sunday night prior to the two contending armies attacking each other again the next day, April 7, 1862. Mr. Charles Demond, of Boston, gave an address at the Closing Exercises of the Commission at the Capitol in which he preserves an incident, showing how some men realized their sinful condition while awaiting battle:

After the first day's fight, Confederates placed a wounded Union soldier on the ground, in the mud, and without care in one of their tents. During the long and terrible night of drenching rain and the roar of artillery fire, the text and argument of a sermon he had heard twenty years earlier came back to him. The next day, Union troops succeeded in battle and rescued this soldier. He was taken to St. Louis, where members of the Army Committee cared for him. The Holy Spirit then drove home the impression of that fearful night and caused the seed of truth, planted twenty years prior, to spring up and bring forth fruit in his conversion. For six weeks, he gave testimony to God's goodness before dying with a sense of abundant joy and hope. His last words summed up the source of this joy. He said, "My God…my country…my mother."

Life of Faithfulness

After the April 6-7, 1862 battle at Pittsburg Landing (Shiloh), Tennessee, Christian Commission delegate, Mr. K. A. Burnell, accompanied the sorrowful Governor of Wisconsin, Louis P. Harvey, and others on a state mission. They were to look after wounded soldiers from their state. Mr. Burnell, who later became the Field Agent of the St. Louis Committee on the Mississippi River, penned these words:

The morning before leaving for home, I visited the hospital tent of the 14th Wisconsin Infantry. As I entered the room, a pale-looking boy raised himself on his elbow and gazed eagerly at me. After addressing each man, I finally came to the young man's cot and offered him my hand. He looked at me earnestly and said, "Don't you know me?"

I could not remember him.

"Why, don't you remember the boy you talked to and prayed with at Milton, Wisconsin, on a Sunday morning about three years ago, as you were going to a meeting? Don't you remember finding me by the roadside and how you talked to me about honoring the Lord's Day?"

As he talked, the circumstances vividly came back to my memory. "Most certainly, I remember," I told him.

Tears came to his eyes as he said, "From that time, I have often thought of you and have wanted to see you again. The moment you came in the door, I knew you. Oh, how glad I am to see you once more!"

Governor Harvey was visibly moved by my account of one of his boys and, the next day, I took him to see the young soldier. It was a beautiful meeting between the weak young man, suffering for the Union flag, and the Honorable Governor who had done so much to vindicate its honor and purity.

Extending his hand and warmly grasping the soldier's, the Governor said, "God bless you, young man from Wisconsin," In tears, the boy—proud and pale—responded, "I am glad to see you, Governor." We then talked about Jesus and, after having prayer, we departed.

It should be noted that, several days later, Mr. Burnell presided over a prayer meeting on the boat that transported the Governor's relief party to Shiloh. This meeting was held within sight of Fort Henry. Unfortunately, this was the last religious service ever attended by Governor Harvey, as he drowned eight days later in the Tennessee River.

Some two years afterward, I held an open-air service on a cotton plantation outside of Vicksburg. While I hurriedly walked away, a soldier came charging after me. He called out, "Mister, Mister!" When I turned, I recognized the boy from the Shiloh tent. By now, he looked healthy and strong. He thanked me once again for the "comfortable words" spoken to him two years ago and for reproving him in Milton. After a few heart-felt words of encouragement, we said good-bye.

Still later in the war, I met him again once or twice. By then, he had matured into a "veteran." It always encouraged me greatly to see him. Each time we met, his words revealed how faithfully he was walking in the upward way.

Finding Peace

The "City of Memphis" arrived at Mound City, Illinois, with more than 750 wounded soldiers. Her lower, hurricane, and upper decks were overflowing with human cargo. Before sunrise on the morning of April 19th, I, along with others, began unloading the boat. We worked until seven o'clock that evening, carrying the disabled on stretchers, assisting those who could walk, and placing the men in various wards of hospitals.

About one hundred men had been comfortably lodged in tents on the hurricane deck. Six badly wounded men occupied one of the tents. Upon entering, I noticed that one man lay very still. The others raised themselves on their elbows and asked eagerly when they might be taken ashore. Because the one man never moved, I asked his comrades why he was so still. With respectful, solemn faces, they said, "He is dead."

I moved the blanket off his face and noticed the kind men had straightened him out. My heart melted as I thought of his loved ones at home. Taking hold of his arm to move it, I discovered his pocket New Testament underneath it. It was open to John 14 and as I looked at the page, these words of eternal consolation to the Christian caught my eye: "Let not your heart be troubled."

Of course, I could not be sure that the soldier had read these words and, yet, it was very moving to think so. His comrades told me how his life had been like a psalm and how his death was like watching someone enter the Kingdom of God.

One by one, the dead man's comrades were taken to the hospital. Each one beseeched me to make sure that he was decently and tenderly buried—for his mother's and sister's sake, that his beautiful life might end in a beautiful grave.

(K. A. Burnell)

Faithfulness in Death

Reverend E. P. Goodwin, Pastor of the Congregational Church, Columbus, Ohio, went to Pittsburg Landing from the State of Ohio after the April 6-7, 1862 battle, on an errand to minister to the wounded. He shared this incident:

Inspector Reed, of the Sanitary Commission, told me this story of a hospital scene in Nashville a short time after the battle:

"Private Andrew McGurk, of the 11th Illinois Regiment, was dying of typhoid fever. He lay near a window of the hospital and, as he looked out, his eye always caught sight of the flag floating from the dome of the Capitol. His regiment had been dreadfully cut up at Fort Donelson and, after Shiloh, they were almost wholly employed as orderlies and for special duty. In his delirium, the poor fellow seemed to get back into the fight again. With his strength gone, he broke out into whispering, 'Fought…till…almost…the…last…man…fell.'

"Then, catching sight of the ever-waving banner on the dome, he hesitatingly articulated,

'Ah! The…old…flag! It…waves…still.'

"Soon afterward, he expired."

Death as Home Going

Returning from the April 6-7, 1862 battle at Pittsburg Landing , Reverend E. P. Goodwin of the Congregational Church, Columbus, Ohio, records these two stories:

On the boat, a very intelligent German was fading fast with pneumonia. We worked with him a long time, trying to restore consciousness, but he was too far gone. We also tried to identify who he was. Searching in his pockets, we found two or three letters. One, written in very broken English, was from his wife of a year or two. Writing without any knowledge of his sickness, she gave a simple, touching account of the death of their little child. Ending the letter, she wrote, "Dear Philip, do come home. If you can't come, I want you to write something to put on the baby's tombstone."

Among these precious letters was a little tract, like many others the Christian Commission circulated. On it, we found the soldier's name, Philip Schaub, and the inscription, "presented by Chaplain Chidlaw."

We knew very little about the dying man. But the discovery of these few pages, wrapped up with the letters from home and lying so close to his heart, gave us hope that the father had gone to the baby's home in the better land.

Honoring the Dead

As we came down the river toward Fort Henry, a number of the poor fellows we had on board died. I told Dr. Smith, our Surgeon-General, how we ought to pay special attention to the sad last rites of these men. One of them, a German, had left some remarkable expressions of attachment to the country of his adoption among his memoranda. As we approached the shore, the steamer's head was put to and the bell tolled. Close to the long ruins beside the bank were the open, fresh graves where we committed "dust to dust, ashes to ashes." While the silent company bowed with uncovered heads, we offered a brief prayer and uttered a few last words. The scene was simple—much too simple to attract the attention of the hurrying world—but it was the burial scene of men who had died that we might live. As we cast our last looks upon the silent, nameless graves, we could not tell how many hearts would ache, how many lives would be saddened to hear of our mournful work.
(E. P. Goodwin)

Answered Prayers

Many of the wounded were brought to Cincinnati after the April 6-7, 1862 battle of Pittsburg Landing, Tennessee. Mr. A. E. Chamberlain, who was later named Chairman of the Cincinnati Branch of the Christian Commission, visited them often in the Fourth Street Hospital. He wrote about this father and his son:

The poor fellow's right arm was almost shot into pieces. I found him to be a very bright Christian. Surgeon Norton felt that death was imminent. He said, "It is no use to take off his arm. It will not save him." So someone telegraphed his father, who arrived the next morning and went in to see his boy. At noon, he stood up in our daily prayer meeting and stated, "Brethren, I have great faith in the power of prayer. I have a son in Fourth Street Hospital. The surgeon says he will soon die. I believe if you will pray for God to restore him to health, He will do it. Will you not pray?"

Being so accustomed to death, the request struck us as very strange. But we offered prayer as the old man had requested.

The next day, I went into the hospital where Surgeon Norton met me. He said, "Contrary to all our expectations, sir, the young man you are interested in is improving." In fact, he grew better with each passing day. One time, I found the father sitting by his son's cot when Dr. Norton came along.

"Tell me, doctor," I asked. "How do you account for this? You physicians told me he was going to die. How do you explain his condition today?"

"Well, sir," replied the Surgeon, "I can only say that I consider it a miracle. It is not anything we did."

"Doctor," said the old man, "I can explain it. God has heard the prayers of His people in behalf of this boy."

After hearing this, the surgeon moved on to his next patient in silence. A week or so passed and the soldier went home on a furlough, safe and sound.

Faith in Jesus

I visited with one soldier whose cot was in the upper ward of the hospital, at the very end of the room. He was a handsome, aristocratic-looking boy. Indeed, his appearance utterly deceived me. He looked like a young man in perfect health and I told him so. He replied, "I suppose I do look well but the physician says I will soon die. My wound is a bad one and I am only waiting here for my life to pass away."

"Are you a Christian?" I asked.

"No, sir, but I want very much to become one."

I prayed with him and gave him Newman Hall's little book, *Come to Jesus*.

"This little book will tell you how to become a Christian, I trust," and after some brief conversation, I departed.

The next morning, I thought about the boy a good deal and finally went back to the hospital to see him. His bed was positioned so that he could see me as I came up the stairway and I discovered that he was anxiously watching for me.

He greeted me by saying, "I was afraid you wouldn't come in this morning." Continuing, he said, "The surgeon says I will probably die during the day and I didn't want to die until I saw you and thanked you for giving me that little book. I want you to know that everything for the future is bright and pleasant now."

The surgeon's words proved to be true. He died that day, "Coming to Jesus," indeed.
(A. E. Chamberlain)

Prophetic Words

A month after Pittsburg Landing, I was getting on a train, headed west, at Seneca Falls, New York. A Baptist deacon of that village, whom I knew well, spotted me and shouted out that his son, George, was in Fourth Sreet Hospital and that he was about to die and was not a Christian.

As soon as I reached home the next day, I went to see him. His right arm had been taken off at the shoulder and he felt very dejected. I talked with him long and earnestly. Later, I mentioned the case to Reverend Mr. Robinson, a Baptist clergyman of the city, and he visited with the soldier many times. Reverend Mr. Robinson told me afterward that George had become a Christian. Just before he died, I asked, "George, don't you think it is hard to die in the hospital?"

"No, sir," he replied. "I thank God I entered the army because, if I had not, I never would have lost this arm and, if I hadn't lost that, I never would have been brought to this hospital and, if I had not been brought here, I probably never would have found Christ."
(A. E. Chamberlain)

Reunion in Heaven

Mr. Robinson was bidding him good-bye, when the man said, "I want to thank you from the depths of my heart for your care and attention." He then prophetically uttered, "It will be but a very few days, sir, before we will be together again in the New Jerusalem. I shall wait for you there."

On the next day, the soldier was buried. Only a few days had passed, when Reverend Mr. Robinson, himself, was stricken with typhoid fever and died. His convert did not have to wait very long for the coming of his guide and friend. The soldier's case, his dying words, and Reverend Mr. Robinson's sudden demise generated a profound interest throughout the city of Cincinnati.

The Deacon's son was the last of a family of seven or eight children to find the Savior. He entered the army from Hillsdale, Michigan.
(A. E. Chamberlain)

Historical Context:

Union General Buell left Corinth, Mississippi in June 1862, moving east toward Chattanooga. General Bragg, the new Confederate commander, devised a bold plan. Near the end of August, he crossed the Tennessee River a few miles north of Chattanooga. He quickly moved northward into Kentucky and, upon meeting no serious opposition, he soon succeeded in thoroughly alarming Louisville and Cincinnati. Buell, leaving Nashville as well garrisoned as he could, hastened to Louisville. He arrived only a few hours in advance of Confederate forces. Bragg retreated slowly with Buell following cautiously until October 8, 1862, when the indecisive battle of Perryville, Kentucky was fought. Bragg continued his retreat but moved more rapidly.

Sinner's Prayer

Reverend B. W. Chidlaw, of Cleves, Ohio, was the well-known Western Agent of the American Sunday School Union and later was connected with the Cincinnati Branch of the Christian Commission. He was also Chaplain of an Ohio regiment, engaged in the battle of Perryville, October 8, 1862. Afterward, he worked untiringly among the wounded and wrote these two stories:

In one of the village meeting houses, where more than a hundred of the battlefield wounded were lying, I was making my way to the door when I felt someone pull at my coat. I turned around and a poor fellow said, "Preacher, are you in a hurry?"

"No, my friend, what do you wish?"

"Well, I am not like John over there. He is ready to die and knows what will become of him after death. But I am in the dark. I am not like him. Tell me, oh, tell me, what I must do to be saved?"

This poor man! He had neglected his soul's salvation and the Bible. A deep darkness brooded over his awakened mind but he was now honestly and earnestly inquiring about the way to be saved. It was my blessed privilege to tell him of Jesus, the sinner's friend, and of the salvation of the dying thief on the Cross, and of the salvation of his comrade John who knew the Lord and trusted in Him. The prayer of the publican, "God be merciful to me a sinner," filled the man's soul. With his lips, he gave utterance to this prayer and who can doubt that it reached the ears of our merciful and faithful High Priest, "…Who can have compassion on the ignorant and them that are out of the way."

Entering the Gates of Heaven

An old tavern at Lebanon, Kentucky was being used as a hospital for the wounded from the battle at Perryville. Here I found a brave young man with an Ohio regiment who was seriously wounded, yet cheerful, patient, and happy. His benevolent friends back home had sent him some money, which enabled me to buy some things to meet his physical needs and bring him comfort while lying on his bed of straw. I discovered that, even though he had become a Sunday school scholar, he had never professed his faith in Christ. Now he was anxious to make this commitment and did so with such clear and convincing evidence of sincerity that I baptized him as he lay among his comrades. Each of them looked upon the ceremony with awe and wonder and silence.

After commending this dear brother in Christ and all of his companions to the care and blessing of the God, I was about to leave the room when another soldier with a booming voice said, "Oh, brother, I am a deserter."

I exclaimed, "Why, no, my friend, you are not a deserter! Where did you lose your limb?"

"It was cut off the night after the battle and I am willing to fight and to die for my country. But three years ago, I joined the church at home in Indiana…but I wandered away from God. I left the ranks and deserted to the enemy. Oh, how I have sinned against God and my own soul! Now I want to re-enlist. Will you muster me in?"

The soldier fully persuaded me that his wish to be "mustered in" again was from a fully repentant heart. I gave him my hand and, after he renewed his vows of fidelity in prayer, I welcomed him back to the Lord's ranks. All the while, I felt filled with wonder and amazement at the mercy of our God who could turn an old tavern into a hospital and a hospital into the very House of God and Gate of Heaven.
(B. W. Chidlaw)

True Contentment

Chaplain J. C. Thomas, afterward the General Reading Agent of the Army of the Cumberland, was at the battle at Perryville, Kentucky with his regiment, the 83rd Illinois, on October 8, 1862. He writes of the following incidents:

While the battle unfolded outside, I was inside a house ministering to the wounded. A soldier, shot through the abdomen, lay writhing on the floor. Stooping down by him, I asked, "Do you love the Savior?"

The look of agony on his face instantly disappeared and a smile of joy lighted up his countenance as he said, "Oh, yes, and even now He does not forsake me."

The next morning, while passing near the house, a hand pressed against my shoulder. When I turned around, the soldier's comrade eagerly said, "You remember the man who lay here in such pain?"

"Yes."

"I need to tell you he is dead."

"How did he die?"

"He died happy in Jesus."

Seeing the Light in the Midst of Darkness

In certain circumstances, the simplest words in a soldier's mouth became pregnant with the history of his soul. When told by the surgeon that he had just five minutes to live, one of the wounded at Perryville replied, "This is the best moment of my life. It grows brighter and brighter."

And then he went away into the country where Light dwells.
(J. C. Thomas)

Historical Context:

When General Buell pushed his Union Army north after Confederate General Bragg's forces, General Rosecrans was in command of the Union Army in Northern Mississippi and Alabama. The Confederates defeated Buell in the Mississippi battles at Iuka and Corinth in September and October of 1862. A few days after the last conflict, Rosecrans replaced Buell as Supreme Commander. The Union Army had been greatly diminished by the withering battles, long marches, and the onslaught of enemy raids, so a strategic reorganization became necessary. When this was completed, Rosecrans moved forward from Nashville against Bragg on December 26, 1862.

On the December 31st of that year, the terrible battles of Stone River began. On New Year's Day of 1863, the two armies watched each other from afar. On January 2nd, the Union forces had the upper hand and, on the night of January 3rd, the Confederate Army evacuated Murfreesboro, Tennessee.

Honoring the Lord's Day

Colonel Granville Moody, better known in the Army of the Cumberland as the "Fighting Parson," relates an interesting piece of history about the movements, which preceded the battles of Stone River:

The advance from Nashville began near the end of the week. Rain, mud, and mist were the order of the day. The enemy's cavalry were harassing the front. Marching under such difficult circumstances made the troops unusually weary. General Rosecrans called a council of war to ask his generals' opinions on various issues pertaining to the movement. Someone asked, "Shall the army march or rest on Sunday?" The decision was far from unanimous. Some thought that, in stopping, precious time would be lost. Others suggested that the troops needed rest.

Toward the end of the discussion, nearly all had voiced their opinion except for General Thomas Crittenden, who had been pacing back and forth under the trees the whole time. When asked for his judgment, he turned toward the group and, pointing his finger solemnly upward toward the wet sky, he fervently said, "Gentlemen, we are going into a battle in a day or two and I always have thought it best to be on the right side of the Old Master. The army can wait." …So that Sunday, the soldiers rested.

Assurance of Eternal Life

At 11:00 P.M. on the first day of the battle at Murfreesboro, Tennessee, July 13, 1862, a well-equipped party of thirty-two delegates started from Philadelphia for the scene of impending carnage. A company of delegates from the Chicago Army Committee, on the same mission, found them at Nashville. This gathering of delegates heralded the commencement of an organized and precious work, soon to be inaugurated in the Cumberland Army. Reverend A. G. McAuley, Pastor of the Fifth Reformed Presbyterian Church, Philadelphia, headed the Philadelphia delegation. He related the following incident:

At this battle, Captain B. F. Haskett, Company C, 51st Ohio Volunteers, was mortally wounded. Some men carried him to an old house, near the battle-field, which was used as a hospital. The surgeon immediately saw that his case was beyond hope and began to ask him for his name, regiment, etc. Unable to speak, the dying soldier signed for writing materials. With a trembling hand, he wrote,

"Take me to my home in Knox County, Ohio, and let me be buried there beside my wife. Let there be a monument erected and, on it, let it be written, 'All with me is well. I died in the cause of my country—a cause second to none, save the cause of my blessed Redeemer in whom I trusted in life and who did not forsake me in death. Meet me in heaven.'" Shortly thereafter, the Christian soldier expired.

Finding Peace

Reverend A. G. McAuley, Pastor of the Fifth Reformed Presbyterian Church, Philadelphia, headed the Army Committee from Philadelphia at the December 31 – January 3, 1863 battle at Stone River, Tennessee. He related the following incident as told to him by Chaplain Crozier, 37th Indiana Regiment:

Sometimes, the blessed peace of God in the heart of the sufferer needed no words to make it evident. Again and again, in hospital and on the field, this peace shone forth in the very eyes of the wounded, leaving the imprint of God upon the body of a departed soul, a picture of Everlasting Hope:

During one of the lulls of the terrible fight, a youthful voice was heard calling for help, a sound quickly drowned out by the tumult of battle. After the fight was over, some soldiers went to look for the sufferer. While searching in some high bushes, they saw a boy of about sixteen sitting up against a tree. As they came near, they found that both his feet had been carried away by a cannon ball. Upon his lap, above the bloody stumps, lay his open Bible. His eyes were fixed heavenward and a look of joy was on his face. His finger, stiff and cold in death, was laid upon this verse of the Twenty-third Psalm: "Yea, though I walk through the valley and shadow of death, I will fear no evil, for Thou art with me. Thy rod and Thy staff they comfort me."

Willing Sacrifice for a Noble Cause.

Chaplain C. C. McCabe, of the 121st Ohio Regiment and member of the Ohio Conference, M. E. Church, gives the story of one of the wounded at Stone River in early January 1863. This soldier was taken to a hospital in Nashville:

A wounded hero was lying on the amputating table under the influence of chloroform. They cut off his strong right arm and cast it upon the pile of human limbs. Then they laid him gently upon his couch. When he awoke from his stupor, he realized his arm was missing. Lifting the cloth with his left arm, he found nothing but the bloody stump.

"Where's my arm?" he cried. "Get my arm. I want to see it once more."

They brought it to him. He took hold of the cold, clammy fingers and, looking steadfastly at the poor dead member, addressed it with tearful earnestness. With tears rolling down his cheeks, he said, "Good-bye, old arm! We have been together a long time. We must now part. Good-bye, old arm! You'll never fire another carbine nor swing another saber for the government."

Looking around at those witnessing this scene, he said, "Understand, I don't regret its loss. It has been torn from my body so that not one state should be torn from this glorious Union."

Was not the poet speaking for him? He wrote:

"Some things are worthless, some others so good,
That nations that buy them pay only in blood.
For Freedom and Union each man owes his part,
And here I pay my share, all warm from my heart."

Good Shepherd Finds a Wayward Sheep

Mr. A. E. Chamberlain, later named Chairman of the Cincinnati Branch of the Christian Commission, met some of the wounded from a Stone River battlefield of early 1863 in the Cincinnati hospitals. He writes of a conversation with one of them:

I found a man from Stone River near the door at Washington Park Hospital, just as I was leaving. I handed him a little book and, without a word, he threw it on the stand by his bed. I had never seen a soldier react like this before. I stepped closer to his cot. In my hand, I held another little book, *The Sinner's Welcome to Come to Christ*. I noticed that the title immediately caught his eye. While I talked with the man, I thought I would hold the book so he could still see it. Overlooking the way he had acted, I told him that I was glad to meet him and asked, "Are you a Christian?"

"No, and I don't want to be."

"Can you give me a good reason for not being one?"

"No, and I don't care whether I can or not."

We talked a little longer and his answers were as curt and unpleasant as possible. He told me that he had a wife and three children and that his wife was a praying woman. Quite suddenly, it occurred to me that he was a "backslider." To test my theory, I asked him a probing question:

"My dear sir, haven't you been a praying man?"

I was wholly unprepared for his immediate shock, which seemed to convulse his whole frame. "Yes, sir, I have. But I have departed further from God than any poor sinner ever did."

He seemed fairly "broken" and told me how happy he was when he had had a family altar:

"First of all, sir, I forgot to pray to God, myself, in secret. Then I threw my Bible away and haven't read one in months."

I observed that he kept looking at the little book I held in my hands, so I gave it to him.

He asked, "Do you suppose Jesus would receive a backslider like me?"

I told him about the "chief of sinners," and kneeling down, I prayed with him. He told me that his wounds had sufficiently healed and that he was returning to his regiment the next morning. Along with the little books, I gave him a New Testament and, after commending him to the care of the Good Shepherd who looks after His wandering sheep, I departed. He promised to read his New Testament often and to be diligent in secret prayer—a promise he evidently meant to keep.

Making a Covenant Not to Swear

All along, Missouri had been plagued with guerrillas and "bushwhackers," as well as by more formidable groups of troublemakers from Arkansas. In the summer of 1862, several new regiments were organized for State defense. Among these was the 33rd Missouri, a St. Louis regiment, recruited by Clinton B. Fisk. He tells the following story:

While the regiment was organizing at Benton Barracks, Colonel Fisk made a habit of conducting religious meetings with his men in the great amphitheatre at the St. Louis Fair Grounds. These meetings generated great interest. Thousands of citizens attended and one of the local clergymen preached. One Sunday, Reverend Dr. Nelson, Pastor of the First Presbyterian Church, was preaching earnestly upon the necessity of a pure life, exhorting the men to beware of the vices inherent to camp life. He especially warned them against profanity.

The Doctor related the practice of a certain Commodore who, whenever recruits reported for duty on his vessel, would enter into an agreement with them that he should do all the swearing for that vessel. Dr. Nelson appealed to the thousand Missouri soldiers in Colonel Fisk's regiment to enter into a solemn covenant that day with the Colonel that he should do all the swearing for the Thirty-third Missouri. The regiment rose to their feet as one and entered into this covenant. It was a spectacular response.

Breaching the Agreement Not to Swear

Several months passed, the meetings had stopped, and no preaching services were held for the regiment. Colonel Fisk was promoted to Brigadier General and followed Confederate General Price into Arkansas. One evening in February 1863, as the General sat in front of his headquarters at Helena, he heard someone down in the bottom lands, near the river, swearing in the most approved Flanders style.

After taking a closer look, he discovered that the swearing party was a teamster from his own headquarters. He was also a member of his "covenanting regiment" and a close personal friend. The man was hauling a heavy load of provisions from the depot to camp when his six mules had rebelled against being overloaded. They ran the wagon into a stump and snapped off the pole. The teamster opened his great vocabulary of wrath and profanity against the mules, the wagon, the Arkansas mud, the Confederates, and Jeff Davis. Awhile later, the teamster was passing General Fisk's headquarters. The General called to him and said, "John, didn't I hear someone swearing most terribly an hour ago down on the bottom?"

"I think you did, General."

"Do you know who it was?"

"Yes, sir, it was me, General."

"Do you remember the covenant you entered into at Benton Barracks, St. Louis, with Reverend Dr. Nelson, that I would do all the swearing for our old regiment?"

"*To be sure I do, General,*" he said. "*But then you were not there to do it and it had to be done right off!*"
(Clinton B. Fisk)

Heart of a Leader

General Fisk related this story in the hearing of President Abraham Lincoln in January 1865 at the Anniversary Meeting of the Christian Commission. This story was part of a speech he gave in the Hall of the House of Representatives in Washington. Judging from his response, the President enjoyed the incident immensely.

The next morning, General Fisk was waiting in the anteroom at the White House to see Mr. Lincoln. A poor, old man from Tennessee, with a very sorrowful look on his face, was moving around the large crowd. The General sat down beside him and asked about his desire to meet with the President. The man had been waiting for three or four days to get an audience. The life of his son, who was under sentence of death at Nashville for some military offense, depended on this meeting with the President.

General Fisk wrote the man's case, outlining it on a card, and sent it in with a special request that the President would see the man. In a moment, the order came. The old man was ushered past impatient senators, governors, and generals, into the President's presence. He showed his papers to Mr. Lincoln, who took them and said, with great kindness, that he would look into them and give him an answer the following day. The old man, with great apprehension, looked up into the President's sympathetic face and cried out, "Tomorrow may be too late. My son is under sentence of death. The decision must be made *right off.*"

The tall form of Mr. Lincoln bent over the old man in an instant. "Come," he said, "wait a bit. That 'right off' reminds me of a story." And then he went on to relate the story of John Todd, which General Fisk had told the evening before. As he told it, the old man listened intently and, for a moment, he forgot about his boy and sorrow. The President and listener laughed heartily together.

Mr. Lincoln took up the papers again, bent over them for a brief moment, and wrote a few magic words. Upon reading them, the old man's eyes filled

with tears. But now they were tears of joy, for the President's words had saved the life of his beloved son.
(Clinton B. Fisk)

CHAPTER IV
THE WESTERN ARMIES

FROM AFTER THE STONE RIVER BATTLES
UNTIL THE SURRENDER OF VICKSBURG

January 1863–July 1863

After the Stone River Battles of December 31, 1862 – January 3, 1863, Union General William Rosecrans and his Army of the Cumberland remained at Murfreesboro, Tennessee until midsummer of 1863. This relatively quiet period afforded the Christian Commission a rare opportunity to inaugurate their work more fully. Reverend Edward P. Smith, Pastor of the Congregational Church in Pepperell, Massachusetts, was appointed the General Field Agent in the Army of the Cumberland. He entered the lines, along with several other Christian Commission delegates, in early April. Organization began immediately and, with Nashville as the center of operations, the work in the army became recognized from "thenceforth rich in effort and in fruit."

Looking to Heaven

Along with their usual supplies, the first delegates carried some children's gifts and letters to soldiers. The history of one of these mementos has been accurately traced and is of particular interest. A seven year-old girl from Philadelphia sent the following letter, along with a New Testament, to "some sick soldier" in the hospitals at Nashville:

PHILADELPHIA, April 17, 1863.

My Dear Soldier,

I send you a little New Testament. I am a little girl seven years-old. I want to do something for the soldiers who do so much for us, so I have saved my pocket money to send this to you. Although I have never seen you, I intend to begin to pray that God will make and keep you good. Oh, how sorry I am that you have to leave your dear mother! Did she cry when you told her goodbye? Don't you think of her often at night when you are going to bed? Do you kneel down and say your prayers? If I were you, I wouldn't care if the other soldiers did laugh. God will smile upon you. I am sorry, very sorry, that you are sick. I wish I could be your nurse. I could wash your head and read to you. Do you know the hymn, "There is a happy land"?

I hope you will go to that land when you die. But, remember, I will pray that you will get well again. When you are able to sit up, I hope you will write to me and tell me all your troubles. Enclosed, you will find a postage stamp. I live at [she gave her address] North Ninth Street, Philadelphia. Good-bye.

Your friend,
Lizzie Scott

Mr. Caleb J. Milne, a delegate from Philadelphia, carried the New Testament and letter to Nashville. Not knowing exactly how to fulfill Lizzie's trust, Mr. Milne determined he would give it to the first man who asked for prayer at the evening prayer meeting in the convalescent ward of Hospital No. 8. When the invitation for prayer was given, the first man on his feet was a Michigan cavalryman. He earnestly inquired about the great question of salvation and, at the close of the meeting, Mr. Milne offered him a few words of counsel and handed him the child's package. What effect the letter had on the cavalryman is evident in his letter, written shortly afterward:

NASHVILLE, TENN, April 24, 1863.

Dear Sister Lizzie,

I received your kind letter from Mr. C. J. M.—a beautiful present, indeed, and I trust that it will be one of the means of converting others, as well as the receiver. May God bless the giver! You have done a good work. Continue to pray, dear sister, and God will answer you. He says so in His Word.

My dear mother is in the grave. Nearly eleven years have passed since she died but she died happy. I trust I shall meet her in heaven. I will try and pray for myself. I have been in the hospital for four months but now I am nearly well. I will be able to join my regiment to face the enemy soon and, if I should fall in the battlefield, I may have the blessed assurance of meeting my Savior in peace.

Yes, "there is a happy land." May we meet some day in that happy land. I do not think that my fellow soldiers will deter me from serving my Master. Many others here are striving with His Spirit.

I expect to go home to see my dear friends once more. I am very thankful that the privilege has been granted and I trust we shall have a happy meeting. Dear Lizzie, I must close. My prayer is that God may bless you. Write me again.

> Your friend,
> Stanley Nichols,
> Company F, 4th Michigan Cavalry, Nashville.

Reverend Thomas Atkinson gives the particulars of a very pleasant interview with Stanley Nichols, at No. 8 Hospital, Nashville, about the time of Chickamauga. His regiment had been at New Albany, Indiana, and was going forward to the front. He stopped at his old hospital overnight to see some friends. Reverend Atkinson gives this report:

"When I first saw him, he was standing late at night beside a cot. A lamp overhead gave a feeble light. He was the very picture of everything manly and noble and Christian. I stepped forward and asked, 'Are you Stanley Nichols?'

"'Yes, sir.'

"'Are you a Christian?'

"'Yes, thank God!'

"'Do you have the letter you got from little Lizzie?'

"'Yes, sir,' he said. He then went on to tell me of the influence it had had upon his life."

Mr. Atkinson's interview resulted in the American Tract Society of New York publishing the original correspondence, which excited such a deep interest throughout the country.

Reverend C. S. Armstrong, Chaplain of Nichols' regiment, writes that, after receiving Lizzie's letter, he always found Nichols to be a true Christian soldier and was of great service to him in his work among the men.

Ministry by the Dying

The chaplains of the army worked most cordially with the Christian Commission delegates and, as they were able, volunteered in the hospitals of Murfreesboro, Tennessee, after the Stone River Battles of December 31, 1862 – January 3, 1863. Chaplain J. C. Thomas gives the following account:

One Sunday, I distributed reading material throughout the nine hospitals in Murfreesboro. At the close of a short service in "No. 8," I glanced along a row of cots to see if there were any bad cases. One face caught my attention.

Approaching, I took a young man's hand, and softly asked, "My friend, are you a Christian?"

Opening his eyes, he gradually entered into the full meaning of my question and answered, "Oh, yes." Then pressing my hand with increasing earnestness, he added, "O, sir, I'm so glad you've come in here."

He was quiet for a moment and then, clasping his hands as though he were beholding the "vision of sanctification," he exclaimed, "Glory to God." His brother, being much affected, stood at his side.

Seeing his brother standing near, the sick man called him to his cot. Taking his hand, the soldier looked up into his face and pleadingly asked, "Tom, won't you go to heaven with us?"

Tom began to melt but was unable to reply. The dying man urged the question with intense, almost painful care and concern. I was moved to tears and, placing my hand gently on Tom's shoulder, said, "Tom, won't you go with us?"

"I will, sir," he responded—when the answer had found its way to his lips.

Trusting Jesus

In two days, I returned for a visit but found the young soldier was with Jesus. I learned from Tom how they both had escaped from the Confederate Army and, after reaching Nashville, had enlisted on the Union side.

Tom gave the following account of his brother's conversion. Sitting in his tent, a large one called a "Sibley," he was unusually thoughtful while the rest of us played cards. During a lull in the game, he broke the silence. "Boys, I've been thinking what kind of a life I've been leading and I'm resolved to quit sinning and begin praying—to try and lead a Christian life."

No taunts ensued, for all respected him as a faithful soldier and kind friend. In no time, he improved at taking every opportunity to talk with his fellow soldiers. In fact, he was so judicious and persevering that, in a few weeks, all swearing and gambling disappeared from the mess hall. We all witnessed my brother as he continued to serve Christ, right up to when he passed through the gates of death.
(J. C. Thomas)

Thankful Heart

Toward the close of April, Reverend Edward P. Smith, Pastor of the Congregational Church, Pepperell, Massachusetts, held a Sunday worship service in the General Hospital, just outside of Murfreesboro, Tennessee. This occurred during the lull in fighting after the Battles at Stone River, December 31, 1862 – January 3, 1863. He writes about the following incidents:

After the service, one of the nurses asked me to go down to Ward E where a sick man wanted a chaplain. Upon going, Mr. Dutton and I found the man, an East Tennessean, prostrate with fever. He was a tall, athletic man, middle aged and wholly unaccustomed to sickness, it seemed. I approached him cautiously, saying to myself, this is one of those cases of someone seeking religion, not because the man wishes for it but because he feels he must have it. He would not have God when he was well so now he wants me to make up for it in this last sickness. I began our conversations with these presuppositions:

"I am sorry to see you in this trouble."

He interrupted me, saying, "I'm sick, parson, but I'm not troubled. Did the nurse tell you I was in trouble?"

His cheerful tone and sweet smile showed me my mistake. This was the voice of a Christian and I immediately became as interested in the present test his faith as I had been before while distrusting his sincerity.

"Are you very sick?"

"Yes, and a heap of men are dying in this hospital but I am not troubled. It's all right, parson."

"Do you have a wife?"

"Yes."

"Children?"

"Six."

"Do they know, at home, how you are?"

"No, sir," he said, showing emotion for the first time. "And I don't know how they are but I ain't troubled about 'em. You see, parson, when the 'Rebels' run me off, my wife fed me out in the bushes. One night, she came to tell me the 'Rebels' were getting hot after me and I must go directly. We knelt down by a gum tree and prayed together. She gave me to God and I gave her and the children to God and then I took off for the Union lines and enlisted. I haven't heard from 'em since—and that was eight months ago. But I am not troubled about 'em. It's all right, parson. It's all right."

"Why did you send for me?" I asked.

"I wanted somebody to pray for me."

"What shall I pray for? You don't seem to want anything."

"Why, parson, can't a man pray without bein' in trouble? My mind is mighty weak and scattered-like. And I wanted somebody to come and help me thank God. You can pray for anything else you reckon I want. But thank Him first."

We knelt on the ground by the cot and, with tears and difficult utterance, I prayed with thanksgiving. The prostrate soldier would occasionally break in, saying, "Yes, Lord. Yes, thank God."

Trusting God

My preaching had taken place in the fortifications to Captain Bridge's Artillery Regiment. I entitled this particular message "Our safety in God's care," taken from Acts 5:17-28, concerning Peter's deliverance from prison. As I walked out of camp, an artilleryman joined me for a visit:

"That was a funny doctrine you preached this morning, Chaplain."

"It is a blessed doctrine," I replied, "and nobody ought to know it better than a soldier."

"I mean to say that it's a strange doctrine and I don't see how it can be true. Don't you think a forty-pounder, when it strikes a fellow, would kill him, whether he was religious or not?"

"Undoubtedly."

"Do you think if a Christian goes out on a skirmish line, a 'Rebel' sharpshooter can't hit him?"

"No," I said. "I think the Christian would be more likely to be hit than a man who was not a Christian."

"Don't the Christians take sick and go to the hospital and don't they carry 'em off just like anybody else?"

"Very often," I said.

"Just so," he replied. "I said to myself while you were talking about always being just as safe as Peter was, 'I'll make the Chaplain take back part of that.'"

"But," I replied, "my doctrine is that a minie ball would not *hurt*, not that it would not *hit*."

"Well, now, Chaplain, I've had a little experience of minie balls and I know they hurt."

"Are, you a Christian?"

"I wish I was but I have to confess, I'm not."

"Suppose you were a Christian, ready to die. What would that forty-pounder do for you?"

"It would take me straight to heaven."

"Would that hurt you?"

"Not much."

"Neither would the minie balls, nor the fever. Now, have you made the Chaplain take back his sermon?"

"Well, but, Chaplain, suppose he should be taken sick and go to the hospital but not die after all?"

Then I told him about my East Tennessee friend, who was "all right" and only wanted help to "thank God." I asked whether the fever was hurting him. Before I finished my story, the artilleryman was in tears. Grasping my hand at his good-bye, he said, "You are right, Chaplain. A man that is a real Christian can't be hurt. The religion in his soul makes the very best kind of a breastwork [a quickly made defense around a gun]."
(Edward P. Smith)

Purifying the Fellowship of Believers

The Christian soldiers in the army found it necessary to meet together in voluntary societies to gain mutual edification and encouragement. Reverend Edward P. Smith, who was Pastor of the Congregational Church, Pepperell, Massachusetts, was also Christian Commission delegate. He recalls his meeting with one of these organizations near Murfreesboro after the Battles of Stone River, December 31, 1862 – January 3, 1863:

On a Sunday morning in May 1863, I was on my way to minister to a regiment, when I discovered a group of soldiers, sitting on logs forming a hollow square under an oak tree. It turned out to be a Bible class of the First Michigan Engineers with a corporal serving as leader. They asked me to assume my usual role as teacher and I took them through the morning's lesson from The Book of James, Chapter One. These soldiers carried no Bible commentaries in their knapsacks but some of them had reference Bibles. The teachings of the hour were from the men's hearts, aided by knowledge they had stored away in early life. The question of sin, its origin and its purpose, was handled in a true soldier's way, from a practical standpoint, rather than according to precise theological terminology and schooling.
(Edward P. Smith)

Need for Purification through Fellowship

After the Bible class, I attended a meeting of the Christian Association of the regiment. Because they had no chaplain, they had formed themselves into a society. The Articles of Faith necessary for admission, to which a candidate must assent, were brief and comprehensive. It included these three points: 1) salvation through the atoning work of the Savior, 2) belief that this salvation must be personally experienced, and 3) proof of this experience, based on the testimony of the regiment.

Several candidates were slated for admittance this particular morning. Each stood up and gave his testimony, followed by the regiment's approval and consent. The candidates were approved one by one. The opinions of their fellow soldiers, as to their fitness or unfitness, were most freely and faithfully given. Few of these men had been accepted into their home churches under such stringent testing.
(Edward P. Smith)

Finding Purification through Fellowship

Sergeant Johansen desired to unite with the Association, as he said, not to help achieve anything but because he needed it: "I am not worthy, my brothers, as you know very well. You know my life has not been what it ought to have been as a Christian man. But if you can take me in and help me, I want to come. I intend to be true and if God and my comrades will help me, I shall be true. But if you think it will be dangerous to receive me, perhaps, you had better let me wait and try again later, even though I do not have much hope unless I have your assistance."

Remarks were called for and most freely given. Sergeant Johansen's life probably will not pass such a severe ordeal again until the final review. Every word was as kind as it was true and every comrade closed with the wish that the Sergeant might be accepted. He was approved by a unanimous vote.
(Edward P. Smith)

Finding Purification through Repentance

When Corporal Stanford spoke, he brought forth a compelling story. His account made his conversion clear, decisive, and rather remarkable. His Christian hopes were delightful. He spoke with deep emotion and moved me to tears. In his case, I figured that the vote on his approval would sail through quickly. But the third major issue—proof before the regiment—was raised by some of the men. They submitted strong objections to his admission. To the grief of many of his Christian comrades, he had persisted in a "gift enterprise," receiving chances from a firm in New York and selling them in the regiment. He insisted that it was not unchristian to do so—that he gave away a good portion of the money and stood a chance for making a large gain.

One after another, his comrades declared that they could not see it in that light and called Brother Stanford to renounce his practice. In the end, he expressed that he was willing to quit selling chances from that day forward, especially since it had been forbidden in the army by General Rosecrans, Commander.

The question arose, "Shall the corporal come in?" One after another, the men declared that he should not only *forsake* the sin but *repent* of it. They said, "Say you are sorry for it, corporal, and we will receive you."

But the corporal had taken a position and could see no way to retreat, nor could the brotherhood see any way to grant his membership. As a result, a committee was appointed to work with him. They did such a wise and faithful job that, at the next meeting, the corporal, after finding repentance and confession, came into cordial fellowship with the Association.
(Edward P. Smith)

Finding Purification through Baptism

At this meeting, the members also received into membership two soldiers who had never united with the church at home. They desired baptism by immersion. So at the close of the afternoon service, we marched to the banks of the Stone River, where we went down into the water. The comrades of the men stood near the side of the stream, singing "Am I a Soldier of the Cross?"

The scene was both strange and beautiful. Those scarred veterans on the bank were cheering for their two comrades who were dedicating themselves to God. But they were doing so in the very stream, which had run red with the blood of their fellow soldiers and enemies mere months before. Just above this point, the Confederates had made their most furious charge in January but were repulsed by Crittenden.

Triumph of Grace

Reverend A. B. Dascomb, Pastor of the Congregational Church, Woodstock, Vermont, came to Nashville as a delegate in early May 1863. The hospitals were filled with wounded from the battles outside Murfreesboro from December 1, 1862 through January 3, 1863. Mr. D. L. Moody, of Chicago, also arrived about the same time. The two of them were successful in establishing a daily prayer meeting, which began on May 10th in the basement of the Second Presbyterian Church of Nashville. This meeting was known for its remarkable character and continued until the work closed in the summer of 1865. Mr. Dascomb gives two accounts of one of the first fruits of this meeting:

I shall never forget one soldier whom I met in Nashville. His name was Jesse Zion. I learned of his story from his own lips after his conversion. His father served as a Presbyterian elder but the son had been disobedient and wicked from an early age. His little brother, who used to sleep with him, made a habit of kneeling by the bedside every night to say his simple child's prayers. This so enraged Jesse that, on occasion, he had been tempted to kill him. Only once did he seem to have been convicted of his wickedness—when his sister died. She had called her wayward brother to her side and tearfully prayed for him to meet her in heaven. He gave her his promise, but after her death, he ran away from home to escape the memory of her request and his parents' entreaties. He became a boatman on the Ohio River for some time after that and plunged into every conceivable vice practiced by the most depraved of these men.

When the war broke out, Jesse enlisted in an Ohio regiment and served at Shiloh, Perryville, and Stone River. At the last battle, he was wounded and no longer fit for active service, so he was sent to the barracks opposite of the Nashville Christian Commission rooms to act as cook. By God's grace, he was drawn into the daily prayer meeting. The words which he heard brought back the vivid memory of thoughts he had had on the battlefield after he was wounded—his sister's tearful prayer, his parents' lessons and unconditional love, his younger brother's bedside prayers. He had neglected so many of his early advantages that he was basically a very ignorant man. But he knew that God, the Deliverer, existed and he cried out mightily for His presence. The Lord heard the poor man's prayer and, in that strength, the soldier renewed the vow he made when his sister died. The change in his life was immediate and manifest. He regularly attended the prayer meetings and became an unofficial volunteer delegate among his fellow soldiers. He brought books and tracts to them and prayed with the sick and dying.

"I have served Satan diligently," he would say. "That's all past now and it can't be helped, God knows, but I want to serve Christ just as diligently." This was his purpose in life now. He was a lion who had become as a lamb. I confess that never, in my lifetime, have I witnessed what apparently was so great a triumph of grace.

Transforming Power of Prayer

While in Nashville, my daily routine included a visit to Hospital No. 20. During one of my visits there, I came upon a soldier obviously near death. I spoke to him earnestly and repeatedly but received no satisfactory response.

I was puzzled in that it was impossible to discern whether he was physically unable or volitionally indifferent to what I was saying. When I urged him to pray, still no answer came. Bending down to him, I repeated my request, giving him these words of petition: "God, be merciful to me a sinner. Savior, pity me. Jesus, save me."

When no reply was forthcoming, I sorrowfully turned to the next cot, occupied by a bright and glowing Christian. His words of faith and hope quickly drew my attention away from the speechless sufferer near me. Suddenly, I heard a low murmur of words from behind me. In a clear but very faint, struggling voice, the words I had said to him were repeated, "God, be merciful to me a sinner. Savior, pity me. Jesus, save me." A flickering glow glanced for a moment into the stony eyes and wavered over the sickly pale cheeks and lips—then went away forever.
(A. B. Dascomb)

Victory in Jesus

Mr. Thomas Atkinson of Chicago, who later would become a member of the Wittenberg Synod (Ohio) of the Lutheran Church, came to Nashville in early 1863. By then, the hospitals were filled with wounded from the battles outside Murfreesboro from December 1, 1862 through January 3, 1863. He tells the story of his first experience as a delegate in the Nashville hospitals:

The morning after Mr. Moody and I reached Nashville, we stood on the hotel steps debating where we should go. Thinking there was no time to lose, we went in different directions—he to Hospital No. 3 and I to No. 8. It was my first venture into my work with the Christian Commission and I scarcely knew what to do or say.

Entering the first floor of the large ward, I wavered with indecision while surgeons and nurses scurried in every direction. Doubt came upon me as to whether I could do this work, which the Lord had placed upon me. Suddenly, I noticed a man attentively observing me from a distant cot. I turned my eyes away from his and let them wander about the room. When I looked at him again, he was still watching me. Uttering a silent prayer to God, I went to him. His name was John Hays. He had a wife and five children.

"You seem to be very low, John."

"Yes, sir, I am."

"Are you a Christian?"

"No, sir, I'm not but my wife is. And just this morning, I asked the Lord to send me someone to tell me how I could get to be like her. When I saw you standing over there, I thought, 'Maybe the Lord has heard me. Maybe this is the man He has sent to help me.'"

The soldier's earnestness, my former indecision, and the evidence of a blessed opening—all these—made me strong in the faith;

"Yes, John, I am the Lord's messenger and, besides that, I have come to tell you that you are to become a child of Christ."

"Do you think so, sir? Then thank God for it!"

"The only way by which you can be made right with God is to trust in Jesus Christ for the forgiveness of your sins. That's what your wife has done." He waited as if I were going to say more.

"Why, sir," he said, "I didn't think that was the way. I thought I had to be sorry for a long time, and...and..." and he stopped here because he hardly knew what more to say.

"Listen," I said,

> "'Just as I am, without one plea,
> But that Thy blood was shed for me,
> And that Thou bidst me come to Thee,
> O Lamb of God, I come, I come.'"

"And will He save me that way for just nothing at all?"

"Yes,

> "'Nothing in my hands I bring,
> Simply to Thy cross I cling;
> Naked, come to Thee for dress;
> Helpless, cling to Thee for grace;
> Vile, I to the fountain fly;
> Wash me, Savior, or I die.'"

"I never knew it before, sir. I never knew it was so easy. Thank God! Thank God!"

A male nurse was standing nearby. The soldier turned to him and said, "Nurse, when this gentleman goes away, I want you to write to my wife and tell her that I have found out how to trust Jesus. Thank God! Thank God!"

During the next five days, he never faltered for a moment. His simple, child-like attachment to Christ carried him forward.

Rectifying Mistakes

At last, the morning came when John Hays' cot was empty. The nurse explained that the dying man had made arrangements for the prompt transport of his remains to his home. They were already en route. Then I discovered that the nurse had neglected the soldier's request to send a letter. His wife's first inclination about her husband's demise would be the arrival of the casket which contained his body. A sad mistake had been made—one without remedy. I wrote a letter to her and gave her the full particulars of her husband's triumphant departure. The answer I received was one of very precious interest:

"O, sir, I didn't think there were any earthly words, which could comfort me as did those in your letter. I am afraid I sinned against God, yesterday, as I stood by my husband's grave. I know I had hard, rebellious thoughts. No one knew about them but me—and God. As the minister said, 'Earth to earth, ashes to ashes, dust to dust,' I almost thought I could stand it no longer. It was hard to be separated from him thus, and to know so little—nothing about how he died. When I got back to the house, your letter was laying on the table. In it, I learned that John had found Jesus and I cried for joy.

"'Children,' I said, 'dry up your tears. Your father is not dead. He is alive in Heaven. Thank God!'

"At the grave, the war had seemed to be very cruel and wicked. It has all changed now. I shall meet John again. That is enough. Thank God for saving my husband."
(Thomas Atkinson)

Historical Context:

In November 1862, General Ulysses S. Grant, after completing his preparations, advanced into Mississippi. At the close of December, General William T. Sherman, along with 30,000 men who were transported down the Mississippi River and up the Yazoo in boats, made an assault upon Vicksburg, Mississippi. This battle continued for several days but proved to be entirely unsuccessful. Arkansas Post, on the White River, was captured in January 1863. During the same month, work began on a canal, intended to render Vicksburg useless but March rains paralyzed this effort to flank the Mississippi. The generals devised various plans to capture the Confederate stronghold but all ended in varying degrees of failure. Grand Gulf, below Vicksburg, was taken in early May, following Sherman's victory at Port Gibson. The Union Army then slowly approached Vicksburg from the southeast. After victories in Raymond, Jackson and Champion Hills, they crossed the Big Black River on May 18th and attacked on May 19th but were repelled. The massive assault on the city on May 22, 1863 taught Grant that it could not be stormed. As a result, he determined that he would lay siege to it. Already low on supplies, the Confederates lasted for forty days then surrendered on July 4th.

Rededication to Christ

After one of the fruitless expeditions "to climb up some other way" into Vicksburg, Mississippi, General Clinton B. Fisk's command was stationed at Helena, Arkansas. The General was also closely associated with the Christian Commission. He relates an incident which occurred here about February 1, 1863 before the surrender of Vicksburg on July 4, 1863:

For a month, our lines of communication had been cut off and we had received no letters from home. Of course, when the route was reopened, our thoughts turned to the mail. I went to the Post Office tent and found my precious allotment from my wife and children. I also received letters from my pastor and Sunday school children—for I had been reduced from the rank of Superintendent of the Sunday school to become a general in the army.

I sat down on a log by my tent to read these messages of love. I had read them thoroughly and was about to leave when an old soldier, seated near me on the same log, accosted me by saying, "Old fellow, I want you to read my letter for me."

Nothing on me indicated my rank. I turned and looked at the man and then reached for the letter, addressed to "John Shearer, Helena, Arkansas." The address began at the top of the envelope and ran diagonally down to the lower corner.

"Can't you read it yourself, John?"

"No."

"Then I will, of course, but why don't you know how to read? The fellows that don't know how to read, rightfully deserve to be found only on Jeff Davis' side."

Even though he was an Iowa soldier, I learned that he had been born in a slave state, which might have helped to excuse him. The letter was from John's wife. After speaking of the gathering in the crops and describing all the little affairs of home—Suzy's new dress, Johnny's new boots, and the baby's teeny tiny socks—the faithful wife launched into a sermon for John along these lines:

"John, the quarterly meeting was held last Saturday and the presiding elder stopped by our house. He told me that a great many men, who went into the army as Christians, came back very wicked because they had learned to swear and gamble and drink. Now, John, I want you to remember the promise you made as you were leaving me and the children about being a good man."

Ah! The soldier wept as he listened. When we came to the dear name that closed the precious letter, he raised the sleeve of his old coat, brushed away the great swelling tears, and said with a full heart, *Bully for her!* This was the soldier's "Amen," eloquent and expressive.

"Well, have you been 'a good man,' John?"

Then came the sad, sad story of profanity, gambling, and drunkenness, into which John had fallen. It also included the humble confession about his forgotten vow and how he would renew it and, with God's help, try to keep it.

I then mentioned my rank to him. This unsettled him at first but he soon got over it. I invited him to my tent and, afterward, he came to all our meetings.

Weeks passed and the horrors of grave-digging on the Mississippi struck thousands of brave men who were laid low with malaria in the swamps. The fever passed through our ranks, sweeping away six hundred of my own men while trying to take Vicksburg. One day, I found John Shearer, laying low with the fever. I moved from my role as the man's general and assumed my role as a delegate of the Christian Commission. John expressed his words of faith in the home beyond and gave me his last messages to wife and children. I then sang by his side the sweet hymn, which began…

> "Jesus can make a dying bed
> Feel soft as downy pillows are."

The soldier's eyes were soon closed in death.

Love for the Lord

General Clinton B. Fisk kept up constant communication with the Western Army Committees and with the Central Commission. He did all in his power to promote the value of the delegates' work in the army. At his urging, The St. Louis Committee of the Christian Commission sent Mr. K. A. Burnell of Milwaukee to Memphis, Tennessee as their first agent. In early spring of 1863, he opened a reading room in Memphis. He writes the following:

During February and March, I spent four weeks with the army before the surrender of Vicksburg, Mississippi on July 4, 1863. Coming back to Memphis, I had an interesting conversation with an aged soldier.

He said, "I joined the army as a Christian, fully expecting to stand up for Jesus. I tried hard but, with no regular Sunday service, no prayer meeting, no closet even for my own prayers, I think I fell back instead of advancing forward. Just before the fight at Arkansas Post, I found this out for certain. So I went to Christ and told Him all about it and He came back to me, brother, and was with me in the midst of that fight in a way I can never forget." The old soldier mused awhile and then continued, "It was peace—a peace in the midst of the battle. Indeed, it passed all understanding."

His countenance glowed as he proceeded, "It seemed as if I wanted to go home in the midst of the fight. I think I prayed that I might. I felt strong and courageous, loading and firing with the calmness of a man alone in a dense forest. Since that fight, I've had no doubts and feel, more and more every day that we boys need to know one thing: in order to fight best, we must know how to love the Lord Jesus with all our hearts."

Power of the Lord in Salvation

In early spring of 1863 and preceding the surrender of Vicksburg, Mississippi on July 4th, the St. Louis Committee of the Christian Commission sent Mr. K. A. Burnell of Milwaukee to Memphis, Tennessee as their first agent.

In one of the Memphis prayer meetings, a man rose and said, "Two weeks ago, I was one of the wickedest men in the army. Nothing was too bad for me to do or say but now, by the grace of God, I can say 'I am a sinner saved.' On guard duty this morning, I forgot my watchword. I was troubled but, as I was thinking about it, I realized, 'I have another countersign—Christ—and with that name, no guarded line on earth or in heaven can keep me from passing through.' When I had thought of that for a little while, my other countersign came to mind and everything was right again."
(K. A. Burnell)

Discharge from the Devil's Army

Mr. William Reynolds, President of the Christian Commission's Army branch, visited the Army of the Mississippi in April and May prior to the surrender of Vicksburg, Mississippi on July 4, 1863. He observed that the soldiers often used the most common incidents of their daily military life to describe their spiritual condition. An example of this took place one evening at a prayer meeting held at Milliken's Bend, Louisiana. He writes of it:

At the close of the meeting, many men asked me to pray for them, saying they wished to be Christians for the rest of their lives. After promising to be back on Sunday, I noticed a man following me as I was leaving. Stopping me, he began, "My friend, I want a discharge."

Supposing he meant a discharge from the army, I said, "I am afraid that would be hard to obtain, as you appear to be recovering from your wounds."

"Oh, that's not what I mean. I want a discharge from the devil's army. I've been fighting and serving in his ranks for twenty-five years and I'm tired and sick of the service. I want to leave his ranks and enlist under the banner of the Cross and fight for Jesus the balance of my life."

I said, "You can have that discharge by deserting the devil's ranks and by coming over to the Lord Jesus." I talked and prayed with him, leaving with him some suitable reading material.

On Sunday, at the close of the evening meeting, he said, "I want you to know that I have come over to the other side and I am now a 'Soldier of the Cross.'"

Conviction of the Holy Spirit

Mr. William Reynolds, President of the Christian Commission's Army branch, also visited the Army of the Mississippi in April and May prior to the surrender of Vicksburg, Mississippi on July 4, 1863. He writes four of the following five incidents:

When I visited an Iowa regiment to conduct a meeting, I was told that no religious services had been held for more than nine months. At the close, all Christians were requested to remain. Nine did so. I asked them if they were willing to live in the future as they had for the past nine months, with no religious services whatsoever. I reminded them of the command found in Hebrews 10:25: "Forsake not the assembling of yourselves together." A deep sense of remorse came over this little company, along with real repentance for their neglect of duty. At the close of my remarks, they all resolved that, with God's help, they would be more fully consecrated to their Savior, whom they had "followed afar off" for so many months.

That evening, a prayer meeting was held at a deserted plantation house nearby. At the appointed hour, the nine appeared as expected, along with two or three hundred fellow soldiers who came with them. As the meeting progressed, weeping ensued. Many who were unused to weeping were bathed in tears. Sobs and crying were heard in every part of the large congregation.

A fine-looking officer rose and said, "Soldiers, you are no doubt surprised to see me here this evening. You will be even more surprised when I tell you that I was once a Christian and now have a Christian wife and three children in Iowa. Before leaving home, my wife made me promise to maintain my Christian character in the army. But I soon forgot that promise. On entering this regiment, I lacked the moral courage to tell anyone I was a Christian. Ashamed to pray, I soon found Christ was ashamed of me. I fell headlong into profanity, intemperance, and gambling. As most of you know, I am now addicted to all these vices. Do you think I am happy? Absolutely not—I have been miserable. My faithful wife writes me a long letter each week and at the close often says, 'O George, if we are never permitted to meet on earth again, how it comforts me to know we shall meet on the other side of Jordan where there are no wars and no partings.'

"Fellow soldiers, how these letters burn my heart! How that wife of mine is so deceived! Many a night, I have laid awake, thinking about my fallen condition and then have drowned my thoughts with liquor in the morning. The day before yesterday, I received another letter from her in which she said, 'George, in looking over your letters, I am surprised you say nothing about your religious condition. O George, can it be possible you have turned your back upon your Savior and that you are no longer living as a Christian? If I thought for a moment you would fall in this war and I should never see you again in this world and that we would never meet in the next, *it would break my heart*.'"

This strong man was utterly broken. After he calmed down, he proceeded, "Now, soldiers, like the prodigal son, I am determined to return to my Father. From now on, I am determined to stand up for Christ as valiantly as I do for my country—so help me God."

From that day forward, his life proved the strength and sincerity of his purpose.

Soldier's Dying Words Bring Comfort

A dying man was brought into the Hindman Hospital at Helena by two soldiers. As soon as he was set down, be reached out his hand to the matron and asked her to shake hands with him, saying, "I am going home to my mansion on high. I love everybody—but, oh, how I love my Savior." A few minutes later, he passed from this life into eternity with a smile on his face and peace in his heart.

On examining his knapsack, we found a very touching letter from his wife. It told how she had just received a letter from him, along with a little book for George, their young son. She mentioned how little George had put the book into the cupboard and had said, "It must stay here till pa comes home."

I took a lock of his hair and cut it, then gathered up some trinkets from his knapsack. I sent them to his wife in Iowa and told her the dying words of her husband. After my return home, I received a letter from her in which she told me that she could not express her gratitude for the little things I had sent— for the lock of hair and, especially, the precious dying words. She mentioned that her husband had been converted while in the army and that the assurance of meeting him in the world beyond brought inexpressible comfort in her bereavement.

(William Reynolds)

Holy Spirit Empowerment

We went down from Helena, Arkansas to Milliken's Bend on a boat, crowded to its utmost capacity with soldiers and a wicked set of officers who were returning to their ranks. They spent their time drinking and gambling. Mr. Burnell and I soon discovered that we were the only Christians on the boat. We felt that, somehow, we must plant the Cross right in the midst of this scene.

Immediately after supper, the tables were cleared and nearly all began playing cards. We went into our stateroom and knelt down to ask God for help, as it seemed to me that anything we could do was utterly useless. When finished, we stationed ourselves in the center of the room. All around us were men intent upon their games—cursing bitterly at losses, laughing loudly over successes, and relating abominable stories. It seemed we were in the very pit of hell. I began by singing the hymn, "All hail the power of Jesus' name."

If a thunderbolt had fallen into their midst, their astonishment could not have been any greater. For a moment, every man stopped and looked at us in utter amazement. After singing two verses alone, Mr. Burnell stated that we were delegates of the Christian Commission. He explained that we were on our way to the army at Milliken's Bend for the purpose of preaching Christ and ministering to soldiers in distress. He then addressed the officers with a few sincere words, reminding them once again of the influence of their example on their troops. He spoke of how demoralizing it sometimes was and he beseeched them to care more about their men's eternal welfare. He mentioned to them about how many sons, given to the army by devoted Christian mothers, had been ruined through the example of wicked officers. For a moment, it seemed to make an impression but soon all were engaged once again in their gambling games. The tide seemed to have rolled back and covered up what we had said forevermore.

The service had been so short that we had little time to notice the effects, such as they were. At a table next to where we stood, one man attempted to resume the game three times during Mr. Burnell's talk but he failed. His muttered curses and jeers did not prevail until we had finished. One of the men at this table looked at us when we began, then dropped his eyes, and sat with bowed head even after we had concluded. Another man rose and left the room.

The next morning, a gentleman came up to Mr. Burnell and said, "You ought to be a general, sir."

"I know nothing of military affairs," was his reply.

"Ah, sir," he said, "but you have moral courage. Any man who could stand up amidst such iniquity and preach Christ as you did last night is a hero. I was a professor of religion before I came into the army but through bad associates and a lack of moral courage to meet my fellow officers as a Christian, I soon fell into profanity, gambling and drunkenness."

He seemed deeply affected and promised that, with God's help, he would show his colors and stand up for Jesus from that day forward.

While at Milliken's Bend, I was holding a meeting in an Indiana regiment. At the close, a man came forward and asked me if I had been on a certain boat two days prior. I told him, yes. He asked me if I was one of two who had sung and preached one evening. I told him I had helped in such a service.

He then explained, "Our first lieutenant has been a very wicked man but he has just returned from home on furlough and seems to be entirely different. He says that, while he and others were playing cards a few nights ago, two men came out of their stateroom and sung a hymn. He said they gave some convincing words about the influence officers had over the morals of their men. They spoke about Jesus. He tried to play after they had gone but it was no use. He lay awake all night. It revived the memories of childhood, bringing back a mother's admonitions and prayers. He then resolved, God being his helper, never to play again and that he would use his influence for good and not evil. And, sir, it has been this way since he came back."

Through all this, God taught me how much might be done even in the midst of sin. He showed me how even a little faith can conquer our spiritual adversary.
(William Reynolds)

Reverend R. Brown, Pastor of First Congregational Church of Oswego, Illinois and delegate in the Mississippi field, relates a similar incident, which occurred as he was returning home. He was on board the steamer *T. S. Arthur* with General McArthur and staff and the First Kansas Regiment. The boat had been fired into from the shore, where Marmaduke had improvised ways for batteries to impede the navigation of the stream. Danger past, the cabin was given up to gambling.

With much fear and trembling, Reverend Mr. Brown proposed to organize a meeting right in the midst of the players. The General consented to preside and a precious service followed. Many Christians on board made themselves known to Mr. Brown and, with earnestness, others promised to change their course of life. "The success of the meeting," he writes, "was a most signal rebuke to our cowardice. For two days we had waited for the devil to give place and, because he did not, we were almost willing to smother our convictions of duty and allow wickedness to go unrestrained."

Dividends of Christian Boldness

Just after arriving at Milliken's Bend, we held a meeting that night in an Iowa regiment. At the close, a man came up to me and said, "Stranger, would you like to come to a little prayer meeting out here in the woods?"

"Certainly," I said.

At about nine o'clock, we went half a mile in back of the encampments and there, under the trees with the moonlight beaming down through the leaves, was a band of about forty men. As we came up, someone was praying. We listened until the fervent "Amen" had sounded throughout the group, and then, without any introduction, I stepped forward and began addressing them. They were amazed at the appearance of a civilian among them but seemed genuinely interested. At the close, they came around me to express their gratitude and comments.

One said, "Stranger, where did you come from? Did you drop down from heaven or from where?"

I told them of my delegate's errand for the Christian Commission. I explained how I had come from their Northern homes to tell them they were not forgotten and how I wanted to encourage them to be soldiers of the Cross as well as for the country. They appeared to be deeply moved.

When I inquired as to why they were meeting out in the woods, they told me that they belonged to regiments, which, predominantly, were opposed to Christianity and interfered with their worship. This included officers as well as the troops. Subsequently, they had gathered together in this secret place of prayer that they might come in quiet to Him who hears and answers all human petitions

After calling upon their commanders and receiving their assurances that these men should be protected in their common devotional exercises, I organized a Christian association in each regiment.
(William Reynolds)

Distributing New Testaments

General Clinton Fisk, in his address at the Anniversary of the American Bible Society, in May, 1866, relates an incident prior to the surrender of Vicksburg, Mississippi on July 4, 1863:

More than 25,000 Bibles and Testaments have been given to soldiers and sailors from my own headquarters. I believed in putting them beside the Tactics and Army Regulations. Let me tell you of a little incident connected with the distribution. There was a brave soldier from Iowa, Colonel Samuel Rice. His name is now honored in the army because of the death of this Christian soldier, who died at Spotsylvania with his face to the foe. Colonel Rice commanded a brigade of my division in the Army of the Mississippi.

In the summer of 1863, the War Department advised us that a new edition of Army Tactics, prepared by General Casey, would soon be issued. We were eager to receive the book and inquiries at headquarters were frequently made about the new Tactics.

One morning, I received a package that contained a thousand New Testaments printed by the American Bible Society. They were placed at my headquarters in a nice little case, showing the backs with the titles in gilt letters. Soon afterward, Colonel Rice came in and, seeing books in the case, said, "So the Tactics have come. I am glad to see them."

"Yes, Colonel," I said, "the Tactics have come."

"Can I make my requisition for them this morning?"

I replied affirmatively.

"General," he said, "have you read these new Tactics?"

"Yes, sir, I have. I have studied them and I mean to study them morning and evening while I live."

The Colonel made his requisition for "forty-two Casey's Tactics" through his Adjutant General. When it was presented, I tied up a package of forty-two New Testaments and sent them out to his headquarters. His officers all gathered around to get the new book. As they opened the package, out came the New Testaments. Of course, a momentary disappointment ensued but it was the human means of leading more than one of them to a saving knowledge of the Supreme Tactician.

Colonel Rice had been spiritually inclined for a long time. He had been to our meetings and had talked to me on the subject at length. He then began reading the Bible from that very day, earnestly and prayerfully. A few months afterward, while leading his courageous boys against the bayonets of General Price, he received a serious wound. I visited him as he passed up the Mississippi River to his home to die and found him rejoicing in hope, clinging to the "sure word of prophecy" contained in the Blessed Book. He was looking forward to the time when he should join the great army above. I sat down with him, and we sang together…

> "Jesus can make a dying bed
> Feel soft as downy pillows are,
> As on His breast I lean my head,
> And breathe my life out sweetly there."

A few days ago, his chaplain sent me a long epistle, telling how triumphantly and gloriously this soldier had left earth for heaven.

Resting in the Lord While Facing Death

Mr. S. E. Bridgman, of Northampton, Massachusetts, preserves a story of the operations of the fleet against Vicksburg, as told by Surgeon Hopkins of the U.S. Navy in a letter to his mother:

You asked for a story, mother. Shall I give you one sad or glad? You remember the sad loss of the Cincinnati gunboat in late May. In the afternoon, the wounded were brought to me for surgery. I will give you the story of one of them. His name was David Hans. He was a handsome, muscular young man of twenty-three or twenty-five years. His left leg was shot off just above the knee but was still attached by a few shreds of muscles.

In this condition he swam ashore, refusing to be assisted. Pale, haggard, and bloodless, he was brought aboard. Not a murmur, not a groan, but such a weary, weary prospect for recovery. He asked, "Can you put me to sleep? I am in great pain."

"Yes, yes, we will put you to sleep right away."

His eyes were large, clear, and blue. They were filled with an unspeakable soul. They continued their wonderful silent eloquence—noiseless, alternating light and shade—until the chloroform closed them.

Another patient, also severely wounded, was brought to me for surgery and he also asked, "Can you put me to sleep?"

So I left the first man, before the amputation began, to give relief to the second. He was of a different temperament from the other and more clamorous but, after a little while, I had him very quiet. Then I said to the nurse, "Watch him for a few moments. If he stops breathing, call me. I must see the other man."

I then attended to Mr. Hans. We completed the operation, applied the dressings, and laid him in a bed. After another amputation, I went to him again. By now, he was awake and in great pain. Again he asked, "I want to go to sleep. Will you put me to sleep?"

"O poor, pale face," I thought. I see it now. Even the tongue was white. I almost wept. Could I even hope for his survival? But I could not hesitate in what I should do. That meek "Will you put me to sleep?" was so very brave, yet bordering on the mournful. It had the slightest touch of self-pity, yet so quiet and so grand! He was teaching me the lesson of suffering quietly.

"Yes, yes, we will put you to sleep."

His eyes opened and closed so wearily, so very wearily! They were wonderful eyes, as clear as two stars in the heavens, and over them the fine smooth brow and wavy hair.

"Will you give me some water?" he asked.

He drank and lay still again. Presently, he took a little stimulant and swallowed it obediently.

"Will that help me sleep?"

"Yes, you will sleep now."

Previously, he had taken a small amount of anodyne powder. Then he was quiet for a while.

I had hope for his survival but with an awful sense that it had no foundation. Very soon he grew restless, a restlessness hard to describe but peculiar. As a doctor for only a year, it was a restlessness I had already learned to dread. The restlessness became extreme. I left him for a while and when I returned, I wondered, "Will he be asleep?" He was quiet now.

The beautiful eyes were beautiful no longer! It was the soul that gave them beauty, so the soul must be very beautiful. Everything is calm now. Is he asleep? Yes, thank God, asleep now. An angel will awaken him soon.

Abiding Faith

The *Congregationalist* of August 14, 1863, contained a short memoir of Captain Henry M. Kellogg, Co. C, 33rd Kellogg Infantry, who was killed May 20th, in the charge on Vicksburg, Mississippi. A few excerpts, prepared by one of the editors, C. A. Richardson, Esquire, occur here:

Captain Kellogg had a strong foreboding of his death and the event did not find him unprepared. The Lieutenant Colonel of his regiment said, "I saw him as he marched to his death. He possessed a clear premonition about his fate, yet, he was calm and resolute. While waiting on the battlefield, he pointed to a little hill and said, 'I shall fall about that spot.'

"Then, as they moved forward to attack, he led at the forefront of his company and waved his sword above his head, calling out, 'Follow me to victory or death.'"

He fell within ten feet of the spot he had pointed out. When he was removed a few minutes later, his grip on his sword was so firm that it required force to unclasp his hand from the hilt.

A brief letter, written only four days before he fell, discloses his hopes for his beloved wife and son and reveals his complete reliance upon God's Divine will:

Christian Father's Testimony

Saturday Morning, 2 O'Clock.

My Darling Ama and Harry,

One more word before I engage in a deadly conflict with the enemy. This may be my last message to you—God knows and will do right. Our heavenly Father has permitted us to spend many happy days together. We shall have even more in heaven.

If I fall, Ama, live and be happy for Harry's sake. Remember I am not dead but have only put off the body to take on a crown of glory. I shall be with you just as much as ever. Try to think so. See me not as dead but ever by your side. Harry, my precious boy, you know not how much your father's heart yearns for you. Meet me, my boy, in heaven. There, we will pick flowers that never fade.

I love you both, my treasures—God knows how much. But if it is best, I can cheerfully die for my country. Ama, let this thought console you when you think of me. I do not dread to die. I do not dread to suffer with wounds, for my body is not me and its pains shall not disturb the peace of my soul. I am ready for God's will.

Good-bye, my Ama and my Harry, my wife and my boy, my father and my mother, my brothers and my sisters. Your

HENRY.

Penetrating Faith

Mr. F. G. Ensign, a student at the Chicago (Congregational) Theological Seminary, was commissioned by the St. Louis Committee of the Christian Commission for the work on the Mississippi. This was about the time of the siege and eventual surrender of the Confederates at Vicksburg, Mississippi on July 4, 1863. He writes the following:

In June, when we were trying to enter Vicksburg from the rear, we stopped by a little spring one day to get a drink. A soldier came down who had a cup in his hand. He gave it to us to use. We thanked him for his kindness and asked if he had drunk of that water of which the Savior spoke.

"No, I have not," he said.

"Well, then, you don't love the Savior. Why can't you begin now?"

"I've been thinking of it, sir, a great deal and know I ought to."

"Why not decide it now?" I asked.

"I don't know," he said. "I can't."

"But God thinks you can and is ready for you now."

He thought for a moment and, then, his reply came firm and clear—"I will."

Just then, some others came to the spring. I gave the soldier a little book and, after commending him to Christ, we separated.

After the surrender, I was back at Memphis in the Soldiers' Lodge, visiting and ministering to all I could. I eventually came to an emaciated-looking young man, who seemed to have gone through intense suffering. Bending over him, I asked what I could do for him. He opened his eyes and, throwing his arms round my neck, said, "Can it possibly be that this is you?"

I said, "I am so very sorry. I do not remember you.

"You don't know me? Don't you remember the soldier you met on Chickasaw Bayou, near the spring? Don't you remember a little book you gave me?"

"Yes, I most definitely remember now."

"Well," he said, "I gave my heart to Jesus because of that book. I am not going to live much longer. I am going to die but, I know that when I die, I shall go up home."

Finding Faith

Reverend Edward P. Smith, Pastor of the Congregational Church, Pepperell, Massachusetts and General Field Agent of the Christian Commission, received instructions from the Central Office. In June, he was to leave his own field temporarily to visit the army at Vicksburg, Mississippi during the siege that ended on July 4, 1863. This was to be done in conjunction with the delegates from Peoria, Chicago, and St. Louis. They were sent there to minister to the troops until the surrender of the city. However, Mr. Smith's health gave way because of the climate. He writes of his sickness and recovery:

I had been in the army but a few days when I was taken sick with malaria and carried to a division hospital. It was my first experience with sickness in camp. When they had carried me into the tent and left me alone, without even a sick comrade, I muttered, "Now you will have an opportunity to test the usefulness of the counsel you have so often given to soldiers in the same circumstances." Many a time, while standing by the cot of a sick soldier longing for home, I had said, "Only trust in Jesus and He will take care of you here, just as much as if you were at home."

But I found this counsel far easier to preach than to practice. I knew that God does all things right and well but I could not help but feeling that a change in my present circumstances would bring great improvement.

I endured a sleepless night—alone and without a light. The more I tried to settle into the conviction that God would provide and make things good for me, the more I longed for a change. My theology said, "It is right and well for me to be sick among strangers, if God wills" and my heart always added, "Yes, but it would be better to be sick at home." While I lay tossing on my blanket and thinking these things in the gray of the morning dawn, the fold of my tent parted and a black face peered through. It was "Old Nanny," a black woman who had taken my washing the day before. I could hear no one else moving about the hospital and wondered what had sent her there at this hour?

Looking tenderly at me, in slave dialect she said, "Master, do you see the bright side this morning?"

"No, Nanny," I said, "it isn't as bright as I would wish."

"Well, master, I always see the bright side."

"You do," I said, "Maybe you haven't had much trouble?"

"Maybe not," she said. Then she went on to tell me, in her simple, broken way, about her life in Virginia. She told me about the selling of her children one by one, about the auction sale of her husband and then about the day she, herself, was sold at auction. She was alone now in the camp, without having heard from one of her loved ones for many years.

"And you say, 'Maybe I haven't seen trouble,' master?"

"But, Nanny," I said, "have you seen the bright side all the time?"

"Always, master, always."

"Well how did you do it?"

"This is the way, master. When I see the great black cloud coming over," and she waved her dark hand inside the tent as though one might be settling on us, "and it appears like it's coming to crush me down, then I just whip around to the other side and find the Lord Jesus there. And then it's all bright and clear. The bright side is always where Jesus is, master."

"Well, Nanny, if you can do that, I think I ought to."

"It appears like you ought to, master, and you're a preacher of the Word of Jesus."

She went away. I turned myself on my blanket and said in my heart, "'The Lord is my Shepherd.' All is right and well. Now, come fever or health, come death or life, come burial on the Yazoo Bluff or in the churchyard at home, 'the Lord *is* my Shepherd.'"

With this came the sweet peace of rest—and God's care and love became very precious to me. I fell asleep. When I awoke, I was perspiring. My fever had broken. "Old Nanny's" faith had made me whole.

Raising Children

Reverend Edward P. Smith received instructions from the Central Office of the Christian Commission to leave his own field temporarily in June to visit the army at Vicksburg, Mississippi during the siege that ended on July 4, 1863. This was to be done in conjunction with the delegates from Peoria, Chicago and St. Louis. They were there to minister to the troops until the surrender of the city. Reverend Smith served as Pastor of the Congregational Church, Pepperell, Massachusetts and as General Field Agent of the Christian Commission.

The following incident illustrates the true manliness of a Christian soldier, the power of early training in righteousness, and the constant solicitude of friends at home. It also shows the way in which the Christian Commission was frequently the direct channel of good news. An example has been preserved by an agent of the Commission, who was for a short time on duty before Vicksburg:

The night scenes were sometimes grand, indeed. Shells discharged from the land batteries traced their beautiful, fiery paths high into the air above the beleaguered city. Here, they met the missiles ascending on the same errand from Commodore Porter's fleet where they crossed paths in brilliant curves. The sight was so spectacular so as to make the beholder almost forget about the mission on which these monsters were sent. On one such brilliant night, I came upon a regimental prayer meeting, under a bluff within short musket range of the enemy's fortifications. Whenever there was a discharge from our batteries, the Confederate sharpshooters along their lines would reply by a shower of minie balls, which cut the leaves over our heads and occasionally ricocheted down to the ground at our feet.

The Brigade commander ordered us to sing the hymns in a low, muffled voice but loud enough to "make melody in our hearts." This was to prevent drawing the attention and, perhaps, the fire of the enemy. The meeting was led by one of the regimental captains. He was both genuine and manly in his piety, which seemed to win the affection and attention of the soldiers. I was so much struck with it that I could not wait to meet the man. After meeting him the next day, we were invited to join the Colonel in his tent.

As was the custom, we were offered a drink from the ubiquitous bottle. As the single glass was passed around the circle and drew closer to me, I questioned in own mind how I should respectfully decline. I was even more interested to see what course my Christian captain would take. When the Colonel called upon him, he declined. When he was invited a second time, he declined again. The third time, he did so pointedly but courteously, so as not to give offense, nor to be imposed upon further.

Afterward, I asked, "Captain, do you always do that?"

"Yes," he said.

"Do you mean that you have never taken any intoxicating liquor?"

"Yes, just that."

"What? Not even to 'correct' this Yazoo water?"

"Never."

"Then I would guess you belonged to the 'cold water army' in your boyhood?"

"Yes. But I learned something better than that. My mother taught me this one thing—'what is right, is right,' and coming to Mississippi don't make any difference. It would not be right for me to accept an invitation to drink at home and I don't believe it would be right here. Therefore, I don't drink."

A few weeks later, while passing up the Mississippi River, I addressed a Sunday evening congregation. After the service, a lady came to inquire about her boy. She said, "I know that in an army of 40,000 men, this is a foolish request. But I want to ask you if you had met my son." She expressed her anxiety for his welfare and how she feared that the bad influences of the camp would lead him astray.

"He promised me that he would do well," she said, "and I have no reason to think he doesn't do well but, if I could only see somebody who could tell me from actual knowledge how he is doing, it would be such a relief."

She told me his name and regiment. Seeking to calm her fears, I assured her that, even in difficult circumstances, many soldiers were becoming better men, growing strong under difficult trials. To illustrate my point, I told her about my captain, without mentioning any names. I told her about the prayer meeting and of the scene in the Colonel's tent.

"Oh," she said, "that's beautiful—that's beautiful. His mother must be very proud of him."

"Yes, she is—and *you are the proud mother!*"

I shall never forget the joy that shone in her face and how she sprang across the carpet. After catching my hand in both of hers, she buried her face in my hand and dampened it with grateful tears. She said, "Is that my boy—is that Will? It sounds just like him. I knew he would do so. He always was a good boy. He told me he always would be—and I knew he would."

Heroic Courage in the Face of Death

Some instances of the heroism and trust of our soldiers and sailors before the surrender of Vicksburg on July 4, 1863 must be told:

In the terrible charge of May 22nd, Sergeant Falmer, of the 18th Illinois Regiment, was mortally wounded. As he lay bleeding to death, he called two of his comrades to his side. They took his last message home:

"I die in peace. You must meet me in heaven."

He called for the flag and they brought it. He looked at the torn banner with all of the love and devotion a soldier can give. He said, "Say to the boys that I am gone. But tell them never to give up the contest until Vicksburg falls."

His voice grew fainter and his comrades bent over to get his last words. They could only hear a murmured request that the flag should fly over him. Silently and solemnly it swayed above the soldier's head until he was at rest. (Edward P. Smith)

Facing Execution with Faithfulness

Reverend W. C. Van Meter, of the Howard Mission, New York City and a delegate of the Chicago Committee of the Christian Commission, relates the following incident:

On my way back home from Vicksburg, Mississippi, I met A. M. Shipman, an Ohio volunteer who was imprisoned for eight months as a hostage in the Vicksburg jail. He was released after the Confederates surrendered on July 4, 1863. A fellow prisoner, who had been forced into the Southern army and had deserted to ours, was recaptured and shot by the enemy. Before the execution, he succeeded in getting into Mr. Shipman's hands the following note:

"Kind friend, if ever you reach our happy lines, have this put in the Northern papers. I want my father, the Reverend Leonard Marsh who resides in Maine, to know what has become of me and why I was shot. I am to be shot for defending my country. I love her and am willing to die for her.

GET THE SHIP BY, BOYS

Tell my parents I am also happy in the Lord. My future is bright. I hope to speak to you as I pass by your cell to die."

JOHN B. MARSH.

One of the guards related to Mr. Shipman that when young Marsh was placed by his coffin and was ready to receive the fire of his executioners, he was told he could speak a word if he so desired. Stepping on his coffin and looking around on that fierce crowd of Union-haters, he cried out, "*Three cheers for the Old Flag and the Union.*"

Of course the patriotic sentiment met no response from that audience. Then, with his hands bound behind him and his eyes lifted as if the flag were in view, he shouted forth his own three cheers, "*Hurrah! hurrah! hurrah!*"

His clear, ringing voice had scarcely died away when the sharp crack of musketry added another name to the long roll of martyrs to the dear "Old Flag."

Devotion to Duty

The heroes were not in the army alone:

During the battle on May 22, 1863, Farragut swept up the Mississippi River, past the batteries at Vicksburg, Mississippi, when Lieutenant Cummings had a leg shot away by a Confederate cannonball. Refusing to go below, he shouted out to his brave sailors, "Get the ship by the batteries. Get the ship by, boys, and they may have the other leg." [*Note to Reader: Another historical account of Andrew Boyd Cummings' gallantry suggests that this incident occurred at Ft. Hudson, LA., March 14-15, 1863 and that he later died of his wounds on March 18th in New Orleans. If so, he never made it to Vicksburg.*]
(Edward P. Smith)

CHAPTER V
THE EASTERN ARMIES

FROM THE BEGINNING OF 1863 UNTIL LEE'S SECOND INVASION

January 1863–July 1863

At the beginning of 1863, the Christian Commission had two headquarters in the Army of the Potomac. One was located at the village of Acquia Creek, Virginia, while the other was at the railroad terminal at Falmouth, opposite Fredericksburg, Virginia. General Ambrose Burnside's second attempt to cross the Rappahannock River was frustrated by rain and sleet, mud and cold. This put thousands of veterans under the surgeon's care in the field hospital at Windmill Point, on the Potomac River, a few miles below Acquia Creek. This headquarters was in operation until the hospital was suddenly shut down and the patients moved elsewhere.

Joy in the Lord

Christian Commission delegate, Mr. T. O. Crawford, of Philadelphia, related these two incidents that occurred in Virginia at the Windmill Point Hospital in February after Burnside's second attempt to cross the Rappahannock River in 1863:

John B. Mitchell, of Mercer, Pennsylvania, was dying of typhoid fever. His tongue was so parched that he could not speak. I thought a lemon might quench his thirst and enable him to converse. After the surgeon gave me his consent, I offered the soldier a lemon. The poor man tried in vain to thank me but, after he had eaten it, he could talk quite easily.

I discovered that even though he had been a Sunday school scholar, he had no sense of the comforting presence of Christ. With great sincerity, I told him the story of how Jesus' crucifixion meant that his sins could be forgiven.

I explained how the agony of that hour brought about the redemption of humankind for those who believed. I told him about the dying thief who found the entrance to paradise, even at such a late hour. My heart yearned for this poor fellow, looking up at me out of his desperate need for help. I asked him if anything would prevent him from adopting the thief's words as his own prayer when the thief uttered, "Lord, remember me when Thou comest into Thy kingdom."

Hope came into his flushed face, as he answered, "No, I would be happy to make that my prayer." I spent a long time at his side, explaining to him the meaning of Christ's atonement and sacrifice. I never had such an intent listener. At last, I turned to go away, saying, "My dear brother, I'll pray for you that God may take you to Himself for Christ's sake."

He looked after me imploringly and said, "Don't go. Don't go. I want to talk more about Jesus."

I returned to his side and stayed with him some time longer. It seemed to comfort him very much. Again, when I tried to leave, he fixed his large, blue eyes on me and exclaimed, "O sir, don't leave me! Can't you stay with me longer? Please, do stay."

I told him about others who might need me just as much as he did. At once, he was quiet about his need for me to stay. Christ's story had taught him the lesson of sacrifice already. Telling him I would come again in the morning and write to his friends, I bade him good-bye.

Early the next day, I hastened to his tent where I found the soldier's place vacant. The nurse told me how he had gone home, saying, "After you left, he began praying and kept on for a long time. About six o'clock, he looked around and asked for you. We didn't know where you were or we would have sent for you. He then asked the other boys in the tent to pray for him but they were too sick or couldn't. So he began praying again. At eight o'clock, he spoke out in a loud voice such that all could hear him. He said, 'Amen, it's all right now. I am ready to die.' In ten minutes he was gone. Chaplain, I've been a nurse for seventeen months but that was the happiest death I ever saw."

Deliverance from Sin

A drum major of the 147th New York Regiment sent for me. The conversation, which followed, was intensely interesting. The soldier opened up to me all the hidden strife and troubles of his heart. He earnestly yearned for some relief and peace. His parents were Christians and his father, who had been a deacon, died when he was fifteen. After that, he had taken counsel from no one but himself. When he was twenty-five years old, he frequented the liquor store and eventually became a habitual drunkard. In spite of all of this, however, he somehow managed to make money at a fast pace. He ignored warnings about severe health problems. He once told his mother-in-law that, if he were to meet God after death, he would laugh to think about the fun-filled life he had led.

He soon became so much of a slave to rum that he could not do without it. In the autumn of 1862, he enlisted in the Union Army, thinking that his worldly possessions would do him little good if the Confederates were victors. He began to try to get along without his stimulant but became weak—almost helpless—and took to the canteen once again. A lieutenant came to his tent every morning for his liquor and the drunkards of the company generally regarded him as their leader. On the march to Falmouth, he severely injured himself in a drunken spree and was compelled to go to Windmill Point Hospital.

Here, a terrible mental and spiritual conflict ensued. One minute, he would vacillate between thinking the Bible was "all trash" and, the next, he would be overcome with its deep spiritual power. His vain objections would scatter in the wind and his desire for deliverance from its judgment or his sin would make him almost insane. He feebly strove to stop his drinking habits. In one moment, he would swear that brandy would not own him—even if it could save him—and, in another, he would take it whenever the surgeon prescribed it. Finally, the meaning of this conflict within himself began to dawn upon him. Far more than temptations were assailing him—there must be a Tempter. Far more than the words of a book were condemning, yet helping him—there must be a Deliverer. He saw that the Tempter had so bound him with the chains of a habit that only this unknown Deliverer could break these chains for him before he could gain the victory. So he called on the unknown Deliverer for help.

It was at this stage that I found him. I told him about Jesus and about the "faithful saying"—the agony and bloody sweat, the Cross and passion, the glorious resurrection and ascension. The surgeon prescribed a substitute for the brandy and the poor, weak, erring man began to retrace the way of his lost life. Next to the Bible, the book which seemed to meet most of his inner needs was James' *Anxious Inquirer Directed*. Slowly, his strength returned and the iron bands of his habit relaxed. He stood up a new man. He spoke earnestly to his former comrades and to the lieutenant who had been his companion in seeking fun. He stood strong in spite of the opposition and ridicule. He proved himself strong by the behavior of his everyday life until the regiment marched to the battlefield. On this field, he really found the Deliverer and really found freedom and peace in His abiding love, indeed. (T. O. Crawford)

Mother's Grief

Reverend Hervey D. Ganse, Pastor of Northwest Reformed Protestant [Dutch] Church, New York City, gave an address at the organizational meeting of the New York Branch of the Christian Commission in 1861. He tells of his experience at Windmill Point Hospital after Burnside's second attempt to cross the Rappahannock River:

Just after my arrival at Windmill Point, I learned of a mother in a neighboring tent who had come from a western county of New York to carry home her sick son. He had died about twelve hours before her arrival. She had looked upon his features, which had wasted to a shadow by the nature of his disease, and declared that she could not recognize him. She had refused to look at him again. I went with others to her tent to offer her sympathy, if not consolation. We found her swaying back and forth in her chair, in the peculiar gesture of distracting grief. There were some Christian ladies in the company and they joined their voices in tenderly singing *Jesus, Lover of My Soul.*

But it was easy to see that her heart was sealed against comfort. We offered to pray with her but she had not come to the attitude of prayer. She spoke of nothing but her child's sufferings. She was sure that he had lacked the most necessary attention. Oh, how she wished that she could have been with him! I strove to console her by appealing to her Christian faith. But she turned upon me fiercely and demanded, "Why did you not give your attention to him?"

I explained that I had just arrived but that others who were present had cared for his comfort. At last, in a quieter frame of mind, she kneeled while we prayed for her. And when we left her she grasped my hand. Looking intensely at my face, she said, "Take care of the rest."

Later, I met her again in Washington. Her last words to me again were "Take care of the rest."

Trusting Christ as Savior

Reverend Edward P. Smith served as Pastor of the Congregational Church, Pepperell, Massachusetts and, afterwards, as the General Field Agent of the Christian Commission in the Western Army. In February and March 1863, he had his first experience of working among the soldiers in the Potomac Army after Burnside's second attempt to cross the Rappahannock River. From his reminiscences, we gather the following incidents:

At Belle Plain, Virginia, while passing over from the First Division Hospital where I had spent the night with some dying men, I met a young soldier assigned to menial tasks in the hospital. Giving him some reading material from my haversack, I asked him about his personal salvation. He gave me an interesting account of his early life in an orphanage, of his education in the family of a kind Christian man who had given him a home, and of the subsequent death of his foster father. He told me of his only surviving friend, his Sunday school teacher, who occasionally had remembered his pupil in the army by a letter. He showed me one of these letters, full of kindness and tender solicitude for his conversion. I said, "Then you are not a Christian?"

"No, but I wish I was. I have been thinking and talking about it so long."

"Do you know that you can become a Christian today?"

"You don't mean so soon as that, do you?"

"Yes, I mean that you can begin a new life and a true life—and that's a Christian life—today. Wouldn't you like to begin today?"

"Yes, I would."

"Well, just over that hill near the run is a place where you will be entirely by yourself. Go and kneel down by that tree and tell your Savior that you want to be a Christian now. Tell him that, from this day forward, you are going to try and do His will. I want you to write to your Sunday school teacher and tell him what you have done. Then find a man in your company you know to be a Christian. Is there such a man?"

"Yes," he said, "there is." And he told me his name. "He is a Christian, I know."

"Well, find that man today. Tell him what you have done and ask him to pray for you. Will you do it? I don't mean, 'Will you think about it?' but, 'Will you do it,' and begin now over by the tree?"

"I will try, sir."

I was in a hurry and bade him good-bye but there was something in that farewell grasp of the hand, in the manly sincerity with which he said, "I will try." I felt that the issue was already settled.

Three days later, just as I was leaving that army, I saw my soldier on the extreme left in a battalion drill. As the line swung past me, I had only time to step alongside and ask, "Did you do it?" His answer was quick and firm. He said, "Yes, sir, I did it."

Conviction of Sin

During the interesting revival meetings held at Acquia Creek, Virginia, in an unfinished hospital building, a Michigan soldier stood up one evening to give his experience. He had enlisted a year before, leaving Katy, his wife, and a little one year-old babe in her arms. She was a Christian and never failed to ask him the great question about when he, too, would become a Christian. He had replied to her letters as often as he could but never said anything about becoming a follower of Jesus.

"Two nights ago," he explained, "I got this letter. It has made me a Christian and I want to read it to you."

He read it as best he could and stopped now and then to wipe his eyes and choke back his sobs. The letter announced, in a most tender and Christian way, the death of "Little Henry." It told of the mother's sorrow and hope. It closed by saying, "Now, Henry," (that was the father's name, too) "I believe I shall not live long and I expect, when I die, to go straight to our dear, little boy. The first thing he will ask me will be, 'Where's papa?' My dear Henry, what shall I tell him? Won't you go with me to see our boy again so we may have our home together in heaven?"

"When I got that letter," he continued, "I could not speak. I read it twice and put it in my knapsack and laid down to sleep. But, somehow, I couldn't sleep. I kept thinking about what my little boy would say, 'Where's papa, where's papa?' I got up, stirred the fire, read the letter again, and then lay down. But I could not sleep. It seemed as if I must see my boy once more. I knelt on my blanket and prayed, 'O Lord, take me to heaven to see Henry. Let me see Henry once more.' I lay down again but couldn't sleep.

Then I prayed once more and, while I was praying, it came over me all at once. Suppose I should go to heaven and Henry wouldn't want to see me. He is an angel now and I am a poor, drinking, swearing, miserable man. He would not know his father and, if he did, he could not love him. Then I began to pray that Jesus would forgive all my sins and make me fit to go to heaven. Somehow, while I was praying, I began to believe and to hope. I laid down on my blanket and dreamed of dying and of seeing my boy and Katy and my Savior. And that's the way I became a Christian. It was Katy's letter that did it."
(Edward P. Smith)

Turning to Christ in Revival

One stormy evening in March, the New York troops, who had been doing manual labor at the Acquia Creek wharf, were relieved by a new regiment. They were not yet accustomed to our meetings. We adjourned the small gathering at the hospital building and resumed at our own quarters, a little building where the delegates lived and slept, wrote and prayed. Some ten or fifteen soldiers were present. The leader of the meeting asked that each one should say a word about his spiritual experience. The speaking process had passed around the room until all the delegates and all, but two, of the soldiers had spoken.

One of the silent ones rose and, pointing to his throat, made signs that he wanted to speak but could not. He was suffering from acute aphonia, a disorder that prevented speech. He laid his hands on his breast and then upon his lips, signifying a full heart that could find no utterance. Then, as if he could not be satisfied without some word spoken for Christ, he motioned for a comrade to stand up beside him. When his proxy spoke, the man gave his approval and dissent by making signs when his proxy was speaking beyond the record. He gave us a very interesting outline of the soldier's trials and triumphs in the army.
(Edward P. Smith)

Revival of the Heart

When he sat down, only one man was left who had not borne testimony. He was a young man who had come late to the meeting. When he saw all of our eyes fixed on him, he rose after a long pause and spoke with deep emotion:

"This is a very strange meeting for me. I came in here to pick up a magazine and get some more reading material, not knowing that you had a meeting here tonight. I couldn't very well go back after I got here and so I have kept my seat—and such a meeting it has been! Memories have come back to me! I have been re-living my life at home while these comrades have been telling their stories. As for my soldier life, how strange and wicked it seems to me tonight!

"When I enlisted, I promised myself, my mother, and my Sunday school teacher that I would be true to my Christian commitment. When we went to camp, I found but one other Christian in my entire company. He was our lieutenant. We soon became fast friends and talked, prayed and read the Bible together. But in the fight at Antietam and the pursuit of Lee, we somehow became separated. After we got back on the banks of the Rappahannock, we were at dress parade one evening when I heard the lieutenant swearing fearfully. I addressed him right out, not remembering that he was an officer and I was a private.

"'Why, Lieutenant! Is that you?'"

"Then he swore at me to 'hush my impudence and keep my place.' His oath and angry look stunned me. It seemed as if it could not be that that Christian man was swearing. I began to doubt whether I or anybody else was a Christian and, in my doubting, I stopped praying. Then doubts grew thick and strong and it was not long before I too began to swear. If you come over to our regiment, you will find no man who can curse harder than I. But I am finished with it now. Brothers, God helping me, I am beginning a Christian life again tonight.

"This is my story. All of my comrades here have asked for prayers. But there is not one who needs your prayers as much as I. I know you will pray for me."

We saw him frequently after this and before the army moved out. He always seemed to be holding onto the true way.
(Edward P. Smith)

Fake Christianity

While visiting in the wards of the desolate hospital at Windmill Point, Virginia, I came upon a man who professed great admiration for the Christian religion without ever claiming to be a Christian himself. He declared himself to be a patron of Christianity—a fit representative of no small class of such patrons. He spoke in glowing terms of the Bible and the intellectual enjoyment it brought him. He referred to its poetry with special enthusiasm. He said his wife was a devout Christian woman. I asked him if he would like me to read to him from the Bible. He gladly assented and said that he always liked to read from the copy which was his wife's farewell gift. He asked me to retrieve it from his knapsack. Opening the book before him, I found a letter addressed to him. He was startled when he saw the handwriting.

"Why," he said with some confusion, "that's from my wife."

He asked me to read it for him. *It was the parting letter his wife had given him ten months prior and this was the first discovery and reading* by this patron of his wife's piety. Her loving words had been left to lie so very securely between the leaves of the unread Bible.
(Edward P. Smith)

Almost Persuaded

In the wards of the Windmill Point hospital in Virginia, I found a Massachusetts soldier. At one time, he was a Sunday school scholar who, unfortunately, was in the last stages of disease. He held in his pale, thin fingers a letter, which had been written by an aged and trembling hand. I read the salutation, which stated, "My dear Son." The letter looked worn, as if it had been read many times. Evidently, he had just read it again. As he lay against his knapsack pillow, something inexpressibly solemn and sad permeated his countenance. Adding to this, the death shadow was overtaking him. I passed my hand softly over his forehead, parting back the hair from as noble a brow as I have ever seen. He looked at me and his eyes filled with tears, a rare occurrence when life is ebbing away. It was a stranger's hand but laid on his head in kindness. Perhaps, it reminded him of a mother's gentle touch.

After casual conversation, softly I said, "You are almost through with this world."

"Am I?" he said.

"Yes, and I hope you are ready for the next."

"No, I am not—not ready, not ready!"

"Well, my dear friend, Jesus is all ready and waiting right here. Come *now*. Shall I pray?"

"Oh no, no. It is too late, too late! I ought to have come long ago."

And then he told me, as calmly as he could, of the time when he "almost became a Christian" but decided to let it pass until another winter. "That was the time. I might have come then but why didn't I? Why didn't I?" He then pulled the blanket over his face and sobbed aloud.

I tried to convince him that Jesus was waiting now to save him but he cried out, "Don't talk to me anymore. It's too late. I can't bear it!" And he motioned me away.

The next morning, bed No. 8 was empty. In the military mailbag was a letter, full of sorrow, on its way to a Christian home in Massachusetts. The old father was expecting an answer to his last letter. This was it. Oh, how that voice falls upon my ears and rings through my soul to this day!

Between those sobs from under that soldier's blanket, I continue hearing, "Too late. Too late! Why didn't I? Why didn't I?"

As I lifted the blanket from his face and took the last look for that far-away father, I saw the manly form on the stretcher, laid out for burial. I thought, "I will tell all my young friends it is not enough to belong to the Sunday school. You must belong to Jesus."
(Edward P. Smith)

Seeker Turns to Christ

Reverend Edward P. Smith, who served as Pastor of the Congregational Church, Pepperell, Massachusetts, had his first experience of working among the soldiers in the Potomac Army in February and March 1863. This occurred after Burnside's second attempt to cross the Rappahannock River. Smith later became the General Field Agent of the Christian Commission in the Western Army. He reminisced about these incidents, which began in Pepperell and progressed to the Gettysburg battlefield:

In 1861, a recruiting officer in a country town in Massachusetts learned that a young man, a farmer's son, was ready to enlist. He was about eighteen years of age—honest, open-hearted, and intelligent—but under the teaching and example of a profane and wicked father. None in the village school, which he attended, could equal him in cursing. He had no inclination for a soldier's life but his sense of duty led him to say that someone in his father's family should go to war. Since he was the only one who could go, he decided he must go. However, when the recruiting officer came to the door, he told him he was not ready to enlist yet and to come back in a few days. This scenario occurred several times, to the great annoyance of the recruiter. The young man's friends were equally astonished because this apparent vacillation was the exact opposite of all their former opinions about his straightforward character.

But his conduct had an explanation. The boy had a praying sister. In the midst of all his waywardness, he had been observing and influenced by her better way of life. In sharing his religious experience later, he confessed that he felt he could not enlist until he became a Christian. He based this on the grounds that he was not ready to die and he would not put himself in peril, from which he would surely run, until he was ready. In his own words, "I am not a coward but I can't go to hell. I know I would turn and run in battle." From this convoluted idea, he started his pilgrimage in the Christian life.

Conviction of Sin

Not being inclined to borrow his sister's Bible, he walked four miles after dark to a neighboring town and purchased one for himself. He read it with this sole purpose in mind—to get ready to enlist by getting ready to die.

"I began to read the Bible," he said, "as I would any other book—at the beginning. It was a very interesting story about the Creation and Abraham and Moses and the rest but, somehow, it didn't help me to get ready to enlist. In due time, I came to the 20th chapter of Exodus. I thought, 'Now I have it for sure. I've got to keep these Commandments and then I can go to war.' I gave myself two days to learn them perfectly. The next step was I knew I had to keep them. Of the ten, I was very conscious of violating only one. I knew what it was to take God's name in vain. That was the sin, which I had to overcome. But the more I tried, the more I swore. I never swore so hard in my life as during that week of trying to keep the Third Commandment. I tried and tried again. Every morning I said to myself, 'I will not swear today,' but I never made it to breakfast without swearing. My great trouble was a vicious, brindled cow that always kicked when she was milked

and put her foot in the pail. Then I kicked and cussed her. Somehow, I had to do it.
(Edward P. Smith)

Seeing the Need for Prayer

"It was getting serious. I had told the officer that I would be ready for him the next week without fail—and I could not fool with him anymore. Then I thought, 'I will enlist now and, the first night in camp, I will begin a Christian life and pray before my comrades.' Having reached this decision, I was feeling quite assured. If the officer had come that day, I would have enlisted. Then it occurred to me that I had better try the praying business in somebody's presence before going to camp. My father's hired man used to go through my room to enter his own. In the evening, just as I had dropped on my knees to try praying, the Irishman opened the door. I jumped up ashamed, as if I had been caught stealing. Then I thought to myself, 'I've been scared out of my senses by an Irishman! A pretty mess I'd make praying in camp!'

So my troubles only increased. I was swearing every day; the recruiting officer was coming soon. Something must be done. I must pray somehow, Irishman or no Irishman. I rose in the night and knelt by my bedside. Perspiration covered my hands and face. I clutched the bedclothes and could only articulate, 'Lord, help—help.' As I lay down that night, there was a strange feeling of relief, as if something had really been done. In the morning, I felt strong for my struggle with 'Old Brindle.' Getting up early, I prayed again, asking God to help me milk that cow without swearing. When I put down my pail, I put both lips between my teeth and said to myself, 'Now, old feller, if you've got any cussin' to do, you've got to do it all inside.' The cow kicked the pail as usual but I didn't swear. The next morning it was not so hard and, lately, 'Old Brindle' has grown quite gentle.

"From that time, I learned to tell God all my troubles and to ask for help. I began to find out that there were a good many things besides swearing for me to learn not to do. When the officer came back, I wrote my name. Now I am ready to face anything—Confederates or death. I know I shall never run."
(Edward P. Smith)

Need for Forgiveness

This was the story of a soul struggling into light, told to his pastor in what was probably the first serious religious conversation he ever had with anyone. Later, when he came to unite with the church and told of his experience before the committee, the pastor said, "You have given us a very remarkable experience but I have noticed that you have never once mentioned the name of Jesus. You say you hope your sins are forgiven but how do you know God can forgive sins?"

"I don't know," he answered, "but I have heard if a fellow wants to do right and is sorry that he has done wrong and tells God so, God will forgive him anyhow. I believe God has forgiven me but I don't know how He did it."

"But haven't you heard about Jesus?"

"Yes, I've heard of Him but, to tell you the truth, I haven't got to Him yet in my Bible. I've only gotten as far as the Psalms. I was thinking the other day I must begin at the other end and read a little about Jesus." He united with the church and, the next day, went to camp.
(Edward P. Smith)

Joy in Christ

His regiment joined the Army of the Potomac and spent the winter of 1862-63 camped on the Rappahannock River. His pastor visited this regiment. On entering the camp, the pastor inquired about the soldier and one of the soldier's comrades said, "He means the happy boy." Another said, "He is looking for the whistling Christian."

"Yes," the pastor said, "he is all that."

And so he was—in his little shelter tent, doing manual labor, on drill, in daily camp-life, singing, whistling, praying—Christian and happy through it all.
(Edward P. Smith)

Endurance in Suffering

After Chancellorsville, in the summer of 1863, his regiment followed Lee through Maryland. Weakened by chronic illness, he fell behind but refused to go to the hospital, even when ordered by the surgeon. Every day, he made his march, living on the rations which the army placed in its path. When he was too weak to carry his musket, he dragged it behind him. He inquired of everyone he met about how soon a battle might take place.

As the prospect of a battle grew imminent, his strength seemed to revive. He pressed forward and actually overtook his comrades, then fell into line as they were coming into position at Gettysburg. That day, he fought bravely enough and long enough to claim a hero's share in the great victory but, before the evening came, a minie ball struck his right leg. His leg was amputated, then re-amputated. He suffered for many long months in the hospital, lingering close at death's door. Writing to his mother from the hospital, he penned, "I have never been happier in my life." To his father, who had steadily opposed his going to war, he wrote, "I am not sorry for anything, unless it is for the poor sneaks who stay at home and wait for the 'draft.'"

He survived his injury and, at war's end, made an honest living on his wooden leg and lived as a most consistent, devoted Christian. When asked how he was cured of the bad habit of swearing, he replied, "By the grace of God and the help of 'Old Brindle.'"
(Edward P. Smith)

Hunger for the Bible

Mr. John A. Cole, of Medway, Massachusetts, had already served as a delegate for nearly six months when he was appointed General Field Agent early in 1863. His district was comprised of the Army of the Potomac and the hospitals and camps of Washington D.C., Maryland and Western Virginia. He vigorously undertook the work of planning and organizing. The first fruit of the plan was to supply every regiment in the army with New Testaments—a plan that was successfully carried out. He asked for an abundance of delegates and supplies, which he received. Six stations were kept in operation successfully until May 3rd. Some of the scenes of distributing the New Testaments and Bibles were very interesting. Reverend E. P. Smith, Pastor of the Congregational Church in Pepperell, Massachusetts writes of the following incidents:

I found one regiment that had thirty Germans in a single company. They had left their homes without the Word of God and had become hungry for it. A squad of these men promised the chaplain that, if he would give New Testaments to them, they would give him their playing cards and play no more.

Sharing the Bible

In another company of this regiment, a single English New Testament had circulated among thirty soldiers in five different tents during the entire winter. It had seldom lain unused for an hour during daylight hours.

The same response often resulted from asking, "Would you like a Testament?" Men would answer, "Yes, I would very much like to have one. I lost mine at Antietam or at South Mountain or at Fredericksburg."
(John A. Cole)

Longing for the Bible

Our prayer meetings are full and solemn. This a serious time for these armed men. They knew from those who fought with "Fighting Joe," as General Joseph Hooker was known, that difficult work lay ahead. The warm days and sounds of spring continually remind them of coming battles, wounds and death. They feel that they must prepare for these realities and, subsequently, they long for the Bible.

Mother's Prayer for Her Son's Salvation

Beginning in January 1863, the Christian Commission worked among soldiers of the Army of the Potomac in the hospitals and camps of Washington D.C., Maryland and Western Virginia. Six stations were kept in operation successfully until May 3rd. Reverend E. P. Smith, Pastor of the Congregational Church in Pepperell, Massachusetts, and later the General Field Agent of the Western Army, writes:

A lieutenant related an incident to the chaplain of the 1st Connecticut Cavalry, which illustrates the potency of appeals from home upon the soldier's heart. To the surprise of all, a young man in the regiment openly embraced Christianity. One day he happened in my tent and I asked, "How is it that your mind was awakened so suddenly?"

Taking a letter from his mother out of his pocket, he said, "There is something in this letter that affected me like nothing ever did before."

The letter said, "We have sent you a box of nice clothes, some fine cakes and fruits, and other luxuries and creature comforts. We hope you will have many good times enjoying them and sharing them with your friends."

Near the letter's close, she wrote, "*We are all praying for you, Charlie, that you may become a Christian.*"

"That's the sentence," said the grateful boy with tears gushing from his eyes. "When I was eating the cookies, I thought, 'Mother is praying for me. I know where she goes to pray and I can almost hear the words she prays.' All the time I was wearing the clothes she sent, I could not help thinking, 'We are all praying for you, Charlie, that you may become a Christian.' How I thank God for such a mother! Her prayer is answered and I am most happy."

Revival at Soldiers' Prayer Meeting

In early 1863, the Army of the Potomac was divided between a number of camps located in Washington, Maryland, and Western Virginia. Reverend William Barrows, Pastor of Congregational Church, Reading,

Massachusetts, gives a graphic account of one of these soldiers' meetings in a letter to the Boston *Recorder*:

A work of revival began at several of the stations of the Christian Commission. What took place became known as "earnest prayer meetings," in which soldiers played the most prominent role. The main feature of this meeting and every subsequent meeting was the manifestation of the Holy Spirit's power.

This particular gathering took place in a large Sibley tent, shaped like an Indian tee-pee. It served as the "upper room" and was warmed by an army cooking-stove. The tent was lighted by three candles and furnished with a long mess table. One real chair and several boxes and chests provided seats for twenty or more of the soldiers.

A minister, unknown to the men and fresh from home, was to lead the meeting. When a hymn was called for, someone began the service by disregarding the normal protocol of agreeing on the tune and humming the pitch when he struck up the words,

"Nearer, my God, to Thee."

The minister prayed and, before he could turn to his Scripture lesson for the morning, they started singing two stanzas of

"My Days Are Gliding Swiftly By."

Then someone read the account of the blind beggar, Bartimeus, and how Jesus healed him and how, afterwards, Bartimeus followed the Master. Someone shared a few words about how poor our estate is, by nature, corrupted by sin. He spoke about how blind we are to our own good and God's glory until we call on Jesus.

Then somebody began to sing

"I love to steal a while away."

Almost all joined in singing, except for one verse. This was followed by a prayer, short and fervent. Then a weather-worn soldier of the Cross and the government gave us an exhortation to serve Christ faithfully. The hymn,

"Jesus, Lover of my Soul,"

then filled the tent and died away on the hillside and among the pines, where the regiment had camped at such a grand and glorious location.

This was followed by a soldier who rose simply to testify briefly that he loved Jesus. He could not have used more than five sentences but it was all testimony to the glory of God. Another soldier prayed for his loved ones at home, the church and Sunday school, and for the prayer meeting. We were all so still that you would have supposed the praying man to have been alone in the tent. His praying voice trembled somewhat and, if we wiped away a tear or two when he said "amen," we were not ashamed to be seen weeping because several of us did so. Our thoughts had taken flight to home also. How could we restrain the tear?

And then, as if some of them might miss the earthly home in the throes of battle, a verse was sung, beginning,

"Sweet fields beyond the swelling flood."

Next, we heard a practical talk about following Christ in the army. The good ideas were put briefly and bluntly—and full of the love of the Lord Jesus. Then a single stanza, entitled "Come Ye that Love the Lord" penetrated outward among the pines again.

Another soldier gave an exhortation to any who had not enlisted under the Captain of our salvation and it was driven home by the sweet words and familiar chorus,

"O happy day that fixed my choice!"

We all knelt down on the clay floor and one soldier prayed in first person singular. It was a short, broken prayer—probably by the brother who had recently learned to pray in that very tent. We have all heard such prayers and none could ever affect us more deeply. This was followed by a sailor who gave us an exhortation on the difficulties of being a Christian in the army. He showed how they tried to do that at sea and illustrated it by a story. Then we sang the hymn,

"Thus far the Lord hath led me on."

The minister remarked that, in order to follow Christ successfully, we must stay in the ranks and witness to everybody, at proper times, that Christ is our Captain. He told us that following Christ by side marches and obscure paths exposes us to the lurking enemy.

By now the hour was almost gone. So we sang the doxology,

"Praise God from whom all blessings flow,"

and the minister gave the benediction.

We thought it would be worth a trip to the Army of the Potomac to learn from the soldiers how to have a good prayer meeting. Their plan was simple: No one was asked to pray or speak. No hymn was suggested. No one said he had nothing to say and then talked long enough to prove it. No one excused his inability to "edify."

Giving the Word of God to Needy Souls

In early 1863, the Army of the Potomac was divided between a number of camps located in Washington, Maryland, and Western Virginia. Here, the work of distributing the Scriptures to the army surpassed all other efforts to introduce the Christian Commission to all the men. This effort was so extensive and thorough and it came at such a time as to command attention, inquiry, and boundless gratitude. Reverend E. F. Williams, Pastor of Congregational Church, Whitinsville, Massachusetts, gives the following account. This work occurred on Sunday, April 12th, at Fairfax Court House in Virginia, where three brigades of cavalry and several artillery companies were stationed close by:

Posters on the village street corners and in the different camps announced our Sunday morning service. We walked out to the grounds of the jail, which was now used as a guardhouse. It was kept by Jackson, the brother of the murderer of Ellsworth, who was the first known casualty of the Civil War. Two or three Confederates, who had been accused of having been guerrillas, asked for reading material. When their request was granted, they asked, "Will you give us a New Testament?"

After we put one into their hands, we spoke a few words about the necessity of trusting in Christ and moved on. Outside of the jail, we met a man who would not accept any of our papers but who wanted a New Testament. His Testament had been drenched in battle—the leaves were falling out and the cover was worthless. He will surely read the new one. Another man lost his New Testament at Bull Run. Still another would not have lost his for a hundred dollars but it was lost with his knapsack on one of his raids. His mother had given it to him as a parting gift. One of ours took its place, although it will never *replace* his old one.

Expecting to die in battle, another man had given his Bible to his sister and was glad to receive a New Testament, which he will most definitely read. In a similar way, two dozen copies were distributed to the few men gathered around the guardhouse and the Post Commissary's quarters. All these men indicated they would attend church and they all wanted to know when they could talk with the delegates about home.

Giving Away Bible

At one of the regimental hospitals we visited, a man was so sick with inflammation of the bowels that we did not venture to speak to him. After talking with each patient and giving something to each one, we turned to leave when this very sick man motioned to his attendant to get him a New Testament.

This done, we asked if he had hope in Christ. He gave us a sign of assent and became quiet again. With the New Testament under his pillow, he lived until the third or fourth day, when his spirit took its flight home.
(E. F. Williams)

Bringing Good News

Reverend E. F. Williams served as Pastor of Congregational Church, Whitins-ville, Massachusetts. He gives the following account of a scene at Fairfax Station in Virginia on April 30, 1863 after a large box of New Testaments arrived for the three brigades of cavalry and several artillery companies stationed there:

When we inquired, we learned that three or four regiments of Pennsylvania troops had not had their share of attention. We loaded up with reading materials and trekked to the top of a hill, where the men were policing and burning brush. They ran to meet us, crying out, "What do you have to sell?"

"Nothing—nothing but New Testaments."

"What do you ask for them?"

"Only that you read them."

"Bully for you." "Give me one." "And me one" "And me." "And me."

A ring is formed and hands press forward for the book. The haversack is emptied in less time than it takes to read this account. The second, third, fourth loads go in the same way. The men had been in so many battles that hardly any of them had a New Testament or anything they had brought from home. The regiment contained a good many Christians, so the privilege of obtaining so much Scripture as a New Testament brought them tremendous joy.

Bearers of Good News

On the same day, we encountered a number of teamsters. Some of them belonged to regiments stationed at Wolf Run Shoals and Union Mills and others to the 5th Michigan Cavalry at Fairfax Court House. Upon seeing the New Testaments, they begged us to allow them to take twenty or more apiece to "the boys." We found it amazing that a dozen swearing teamsters wanted the task of being "Bible distributors" but they did their part and faithfully carried out their duty. In some of these companies, they generated an interest in religious matters.
(E. F. Williams)

Trusting Christ

In early 1863, Reverend John O. Barrows, Pastor of the Congregational Church, Northampton, New Hampshire, spent a few days of his term of service with the 18th Maine Regiment. They were camped slightly above the old village of Falmouth, Virginia. He wrote about a visit to a Rhode Island Battery nearby:

Each day, I watched these artillerymen as they galloped their horses past my tent door to the brook below. So after filling my haversack one afternoon, I paid them a visit. I found them more than ready to tell me about hard fighting and deep mud, long marches and lonely days—but none could tell me of Jesus' love. This was very unusual. Never before had I turned away from a company of men with so sad a heart. Suddenly, someone called after me. A young soldier came running toward me. A little out of breath, he asked, "Do you belong to the Christian Commission?"

Almost before I could answer, he said, "I saw some of your men at General Stoneman's regiment the other day and I got a book from them."

All of this was introduction. Then with trusting simplicity, he began to open up the story of his heart:

"I was as hard as any of them when I joined up but I had a praying mother. It almost broke her heart when I left home because she knew I was wild and reckless—but she kept praying for me anyway. In her letters, after whatever else she said, she always told me she was praying for me. But I didn't trouble myself much about it until one day a letter came to me at Poolesville. It wasn't very long but it took a long time to read it. Mother was dead.

"After that, I could see her, see the tears on her cheeks and hear her say the old words, over and over again, I'm praying for you. All through the Peninsula, it was still the same. She was right before my eyes continually—but I still didn't give in until I came to Fair Oaks. I had worked hard all day at our gun and, when the firing stopped, I sat down on a log by the road all alone. They were taking away the dead and wounded right in front of me. I thought about how I had been spared and then the question came, 'What has God spared me for?' Then another question came, 'Did my mother's prayers have anything to do with it?' They were solemn questions, Chaplain.

"Across the road, the only Christian in our battery was sitting against a tree. He saw I was thinking seriously, so he came over and asked me what was bothering me. I told him. He was quiet for a little while and then he asked me to go with him to a still place to pray. I went with him, knelt down, and I gave my heart to Jesus. You don't know how I love my Jesus, Chaplain. My friend has been with me ever since. He's been a great comfort when the boys laughed. Ridicule isn't much anyways, if I can keep remembering how my mother's prayers saved me."

He led me to the friend who had prayed with him at Fair Oaks. Their hearts seemed knit together, like the heart of one man. But it was, indeed, "rivers in a dry place and, to a thirsty land, streams of water," to find another with whom they could share a little of their Christian pilgrimage. Tears came into their eyes and mine as they told me how it seemed as if I must have come to the army, especially, to meet *them* and to hear their story.

I then returned to my tent. Somehow, my sorrow and sighing had fled away.

Comfort from Christ in Midst of Battle

Reverend Franklin Tuxbury was a Congregational Minister, residing in Exeter, New Hampshire. Writing in April 1863, he narrated a soldier's history, given at the close of a meeting in Washington:

A Lieutenant Colonel came to me with his story. He had a Christian mother and a praying wife, though he himself had been, as he said, "a very bad man." His narrow escapes in battle had awakened him. While going into the thickest of the fight at Antietam, he had been appalled by the thought of death without Christ. He had resolved to seek and find Him but, when the hour of danger passed, his impressions vanished.

At Fredericksburg, in greater danger than ever, his feelings of conviction returned. This time they were deepened by noticing the peculiar firmness and steadiness of several Christian men under fire. He was especially struck by the noble courage of a corporal who, after several standard bearers had been shot down, had seized the flagstaff and bravely bore it to immediate death. Calmly, he spoke to a friend, saying, "If I fall, tell my dear wife that I die with a good hope in Christ and that I am glad to give my life for my country."

"I cannot forget that," said the Colonel, "and I want to become a Christian for I know there is a reality in the Christian religion."

Thanksgiving

Near Washington in the spring of 1863, a work of grace was taking place at Camp Convalescent. The scenes at some of the meetings were thrilling with their emphasis on pathos and conviction, repentance and gratitude. No pen can ever adequately tell their story. Reverend George J. Mingins, then Pastor of (O.S.) Presbyterian Church, Huntingdon Valley, Pennsylvania, details an account given by a soldier at one of the gatherings:

One evening, those who had seen the Christian Commission's work and had benefited from it were invited to rise and tell their story. One after another delivered their testimony in the straightforward, manly, candid style—so much a trait of a soldier. The first man rose to his feet and said, "I hear say, Chaplain, that you are going East to Massachusetts. Well, tell them there that a Yankee of the Yankees, who never prayed at home, has learned to ask God morning and night to 'bless the Christian Commission!'" He sat down.

The next soldier that stood up was a young man, with his hand in a sling and his face pale from a long-lasting illness from a wound. He was touched deeply and could hardly speak. At last he said, "Chaplain, you will know what I think of the Christian Commission when I tell you my simple story. I love it and my dear old mother, out West, loves it. I know she prays night and morning for God to bless it because it saved her boy's life.

"After I was wounded, I lay all night on the battlefield. I shall never forget that night. Oh, what a long, terrible night it was! The stars were shining brightly but I could not enjoy them. I was dying of thirst. Oh, how I prayed that somebody would come near me—that God would send me relief! How my mind went home to my dear, old mother! O Chaplain, I thought it was hard to die when I knew all I needed was somebody to help me. But nobody came near me. I prayed that God would shut out the stars and let the sun come once more, bringing light and morning and relief.

"After awhile, I saw a light glimmering on the field. I wondered what it could be. Finally, I saw the shadow of a man carrying a lantern in his hand. I saw him stoop down, then get up, move along a little further and stoop down in another place. I knew he was lifting wounded men up and giving them something to drink. Then I began to pray with all my might that he would come near me and give me a mouthful of water. I tried to cry out but my tongue stuck to the roof of my mouth. The man came nearer and nearer. At one time I thought that he did not see me and was turning another way. O, how my heart was sickened! But he came nearer and I hit my arm on the ground so that he heard me.

"In a moment, he was kneeling by my side and pouring what, *I thought, was heaven, down my throat!* It was cool lemonade. The very moment my tongue was loosed, I exclaimed, 'God bless you! God bless you! Who are you, sir?' He lifted my head and, on the lapel of his coat, flashing in the light of the lantern, I saw the badge of the Christian Commission. I could not help it, but I cried out, 'Hurrah, boys! The Christian Commission has come! We are all right now!' The men answered back. 'Thank God! Thank God!' Ah, Chaplain, the Christian Commission saved my life that time and it has saved many a life, many a time." And he sat down amid a tearful audience.

Conviction Leading to Conversion

Reverend George J. Mingins, Pastor of (O.S.) Presbyterian Church, Hunting-don Valley, Pennsylvania, began a series of services in June 1863, at the chapel at Camp Convalescent near Alexandria, Virginia. About three hundred men attended the first meeting and about five hundred the second. On the third evening, the chapel was entirely too small to handle the crowd. Afterward, the meetings were held outside where the nightly attendance reached two thousand people or more. Reverend Mingins told of this incident:

"One evening, after a hard day's work of preaching and talking privately to the men, I retired at a late hour. Someone came to the tent door and wanted in. I asked, "Who's there?"

A voice replied, "Open the door, won't you, Chaplain?"

I did as requested and three men stood before me. One of them, a young soldier, spoke up and said, "Chaplain, it's a shame to come at this time of night but I couldn't help telling you how happy I am. O Chaplain, I've found Jesus."

I invited them in. The young man spoke again, saying, "Tonight, while sitting by the cookhouse door, I heard your voice as you were speaking. I said to a comrade, 'That fellow has a loud voice. Let's go and hear him—and have some fun at the meeting. We came to the meeting, Chaplain, to make fun. Then I heard you say, 'When the Lord riseth up, what will you do? When God visiteth, what will you answer?' These words rang in my heart. I couldn't make any fun anymore. I was thinking all the time about God and judgment and what I should do to answer God for my wickedness.

When the meeting was over, I was so miserable I did not know what to do. I tried to go to the tent. I tried to come and see you but I was afraid to do either. So I went into the woods and began to pray. My good, old mother taught me long ago what I must do to be saved. So I cried like the publican and, like him, I was accepted. After awhile, I heard other men praying near me and found these two. Speak to them, Chaplain. They want Jesus."

I spoke to them about Jesus and, before I left the camp, they had found Him precious.

Historical Context:

General Joseph Hooker's arrangements for crossing the Rappahannock River were carried out successfully at the close of April 1863. On May 1st, the disastrous battle of Chancellorsville began. It ended on the evening of the 4th with the hasty retreat of our left wing back across the Rappahannock with heavy loss. On May 6th, the entire army had fallen back to the old position. Field hospitals for the various corps were established quickly. They were immense and widely scattered, which called for new Christian Commission stations to be established immediately. These were located at Potomac Creek and at Howard and Brooks' Stations. A relief work of great scope and variety sprang up quickly.

Enduring Hardship

Reverend W. H. Eaton, Pastor of First Baptist Church, Nashua, New Hampshire, gives many interesting reminiscences of his hospital work after the battle of Chancellorsville, May 1-4, 1863. He was especially struck with the unfaltering courage of the men in these incidents:

About fifteen hundred of our wounded were left on the battlefield over the river. For *twelve days or more* they had little or no attention. Their wounds were, in many cases, dressed only once. The men had no shelter from the rain and sun, except for the scattered trees. When brought to the hospital, they were in a pitiful condition. Many died quickly thereafter. Others had wounds, filled with loathsome worms. "I don't expect to live," said a New Hampshire man who was in this condition. "All I ask is to be kept clean while I do live."

Reverend John M. Durgan, a Freewill Baptist Minister, who was also a Lieutenant of Company B, 12th New Hampshire Regiment, was severely wounded just below the heart. On the twelfth day, he was brought over the river with the rest. His rescuers feared he would not live to reach the hospital. When they proposed to take him from the ambulance on a stretcher, the brave man utterly refused all assistance. Getting out alone, he walked into the ward to his bed. He is still alive and able to preach the gospel.

Another had lost both legs by amputation. The next day, I saw him leaning nonchalantly on one arm, perusing the *Philadelphia Inquirer*.

Relying on God During Hardship

Still another had been very severely wounded but, after falling, he had succeeded in crawling under some trees. His was a golden testimony. He said, "Those twelve days were among the happiest of my life. I had my New Testament with me. All the strength I had was devoted to prayer and the reading of the Blessed Book. Never before did the Savior seem so precious or His Word so sweet. I would not part with this little book for any amount of money. It was my light and joy in those days of darkness and loneliness." (W. H. Eaton)

Enduring Hardship with a Hymn

Major Whittlesey, of General Howard's staff, told us of a chaplain who, for several days, had tried to save the limb of a wounded soldier. The surgeon decided that the leg must be taken off. The soldier wanted his chaplain to be present during the operation but felt the chaplain could not bear the sight. When the suffering man was put on a stretcher and taken to the amputating table, the chaplain remained behind. As he waited sadly, the chaplain was both surprised and electrified to hear the voice of his friend sounding forth from the room of pain, singing those precious lines—

> "How sweet the name of Jesus sounds
>   In a believer's ear!
> It soothes his sorrows, heals his wounds,
>   And drives away his fear."

(W. H. Eaton)

Reverend I. O. Sloan relates a very similar incident, which occurred during his experience as a delegate at one of the hospitals after Antietam. A young Massachusetts soldier, named Charles Warren, had given himself up to Jesus through the unremitting care and faithful admonition of this delegate's work. Mr. Sloan, unwilling to witness the scene, turned away as they carried the soldier to the operating table. Sloan had not walked far when he heard Warren's cheerful voice, singing,

> "There'll be no more sorrow there;
> In heaven above, where all is love,
>   There'll be no more sorrow there."

He returned to find the soldier drowsy from the chloroform. He remained in this condition, as the operation proved useless, until he passed away.

Victory in Death

Reverend E. F. Williams was Pastor of the Congregational Church, Whitinsville, Massachussets, and a Christian Commission delegate. He tells the story of the death of Captain Isaac R. Bronson after the battle of Chancellorsville, Virginia, May 1-4, 1863. He was shot in the shoulder on the May 3rd but lingered until the 20th:

Death held no terror for him but his struggle was one that only a parent's heart can know. He said, "Oh, if I could only get inside the old homestead and look into the faces of my little ones and my parents and George and Lottie, I would be satisfied."

I replied, "We shall see them pretty soon."

Pointing upward, he answered with a smile, saying, "Yes, only a little further to go."

Shortly before he breathed his last, he said, "Sing me one of the songs of Zion."

His wife, who had arrived to be with him, asked, "What shall we sing? 'Rock of Ages?'"

"Yes, 'Rock of Ages.'"

We sang that song and "Come sing to me of heaven."

For a moment, he appeared to be asleep. Bending over him, my ear caught the word "Glory," quickly followed by a loud, distinct voice, saying, "Death is nothing compared to the glory beyond."

I asked, "Is death swallowed up in victory?"

His answer came back from the threshold of the heavenly door as he said, "Death is swallowed up in victory."

Holy Spirit's Leading

The incident that follows was related by Mr. George H. Stuart, Chairman of the Christian Commission, after the Battle of Chancellorsville, Virginia on May 1-4, 1863. It presents a strange sequence of events in leading a soldier to Jesus:

After the battle, Private D_____, of the 68th Pennsylvania Regiment, a typesetter from Philadelphia, was detailed for service with the Ambulance Corps. Passing over the bloody field covered with all the valuable wreckage of battle, he saw a little, torn book lying on the ground. Picking it up, he put it in his pocket and soon forgot it.

Afterward, he was moving a wounded soldier onto a stretcher to be carried to the hospital when the man exclaimed, "Don't move me. I'm dying. My name is Jesse Stevens, of the 1st Massachusetts Regiment. I want you to pray for me."

Private D_____ did not know how to pray but it suddenly occurred to him to look at the little book he had picked up. To his great astonishment, he found on the outside page a prayer, entitled "After sudden visitation. At once, he knelt down and read in the ear of the dying man the words of the petition:

"O most gracious Father, we fly unto Thee for mercy on behalf of this Thy servant, here lying under the sudden visitation of Thy hand. If it be Thy will, preserve his life that there may be place for repentance but, if Thou hast otherwise appointed, let Thy mercy supply to him the desire for the usual opportunity for the trimming of his lamp. Stir up in him such sorrow for sin and such fervent love for Thee that Thy hand, in a short time, may do the work of many days. We pray for him so that, among the praises which Thy Saints and Holy Angels shall sing to the honor of Thy mercy through eternal ages, it may be to Thy unspeakable glory that Thou hast redeemed the soul of this Thy servant from eternal death and made him partaker of everlasting life through Jesus Christ our Lord. Amen."

During the prayer, the Confederates had arrived, posting themselves in the immediate area. They made D_____ their prisoner. During his confinement in Libby Prison in Richmond, the words of the dying man kept ringing in his ear: "I am dying. Pray for me." His sins came to mind but he found no peace. Subsequently, after arriving at Camp Distribution and hearing of a prayer meeting, he resolved to attend it. He was one of more than a hundred and twenty men who, that evening, rose to ask for prayer. His anxiety was further heightened after hearing from his wife who had become a Christian since he had left home. In all her letters, she urged him to give his heart to Christ. Shortly thereafter, he followed her advice and example.

Mr. Stuart bore the message of the soldier's decision to his happy wife. He still keeps, as a memento of solemn interest, the tattered leaves of the torn Prayer Book.

Work of Prayer

The work of holding prayer meetings among the men began as soon as possible after the Battle of Chancellorsville, Virginia on May 1-4, 1863. Reverend W. H. Eaton, Pastor of First Baptist Church, Nashua, New Hampshire, gives a graphic account of meetings at Potomac Creek Station:

Our station was on the thoroughfare between the hospitals of the 3rd and 6th Corps, one mile from Potomac Creek. We had three large wall tents put up in such a way as to make but one spacious room. On one side, we kept our books, papers, and hospital supplies. The other was used as a parlor by day, a chapel in the evening, and a sleeping room at night. For our parlor chairs we had rows of planks, five deep, resting on empty wooden boxes. In the evening, they were used as chapel pews and, at night, for spring beds. Colonel Bowman allowed us to have a small tent, close by, that we used as our kitchen. Joseph Jones, of the 84th Pennsylvania Volunteers, was in charge. Joseph was a committed Christian. During the previous winter, he had been converted at one of our stations. His work in his post as cook to the Christian Commission made him a very happy man.

Results of Prayer

Our prayer meetings began at early candle-lighting, although some of the soldiers used to come in a half hour or so before sunset. Some came on crutches and others with canes. Some had bandages around their heads while others had their arms in slings. All were sore and lame from recent wounds but able to move about. A hundred or more filled our chapel. At twilight, one of us would take a half dozen candles from the box but, lacking candlesticks, we put one into a potato, prepared for such a purpose, and suspended it from the roof by a wire. We placed another into a piece of board and put two or three more into small boxes, filled so as to keep the candles upright. Then the meeting began.

How the men turn their hearts back to their homes! "When I left home," says one, "my father took me by the hand and told me, 'It would not be half so hard to part with you if I knew you were a Christian.' I made up my mind to seek Christ then and I think I have found Him."

Another said, "I once had a hope but I have gone astray. The dangers of war did not awaken me. I have been in the habit of gambling since I was wounded. Today I got a letter from home with the sad news of the death of a dear sister, who was baptized on the same day I was. Ever since I have been in the army, she has written to me and has prayed for me that I might not bring shame to the cause of Christ. She has gone to heaven now and I want to forsake my sins and lead a Christian life. Won't you all pray for me?"

"I was wounded on the field," said another. "As I staggered off to the rear, the bullets kept singing past me and burying themselves in the ground all about. I expected immediate death. When I got beyond the hill, mostly out of danger, I fell on my knees and gave thanks to God. Now I mean to be His forever." (W. H. Eaton)

Kindnesses Reap Dividends

The following incident occurred at Falmouth, Virginia in the month of June, following the May 1-4, 1863 Battle of Chancellorsville. It shows how the soldiers were touched by little kindnesses—their very lives sometimes turned to Christ by them. This story was told by Reverend George N. Marden, Pastor of the Congregational Church, Boxborough, Massachusetts and a delegate at the Acquia Creek Station:

A vigorous-looking soldier came in, asking whether we had any sewing kits with needles, buttons, etc. He said, "I belong to Company B, 78th New York Regiment and I lost everything in the battle of Chancellorsville. I was lying down when a piece of shell struck me on the cartilage of the nose. It's all healed now but it was a close hit. I was very near death then but I thought of God all the time and prayed and trusted Him as never before. A man lying three feet from me was killed by the same shell. Oh, I hope I love the Lord. I try to serve Him. He seemed near me all that dreadful day."

I handed him a comfort-bag and told him it was from a little, motherless boy in my own Sunday school. He asked, "And could you let me have one for McClusky, my tentmate?"

"Oh, yes, with pleasure.

"Well, sir," he told me, "we'll write to these little boys. It's about all we can do in return for their kindness."

"Is McClusky a Christian?" I asked.

"He is leaning that way since the last battle. I have persuaded him to try to become one. He and I go out a little way from camp and pray together. One of your little books may help him."

I gave the veteran a book for his friend, entitled, *Come to Jesus*, and gave him some papers for himself. He departed after bestowing upon me the warmest, most solid handshake I had yet received in Virginia, along with an earnest "God bless you!"

Heart Melted by Kindness

This incident shows how the soldiers were touched by little kindnesses—their very lives sometimes turned to Christ by them. This story is from the pen of Reverend George H. Morss, Pastor of the Congregational Church, Abington, Connecticut. At the time, he was laboring at the Division Hospital of the 2nd and 5th Corps near Falmouth, Virginia:

An old soldier from Connecticut visited us one morning. He was acting as orderly for his Colonel. Our breakfast was ready and we invited him to stay and eat with us. At first, he objected because he was not accustomed to eating with others. However, he finally did join us and seemed to enjoy himself greatly. He said he had not sat down to eat at a table with anyone since he had been in the service

He said, "I have three sons in the army. When the third one enlisted, I felt that I could not remain alone but must join up myself. I have been a very hard man and much given to swearing." Even talking about it, he proceeded to prove his point by swearing and we had to reprove him mildly for it once.

He seemed touched and melted by our kindness. After breakfast, I told him that we were accustomed to having our devotions then and asked him to remain. He did so. After reading a portion of Scripture, we sang a hymn. I then offered prayer, commending the soldier and his sons to the Lord. He came to me afterwards, took me by the hand, and with the tear glistening in his eye, said, "You are the first man that ever prayed for me in my presence and I want to thank you for it. I am determined now to live a different life. Old John Perkins shall be a better John from this time forward. I will never swear again."

He then left our tent. Our hearts rejoiced before God that He had made use of our simple acts of kindness to reach the heart of the old man.

Historical Context:

The work of quieter Christian effort was soon brought to an abrupt end. Lee, strengthened by Longstreet's Division, called from the siege of Suffolk, Virginia because of the crisis on the Rappahannock River. Early in June, he concentrated his army at Culpeper in preparation for another invasion of Maryland. His troops traveled rapidly up the Shenandoah, scattering Milroy's army before them. General Ewell's Corps crossed the Potomac at Williamsport on June 16th, only three days after "Fighting Joe" Hooker had started from his lines in front of Fredericksburg. It soon became evident that the enemy did not intend to attack Washington but was heading into Pennsylvania. Hooker crossed the Potomac on June 26, 1863. On the 28th, he was relieved and General George G. Meade was placed in command.

When Hooker's movement began, the Christian Commission supplies were safely moved from the old stations to Washington. Messengers found the army at Fairfax Court House, where a station was already in operation. It did not remain long but delegates worked diligently, both there and at Fairfax Station. They worked especially among the wounded in the cavalry because of the skirmishes and battles so frequent at this juncture of the war.

Ladies Show Kindness

In June, prior to the July 1-3, 1863 Battle of Gettysburg, Field Agent E. F. Williams took part in this incident during this crisis. It was peculiarly characteristic of an American army:

In the midst of our work, two soldiers of Company I, 2nd Pennsylvania Cavalry, came into our room in the old church at Fairfax Court House. They carried a library of a hundred volumes, neatly packed in a box on their shoulders.

They had carried this library around for eighteen months. The boys in their company had read these books over and over, yet the books were still in good condition. Hardly a book had been lost. At this point, they had no means of transporting it and could not bear the prospect of throwing it away. Ladies in Philadelphia had given it to them while on their way to the front.

They asked, "Will the Christian Commission take it and get it to Washington? After the present movement is over, perhaps, you can find some regiment that would like to have the library. There's not much use thinking we shall see it again. The destiny of the cavalry this summer is to be pretty busy. Better give the books to a regiment of infantry."

"And here is my singing book," added one of the soldiers. "I have carried it ever since I came into the service. I must give it up now. Will you take it and give it to somebody to whom it will do some good? I can't bring myself to throw it away."

We received the gift, marked the box, and assured the soldiers that we would get the books to Washington. We said, "We want you to know that, if possible, we will return them in more favorable times."

Showing Kindness

Mr. E. F. Williams, Field Agent and former Pastor of the Congregational Church, Whitinsville, Massachusetts, adds his interesting reminiscences of the Christian Commission movement. Prior to the Battle of Gettysburg, July 1-3, 1863, the following incidents began at Fairfax Court House in Virginia:

On June 23rd, two hundred men were being taken in ambulances from the skirmish field all along the Blue Ridge. They had traveled over the roughest of roads and passed by our doors on their way to the railroad station. Still, they have four miles of terrible road before them and have had no food or drink since they were wounded. They cannot stop now for us to prepare them anything. A Commission agent rode rapidly to the train station, where he had fires kindled, coffee prepared, and bread sliced—buttered and spread with jelly. Water was brought in, along with tin cups and sponges. The delegates prepared to give aid and comfort to the men as they are taken from the ambulances and placed upon the railroad cars, headed for Washington. The work continued all afternoon and far into the night, because the train was delayed.

Prisoner of War Receives Kindness

Confederate prisoners were not overlooked. After being handed a cup of coffee, one of their Colonels asked, "Is this for me?"

"Yes, sir. Will you please drink it?"

"Well, this beats me. We don't treat our prisoners this way."

"We make no distinctions," was a delegate's only answer.

With tears in his eyes and wonder in his heart, the Colonel drank his coffee and ate his bread and jelly in silence.
(E. F. Williams)

Effects of Kindness

One worker at the station had been a disbeliever in the Sanitary and Christian Commissions and considered them as imposters and deceivers. Seeing these things, he began to change his mind somewhat. It was wonderful to see how the unfolding of these events gradually conquered him. With tears in his eyes, he finally said, "That's what I call the gospel. God bless you! I will tell them at home to do all they can for you."
(E. F. Williams)

CHAPTER VI
THE EASTERN ARMIES

GETTYSBURG

July 1863

The great battle of Gettysburg began on the first day of July, with Ewell and Hill's Corps of the Confederate Army forcing back our 1st and 11th Corps. Each side spent the greater part of the second day waiting for its absent divisions. Then the well-known battles of Round Top, Peach Orchard, and Cemetery and Culp's Hills took place. The evening's fighting went to the enemy's advantage, even though it welded our line together for the struggle the next day. The sun went down on July 3rd with a decisive Union victory for General Meade and the Union troops. General Lee began his retreat on the following day. General French captured and destroyed the bridge over the Potomac at Williamsport. It took some time before the enemy could rebuild it but their task was completed on the 13th. That night, Lee's men safely crossed the swollen river.

Before the battle closed, delegates of the Christian Commission were on the ground. Immediately, they began the most successful and extensive work yet attempted—a work rich in incidents of sacrifice, devotion and Christian ministry. A supply station was established in the village.

From there, supply stores sprang up from the Christian Commission offices and from the whole surrounding country. More than three hundred delegates, of all ranks and occupations, were sent to distribute the gathered bounty. Before they had concluded their work, supplies valued at more than $80,000 had been distributed. No amount of gratitude can be given to the people of Gettysburg for their kindness to the delegates, whose accommodations were very limited at first. Nor was their kindness confined to the delegates. The residents were untiring in their efforts to alleviate the needs of the wounded and dying until the hospitals were withdrawn from the area.

Ministry to the Wounded

After the July 1-3, 1863 Battle of Gettysburg in Pennsylvania, Mr. Enoch K. Miller, a private of Company F, 108th New York Volunteers and who later became a chaplain in the Army of the 25th U. S. C. T., addressed a letter to Reverend R. J. Parvin. He related how his life was saved at this famous battle:

"It was dark when they laid me under a tree, surrounded by hundreds of my comrades who were wounded and dying. As my Chaplain, the Reverend Thomas Grassie, bent over me and asked where my trust was placed, the Psalmist's words came involuntarily to my lips: 'Yea, though I walk through the valley of the shadow of death, I will fear no evil, for Thou art with me, Thy rod and Thy staff they comfort me.'

"A minie ball had pierced my breast, passed through my left lung and came out a little under my shoulder blade. When the surgeon of our regiment came to examine me, I thought that the ball was still in me. So he only looked at my chest wound and gave me a sleeping powder. Throwing his rubber blanket over me, he left me to die. During the next three or four days, I had no pillow or sufficient covering, my clothes were saturated with my own blood, and I had no proper food. Attended by a faithful comrade, Sergeant John O'Connell, I lay hardly daring to hope for life.

"About noon one day, I saw the silver badge of a Christian Commission delegate in the distance. After sending my friend, I soon had a delegate by my side. Seeing that delegate's face, I immediately recognized Brother J. B. Stillson, Esquire, of Rochester, New York. He was an old friend of mine and we had been co-laborers in Sunday school work before the war. He knew me in an instant and, without wasting words, he supplied me with a feather pillow (the first I had had in a year) and a quilt, a draught of wine and some nice soft crackers, as well as a cup of warm tea. After offering up an earnest prayer on my behalf, he hurried off to secure some clean clothes. He then removed my filthy garments. It was then that we discovered that the ball had passed through me.

"After all this had been accomplished, I felt as though I was at home. My dear friend and delegate of the Christian Commission acted the part of a willing father, a loving mother, an affectionate sister, a sympathizing brother, and a beloved pastor.

"I lay on the field until July 15th and received everything that could bring comfort in such a situation. Most of my needs were met by the Christian Commission. For a few days, a surgeon, affiliated with your society, tended to me. Had it not been for these comforts and necessities, I would have died. However, your agents were on the ground to care for such cases as mine and, as great Providence ordered it, I survived."

The soldier's words of gratitude to the Commission and to Reverend Mr. Parvin, who had written the orders for the supplies which relieved him, need not be added.

Labor of Love

Mr. Charles Demond, from Boston and an original member of the Christian Commission, related this story in his address at the last Anniversary of the Commission. After the July 1-3, 1863 Battle of Gettysburg, Pennsylvania, he tells of the relief work, performed by Mr. John C. Chamberlain. He attended Bangor Maine Theological Seminary and was brother of the gallant General Joshua Chamberlain. It illustrates the spirit animating the delegates and of the good brought about by even a very small service:

At nightfall, John Chamberlain heard of a hospital, several miles away, that had not been visited. Though wearied with the labors of the day, he walked to it at once. He found that the surgeon in charge was sick and the assistant was overwhelmed with the care of some two hundred wounded. They also had no supplies or comforts. He asked, "Doctor, why haven't you gotten supplies? A station of the Sanitary Commission is less than a mile away." The doctor said he did not know how to get them. Mr. Chamberlain wrote an order for the Sanitary Commission, the doctor signed it, and the delegate went to the station. Unfortunately, he found that the Sanitary Commission had moved elsewhere.

What was to be done? It was late. He was very weary. The Christian Commission was stationed at Gettysburg, nearly five miles away. The road was hard and all the streams were overflowing the banks. But the men were suffering and no one was there to help but him. He took the long and lonely walk and, very early the next morning, a wagon, laden with supplies and comforts from the Christian Commission, arrived to care for the heroic sufferers.

Practical Kindness

One day, Mr. John Chamberlain came upon an out-of-door's hospital, where the men were lying in the July sun with no shelter. After looking for a moment, he took a stone and stick and arranged the blanket of a soldier so as to shield his face. Others caught the idea. Soon, everyone in the hospital was sheltered from the burning and torturing blaze of the sun.
(Charles Demond)

An Amputee Receives Kindness

Reverend George Bringhurst served as Rector of All Saints' Protestant Episcopal Church, Moyamensing, Philadelphia and as a Christian Commission delegate. After the July 1-3, 1863 Battle of Gettysburg in Pennsylvania, he tells of a little incident about one of their small acts of kindness:

One very dark night, I met a soldier whose arms had both been shot away. He was going to his tent and I asked, "What can I do for you, my friend?"

"Oh, nothing, Chaplain," he said cheerfully, "Unless you would tie my shoes for me. They have been bothering me a good deal."

As I stooped down, I thought of the latchet which the Forerunner John the Baptist was not worthy to loose on the feet of the Lord Jesus Christ and the little deed became a great joy.

Faith in God

After the Battle of Gettysburg in Pennsylvania on July 1-3, 1863, Reverend E. F. Williams, Pastor of the Congregational Church, Whitinsville, Massachusetts and Christian Commission delegate, tells this story of faith and its result:

Our storekeeper, an Englishman, was a hard-working, patriotic, Christian man. One day, when our supply of provisions was getting very low, he was asked to cut thinner slices of bread for the boys.

"Oh, no," he said, "I can't. The poor fellows are so hungry."

"But our bread will soon be gone."

"Well, I have faith that the Lord will send us more before we run out."

He was allowed to take his own course, though advised to be as sparing as possible. The day wore away and still the crowd of hungry soldiers pressed around our doors. When the last loaf was taken from the shelf, a hundred delegates were waiting for their supper. We had no crackers, no meat, or no bread for them. To make matters worse, we still had unfed soldiers who were weary from their wounds and their long, grueling march from the field hospital. They lingered for a morsel of food and a cup of coffee, as they awaited word about the trains for Baltimore and Philadelphia.

Just at the last moment, when our faith was almost exhausted, an immense load of provisions stopped before our quarters. The drivers asked for the agents of the Christian Commission station. They said, "We have brought bread, dressings and bandages, jellies and wines. We don't know who are most needy but we have confidence in you. Will you distribute these things for us?"

These supplies had been transported one hundred and three miles. Two ministers, German Reformed and Lutheran, were with them. Our profound thanks can better be imagined than told. Never again did we chide the storekeeper for his faith for he knew the Lord, in His perfect time, would send just what we wanted and needed. Never did our stock of provisions ever run out while we remained at Gettysburg.

Sacrifice in Acts of Ministry

After the Battle of Gettysburg in Pennsylvania on July 1-3, 1863, an incident of noble Christian fortitude and heroism was related about Chaplain Eastman, son of Reverend Dr. Eastman, Secretary of the American Tract Society. This story was told by Reverend Joseph T. Duryea, D.D., Pastor of Collegiate Reformed (Dutch) Church, New York:

Chaplain Eastman's kneecap was severely damaged when his horse went down during the battle. His leg swelled and stiffened until the pain became almost unbearable. When he could no longer stand, he gave his horse to a servant and laid himself down on the ground. All alone, he had to experience what a wounded soldier experienced that night. As he laid suffering and thinking, he heard a voice say, "O my God!" He thought, "How can anybody be swearing in such a place as this?" He listened again and a wounded soldier began offering a prayer.

His first impulse was "how can I get to him?" He tried to draw up his stiffened leg but he could not rise. He put his arm around a sapling and tried to stand on his well foot. He tried to extend the other without bending at the knee but he fell back and jarred his leg as if he had been stabbed. He thought, "I can roll." So over and over, he rolled in pain through blood and past dead bodies until, at last, he fell against the dying man. There he preached Christ and prayed.

After awhile, one of the line officers came up and said, "Where's the Chaplain? One of the staff officers is dying."

"Here he is, here he is," cried out the sufferer.

"Can you come and see a dying officer?"

"I cannot move. I had to roll myself to this dying man to talk to him."

"If I detail two men to carry you, can you go?"

"Yes."

They lifted him up gently and carried him. And throughout that live-long night, the two men bore him over the field and laid him down beside bleeding, dying men so he could preach Christ and pray for these men. Lying flat on his back, the wounded Chaplain could not even see his audience of the dying but looked ever heavenward into the eyes of the peaceful stars—emblems of God's love, which even on that day of spilled blood had not been soiled nor made dim.

God's Supernatural Protection

Mr. J. B. Stillson, Esquire, of Rochester, New York and delegate of the Christian Commission, gives a detailed account of the adventures and escapes of John Burns, of Gettysburg, Pennsylvania. He acted as a volunteer soldier through part of the crucial battle of July 1-3, 1863:

John Burns was two months shy of his seventieth year when he volunteered as a Union soldier. Dressed in the Continental coat, vest and corduroys that he had worn in the War of 1812, he offered himself to General Wister, who commanded what was known as the "Iron Brigade." Approaching the officer, Burns said, "General, I fought for my country in 1812 and I want to fight for it again today."

The officer gazed at him intently from head to foot. Seeing he was in earnest, the General extended his hand and said, "God bless the old soldier. He shall have a chance."

Joining the 7th Wisconsin Regiment, he performed a brave man's duty until the close of the first day's battle, when, after being struck four times, he fell into the enemy's hands. How he escaped death four times had been truly marvelous. The first ball struck his side and was turned away from his body by the intervention of a pair of old-fashioned spectacles in his vest pocket. The second struck a truss, worn for an abdominal injury. It glanced off, cutting away the flesh from his thigh about two inches below the top of the hip-bone. The third ball passed through his leg, between the large and small bones, without injuring either of the bones or the arteries. The fourth went through the fleshy part of the left arm below the elbow, also without breaking bones or rupturing arteries.

He lay on the field during the night until the next morning. Through the kindness of a neighbor, he was removed to his own house in Gettysburg. A Confederate officer, accompanied by a soldier, visited him there and questioned him at length about his part in the fight. Burns made no replies. The window of the room opened out toward a distant house, occupied by Confederate sharpshooters. The old man's bed was within range. Shortly after the officer and soldier left, a ball from the house entered his window, grazed his chest, and buried itself in the wall. Only a moment before, the wounded man, weary of lying on his side, had turned on his bed to lie on his back. In the former position the minie ball would have passed directly through him.

Turning to Christ in Repentance

The most precious reward for a delegate was the privilege of turning a wandering soul to Jesus. This occurred often in the Gettysburg hospitals following that fateful battle of July 1-3, 1863. Reverend R. J. Parvin, Rector of St. Paul's Protestant Episcopal Church, Cheltenham, Pennsylvania and delegate of the Christian Commission, narrates one such incident:

On the field of battle, I found a Michigan soldier named David Laird and visited him regularly while I was at Gettysburg. One day, after writing home at his request, he told me of his early training, of his wandering, and of his longing to return. We prayed together, read Scripture, and talked until, at last, the Spirit took possession of his heart. At first, he was very much troubled because his wound—a serious one received while the regiment was falling back under orders—was in the back. I reassured him and explained all the circumstances to his parents in my letter. I received answers from each of them, thanking me for my little ministries to their son. But the mother's letter to her boy epitomized perfect tenderness and love:

"DAVID, MY DARLING BOY: What can I say to you, my son! my son! Oh, that I could see you and that I could minister to you! I think your father will probably be with you soon. My dear one, you have done what you could to suppress this cruel rebellion. May God comfort you! You are still serving the country so dear to your heart. For thirty months, you have been an active volunteer. Now you are a suffering one. Still there is an army in which you may enlist—the army of the Lord. All, yes, all are welcome there. You will find kind friends who will keep us advised and please request them to give us all the particulars of your situation. God comfort and sustain you, dear one, is your mother's prayer!"

His father wrote about the wound:

"As to David's wound in his back, it need give him no uneasiness. None who know him will suppose it to be there on account of cowardice."

The weeks passed by and the pleasant September days came but David was worse. His father came in time to see him die. When it was all over, I tried to comfort him for his loss but he put the words kindly aside: "I don't need any comfort from man for God has given me so much in seeing the happy death of my boy that I am perfectly content."

Finding Peace Amidst Trials

Professor M. L. Stoever of Pennsylvania College, Gettysburg, remained in the town throughout the terrible days of July 1-3, 1863. Afterward, he became a member of the Christian Commission and was a frequent and effective delegate. At much personal risk, he, along with other citizens, strove to do what he could for the many wounded sufferers. His reminiscences of the battle are exceedingly rich and valuable. In the following stories, he illustrates some aspect of the Christian soldier's peace in the hour of deepest trial:

One of the most touching scenes I remember was in attending to a man who became a Christian as he lay wounded in the college edifice. As I read the precious promises of God's Word to him, his joy seemed unspeakable and his countenance beamed with delight as the hour of his departure drew near. While giving me his dying messages to his family, he spoke with strong confidence of his acceptance of the Savior's love. After I had closed the letter, he said, "Please add a postscript. Tell mother to urge my brothers to serve the Lord." His earnestness in this regard during the midst of his sufferings was deeply moving.

Farewell in Midst of Trials

Captain Griffeth, of General Howard's staff, was mortally wounded in the battle. Amid army associations and perils, a warm personal attachment had grown up between the General and his Adjutant. When the command came to pursue the retreating foe, the General hastened to take his last farewell. The hospital door was closed. Words of sympathy were necessarily brief but none were better than Christ's own words. General Howard read the Fourteenth Chapter of St. John:

"Let not your heart be troubled: ye believe in God, believe also in Me. In My Father's house are many mansions; if it were not so, I would have told you; I go to prepare a place for you. And if I go and prepare a place for you, I will come again and receive you unto Myself; that where I am, there ye may be also."

Then bowing upon the floor, the General commended his wounded friend to the compassionate God and Father of all who trust in Him. Rising from his knees, he clasped him in one long, fond, weeping embrace. Thus the heroes parted—one to pursue the Rebellion to its death, the other to enter into God's eternal rest within in a few days.
(M. L. Stoever)

Finding Christ in the Midst of Trials

In the schoolhouse, Professor Stoever found two interesting and intelligent young men, who had just had amputations performed and were recovering side-by-side. They were Confederates and they both were from Lutheran colleges—one from Roanoke College, Virginia, the other from Newberry

College, South Carolina. Their teachers had been students in the college at Gettysburg and were well-known to the Professor. One of them was already a Christian and the other had found Christ on the Gettysburg battlefield.

"Tell my father," said the first, "if you can get a letter to him, tell that I am leaning on the strong arm of Jesus. He comforts me. All my hope is in Him."

The other said, "Write to my mother and tell her that I have found the Savior. He is precious to my soul. Say to her, 'If I meet you, mother, no more on earth, I hope to meet you in heaven.'"
(M. L. Stoever)

Answered Prayer

Throughout the terrible days of July 1-3, 1863, Professor M. L. Stoever of Pennsylvania College, Gettysburg, remained in the town. Afterward, he became a member of the Christian Commission and was a frequent and effective delegate. He narrates a striking instance of the way in which all Christians are made one through Christ Jesus:

On the Sunday after the battle, wounded and dying soldiers filled the Roman Catholic Church in Gettysburg. On entering the building, I was met by a Roman Catholic lady who was longtime friend. She was a good Christian woman but very rigid in practice. Immediately, she said, "Do come and speak to this man. The surgeon says he will die and he is unconverted."

I followed her to the chancel where the man lay dying. She introduced me by saying, "Sir, this is Professor Stoever from the college and he is a Protestant. He wants to speak with you." She then left him to my care and I presented to him the only open way for his return to God. Kneeling by his side, I offered a prayer—the first prayer, no doubt, ever offered by a Protestant in that church and even requested by one of its members of all things! The man died most peacefully shortly afterward, having trusted in Christ and assured of eternal life. Although he had never before made a profession of faith, he was the son of a praying mother, whose early instructions had prepared his mind to lay hold of the Cross and to embrace the Savior.

Answered upon Death Prayer

Near the altar of the Roman Catholic Church in Gettysburg, Pennsylvania, Mr. George Stuart, Chairman of the Christian Commission, ministered to a soldier, following the famous battle of July 1-3, 1863. This man took Christ Jesus as his Lord and Savior. Mr. Stuart recorded the scene:

As I was passing, a man near the altar looked up at me and imploringly asked, "Ain't you going to stop and talk to me?" I went to him and he introduced himself as William O. Doubleday. He explained that his wife was a Christian. She had taught each one of his children to pray as soon as they could utter the words. He had never made a profession of faith himself but that people would not call him a "wicked man."

He said, "When I enlisted, I did it because I considered it a disgrace to be drafted. Just as I was leaving for the war, my wife said, 'I hope you will come back all right and as a good Christian.' It touched my heart. We went into the room with the family and there she prayed for me. Then she asked me to pray. I struggled to offer a few broken petitions. My little boy, only thirteen-years old, then offered a most sincere prayer for me and for our distressed country. I don't know where he learned to pray like that, unless it was in Sunday school."

When he learned how I was connected with the Christian Commission and saw the badge, tears came to his eyes. When I spoke to him of Jesus, he took hold of my hands and the tears came as fast as rain. I prayed with him and then he asked me to bend down and kiss him on the forehead. He died soon afterward from the effects of an amputation.

I later received a letter from his wife, who came to him before his death. She was very sincere in her expressions of thankfulness and told me with loving sorrow and joy about how her husband's peaceful death had answered her prayers.

Inspired by the Example of Christ's Endurance

Mr. George Stuart, Chairman of the Christian Commission, ministered to the wounded and dying, following the Battle of Gettysburg, July 1-3, 1863. At a private residence, he visited with Lieutenant William Henry Walcott of Providence, R. I., 17th Regiment, U. S. Infantry, and afterwards a Brevet Major. Walcott told him how he had been encouraged in the midst his pain and suffering:

Through his window, the Lieutenant had heard me addressing a large congregation in the "Diamond," the public square of the town. Thinking I was a clergyman, he sent for me. This is his story:

"My wife died a month before the war began and, since leaving home, my little child has also died. I led thirty-nine men into battle in my company. Twenty-nine of them are either killed or wounded. I fell on Thursday near Round Top, at a very exposed spot, which was alternately lost and won by our troops. My own men could not carry me off the field, so I signaled to the Colonel by waving my handkerchief and he sent help. In being carried to safety, my wounds and pain were severely aggravated. I had been lying across two men, one dead and the other dying, but I was unable to move. The dying man was one of the best soldiers in my company. I had often taken the men to church and now, amidst the roar of battle and danger, I prayed with him. Very soon he was gone.

"Later, I was carried to the regimental hospital but they could do nothing for me. Then I was taken to the division hospital where the surgeon examined my wound and amputated my foot. On Friday, the Confederates shelled the hospital and I was taken a great distance into the woods. The stretcher bearers, without thinking, placed me near the foot of a little hill. When the rain came, streams of water poured along the ground under the shelter tent, which had been pitched over me. On the battlefield, I thought I could not endure my sufferings but then I recalled what Jesus had endured. It came to my mind that, while I had water to drink, He had vinegar and gall offered to Him."

This soldier's thoughts continually traveled to this scene from long ago. His reflections enabled him to keep up his sagging spirits until relief came.

Ministry in Times of Death

Reverend Mr. Parvin, Rector of St. Paul's Protestant Episcopal Church, Cheltenham, Pennsylvania, chronicles the testimony of Captain Billings. He served with the 20th Maine Regiment after the battle at Gettysburg, Pennsylvania on July 1-3, 1863. The story's close tells of one of the hardest tasks of a delegate:

A captain was brought into the old barn, where sixty-five of the worst cases in the Fifth Corps were lying in pain. Some of his own men were lying on the floor not far from this brave man. He loved them with a father's love. As one after another died before his eyes, it worked on his mind in such a way that he became delirious, to the point that it took four or five men to hold him down. With great difficulty, we moved him away from his men into a place by himself, where he rallied and became a little better.

Once, as I was about to go into his tent, the surgeon came out and told me that the Captain will die very soon. As I entered and took him by the hand, he asked, "Chaplain, what did the surgeon say?"

"Why, Captain, you are in critical condition."

"I know that, Chaplain, but does he think I can live?"

"He thinks that it is hardly possible that you will."

"Have you heard from my wife, Chaplain, since your message yesterday?"

"No, the telegraph lines are in the hands of the government but I hope she will be here."

"Does the surgeon say I cannot live long, Chaplain?"

"Yes—but, thankfully, you are a Christian, Captain."

"Yes, Chaplain, I have no fears. I left my place in the Sunday school for my place in the army. My hope is in the Lord Jesus Christ. I have tried to serve Him in the army and He will not forsake me now—but I would like to see my wife."

"Well, Captain, if you have anything to say to her, will you send the message by me?"

He asked me to give her his haversack, sword and some other little things, with a message. Then, while dismissing all earthly things from his mind, he said, "Don't stay any longer with me, Chaplain. Go help the boys and run in here, as you can, to read a few words from the Bible."

After one visit, he asked me to have his body embalmed and sent home. I promised to do so. He did not even refer to it again but passed away in triumph.

He died at eleven o'clock in the morning. At five that afternoon, his body was sent to the embalmers. Late that night, I was busy writing letters from memoranda taken throughout the day when I heard a knock at the door. In came a man inquiring about Captain Billings. What a coincidence for us to meet! I thought of the home link.

"Who are you?" I asked.

"I am his brother. I have his wife with me! I have kept her up her spirits all the way here with the hope that we would find the Captain in good condition. Where is he, sir?"

"You have not brought the Captain's wife out here tonight, have you?" The Corps hospital was four miles from Gettysburg.

"No, I left her in town until morning."

"That was a good decision. The body of your brother was sent to the embalmers this afternoon."

"Oh," he said, "I cannot tell her. I cannot trust myself even to try to tell her— or even to see her again tonight." The poor man broke down in his grief. After a while, he was able to say, "I have brought her all the way to Gettysburg for this and now you must … you must tell her everything."

So often our duty as delegates called for us to visit the bereaved wife and deliver messages and tokens of love from her deceased husband. We would speak words of comfort to her in the name of the Lord.

Holy Spirit Descends on Place of Death

Reverend W. T. Eva, Pastor of (N. S.) Presbyterian Church, Kensington, Philadelphia, Pennsylvania, tells the story of two soldiers who seemed to have entered into the meaning of the Father's promises of eternal care:

Over in the corner of a shed crowded with wounded, I found a dying man. His limbs were already cold and the death-damp was upon his brow. Fellow sufferers surrounded him and, yet, he was dying alone. He was still conscious when I came to him—not only conscious but happy in the love of God. I can truly say that nowhere have I witnessed a more triumphant peace than his. We prayed by his side and then sang and hymn and a chorus.

> "Just as I am, without one plea,"

> "Happy day, happy day,
> When Jesus washed my sins away."

As we prayed and sang, the Holy Spirit seemed to come down, not only upon the dying man but on all in that sorrowful place. As they lay upon the floor here and there, one of the wounded would utter aloud the earnest cry, "God have mercy on my soul!"

Grace of God Evident Even in Wretchedness

In a barn, lying upon a slab floor, with nothing under him but a little wet hay, and with scarce a rag to cover him, I found a middle-aged man shot through the body and so paralyzed by the shock of an exploding shell that he was entirely unable to move—the most abject picture of utter wretchedness I had ever seen. He was quite sensible however and, having done what I could to make him comfortable, I spoke of his heroic devotion to the flag, of the love of God and of the Savior's death. A flood of tears welled up in his eyes and rolled down over the bronzed face. He was too overcome to speak but it was evident that, even in that forlorn man, I had found not only a true patriot but also a lover of Jesus—a blessed witness to the triumph of the grace of God.
(W. T. Eva)

God's Grace Revealed in Creativity

Reverend Mr. R. J. Parvin, Rector of St. Paul's Protestant Episcopal Church, Cheltenham, Pennsylvania, tells of a few short incidents after the battle at Gettysburg, Pennsylvania on July 1-3, 1863. They tell their own story of sacrifice and Christian victory:

After the battle, the ground was soaked by heavy showers. Many of the wounded were on the bank of a brook where the rapid rise of water put them in danger of drowning. No stretchers were available and some of the badly wounded could not be carried in the arms of the men without great pain.

Going into the water on his hands and knees, one delegate said, "Lay them on my back." Then, bent with his face to the ground, he tenderly carried them out of the reach of danger.

Offering One's Own Comfort As a Sacrifice

The storehouse was some distance away and I had but one bottle of blackberry cordial left, so I called out, "Boys, I've got one bottle of nice cordial here. Who wants it?"

A brave fellow near me replied, "You'll find others not far away who need it more than we do, Chaplain. Keep it for them."
(R. J. Parvin)

Seeing the Benefits of Hardship

I can never forget how the heroes greeted me that morning, as I passed along a line of shelter tents, flooded by last night's rain. They said, "Never mind, Chaplain. We don't care about our soaking. If the Potomac is full, it means that Lee can't cross it."
(R. J. Parvin)

Giving One's Life as a Sacrifice

This was the last message of a Maine soldier, "Charley" as his comrades called him. "Tell mother I received my wound on my twentieth birthday. I give my life for my country. If I had another, I would give it too."
(R. J. Parvin)

Mother's Request Brings Sacrifice

A great favorite among his comrades was M_____, a soldier from Massachusetts. After his death, his mother wrote me, begging for "only one lock of his hair." A comrade of the dead soldier went down into the last resting place and severed a damp lock. It then was sent on its mournful errand.

Finding God

Reverend Mr. Parvin, Rector of St. Paul's Protestant Episcopal Church, Cheltenham, Pennsylvania, served as a Christian Commission delegate after the battle at Gettysburg, Pennsylvania on July 1-3, 1863. He tells about a soldier's pilgrimage to peace with God and eternal life:

A soldier, only seventeen years old, had run away from his employer in Camden, N. J. to join a Philadelphia regiment. He was found on the field with seven bullet holes in his body and had but a short time to live. I knelt down on the ground by him and asked for his mother's name and residence.

He replied, "I have no mother, Chaplain."

"A father?"

"No."

"Any brothers or sisters?"

"No relatives in the world," he said.

Poor fellow! He seemed so alone, indeed. I took his hand in mine. Martin, you've been at Sunday school. Right?"

"Yes, sir."

"Well, sir, you have forgotten *one* relative."

He looked at me inquiringly, when, pointing upwards, I added, "'Our Father, who art in heaven.' You have a Father and a home up *there.'*"

Doubtfully at first, then increasing slowly in assurance, he received the precious truth. In a broken, child-like way he learned to pray to this, his Heavenly Relative. Soon, his face grew bright and glad and the fearful look in his once restless, homeless eyes was now one of trusting peace and joy.

Care for Orphans and a Widow

Perhaps, no incident of the war became so widely known and elicited such deep sympathy as the story of the Humiston children, following the battle at Gettysburg, Pennsylvania, July 1-3, 1863. The main facts of the narrative are set forth here:

Dr. J. Francis Bourns, of Philadelphia, was crossing the mountains on his way to Gettysburg, as a volunteer surgeon and delegate of the Christian Commission. After his vehicle broke down, he and three of his fellow travelers on the same mission were forced to stop at Graefenberg Springs. Mr. Schriver, the proprietor of the hotel, showed them a beautiful photograph of three lovely children. It had been found, clasped in the hands of a soldier dead on the battlefield. Reportedly, the soldier held the picture so that he must have gazed at it while dying. No other memoranda, relics, or even equipment were found on the body, making identification impossible.

Dr. Bourns obtained the photograph with the intention of using it, when his delegate work was finished, to find the little fatherless children. He

THE HUMISTON CHILDREN

persevered in overcoming all the obstacles to obtain a picture, suitable for reproduction purposes. Some Philadelphia artists helped to produce this picture. Bourns then furnished the press with all he knew about the story, along with a copy of the photograph, which by now had become well-known.

Week after week passed and the mystery of the dead soldier was still unsolved. Inquiries poured in but no identification was forthcoming. Dr. Bourns began to despair. A copy of the *American Presbyterian*, containing a description of the picture, found its way to a little town on the Alleghany River in Western New York. The emotional story was repeated through the village for several days, eliciting the warmest sympathy.

A lady carried the paper to a friend, who had not heard from her husband since the battle took place. The narrative included the perfectly reproduced picture, which the wife had sent her husband just before Gettysburg. This information reached Dr. Bourns, who then sent a copy of the picture in reply. This publication brought the first news that her children were fatherless and that she was a widow. Dr. Bourns found that the name of this unknown soldier was Amos Humiston, Sergeant, 154th N. Y. S. Volunteers, of Portville,

N. Y. The sale of copies of the famous picture afterward became the source of great good.

In March 1868, Dr. Bourns wrote, "The founding of the 'National Orphan Homestead' at Gettysburg, is the sequel to the story of the Humiston children. About seventy soldiers' orphans have been received into the institution, and there are many more fatherless little ones who are awaiting its enlargement of accommodations." Furthermore, the Humiston children came to live at the "Homestead" and their mother became a housemother. The morning after the children arrived at their new home, they were discovered while quietly adorning their father's grave with beautiful flowers.

Effects of Caring for Enemies

No result of the Christian Commission ministry that took place after the battle at Gettysberg, Pennsylvania, July 1-3, 1863 was more marked than that manifested in the altered feelings among the Confederate prisoners. The delegates continually allude to this in their reports. We can present but a few of the numerous instances. Mr. Charles Demond, of Boston, was one of the original members of the Commission. He offers the following account:

While passing among the wounded, giving sympathy and aid, a delegate came to an officer from South Carolina. He asked, "Colonel, can I do anything for you?"

With stubborn defiance, he replied, "No."

He passed on by. Awhile later, he came around again, made a similar inquiry, and was rebuffed once again. Yet, he came again the third time. The air in the room had become offensive from heat and wounds. He was putting cologne on the handkerchiefs of each man as he passed by.

The delegate asked, "Colonel, can I put some of this on your handkerchief?"

The wounded and suffering man burst into tears. He said, "I have no handkerchief."

"Well, you shall have one," and wetting his own with cologne, he gave it to him. The Colonel was now ready to talk.

He said, "I can't understand you Yankees. You fight us like devils and then you treat us like angels. I am sorry I ever entered this war."

Benefits of Laughter

Mr. John Patterson, of Philadelphia, was described as "an earnest and indefatigable delegate of the Christian Commission from the beginning to the close of its work." After the July 1-3, 1863 Battle of Gettysburg, he tells of the rather amusing little conversation between some soldiers, Union and Confederate, and himself:

Quite a number of us had been busy aiding the surgeons, who had performed about two hundred amputations that day. When the men were washed and dressed, they began bragging at supper about our good butter.

"Let us see, boys," I said, "which of you can make the best wish for the old lady who made the butter."

"And sure," replied an Irishman in thick Irish brogue, "may every hair of her head be a wax candle to light her into glory"—a kind of beatified Gorgon, one would say.

Then another Irishman offered, "May she be in heaven two 'wakes' before the devil knows she's dead."

The third and last was also from a son of the Emerald Isle. His wish was addressed to me. He said, "And truth, sir, I hope God will take a liking to yourself."

Expressions of Thankfulness

The letter, which follows, was written in response to a note found in a comfort-bag, sent to any wounded soldier from the July 1-3, 1863 Battle of Gettysburg by a little girl from a town in Massachusetts:

GETTYSBURG, PENNSYLVANIA
August 7, 1863.

My DEAR LITTLE FRIEND: I received your present, the comfort-bag, and it is thrice welcome, although it was intended for Union defenders. It was given to me by a Christian woman, who lost her holy anger against Confederates—for such am I—in her bounteous sympathy for the unfortunate. My little friend can only imagine my thankfulness for the favor when I inform her that I have no friends this side of heaven, for all are gone— father, mother, sister and brother—and I alone am left.

I shall always keep the dear comfort-bag as a memento of true sympathy from a generous heart in the loyal State of Massachusetts. I hope you will not be disappointed by this, coming as it does from a Confederate. You should know that I was forced into the ranks at the point of a bayonet, for I would not willingly go to fight against the dear old flag, whose ample folds have always shielded the orphan and made glad the oppressed.

I have read your note many times over and have wished it could rightfully be mine. "Do they think of me at home?" Silence—all is silence! Not so with the Union soldier. A thousand tokens tell him "yes."

I was wounded in the second day's fight and am now packing up my weapons to be exchanged or sent back a cripple for life. I am seventeen years old and now am turned out with one arm to carve my way through the world. But my trust is in my heavenly Father who will forgive and bless. Hoping that God may, in His mercy, reunite us all again as brothers and sisters, I am your unworthy friend,

E_____ A_____,

Company _____, Mississippi Volunteers

P. S.—May God guard and bless you!

Comfort Even in Death

Mr. J. B. Stillson, Esquire, of Rochester, New York, served as a Christian Commission delegate following the Battle of Gettysburg, July 1-3, 1863. He writes of the following incident:

The sufferers always hailed the morning with a peculiar satisfaction. During the weary night hours, the badly wounded would often ask, "How long until the morning will be here?" They often said that its beams of sunlight would bring deliverance.

An old Confederate, suffering from two flesh wounds, beckoned to me very early one morning as though he would ask, "Watchman, will the night last much longer?" I had already ministered to his wants and had been impressed with his venerable look that radiated the countenance of a peaceful and trusting heart. With a subdued voice and gentle as a child's, he spoke of his only son, Thomas, who also had been in the fight and, he feared, was either killed or wounded. He told me the boy's company and regiment and, upon inquiring, I soon found him very close by but mortally wounded. The son, in turn, was deeply concerned about his father. When told he was very near, he quickly said, "Oh, I wish I could see him once more." With assistance, I bore him to his father's side.

As they were brought face to face, tears flowed freely before ever speaking a word. The old man greeted his son by saying, "Thomas, my son," and, being overcome, he could say no more.

The boy immediately asked, "My father, are you badly wounded?"

I responded, "Your father's wounds were not serious." A thankful smile lit up his face until the father recovered from the first effects of his emotion.

He inquired, "Thomas, are your wounds bad?"

"Yes, I fear they are mortal."

The sad story of their parting then took place. The son was pointed to the Cross. His every temporal want was supplied but, before midnight, he died.

The old man, bereft of wife and children, mourned as did Jacob of old for his son, Joseph. The soldier prayed that he, too, might depart. I comforted him with precious Gospel assurances and told him how "our light affliction, which is but for a moment, works for us a far more exceeding and eternal weight of glory." A few days afterwards, the cloud, which had seemed so impenetrable, was scattered before the brightness of the rising "Sun of Righteousness." Rejoicing in faith that comforts, the old man said, "He doeth all things well."

Praying for Enemies

Reverend George Duffield, Jr. labored on the field after the July 1-3, 1863 Battle of Gettysburg in connection with Mrs. Harris and the Christian Commission. He served as Pastor of the (N.S.) Presbyterian Church, in Adrian, Michigan, at that time, then later in Galesburg, Illinois. Mr. Duffield's observations were published in letters to his brother in the *Detroit Advertiser* and *Tribune*. He spent a large portion of his time in looking after the Confederate wounded in Union confinement, as reflected in this incident:

Known to her neighbors as "the faithful creature," the poor woman said, "Oh, come, mister, and see them in the cow stable. Some of them are worse off than these."

Sure enough, it was so. They were not wounded any worse than the others nor were they more utterly helpless or destitute of decent clothing. In these respects, all were on a common level. But, at least, those in the wagon shed had the advantage of lying in comparatively clean dirt. In the cow stable, the filthy water of the dung heap had dammed up and backed in upon them. It had saturated the straw, the blankets, and everything else within its reach.

Yet, another and more painful difference existed. On account of the water, most of the scanty hay had floated away and left the poor sufferers lying upon the bare rails of the floor. In some cases, the men had not so much as the thickness of a single blanket between their emaciated bodies and the sharp, knotty wood. These men were the elite of the Southern army—lawyers, planters, men of wealth, intelligence and refinement. Some of them,

I learned afterward, had been ruling elders in the Presbyterian Church and members of its General Assemblies.

At first, the distribution of bread was carried out in solemn silence, reminding me strangely enough of distributing the emblems of Christ's body and blood on Communion day. It also reminded me of the command, "If thine enemy hunger, feed him; if he thirst, give him drink." But misery soon found a spokesman. The first man who spoke to me was from Georgia, apparently about twenty-five years of age. His language and graciousness led me to believe that he had known what home and generous hospitality were all about. Over the course of a twenty years' ministry, I had served for ten years in the city of Philadelphia, in times of cholera and famine, in the most obscure alleys, in the court within the court, in the Penitentiary, in the incurable wards of the Blockley Almshouse Hospital, and in Bedlam. I have often looked on sad and despairing faces but never have I seen in any man who retained sanity with such a face of blank hopelessness as this.

"O sir," he said, with an expression of agony that anguished me, "as much as I thank you for this bread, which is the first mouthful of anything I could eat since I was wounded, I would rather do without it and starve outright, than remain any longer in my present position. Just look at me. I am shot through the lungs and spine and cannot move myself a hair's breadth. And here I am, bent across this rail as if on a rack with not a handful of hay or even the thickness of a blanket under me. I shall die if I do not gain relief—immediate relief, sir—from this unbearable torture."

To help this pitiful sufferer was no very easy matter. On one side, almost touching him was a man whose right leg was missing. On the other side, another man had lost his left leg. Anyone who, in passing through a hospital and ever touched the blanket of such a man, will be careful forevermore after hearing his piteous cries. After finding a place for my feet, one on each side of him, I reached over to the trough for support. With one of his arms around my neck, I managed somewhat to raise him up. While beginning to push a little hay under him, I heard a feeble, pettish voice exclaim, "Don't you steal my hay."

Another man on the other side and in a similar tone exclaimed, "And don't you steal any of mine."

A bale of such hay could not have been bought with all the gold in California. With great difficulty, I gathered up the little portion of hay properly belonging to the man, added some of the reeking straw, and adjusted his blanket so as to cover his whole body. With an air of inexpressible satisfaction, he laid himself back in his new position and a gleam of hope lit up his face as if the sun should dawn at midnight. Seizing my hand with passionate gratitude, he was about to shower it with kisses.

"No, sir," I said, while gently pushing back his head. "If you have any thanks to give for so small a favor, then give it to God, not me."

In an instant, he took me at my word. His short but sincere prayer for himself moved me to pray for all his suffering comrades. The Master prayed for His enemies, "Father, forgive them." Why should not I, a poor sinner myself, offer a similar petition for mine?

Freedom from Bondage

After the Battle of Gettysburg, July 1-3, 1863, Reverend George Duffield, Jr. labored on the field in connection with Mrs. Harris and the Christian Commission. He served as Pastor of the (N.S.) Presbyterian Church, in Adrian, Michigan, at that time, then later in Galesburg, Illinois. He spent a good portion of his time tending to Confederate wounded who had fallen into Union hands. This incident and others were written in letters to his brother and published in the *Detroit Advertiser* and *Tribune*.

Although these Confederate soldiers were in such a sad plight, they were outspoken in expressing their attachment to the South. Indeed, the ministry of kindness affected the political tendencies of the privates but touched the officers much less. Reverend Mr. Duffield said that after hearing them talk, he could hardly keep from telling them this very recent experience of his:

The day before, near Dillstown, on my way from Carlisle, we stopped at noon to feed our horses. Off in a far corner of the porch, two black men were sitting very quietly and were apparently very tired and hungry. One was a splendidly muscular man, about six feet two inches in height, named Harrison Ash. He must have been a very valuable chattel to his master, a Mississippi colonel, when human flesh was at a premium like gold.

Spoken in heavy black dialect, Mr. Ash's story was as follows:

"I came here with the Southern army and I've been with it ever since the war begun. Friday, we had a big fight, the biggest fight yet, and we got an awful big lickin'. Friday night, we had a retreat. Me and Druro here was asleep under a tree. Rain poured down powerful and they left us. So in the morning, when we woke up, they were gone."

"Why don't you follow them?"

"Followed them long enough. Besides, they travel too fast and we can't catch up."

"That is, you didn't want to follow them. Right?"

"No, sir."

"Wasn't your master kind to you?"

"Yes, most times. Though the hardest lickin' he ever gave me was for what he did hisself."

"Then you would rather stay in Pennsylvania?"

"Yes, sir. They tell us there in Mississippi that at the North there's nothing but snow and ice all the year round but this doesn't look much like it, I reckon, and I'd as soon live here as there, I'm thinking."

"Harrison, you've been thinking of a good many things today, I suspect. Let me see that big hand of yours and feel the grip of it. Who owned that hand yesterday?"

"Master did."

"He made it work for him. Who owns it today?"

"Reckon Harrison does himself."

"Stand up, Harrison. Do you know…you are a freeman? Both the laws of God and man say so. What work you do, you will be paid for. What pay you get, you can put in your own pocket instead of into your master's."

Like one awaking from a dream, or like the man in the "Christus Consolator," long shackled and lying in a dungeon, just beginning to move his unfettered limbs and to look upon the light of day, so was it with poor Harrison.

Supposing, from an incidental remark, that he was not altogether destitute of God's grace, I asked, "What do you know about religion, Harrison?"

"I know that Jesus came to save sinners."

"What did He do to save them?"

"He died for them."

"Did He die for you?"

"Yes, He died for me as for any sinner."

"Did you ever feel that you were a sinner?"

"Oh, yes. Very much one time, when I was about sixteen years old."

"How long did you feel this so much?"

"'Till I experienced the new change."

"What change?"

"Why, the change in the heart, you know, when we begin to love the Lord Jesus who died for us."

This was religion in its pure essence: the work of Christ for us on the Cross, the work of the Holy Spirit in us, a change of state and a change of nature, and the prisoner not only pardoned but the jail fever arrested and put in the process of cure. Surely, if these things are hid from the worldly-wise and prudent, who through their own pride and folly will not stoop to even pick them up when they lie at their feet, yet, blessed be the name of the Lord! They are still revealed unto those who seek.

Sinner's Prayer

Reverend George Duffield, Jr. labored on the field in connection with Mrs. Harris and the Christian Commission after the Battle of Gettysburg, July 1-3, 1863. At that time, he served as Pastor of the (N.S.) Presbyterian Church, in Adrian, Michigan, then later in Galesburg, Illinois. He spent a good portion of his time tending to Confederate wounded who had fallen into Union hands. This incident and others were written in letters to his brother and published in the *Detroit Advertiser* and *Tribune*. He tells this incident:

A number of Confederates were found in a barn. Some of the poor outcasts were in great bodily distress, continually crying out, "O Lord, bless my wounds!" Still others were in even greater mental distress. One fatally wounded man was groaning heavily. As Mrs. Harris was tending to his needs, he said, "O ma'am, if I was only sure that my sins could be pardoned, so that if I died I might go to heaven, I would be more reconciled to my fate."

Pointing him to the mercy of God in Christ Jesus, she recommended for him to seek it in prayer. Strange enough was the petition of this poor Publican as he prayed, "O Lord, save my body! O Lord, save my soul! And if You do, O Lord, I'll knuckle to You to all eternity."

Finding Peace

Following the Battle of Gettysburg, July 1-3, 1863, Reverend George Duffield, Jr. labored on the field in connection with Mrs. Harris and the Christian Commission. He served as Pastor of the (N.S.) Presbyterian Church, in Adrian, Michigan, at that time and later in Galesburg, Illinois. He spent a good portion of his time tending to Confederate wounded who had fallen into Union hands. This incident and others were written in letters to his brother and published in the *Detroit Advertiser* and *Tribune. He tells this incident about a scene from the battle and one man's perspective:*

"The fruitful place was a wilderness and all the birds of the heaven were still." Whether it was because of the noise, the smoke, the universal presence of the soldiers, or the noisome and pestilential atmosphere, I do not know. But one thing is certain. The orioles, robins, and other birds—so plentiful around the cemetery before the battle—had entirely disappeared from it. Strangely enough, the very first, and indeed the only bird I saw on the battlefield, near the extreme edge, was a solitary turtledove. It sat in perfect silence, with its head turned toward the path of strife, as if in mute contemplation of the scene of carnage.

"Surely that bird is strangely out of place and has no business here," said one soldier.

"Not so," was the reply of another. "May we not accept it as a happy omen but may we see in it the joyful harbinger of the return of peace—a peace on the sure foundations of truth and righteousness?"

Unusual Conversion

Reverend George Duffield, Jr. served as Pastor of the (N.S.) Presbyterian Church, in Adrian, Michigan, and later in Galesburg, Illinois. He labored on the field in connection with Mrs. Harris and the Christian Commission after the Battle of Gettysburg, July 1-3, 1863. He spent a good portion of his time tending to Confederate wounded who had fallen into Union hands. This incident and others were written in letters to his brother and published in the *Detroit Advertiser* and *Tribune*. He tells this story of an East Tennessee loyalist, furnished by a lady not connected with the Christian Commission, who requested that names be withheld:

While moving through one of the field hospitals a few days after the battle of Gettysburg, a lady from Philadelphia had her attention drawn to a young Confederate asleep and dreaming. He was talking aloud. Going to his cot, she gently fanned away some flies which were buzzing about a bandage concealing the lower part of his face. One hand was pressed tightly against his chest. A kindly but rough Irish nurse came by and the lady inquired about the wounded man:

With a strong Irish accent, she said, "Indeed, mum, he baffles me entirely. His clapper's half shot out, mum but he's forever gossiping with himself and the Virgin only knows what he's saying. It's all about his book with a 'bit rag' around it and he'll let no one touch it, mum. He's a strange creature, mum, that's for sure."

No one knew his name and the lady discovered that his wounds were pretty certain to prove fatal. Unwilling to disturb him in his troubled sleep, she passed on.

The next morning, a surgeon stood by the soldier's bed. The poor, unknown boy was dying. His two weak, sad, and wandering eyes were opening and closing restlessly. It seemed very mournful that one so young, nameless and alone should die this way among strangers. The Irish nurse was much affected:

"And sure, now, if we only had the book, it would have the poor creature's name inside." But no coaxing or efforts could get the book away from him. The surgeon said he would awaken from his long stupor before death—and, indeed, he was already beginning to do so. The lady sat down, fanned him and gave him what gentle care she could. After awhile, he began muttering to himself but his words were so indistinct that no one could understand him. Suddenly, he turned his head a little and spotted an old Union flag, hanging temporarily at one end of the ward. He gazed at it earnestly for a moment. The lady was watching him with intense interest when a great change came over his face. The dull, unconscious look passed away. Pointing to the flag, he turned painfully and clearly asked, "Why do they let it stay there for?"

The question was not a pleasant one for the lady to answer for several reasons but she replied, "Because General Lee was beaten the other day and has retreated. Don't you remember?"

The answer seemed to confuse him. He looked back and forth from the lady's face to the flag, murmuring, "Beaten? …General Lee? …Retreated?"

All of a sudden, the meaning appeared to grow plain. A look of joy covered his face and he turned back to the old stripes and stars. Tears flowed out of those poor, sunken eyes, and fervently, he said, "Thank God! Thank God!"

The lady thought this strange for a Confederate soldier to say. Supposing he had misunderstood her, she explained her meaning again but the poor fellow's eyes closed. The old, hopeless, blank look settled upon his face and he seemed more puzzling and strange than ever.

He began to dream now. His face grew bright and he resumed the old, muttering noise once again but, this time, much more distinctly. He seemed to be back at his home again. He talked first of someone whom he called "Mama Tilly," his mother we found out afterward. Then he spoke about "Nettie," his wife. The soldier's face soon became positively radiant because he thought Nettie had come, that she was with him! He told her how glad and happy he was to see her and asked about Harry, their little boy. The invisible Nettie seemed to be answering his questions, for he would look up now and then and laugh—sadly it seemed because of his wounded mouth. Still dreaming, he opened his shirt, brought out the precious book with the "bit rag" around it. Then, looking up again into the eyes "so near, and yet so far," he laughed a low, happy laugh, and said, "Nettie, darling, there it is yet good Minister _____'s New Testament, with the old flag around it still."

The lady bent forward eagerly and saw a little well-worn and well-marked New Testament and wrapped around it very carefully a torn bit of the *Union* flag.

The dream of Nettie seemed to be lost for a while and another replaced it. The soldier's mutterings were still indistinct but, pieced together, they appeared to be a kind of history of the flag-shred. He told about how the Confederates had come into the village, pulled down the Union flag, torn it into hundreds of fragments, and trampled these shreds into the dirt. He spoke about how he had gone out during the night at peril of his life, had picked up a piece of the dishonored banner, had taken it home and cherished it. He explained how he was driven from his home and forced into the Confederate Army but how he had clung silently, through all the months of drill and march and battle, to the old symbol which he so dearly loved. It was a thrilling story, as the lady gathered the facts, one by one, from the lips oblivious of the tale they were telling. She understood now the noble soldier's unexplained conduct and words.

After reminiscing about the flag, Nettie came back again—only for a few moments, however, little more than for a kiss and a farewell—a kiss given by no human lips, a farewell uttered to no visible, human presence. Yet, it could not have been an unconscious pantomime as mere shadows could not have cheated that dying man. It must have been real, no less true than St. Paul's experience—even if invisible. And then came another, brighter vision—a vision which none may smile at, thank God, or call untrue. This vision has been seen by too many glad eyes over eighteen hundred years. For men to be deceived by it now is unthinkable—the vision of the Crucified One. The man uttered only two words but who can dispute them? He said, "Jesus...dear."

And so this portion of the story ends. The soldier went away to be forever with the Lord.

The little New Testament told the whole story in a few simple dates. The date of his confirmation was given, along with the name of the beloved clergyman who had given him the Testament, and who had written in the front the words of the Collect for the second Sunday in Lent:

"Almighty God, who seest that we have no power of ourselves to help our-selves; keep us both outwardly in our bodies and inwardly in our souls; that we may be defended from all adversities which may happen to the body, and from all evil thoughts which may assault and hurt the soul: through Jesus Christ our Lord. Amen."

The sentences had been written two years before the war. However, it would have been difficult to have chosen more appropriate words for all the unforeseen conflict and toil between then and now.

The date of the soldier's marriage was recorded—only a month or two before the war began. On one of the flyleaves, these words of Isaiah were written, "Is not this the fast that I have chosen? to loose the bonds of wickedness, to undo the heavy burdens, and to let the oppressed go free; and that ye break every yoke?" After these words came the date of the firing on Fort Sumter. This, along with other plentiful remarks, showed that the brave Tennessean had entered into the full meaning of the struggle. The birth of little Harry was chronicled and dates attached to passages all throughout the book showed how the noble loyalist had followed, amidst enemies, the varying fortunes of the war. Toward the close of 1862, the Confederates had entered the village in East Tennessee, which had been his home. Here he began his love of the flag. He had fled with Nettie and Harry into Northern Alabama and, there, he was forced into the Confederate Army. The date of his separation from his family was appended to these words of St. Luke: "Be not afraid of them that kill the body, and after that have no more that they can do."

Several letters from his wife, who found her way back to their wrecked and ruined home in Tennessee, were tucked away carefully at the back of the book. After reading them, one might struggle to discern which of the two had the firmest faith in Christ and in the final triumph of the right cause in the war.

The treasured relics of the dead soldier were gathered and kept. When East Tennessee was opened, they were sent safely to Nettie. Little Harry had died but a sweet little girl had come in his place.

For all that had been done for her husband, Nettie sent a touching letter of thanks. She wrote, "It had been such a long time since I got a letter from him that I had given him up entirely, even before your good, kind letter came. I am glad that I know now just how he went away. I want to live long enough to tell little Alice all about it when she can understand better than she does now."

She did not live long enough for this, however. A few months passed and Nettie went to be with her husband. After their weariness and separation, their bodies now rest, side by side with little Harry's, amidst the sunny goldenrod on the banks of the Clinch River in Virginia. Little Alice has been brought to the home of the lady who was at her father's bedside in the Gettysburg hospital. She has a middle name now, which her friends love to call her. She is known as "Loyal."

The lady who tells this story was herself neither loyal nor a Christian when she was at Gettysburg. In death, the East Tennessean taught her to be both an earnest lover of her country and to be Christ's child. She feels such deep gratitude for the lessons both Nettie and her husband taught her that she feels wholly inadequate in repaying this debt of gratitude to little Alice.

CHAPTER VII
THE EASTERN ARMIES
FROM GETTYSBURG UNTIL GRANT'S ADVANCE ON RICHMOND
July 1863–May 1864

For several months after the Battle of Gettysburg in Pennsylvania, the movements of the armies in Virginia needed no chronicling because their ranks had been devastated and so many men were laid up in hospitals. Stations of the Christian Commission were established at Germantown, Warrenton, and among the First Corps hospitals on the Rappahannock, at Bealeton, and in the Third Army Corps. The sick were promptly taken to Washington, so the main work took place among the able-bodied for some time. In September, the strange retreat of the entire army to Centreville Heights occurred. Tedious days of slow advance followed. A station that was established at Gainesville was moved to Manassas Junction in October and then was transferred to Warrenton Junction in November.

Life Transformed by Faith

After the Battle of Gettysburg, Pennsylvania, July 1-3, 1863, Mr. A. D. Matthews, of Brooklyn, served as a delegate in October at Winchester Seminary Hospital at Frederick, Maryland. He relates a touching story of a mother's courage and of a soldier's faith:

After the service on Sunday morning, I found Henry Morton in the hospital, dreadfully wounded in the chest. He was one of three brothers, all of whom were Sunday school scholars at the time of their enlistment. Two or three weeks prior, Henry's mother had been called to Washington from her home in northern New York to see Willie, one of the brothers, who was at the point of death.

After her arrival, he lingered but a few days, then sweetly fell asleep in Jesus. Efforts to embalm the body failed and, after following it to the grave so far from home, the broken-hearted mother was summoned in haste to Henry's cot in Frederick. The surgeon cautioned her not to mention Willie's death, as the soldier's wound in the chest would likely open during any fit of sobbing or crying, likely causing his death. Of course, one of Henry's first questions was about his brother.

The mother replied, "Don't be troubled about him, my son. Keep perfectly quiet. Willie is in good hands and well cared for."

With heroic fortitude, she kept the mournful news pent up inside for several days until someone, not knowing the situation, alluded to Willie's death. Henry looked into his mother's face and asked, "Mother, is Willie dead?"

Since concealment was no longer possible, she was telling the sad story when surgeon's fears came to pass. The wound reopened. For several days, Henry hung to life hung by a slender thread. By Sunday morning when I visited him, he had begun to mend. With a smile on his face, he told me how his once feeble hope had become his present glorious prospect.

"Since I have lain here, the old lessons of faith have come fresh and new to my mind. I am now sure that Jesus is my all."

Fortunately, the mother's heart was spared the loss of her second son but, even before Henry had entirely recovered, news about her third son brought her anxiety again. Even though he also was wounded in battle, he was able to return to his regiment quickly.

Victory in Spiritual Struggles

Reverend Luther Keene, Pastor of the Congregational Church, in North Brookfield, Massachusetts, also served as a Christian Commission delegate following the July 1-3, 1863 Battle of Gettysburg. He worked among the wounded in and around Washington during October and November and furnishes the following sketches of hospital work:

A young German, who was later baptized by Reverend Colt of South Brookfield, Massachusetts, came to talk to me about his spiritual struggles:

"There are two voices within me. One voice tells me to play cards and swear while the other tells me to go to the meeting." He vividly described his last conflict in minute detail. It was as real to him as if the voices were actually audible, indeed, it could not have been more real.

I asked, "Which voice are you going to obey?"

With decisiveness in his animated face, he replied, "The good voice."

I then showed him St. Paul's words in Romans Chapter 7 and how he had unconsciously quoted them.

Guiding Another into Salvation

After the young German was baptized by Reverend Colt of South Brookfield, Massachusetts, he gave a precious testimony of his love for Christ and souls one evening. Going to a comrade at the meeting's close, he led him forward to where the men were kneeling to be prayed over. It was a beautiful sight to see him make room among the company for the unresisting soldier and then help him down upon his knees. Coming to where I stood, he told me the man was almost deaf. I then went over to him and, putting my mouth close to his ear, I prayed with him. The last I saw of them, they were leaving the meeting together—the deaf soldier leaning on the German who seemed to be tenderly and solicitously helping him into the kingdom of God.

(Luther Keene)

Ministry of Writing Letters

Those letters written for soldiers—how precious they were sometimes! I met one poor little English boy in the hospital. His face was sorrowful with homesickness. "I would give all I have in the world," he said, "if only I could hear from home." For some reason, all his letters had gone unanswered. I wrote a letter to England for him and, a few weeks later, the army had at least one happy heart when the answer came.

In another instance, I had visited a dying soldier named Hill and written home for him. One morning, I found a young stranger kneeling by Hill's cot. The man was Hill's brother. Shall I ever forget the grasp of that man's hand and the light in his eyes, as he told me about those letters home, narrating so simply the story of a soldier's endurance and victory over sin? Or, shall I never forget another scene—over which there was great joy elsewhere, if not there—when the brother of one maimed in the service of the government followed the dead soldier to the grave and wept there with me? We were the only mourners and, yet, many of the poor boys had fewer still.

(Luther Keene)

Historical Context:

In November, the Union Army moved against Lee in Virginia. They crossed the Rappahannock on the 7th and, after bridges were rebuilt and communications opened, they crossed over the Rapidan River on the 26th. The armies then faced each other along Mine Run for several days. Finally, on December 1st and 2nd, our forces were withdrawn and the campaign of 1863 ended.

A few days before the advance to Mine Run, Brandy Station became the hub of supplies and communication. With instructions from the Christian Commission Field Agent, Reverend E. F. Williams and six delegates proceeded there. The first Sunday's service foreshadowed the great winter harvest to be gathered there. Several weeks earlier, an interesting work of grace had begun among the unorganized recruits at Warrenton Junction.

Dying with Grace

Chaplain Norman Fox, of the 77th New York Regiment, sent a story to the *New York Examiner* about the evening after the battle of Rappahannock Station:

I found a young man of the 10th Massachusetts Regiment whose leg was crushed and mangled by a piece of shell. The injury had been so severe that amputation was useless and he was sinking rapidly. I asked the man about his religious background. It was the old story—a bright hope, active church membership, army life and irregularities, and finally the abandonment of his profession of faith. "And now," he said, "if there can be forgiveness for such a wanderer, pray for me."

I confess I felt more awkwardness than I should have. Standing nearby, a circle of rough soldiers surveyed the solemn scene with nothing more than morbid curiosity. Beside them, stood a more educated and refined group of surgeons, some of whom I knew had no belief in God or eternity. Without a doubt, I knew they considered my interview with the dying man as nothing but amiable uselessness. But before me lay the sinking sufferer and I wore the uniform of a minister of Christ. Bending over the table where he lay, I asked the Good Shepherd to pardon the returning wanderer. The man murmured responses throughout the prayer, emphasizing his own earnestness in the petition. The smothered hope, faint at first, was revived and grew brighter and brighter until, finally, his face beamed with the full radiance of faith and hope, which supports the bearer in such a stern hour as this.

Meanwhile, standing by the table was a noble-looking soldier, a little older than the dying man, who moistened the lips of the dying man and affectionately smoothed his hair. He was so perfectly calm and collected that I supposed he was merely a hospital attendant. A casual remark caused me to change my mind and I asked, "Is this a friend of yours?"

"He is my younger brother," he replied.

Stooping over him, the brother said, "Sam, what shall I tell mother for you?"

"Tell her I died for my country" was his prompt, cheery reply.

"Give me a kiss for her," said the other and the bronzed face bowed down to brother's pale lips as tenderly as if they had been an infant's. More than one turned to hide his tears but the brothers seemed least moved of all.

The dying boy sank rapidly but all clouds vanished and his faith grew bright and strong. I recited various passages, including, "I know that my Redeemer liveth," "The Lord is my Shepherd," "In My Father's house are many mansions," and the beautiful hymn "Rock of Ages." But the lines of a hymn—especially dear when the couch of departure was a rough board table in a cold, dark tent, with only a knapsack to lay his head—were so very dear to his heart: *"Jesus can make a dying bed feel soft as downy pillows are."*

He tried to repeat, "Jesus, lover of my soul" but I had to finish it for him. This seemed to strengthen him even more than the others. But his voice was already beginning to fail. He said, "There's … a … silver … pencil … in … pocket … silver … pencil … in … pocket …."

With deepest sorrow, we saw that he could not speak friendship's last message. There was but one Friend of whom he could speak now. We watched him silently as he lay motionless for several minutes. I thought all was over but, rousing suddenly, he said,

"'Jesus, lover of my soul,'—oh, repeat that again!"

My voice choked up so that I could hardly speak. I do not know if he heard me because, before I reached the last verse, "the storm of life" was over, "the haven" was reached, and "the billows" had died away in eternal peace.

Preach the Word

Reverend Amos H. Coolidge, Pastor of the Congregational Church, Leicester, Massachusetts, was also a Christian Commission delegate. He served after the July 1-3, 1863 Battle of Gettysburg about the time of Mine Run. He gives an interesting narrative of a Sunday's work:

I started out after breakfast. My horse made what time he could in the deep, sticky mud. Spending a short time in the Contraband camp, helping the eager scholars in their efforts to read, I hastened to my first preaching service among several detached companies of artillery. Following this, I took the long ride to my second appointment with a regiment.

The regiment was drawn up in line. Leave was granted to any who wished to retire from the ranks and the sermon if they wished. Only two left. On my return, at a little picket station, the men begged for a service. So again, the Word was preached. At another picket station on the way, we held another service. Without dismounting this time, hymns and prayer and the proclamation of the blessed Gospel went forth for the fourth time. The men were hungry and grateful for the truth. Down the road was a wood station where were several hundred men were located. Night was descending. But upon meeting a friend, we made arrangements for my fifth preaching service.

"All hail the power of Jesus' name" rang out as the "church call." Instantly, men came pouring from every direction. Fuel was added to an already immense fire and a great army of flames sprang skyward, sending a rich tinge over the darkening woods and ground. Sounding forth over the multitude, the Good News traveled on its heavenly errand once more. Indeed, it was a solemn assembly. Many days afterward, I heard of some who gave themselves to Jesus.

As I rode away into the night and looked back on the diminishing blaze, I thought of the "heavenly City" where "there shall be no night," where "they need no candle, neither light of the sun." I was more glad than tired when I came to the Christian Commission quarters. I prayed that the five services might be blessed of God, even though the congregations had not sat in cushioned pews and I had preached from strange pulpits—three stumps, an old plow, and a tired horse's back.

Historical Context:

During January 1864, the Christian Commission's work was mainly that of an organizing, preparatory nature. The troops were in, what proved to, be "winter quarters," even though the men did not know it, nor did the Commission have tents or delegates for its fifteen army stations until the month had nearly passed. Yet, the soldiers welcomed the agents everywhere we went. They came to the depot at Brandy Station and begged for brigade and division chapels in which to hold preaching services. During the winter, not less than sixty canvas coverings were issued. Under these tents, the chaplains held their Sunday services and nightly meetings. Without them, there would have been very little opportunity for religious gatherings during the winter months.

The great work of revival began at once. Meetings at the stations and in the chapels were soon crowded and, again, the men were furnished with New Testaments and hymnbooks. Bible classes were formed—some taught by delegates, others by chaplains, and still others by the soldiers themselves. For a great many wanderers, whose number can only be known when the books of heaven are opened, the winter camps became the "gate of heaven."

God's Hand upon Ministry

Following the July 1-3, 1863 Battle of Gettysburg, a Bible class was organized in February 1864. Reverend J. B. Davis, Pastor of (O. S.) Presbyterian
Church in Bridesburg, Philadelphia, and Mr. Johnston Calhoun of Hook-
stown, Pennsylvania, served as leaders. This class took place among the 1st
Brigade, Horse Artillery, encamped not far from Brandy Station and met
at the Christian Commission "Artillery Reserve Station, No. 2" and numbered forty-six soldiers. The work among these men and in the chapel services
was especially blessed of God. Reverend G. S. Stockwell, a Baptist clergyman from Springfield, Massachusetts and Messrs. Davis and Calhoun were
associated in this work. Reverend Davis' preached his first sermon here to
about seventy-five listeners, standing in the mud. Later, the soldiers brought
boughs of evergreen from the riverbank to serve as a carpet and lumber for the
seats. The chapel became comfortable. Night after night, the meetings were
crowded and many were converted.

The artillery stood in special need of spiritual ministry and effort, as they had
no army chaplains assigned to them. Therefore, a special effort took place
throughout the winter to reach the men in this branch of the service. The
Bible class scholars asked the Central Office for books to aid them in a critical study of God's Word. Their requisition was approved and the meetings of
earnest Bible students became a source of great delight to the students and of
much encouragement to the delegates. Several of these students were college
graduates and a number of them decided to prepare for the ministry when
their army service was over.

New Christian's Zeal

Following the Battle of Gettysburg on July 1-3, 1863, Reverend E. F. Williams, wrote the following incidents from Brandy Station, Virginia in February 1864:

A "sutler" was someone who followed the army and sold food and liquor
to the soldiers. One particular sutler told me today about a member of his
regiment who could not read but had recently been converted at one of
the soldiers' chapels. The new Christian was so anxious to hear the Savior's
words that, day after day, he had hired his comrades to read to him. Only
yesterday, he had given a swearing acquaintance ten cents—all the money
he had—to read to him the fifth chapter of St. Matthew's Gospel. He would
ask for the reading of passages which he had heard in the meetings. He
was continually on the alert to discover the names of books and numbers

of chapters that had impressed any of his comrades or which he had heard about in some incidental way.

Seeking Joy

A German was converted here, who seemed utterly surprised at the goodness of God to him. One day, he was overheard, praying, "O Lord Jesus, I didn't know You were so good." And, yet, as happy as he was, he was anxious for more of Christ's presence and kept praying, "God, I pray You would add as much to this present joy as You gave me when I trusted Christ."
(E. F. Williams)

Trophy of God's Grace

During the winter of 1864, following the July 1-3, 1863 Battle of Gettysburg, a station was established and manned by two Christian Commission delegates. This occurred in the Second Division of the First Corps, on Sperryville Pike. The usual scenes at other stations were witnessed here as well. Reverend E. F. Williams, Pastor of the Congregational Church, Whitinsville, Massachusetts and delegate of the Christian Commission, writes of the circumstances surrounding the conversion of a soldier at this place:

Born of pious parents in the State of New York, Charles Rockwell spent his early boyhood in Connecticut in every kind of wickedness. At one time, his parents, thinking he had been converted, forced him to join the church contrary to his will. But his vows were never kept. When he had been disturbing a meeting, a most injudicious and sinful prayer for his "damnation," by an officer of the church had thoroughly hardened him. Afterward, he considered himself condemned to hell and met every effort for his reformation with unwavering conviction about his doom.

During a long, perilous whaling voyage, he had a very narrow escape from immediate death but the warning had no effect upon him whatsoever. Some remarks of another officer of the church, with which he had been connected, set him thinking seriously about marriage and family and home. Soon afterward, he married a gentle, loving Christian woman and they settled in Pennsylvania. His wife would go away alone, day after day, to read the Bible and pray. Her husband followed her once to listen and she was praying for him. He was deeply affected but fought hard to avoid discovering himself.

When she came into the other room, he asked why she had gone away by herself. When she hesitated and was confused about answering, her husband said, "Well, never mind. I know because I followed you upstairs today. If you want to pray, you may do it down here before me and not go up there into the cold."

Consistently, the wife maintained family prayers. But the husband continued in his intemperate and profane ways.

When the war broke out, he enlisted as a cavalryman. He was soon made Orderly Sergeant for his skill and knowledge but was reduced in rank again and again for committing crimes. It was his ambition to drink more whisky and play a better game of cards than any other man in the 17th Pennsylvania Regiment.

In January, a delegate was sent from Culpepper, Virginia to preach to the regiment. Charley Rockwell thought the sermon—on small sins—was a feeble one and fit only for ridicule. Later in the day, he heard another sermon in a neighboring regiment, which drove home the words of the earlier sermon into his conscience. He went back to his tent with little peace.

A few days earlier, two pious soldiers, hungry for a prayer meeting, had begun one in their own tents. The regiment had no chaplain, and this little soldiers' meeting grew so large that the colonel gave them a tent, which held about thirty men. Many more used to crowd around the entrance until, finally, the men petitioned the Christian Commission for a "fly." They not only received this but they also acquired occasional help from delegates working at the nearest station. Their meeting had grown until some twenty men attended it.

To escape the sermon, Rockwell wandered around looking for excitement. Hearing singing, he stumbled upon this little Christian company and, before the meeting closed, he rose and asked for prayers. However, it was not God's time yet. Regretting what he had done, he became drunk and remained so for several days. Coming to himself, he recalled a scene at home during his last furlough. He had been urging his wife to go to a ball. Putting her arms around him, with tears pouring down her face, she said, "Charley, I'm trying to live as a Christian. I wish you were one. But I can't be a Christian and a ball-dancer too."

In great agony of mind, he sought the prayer meeting again. The struggle was a fearful one but, at last, God's peace came. Describing the close of the strife, he afterward said, "I had been praying all night until about two o'clock, when I began to feel strange. I kindled a fire, not sure whether I was alive or dead. Then I lay down, slept soundly, and woke early. First of all, I prayed and then went out to attend to my horse—usually a vicious animal.

This morning, he was kind and gentle. I put my arms about his neck and said, "Well, old horse, have you got religion too?"

At roll call in the evening, Charley stepped forward from the ranks and asked permission to say a few words. Imagine his comrades' surprise when they heard his simple, brave speech: "Comrades, you know how wicked I have been—what a life I have led in this regiment. With God's help, this day Charley Rockwell turns over a new leaf and begins to live as a Christian. He wants your forgiveness for the wrongs he has done and asks you to join him in trying to serve Christ."

Ever afterward, he was an earnest Christian, cheerfully giving up his wicked companions and returned, as far as it was in his power, his gambling gains. He used to tell me sadly of his past life. He once said, "I fully expected to go to hell. I wanted to go there. I used to think I would get Satan to make me his prime minister. Then, what fun I would have in raking up the coals and heaping them on the heads of old religious hypocrites!"

His faith in the power of God's grace was boundless. When he became interested in studying for the ministry, Christian Commission delegates furnished him with books, which he diligently used to direct his course in life. But the book of greatest delight to him was the Bible. He spent every spare moment in perusing its pages. He continued steadfast as long as I knew him. Then the Wilderness campaign began.

Needing Spiritual Food

Following the July 1-3, 1863 Battle of Gettysburg and during the early months of 1864,

Reverend E. F. Williams, Pastor of the Congregational Church, Whitinsville, Massachusetts served as Christian Commission delegate. He was in charge of Culpepper Station, the headquarters for work in the First Corps. He tells of a particular man:

Every night, a Pennsylvania soldier regularly traveled two miles to the meeting at Culpepper. Storms, mud, and swollen streams could not keep him away. When his turn came to man the picket, he paid a companion to take his place, rather than miss his favorite meeting. He could not read so, in his quest for spiritual food, he could only find this kind of nourishment at the evening services and in conversation with Christian friends.

True Christian Unity

Following the July 1-3, 1863, Battle of Gettysburg, Reverend William M. Taylor, Pastor of (O. S.) Presbyterian Church, Mount Jackson, Pennsylvania served as a delegate for the Christian Commission. In March of 1864, he wrote:

Toward the close of my labors at Vermont Station, near Culpepper, I administered the Lord's Supper. Reverend George Mure Smith, Pastor of the Congregational Church, Rocky Hill, Connecticut, assisted me. One thing in connection with this service is most noteworthy. Even though the administration of the elements was given to members of eight different denominations, not one communicant belonged to the (O. S.) Presbyterian Church where I served. This typified the mighty power of God in using the Commission to break down sectarian prejudices and barriers.

Work of the Holy Spirit

After the July 1-3, 1863 Battle of Gettysburg, Reverend Benjamin Waddle, of Kenton, Ohio, served as a delegate with the Christian Commission. In February 1864, he worked among the men of the Fifth Corps at Nelson Station, Warrenton Junction, Virginia. He writes of the following incident:

The corps of drummer boys at the station numbered ten. One became deeply convicted of sin. Ashamed to let the fact be known, he sought solace and secrecy in the woods for prayer where he found Jesus. His older brother imitated his example. One after another followed, until all ten "rejoiced in hope of the glory of God" and began sounding out to all around them a new martial call—"To arms for Jesus!"

Coming to Christ because of Christian Unity

Following the July 1-3, 1863 Battle of Gettysburg and during the early months of 1864,

Reverend E. F. Williams, Pastor of the Congregational Church, Whitinsville, Massachusetts served as Christian Commission delegate. He tells of the influence that the Warrenton Junction Station had upon soldiers by reporting the soldiers' own statements:

One said, "Before the meetings started, all my comrades were profane and gambled. But now, not an oath can be heard, nor a card seen in our camp."

In one of the meetings a soldier rose and said, "The sectarian jealousies of denominations at home have been a stumbling block for me but here, in the army and in your Commission meetings, the corners have been rubbed off.

There is no excuse left for me. With God's help, I intend to begin living a Christian life from this day forward."

Power of Prayer

Reverend J. B. Pearson, Pastor of the Congregational Church, Plymouth Hollow, Connecticut served as a Christian Commission delegate following the July 1-3, 1863 Battle of Gettysburg. He relates an incident, which came to his knowledge, at the Warrenton Junction Station in March 1864:

On parting with their son and brother who was soon to lead his company into battle, a mother and sister said to him, "We shall pray for you every night at seven o'clock." The Captain was not a Christian but he rose in our meeting and said, "Not a night goes by but, at the hour of seven, I remember my praying mother and sister. Once during a severe skirmish, lasting into the evening, for some reason I looked at my watch. It was nearly seven. Though I make no claims on God's favor and have never sought His care, yet it seemed to me that I was being upheld by the prayers of my mother and sister. In answer to them, I had assurance He would bring me safely through the fight."

He told his story with deep feeling. I trust he soon found Christ.

Powerful Preaching

After the July 1-3, 1863 Battle of Gettysburg, Reverend E. F. Williams, Pastor of the Congregational Church, Whitinsville, Massachusetts served as Christian Commission delegate. Warrenton Junction Station was established in February 1864 and Reverend Williams writes of its beginning:

A delegate preached on Sunday and a captain invited him to share his tent at night. Before retiring, the delegate learned that the captain was a backslider but he promised the delegate from that day forward, he would be faithful in secret prayer and correct in outward life. I can never forget the depth of feeling with which the captain, in one of the meetings at Warrenton, gave thanks for the good, which that delegate had done him. Through the Divine blessing upon his amended life and his renewed efforts for Christ, every member of his company had become a child of God.

Profound Work of the Holy Spirit

Reverend E. F. Williams, Pastor of the Congregational Church, Whitinsville, Massachusetts served as Christian Commission delegate, following the Battle of Gettysburg, July 1-3, 1863. Perhaps, the most marked work of the Spirit during the winter and spring of 1864 was begun in March at Bristow Station, Virginia.

It began in the 11th Pennsylvania Reserve Regiment. Reverend Williams gives the following account of it:

Its origin, under God, was in the prayers and efforts of a private of the regiment. Day after day he went alone into the woods to pray. His comrades scoffed but he persevered. At last, one friend found him. This man bad been converted by the memory of a conversation with a pious mother on a Sunday long ago. His mother's sudden death had brought back to memory the almost forgotten words. The two pious men together felt strong; in faith they waited for a blessing. Others joined them, and when the Commission chapel was set up, "It seemed," said the Chaplain of the regiment, "as if God's Spirit descended at once." Prior to the opening of the tent there were seven who had placed their hope in Christ; within four weeks there were sixty-one.

Touching Work of the Holy Spirit

A German, deeply interested in religion, went home on a furlough. His chief regret, when returning to his regiment, was the thought that he could no longer enjoy meetings for prayer. Some of his companions, converted during his absence, surprised him as he came into camp when they inquired, "Are you going to the meetings?"

"What meetings?"

"Why, at the Christian Commission meetings—we have two every day. Will you come?"

The German's heart was too full for speech. Describing the effect of their words upon him, in heavy German dialect, he afterward said,

"I jus' cried for 'glad.' I could jus' see Jesus in the boys' faces."
(E. F. Williams)

Moving Work of the Holy Spirit

A soldier was greatly interested in reading from an old paper, which his chaplain had given him. It told a story of some poor children in Germany, who, while eating the bread of charity, denied themselves their evening meal. Instead, they sold their food and gave the proceeds to a missionary endeavor. He was so moved by the account that he came at once to the chaplain and told him of a vow he made during the battle of Gaines' Mills. He had prayed that, if the Lord would spare his life, he would give a certain amount of money to some benevolent cause. Afterward, he paid the vow with a hundred percent interest and lived a devoted Christian life.

Unusual Timing of the Holy Spirit

Many who were converted here immediately wrote to their friends of the change they experienced. As a result of these letters, several revivals began in different parts of Pennsylvania. One soldier wrote to his betrothed, telling her of his conversion and praying she would give herself to Christ. But his letter and one from her, telling of her conversion and begging him to live for Christ, crossed in the mail. The man was so overjoyed that he came and woke up a Christian Commission delegate to hear the story.

A similar incident came to our knowledge in the case of a husband and wife whose letters crossed in the mail. Each contained an account of the writer's conversion, along with a prayer that the other might find peace in Jesus.

Power of Christian Unity

After the July 1-3, 1863 Battle of Gettysburg, Reverend E. F. Williams, Pastor of the Congregational Church, Whitinsville, Massachusetts served as Christian Commission delegate at Bristow Station, Virginia. In the winter and spring of 1864, the result of six weeks work was the formation of a "Christian Union," numbering more than one hundred and twenty members. Mr. Williams' narrative explains its origin:

A missionary concert, which was held the first Sunday in April, gave the soldiers zeal and a vision of working for the salvation of others. They rejoiced in giving up, for a time, one of our delegates to look after destitute regiments. The subsequent reports from these efforts generated intense interest. Through constant attendance at our meetings, which centered on the means of grace and on zealous work, the young brethren were built up in a wonderful manner and were drawn together into a precious Christian communion. All this prepared for the formation of a "Christian Union," which occurred on April 18th. Believers from eleven different denominations worked together in complete harmony, without a dissenting voice. Forming such a brotherhood was a delightful testimony to the oneness and strength they found in Christ.

Trophy of God's Grace

Following the Battle of Gettysburg on July 1-3, 1863, Mr. J. H. Morley, of Andover Theological Seminary in Massachusetts, labored at Sperryville Pike Station in Virginia. During his term of service with the Christian Commission, the following incident took place:

One of the most interesting cases of conversion I encountered was that of a German named Bolick. He served with the 17th Pennsylvania Cavalry. Seven years prior, he thought that he was a Christian. Although he was the son of pious parents, he took no definite stand for Christ. So he lived in darkness and soon gave up his hope of knowing the Light. He became, as he himself said, "a drunkard, a gambler and as bad as a man could become." He came to a chapel meeting one evening but made up his mind that it was no place for him. He concluded, "I must get out of that meeting or else come back to Christ."

For several evenings, he stayed in his tent gambling. One day, someone handed him a petition and asked for his signature. The soldiers were requesting an army chaplain for their regiment. He was a habitual gambler but signed his name anyway. He then began to think about the incongruity of a gambler signing a petition for a chaplain. He was troubled and determined to go to a meeting but, for some time, was kept back by his companions. At last, he came and, for two successive evenings, asked us to pray for him in terms, which convinced all of us that he was in earnest. On the third evening, he told us in broken English that he had found the Savior and must forsake his old habits. Upon hearing of his confession, his old comrades abused and ridiculed him. But he stood firm and asked our prayers for them. For as long as I was with the regiment, Bolick stood well and was always ready to take up his Cross and follow Christ.

Ministry of Penetrating Hardened Hearts

After the Battle of Gettysburg, July 1-3, 1863, Mr. H. Morey, a City Missionary from Brooklyn, New York, served at Warrenton as a Christian Commission delegate. The duty of the delegate was to minister to men of every rank. Mr. Morey writes of an interview near Warrenton with a captain and a surgeon returning from their leaves of absence:

The surgeon's appearance indicated refinement and education but I noticed that both he and the captain frequently swore as they talked. I reproved them, somewhat to their astonishment. The surgeon replied, "I meant nothing by it. It is a habit—I didn't even notice I was doing it."

I asked, "Are you satisfied with such an apology? If you are, I am not."

"Oh, I'm going to stop and be good one of these days," he replied.

"That's all very well but you have confessed that the habit is so deep that you don't even know when you are indulging in it. It will be harder to break when you 'stop' and 'get good,' my friend."

In the course of conversation, he said, "My father is a clergyman and my mother is a fine Christian woman. I grew up in a Christian home."

I replied, "You have yet another Father whom you are offending." He was somewhat repentant and thanked me while I prayed inwardly that the words said might, indeed, profit him.

The captain said, "I was a 'professor of religion' before entering the army but I found that swearing is necessary to govern my men, so my profession has been relieved from duty."

I replied, "Sir, I have often seen people swearing at horses and mules but I have never noticed either a horse or mule being improved by such language and I am quite certain the users of the language had not been."

We parted company and, months later, I met the captain near the Weldon railroad station. He introduced himself by asking if I remembered our conversation near Warrenton. I told him I did.

He replied, "I am the captain you spoke to and I want you to know that your words were not forgotten. I have come to think as you do about swearing at men and mules too."

Work of Revival

Reverend E. F. Williams, Pastor of the Congregational Church, Whitinsville, Massachusetts, served as a Christian Commission delegate, following the Battle of Gettysburg, July 1-3, 1863. The Commission's work in Washington took place primarily at Camp Convalescent, where there seemed to have been a continuous revival. Agents might be called to other fields and new delegates might take their place. Still, the precious work of the Spirit continued. Reverend Williams, who visited the camp in January 1864, gives the story of one of the nightly gatherings:

The bell was ringing for a meeting as we were eating a hasty dinner. Entering the chapel, we found it filled with an audience of at least eight hundred people. Within an hour, forty-three had given a word of testimony, we had sung ten or twelve hymns, and several prayers had been offered. It was a memorable meeting, as the soldier's expressions were peculiar and striking.

One said, "Brethren, I *know* I have passed from death unto life, for I love the brethren. I feel the need continually to pray 'Create in me a clean heart, O God, and renew a right spirit within me.'"

Another said, "One year ago, I could drink as much whisky and swear as much as anyone in my company. Now I trust I am a Christian."

In a similar, straight-out soldier's way, they spoke until the hour had passed. At the close of the meeting, a good many came forward. They shook hands with us as if they had always known us and told us more of their religious experiences. Among these was a man whom we had known a year before, at the hospital of the First Corps near Acquia Creek. At that time, he was an infidel, awfully profane, unwilling to attend any meeting, or to converse upon any religious subject. Now, he was a believer, ready to testify for Christ, and anxious to atone for past neglect and sin through hard work.

Difficulty Understanding New Testament

Following the Battle of Gettysburg, July 1-3, 1863, Reverend F. N. Peloubet, Pastor of the Congregational Church in Oakham, Massachusetts, worked as a Christian Commission delegate. He gives a graphic account of work at the Deserters' Barracks at Camp Convalescent in Washington during February and March of 1864. It shows the varied work of the delegate and the difficulties and temptations of the soldier:

I went, as usual, to the Deserters' Barracks on the morning of March 2nd. I took out a little tract, entitled, *Will You Enlist,* to read aloud. Some objected, saying, "We've heard it before. We can read that any day. Let's hear the New Testament."

I replied, "Why, you can read *that* any day."

"Yes, but we want it explained. We've read it but don't understand it. The other things are made up and we want something we know is true."

Difficulty of Living a Righteous Life

While standing on a board between two bunks, I read two chapters in St. John's First Epistle. Before long, a young man named Isaac Free objected, saying, "Seems to me a man must be perfect, else he can't go to heaven."

I said, "That can't be, for then none would go there, since none are perfect."

"Well, you said so last Sunday, anyhow."

I read the 8th and 10th verses of the 1st chapter, then the 6th verse of the 3rd chapter—comparing them.

"Well, they contradict, don't they?" Isaac asked.

As forthrightly as I could, I showed that they did not contradict. I also stated how Peter and David, though sinners, went to heaven.

"But it says there, 'The soul that sinneth, it shall die.' How's that?"

I told him about Christ's salvation and how pardoning a criminal did not make a judge a liar. Isaac then came back to the strife within his own heart.

He said, "I've tried to be good and I can't. I've suffered a good deal and sin don't give any peace. That's all the hell I believe in."

"Isn't that enough to make you want freedom from it?"

I told him of my own experience once—how the more I had tried to be good, the worse it seemed.

"That's it," he said. "Who can live like a Christian here?"

"But you *can*. Only you must find the Way—Christ, whose blood cleanses from all sin. Do you really want to be a Christian? Do you ever pray?"

"No."

"And do you expect to become a Christian without asking?"

Here our conversation rested.
(F. N. Peboulet)

Difficulty Becoming a Christian

Before I left the barracks, he came to me and told me his story. Born in New York to Christian parents, they had died when he was quite young. He went to live with an uncle, who ran a household without any restraints upon his actions. Enlisting in the regular army in 1859, he met much hard company. During the New York riots, his regiment was sent to quell the disturbance and was stationed at the Battery. A comrade persuaded him to go AWOL one night and they passed the hours in sin. Being drunk for the first time in his life, his false friend enticed him to go to Philadelphia. He did not dare to return to New York but found work. He was soon arrested.

"I haven't known an hour's peace since I deserted," said the poor fellow.

I asked, "Is the punishment hard here?"

"Oh, it isn't that. It's the disgrace, *the disgrace of* fighting well and then coming to this!"

He had already sworn never to touch drink again. I strove hard to persuade him to pray but he replied, "It won't do for me—a deserter become a Christian! They'd always throw it in my face."

"But Christ knows better than 'they.' He will forgive you and befriend you."

Eight days later, I saw him again. He had been praying all night but there was no answer forthcoming. I told him to keep praying and the light would come. He pressed my hand and asked me to add my petitions to his own.
(F. N. Peboulet)

Difficulty Choosing the Right Way

Reverend Edward Hawes, Pastor of the Congregational Church, Waterville, Maine, preached at the Deserters' Barracks in Washington one Sunday morning in March 1864. After the service, we distributed one hundred *Black Valley Railroad Guides*—a vivid picture tract, illustrating the evils of intemperance. It had an amazing effect. A deserter, who had been an engineer once, said they were asking him to run on the *B. V. R. R.* at good pay. Since he thought he wouldn't get his wages and would have to go on the train anyway, he was holding on to the other road. Pointing upward, I asked if the road he had chosen ended *there*. He answered, "Yes."
(F. N. Peboulet)

Difficulty Caused by Drunkenness

In another story, a soldier at the barracks fell into a drunken fit and persuaded a comrade to write to his betrothed that he was dead! A short time later, letters of grief and inquiry came at once. He himself replied to these, explaining that he had only been dead-drunk! In a few days, he learned to his horror that the poor girl died from the shock brought on by the first letter!
(F. N. Peboulet)

Becoming a Child of God

Following the Battle of Gettysburg, July 1-3, 1863, Reverend F. N. Peloubet, Pastor of the Congregational Church in Oakham, Massachusetts, worked as a Christian Commission delegate. While laboring at Camp Convalescent in Washington, Mr. Peloubet met a Pennsylvania cavalryman from Carbon County, named Sergeant Marcy, who told him his story:

He had once joined the church but was only half persuaded at the time. Afterward, he opposed religion in numerous ways. His wife, a committed Christian, strove in vain to restore him. In the army, he was deeply shocked by much of the wickedness around him. He and a comrade mutually agreed to write down the number of times they swore during each day. The result appalled him and he determined to stop.

His wife's letters made him uneasy, so one Monday evening he went to the prayer meeting. The sermon made no particular impression but some remarks following the meeting deeply affected him. He determined to attend the meeting every night that week. Once or twice, he regretted his resolve but attended anyway. His mental agony and darkness were increased by certain morbid reflections about committing the sin against the Holy Ghost.

A Christian bunkmate was very distressed on his account. Finally, the Lord's words, about no man entering the Kingdom of Heaven unless he became like a little child, brought him to see that he was helpless as a child. His only option was to put his hand into Christ's hand and say trustfully, "Lead Thou me on." At once, his whole life was illuminated. One day, while repairing and cleaning the stables, some of his comrades were swearing and finding fault at the dirty work. He did not like the task but suddenly it occurred to him that Jesus was born in a manger and, at once, his work grew bright and glad.

Entering the Kingdom of God As Children

Following the Battle of Gettysburg, July 1-3, 1863, Reverend F. N. Peloubet, served as Pastor of the Congregational Church in Oakham, Massachusetts and worked as a Christian Commission delegate. Possibly the Lord's words about children only entering the Kingdom of God were never more clearly illustrated than in the hour of the soldier's death:

In Camp Stoneman Hospital, Washington, a soldier lay dying in March 1864. He was from Michigan and was but eighteen years of age. Mr. C_____, a delegate, learning that the soldier would not recover, hastened to his side.

"I am very sick. Pray for me," said the soldier.

"Do you have a Christian mother?"

"Oh, yes. My father and mother are both Christians and so are my sisters. My brother is a minister. I wish I was a Christian but, I'm afraid, I'm not."

I prayed with him, after which he himself offered a most fervent petition. As I read St. John's 14th chapter, he anticipated me, showing his knowledge of the Bible. I stayed with him a long time. Together we sang "There is a fountain filled with blood" and "Rock of Ages, cleft for me."

Just before he died, he called the ward-master over and, lifting his weak arms, put them round the man's neck and kissed him. Looking up, he said, "I love everybody." He prayed again and afterward felt exhausted. The nurse told him to try and sleep a little. They lifted him gently upon his left side. His thoughts went back to her whose memory lingers longest upon earth. Like a child might have done, he folded his arms across his chest and, in a very low voice, distinctly repeated,

> "Now I lay me down to sleep;
>   I pray the Lord my soul to keep.
> If I should die before I wake,

I pray the Lord my soul to take."

The light went out of the dying eyes. The pale lips never moved again—the answer to the simple petition had come quickly indeed. "Except ye be converted, and become as little children, ye shall not enter into the Kingdom of God."

Ungodly Man Moved by the Holy Spirit

After the Battle of Gettysburg, July 1-3, 1863, Reverend Edward Hawes, Pastor of the Congregational Church, Waterville, Maine, served as a Christian Commission delegate.   Reverend Hawes worked at Camp Convalescent in Washington in the spring of 1864. He writes these incidents:

Many hearts rejoiced one evening upon seeing Sergeant Morrison kneeling for prayers. He was well-known throughout the camp as a wild, reckless man. His Christian wife missed no opportunity to write to him about coming to Jesus. In answer to her entreaties, he had determined to attend the evening meetings at the chapel regularly. To many of us, his unexpected act was surprising. Afterward, he told me:

"I had more feeling than many supposed, for I knew that I was a sinner who needed a Savior. While you were preaching that night, I was continually thinking, 'Well, I stand up pretty well in that' but, toward the end, you said you wanted to hide yourself behind Christ and let Him speak through you— and He did speak and I couldn't stand under it."

At another time, he referred to his conviction. Speaking to me, he said, "I was trying to do something myself but it is good to become a little child and cry for one's own helplessness."

He was so strong, stalwart, and large that the words seemed to have an added meaning in his case. He often came to visit with me and I always enjoyed the conversations. At our final parting, he said, "I shall never, never forget the time when you 'hid' yourself behind Jesus."

Converted by Work of the Holy Spirit

Some of the expressions of the men in the meetings were wonderful for their conviction of feeling and power. A soldier once rose to speak only these solemn words, "I left a gray-haired mother at home praying for me. As I was leaving home, she said, 'You have enlisted in the service of your country. Now I beg you to enlist for Christ.' All her letters asked the question, 'Have you enlisted for Christ yet?' I thank God, Jesus has found the way to my poor heart."

(Edward Hawes)

Soldiers Moved to Pray by Work of the Holy Spirit

At a meeting in the Cavalry Camp, a new convert rose to say, "I rejoice that I have found the Savior but my wife is not a Christian…." and then he broke down.

A comrade of his rose to the occasion immediately. He said, "Boys, let's get right down here and pray for his wife." And kneel they did, while a fervent prayer ascended.
(Edward Hawes)

Learning to Trust by Power of the Holy Spirit

A Maine soldier who was in the hospital said, "If I had been impenitent since being a soldier, I don't think I would be alive. I would have been so impatient and restless. But I have tried to give up everything to God and, even when sickest, to trust Him."
(Edward Hawes)

Broken by the Holy Spirit

At one of the meetings, a soldier prayed in his mother tongue—German—and then told us about his experience: "Brethren, I shall try to say a few words. The English goes rather difficult for me but I want you to understand that I love Jesus. I was once very wicked. God took away a child and I promised to reform but didn't. Then He took away another. That's when my stubborn heart was broken, when I found Jesus."
(Edward Hawes)

The German told us of a sermon preached by a minister who was "hard as nails on sinners." He told us that he was afraid to pass by the minister's house, fearing that he would come out to talk with him. After his change, he successfully awakened his wife and children to the things of God and, before leaving for war, he sat down with them at the table of the Lord.
(Edward Hawes)

Singing in Power of the Holy Spirit

During a prayer meeting at Cavalry Camp the night before some of the men were to join General Judson Kilpatrick, they put their arms around each other's necks and, with deep feeling, sang,

"Shall we know each other there?"
(Edward Hawes)

CHAPTER VIII
THE WESTERN ARMIES

THE CAMPAIGNS IN TENNESSEE AND GEORGIA
July 1863–December 1863

The demands of General Rosecrans' position and poor communications had dictated his long delay at Murfreesboro, Tennessee after Stones River. In June 1863, he found Bragg's army entrenched in front of him at Shelbyville and Tullahoma. Toward the end of the month, he began a campaign to dislodge him. In spite of a continuous rainstorm, which materially delayed Rosecrans' advancing columns, Middle Tennessee was cleared of the Confederate Army within nine days. His army occupied Shelbyville and Tullahoma without any serious engagement. He then pushed his light troops forward to Stevenson, Alabama and began repairing the railroad to both Stevenson and Bridgeport. In the middle of August, the Union Army once again moved forward in force.

Claiming Promises

The General Field Agent of the Christian Commission, Reverend Edward P. Smith, who also served as Pastor of the Congregational Church, Pepperell, Massachusetts, returned from his visit to the forces operating against Vicksburg in July 1863. From Murfreesboro, Tennessee, he writes about the grand army center before Rosecrans' move against Tullahoma:

Late one afternoon, a soldier from the Anderson Troop, 15th Pennsylvania Calvary, was brought to the General Hospital outside of Murfreesboro, Tennessee. It was his first experience of this kind. He was far more despondent than any picture a writer can paint. Weak and desponding, he had been taken from his comrades, who enlisted with him in Philadelphia, and brought into the company of strangers. The male nurse, who had lifted him from the ambulance and laid him on his cot, was helping him undress when the cavalryman hesitatingly asked, "Nurse, do you ever read in the wards?"

The nurse replied, "Yes, most definitely."

"Well, nurse, I wish you would read a bit for me this evening."

"What shall I read?"

The soldier asked him to take a Bible from his knapsack and said, "Find that chapter about 'Coming to the waters.'"

The nurse, who was a Christian, immediately turned to the 55th chapter of Isaiah, and read the first verse: "Ho, every one that thirsteth, come ye to the waters, and he that hath no money; come ye, buy and eat; yea, come, buy wine and milk without money and without price."

"That's it," says the sick man, "that's it, 'come to the waters.'"

As the nurse continued to read through the chapter, the cavalryman stopped him and said, "Read that verse again, nurse, 'Ho, every one that thirsteth.'" He read it to him again and then again at the man's earnest request.

"Now, that'll do, nurse. Do you ever pray?"

"Yes, I can pray."

"Will you offer a little prayer for me?"

The nurse knelt by his cot and offered the soldier's spoken request. The next morning, he asked again for the reading of Scripture and the nurse asked, "What shall I read?"

"I want to hear again about that 'Coming to the waters.'"

He read it to him twice that morning, twice in the evening, and prayed also with him. The next morning he read it again.

"I must pray for myself, nurse," the cavalryman said, "and I want to be placed in the attitude of prayer on my cot."

The man would not be denied the privilege, so they placed him on his knees with his hand on the head of his iron cot. He began praying for himself in the words of the petition of Our Lord and, thus, the angelic messenger found him. Taking him up home, He showed him "a pure river of water of life, clear as crystal, proceeding out of the throne of God and of the Lamb."

A week or two before this incident, I had met a relative of this cavalryman in Louisville. This man was desperately trying to get through the lines to minister to him. I wrote the soldier's name and address and visited the Murfreesboro Hospital in Tennessee shortly thereafter. The nurse then related the cavalryman's moving story, which I immediately communicated to the soldier's mother in Philadelphia. More than likely, she never would have learned in any other way how her boy died. Certainly, in the last great day, the mothers and fathers and friends of many a soldier will be surprised with the unveiling of histories told to no human ears—stories noted only by Him, who "shall bring into judgment every secret thing."

Love for the Word of God

In July 1863, Reverend Edward P. Smith, General Field Agent with the Christian Commission and Pastor of the Congregational Church, Pepperell, Massachusetts, wrote to the *Bible Society Record* about the distribution of the Scriptures at various points throughout the army. He mentioned this incident, which occurred at a meeting in Convalescent Camp, Nashville:

A middle-aged man rose in the crowd and held up a little book and said, "Soldiers, I have a book here, which I suspect none of you have money enough to buy. I never read it. I don't know how to read but I couldn't let this book go. They tell me it is God's Word and that this is where we find what Jesus says. I love to feel it in my hands and press it to my heart and put it under my head at night. It reads of Jesus! What could I do without Jesus and how should I know about Him, if it was not for this book!

"Since I cannot read, I sometimes find a good friend and take him by the arm and say, 'Come, go with me a little way;' and, when we get by ourselves, I pull out my little book and say, 'I have a nice book here and I want you to read a little with me.' He says, 'Where shall I read?' and I say, 'Read the 7th chapter of Matthew.' Then, when he has read that, I say, 'Just a little more—the 1st chapter of James.' I have almost memorized these two chapters and, when I do, I am going to learn another. I want to advise all of you to get a New Testament from the Christian Commission."

He spoke modestly but with deep feeling. When he held up his book and pressed it to his heart, the tears flowing down his cheeks told how deep was his love for the Book that "reads of Jesus."

Loving Your Enemies

In the hospital at Tullahoma, Tennessee, Reverend Edward P. Smith, Pastor of the Congregational Church in Pepperell, Massachusetts and General Field Agent for the Christian Commission, found a Confederate prisoner during the summer of 1863. This soldier's story illustrates the influence of God's Word over angry passions and a wandering heart:

He was lying side by side with our own soldiers and, judging from his treatment and appearance, I had no way of knowing that he was not one of them. When he learned that I served with the Christian Commission, he pressed my hand very earnestly, saying he was glad to see me. Turning to the nurse, he asked, "Nurse, has my bundle come yet?"

"It will be here shortly," replied the nurse. "Don't worry about it. It's all safe."

"I suppose it is but I wish it was here." Turning to me and speaking in his Southern dialect, he added, "When they brought me here, I felt scattered-like and I left behind my bundle of things. My hymnbook and New Testament are all tied up in it. I have been looking and waiting for them and it appears like I am lost when they don't come. One of your Commission gentlemen brought 'em to me when I was under guard. I have read 'em over a heap of times and it appears like I wasn't the same sort of man I am now.

"Last month, I wouldn't have believed that I should lie in my bed and pray for Dalton. He is a very bad man and it's because he has told lies on me that your soldiers had me arrested. But I have been praying for him and, just now, when you came to the door, I was asking God to forgive old man Dalton and bless him like He does me. You see, I've been reading where it says, 'Love your enemies and pray for them' that is spiteful against you. My wife's been a praying Presbyterian ever since I knew her. I want to see her now more than ever. If allowed, she'd put a heap of money on that New Testament and I'd be able take it home with me."

I took down the address of his wife and, by means of our network of couriers, sent a letter with the glad news of her husband's conversion direct to her own door.

Praying for Endurance

Reverend Benjamin Parsons, Pastor of the First Congregational Church, Windsor, Connecticut, was placed in charge of the Christian Commission's field work at the front during the temporary absence of the General Agent. He moved forward with our forces while they followed Bragg's retreat from Tullahoma, Tennessee to Cowan and Stevenson. He relates a soldier's testimony at a meeting at Tullahoma in August 1863:

"I am glad, my comrades, to be here. When I enlisted, I had many companions whom I knew well. Several of us entered into a covenant to hold together in the Christian life while in the army—and especially to hold on to Christ. Nearly all of them are gone. Some lie at Shiloh. Some fell at Perryville and some are sleeping their last sleep at Stones River. I feel quite alone and feel that I, too, shall soon join my companions who are now where war and bloodshed are forever unknown, where there shall be no broken bond, no partings, and no more death. Comrades, pray for me, that I may hold on and hold on faithfully to Christ, even to the last."

Eternity Apart from Christ

Reverend Benjamin Parsons was placed in charge of the Christian Commission's field work at the front during the temporary absence of the General Agent. He also served as Pastor of the First Congregational Church, Windsor, Connecticut. He went forward with our forces while they followed Bragg's retreat from Tullahoma, Tennessee to Cowan and Stevenson. He writes that sometimes he heard sad testimonies:

I was holding the chilling hands of a soldier of the 75th Indiana Regiment in the Tullahoma hospital in Tennessee. I bade him instantly to cast himself into Jesus' arms, telling him that He was near to receive him. I said, "My dear boy, trust yourself to Jesus." He opened his eyes wearily, looked at me, and said, "He is not here! He is not here!"

"Yes, yes, He is here. Believe in Him and thou shalt be saved."

Once more he articulated, "Not here! Not here!" …And with these hopeless words upon his lips, he died.

Love for One Another

A drummer boy came into our office and told us he had received no letter for two years. He explained he was an orphan and had lived in Brooklyn. We asked, "Wouldn't you like to get a letter?"

"Oh, yes, indeed I would."

"Well, well, my son," said Reverend Mr. Cushing of Shrewsbury, Massachusetts and member of N. E. Conference, Methodist Episcopal Church, "I think I have one for you."

Opening a comfort bag, he took out a letter written by a Sunday school pupil in the North and gave it to the lad. As he received this token of appreciation that even he had been remembered by somebody, he wept freely.

Faithful Reading of the Scriptures

During the temporary absence of the General Agent of the Christian Commission, Reverend Benjamin Parsons, the Pastor of the First Congregational Church, Windsor, Connecticut, served as head of the field work in the summer of 1863. On August 2nd, he wrote from Cowan Station in Tennessee:

This afternoon, several officers called on Colonel Scribner, Commanding Officer of First Brigade with General Rousseau's Division, with whom I was staying. In the midst of a varied and interesting conversation, Colonel Scribner teased Brigadier General Beattie, who had recently been elected to Congress from the 8th District of Ohio, regarding a Bible given to him by his wife. Scribner playfully said, "It's just as fresh and clean as when you received it from her hands, isn't it!"

"Colonel," replied the General, "I can say what I fear you cannot. I have not let a single day pass since I entered the service without reading it."

"Upon your honor?" Colonel Scribner asked.

"Upon my honor, sir."

"What about in those fighting days at Stones River?"

"Yes, sir. In those fights, I did not fail to read my daily chapter and, if you'll examine my Bible, you will find every chapter marked in daily order."

The answer was so calm and serious that no one present could doubt the words of the speaker.
(Benjamin Parsons)

Hungering for the Word of God

In Louisville, Kentucky, the reminiscences of the Union Army are rich with Bible incidents, on account of the constant work of Scripture distribution. Reverend Edward P. Smith, General Field Agent of the Christian Commission and Pastor of the Congregational Church, Pepperell, Massachusetts, related the following story in the *Bible Society Record:*

Last Sunday in Louisville, I found a German orderly in the barracks and I asked, "Would you like to have a New Testament?"

He replied with a very doubtful query. He said, "You have no *Bible*, I suppose?"

"No, I only have only the New Testament."

"I have *that*," he said. "I want a German Bible. I would give my next month's pay, when I get it, for a Bible in my pocket today."

I responded, "Call upon me at the Bible Depository in the morning. I will give you one then."

At breakfast the next day, I was summoned to the door. It proved to be the orderly who had come for his Bible. I gave him his choice out of the stock—and a happier man I have not seen for months. He had brought along with him another orderly, who was formerly a preacher. While on duty at a hospital in Louisville, this man had loaned out his Bible—the only one there—until it was so worn that, with his poor eyesight, he could no longer read it. The convalescents, he told me, used to take turns with his Bible, and sometimes *five or six applicants would put down their names for the next reading.* I also gave this man a Bible of his own selection.

Historical Context:

On August 16, 1863, the advance from Stevenson upon Chattanooga began. Movements were so prompt and well-arranged that, when Bragg saw the last corps of Rosecrans' army crossing the Tennessee River, he abandoned his stronghold on September 8th and retired southward into Georgia. Following too hastily, Rosecrans soon realized that reinforcements were coming into the Confederate Army from all directions: Buckner had been called from East Tennessee; Walker's Division from Johnson's army in Mississippi, and Longstreet's veterans from the Army of Northern Virginia. The Union forces were rapidly concentrated along Chickamauga Creek and here, on September 19th, the battle began.

On the evening of the 20th, the enemy conclusively took control of the battle and Rosecrans withdrew to the Chattanooga entrenchments. Bragg followed but, finding the city strongly fortified, he attempted to starve out the Union Army. In October, Rosecrans was relieved by General Thomas. Shortly thereafter, the Armies of the Cumberland, Tennessee, and Ohio were made into the Military Division of the Mississippi—all under the command of General Ulysses S. Grant. In the meantime, two corps from the Potomac had reinforced the Army of the Cumberland.

Comforting One Another

Early in October, Reverend B. W. Chidlaw of Cleves, Ohio, the well-known Western Agent of the American Sunday School Union and now Chaplain of an Ohio Regiment, wrote from Stevenson, Tennessee. He tells a story of the value of some little hospital comforts:

One Hoosier boy, not even twenty years old, lay sick with a touch of the fever and chills, an affliction from which I myself had suffered sometimes at home

"What did mother do for you when you had these spells at home?" I asked.

"Oh, she used to make me a good cup of tea and such nice toast."

"Why, that's just what my mother used to give me. And didn't it help you?"

"Yes, almost always."

"Why don't you ask for the tea and toast here?"

"Oh, the tea isn't what mother used to give me and the toast isn't the same at all."

"Well," I thought, "you shall have some that's good, if it's available."

So, going to the Commission's quarters, I soon found myself dipping into a chest of real, genuine black tea, and a cask of sweetest loaf sugar by its side, and a box of condensed milk. Then, upon entering the government bakery, I secured a nice loaf of bread and took it to the back where the cook was. I began telling him what I wanted and asked for the privilege of using his fire and utensils to do my work. He interrupted me and, in strong Black dialect, said, "In dis kitchen, I cooks and you talks."

So he took the knife, sliced the bread and toasted it, while we talked of Jesus and His religion. At last, the tea and toast were made, the condensed milk was used instead of butter, and a delicious-looking meal was ready to carry to the hospital.

"My friend," I said to the Indiana boy, "wake up, I have something nice for you."

"Why, preacher, ain't there milk in that tea?"

"Certainly."

"Why," he asked in astonishment, "*does the Christian Commission keep cows down here?*"

"Better than that, my boy. They have gone all the way home to get the old cow. Now sit up and eat and drink."

And he did so to his heart's content until, I am afraid, he ate too much. A soldier close by said, "Chaplain, can you give me a little tea and toast, too?" "And me, too?" said another, and another, until it was like a chorus all through the room.

"Certainly, certainly! We'll have a general tea party."

And that we did! We notified the old cook, he did the toast up brown, and the hot, smoking tea was delicious. We had a glorious tea party that day!

Perspectives on Eternity

Reverend Mr. Edward P. Smith, General Field Agent of the Christian Commission and Pastor of the Congregational Church, Pepperell, Massachussets, relates a Nashville story that occurred in October 1863:

Standing atop Fort Negley, he noticed a squad of soldiers following an ambulance to the grave of a comrade. Two of the artillerymen belonging to the fort commented upon the burial.

"There's another poor fellow that got his discharge," said one.

"Not that," replied his comrade.

"Well, if not discharged, I'd like to know what is he?"

"Only transferred."

"Transferred where?"

"To the other department."

"What for?"

"For duty."

"What duty?"

"Don't know. That all depends on what he's fit for."

Time and Place for an Altar Call

Mr. Thomas Atkinson of Chicago, and afterward a member of the Wittenberg Synod (Ohio) of the Lutheran Church, tells of an incident in his service in the Nashville hospitals. He writes about some of the wounded from the Battle of Chickamauga:

I found a young man dying in the upper end of the long first ward of Hospital No. 19. Putting my mouth near his ear, I whispered to him words of Scripture until his spirit departed in peace. Then, after gathering about sixty of the convalescents around the cot, I preached Jesus to them. Down in the middle and lower end of the long ward were many who could not stir from their beds. As I went along among them, I told them of the soldier who had gone up from their midst into the City of God.

It was time for our daily prayer meeting but, before I went away, I thought that some of the maimed company might be comforted to know that God's people were praying for them somewhere. So I said, "Boys, I'm going to the prayer meeting now and I would like to know if any of you are anxious to be saved. If you are, please hold up your right hands."

Hands went up all around. Here and there, a stump was raised. One man had neither hand remaining, so he raised two poor stumps in token of his desire for Christ. Another had no stumps, so he turned his head and, with great difficulty, said, "Me. Me."

Ministry of Replacing a New Testament

Reverend Edward Hawes served as Pastor of the Congregational Church, Waterville, Maine. He recalled these scenes of his service as Christian Commission delegate at Chattanooga after the Chickamauga Campaign, September 19-20, 1863:

I enter a hospital tent. A wounded man was lying in one corner. I asked, "Can I do anything for you, my friend?"

"Yes, sir, if you please. I have lost my Testament and would like to get one." I gave him one.

Comfort for Wounded Soldiers

On the next cot, a man was lying quietly, seemingly without pain, except that his face was covered. I said, "You are not injured very badly, are you, my dear fellow?" He looks up with a faint smile and responded, "Not much, sir," but he had, in fact, been hit in *nine* places by a bursting shell!
(Edward Hawes)

Blessing the Dying

I passed along and the steward said, "Chaplain, won't you come here? We think this man is dying. Can't you say something to him?"

I bent over him and noticed the cold sweat was already on his brow. His eyes are fixed, fastening themselves in death, but they grew brilliant and he mutters, "See! A star! There's a star! Oh, how bright! It's the star…" and his voice dies away in death. Perhaps, he is thinking of the Star of Bethlehem. We hope so—and that it will light him through the dark valley.
(Edward Hawes)

Ministry of Comforting the Sick

I went to another man in the next tent and, with the surgeon's permission, gave him a single swallow of wine. His brightened eyes gleamed beams of gratitude!

"O sir, that's good. What is your name? I shall always remember you."
(Edward Hawes)

Ministry of Writing Letters

"How are you getting along, my brother?" I said to the next.

"Oh, very well, thank you."

"Do you have a family?"

"Yes, a wife and two little children in Ohio."

"Have you written to them since the battle?" I saw in a moment that I had asked a foolish question. His right arm was shattered. "Shall I write to them for you?"

He hesitated and I wondered why he didn't gladly say, "Oh, yes, sir, if you please." I repeated the question, thinking he did not understand.

He looked at me strangely and asked, *"How much do you charge, sir?"*

Oh, how those words cut to my heart! I responded, "My dear soldier, the reason I am here is to write for you or to do anything for you. I will thank you for the privilege."

"Oh, thank you! Thank you! I will be so glad."

We got paper and pen ready and I asked, "What shall I write?"

He began with expressions of Christian trust and then briefly described his condition related to the shattered arm. I read to him what he had dictated. But the soldier did not respond. His eyes were shut. Big tears rolled down from beneath the closed lids. He made no effort to wipe them away. I thought it must be the shattered arm but, no, that was not the reason. His mind was back in Ohio with his dear wife and children. I did not disturb his dreams. After a pause, he opens his eyes and I told him the letter was finished. "Will it do?" I asked. With a look of overflowing gratitude, he answered, "Oh, yes, sir. Yes, sir. Thank you!"

(Edward Hawes)

Ministry of Evangelism

In the corner, a man was lying, burdened with a sense of his guilt. After talking some time, I asked him, "My dear friend, can't you trust Jesus now?"

"Oh! If only I could! It would be the happiest day of my life. Won't you pray for me?"

I knelt at his side. God's Spirit was with us, prayer ascended to heaven, and God heard us. I then departed, leaving the soldier with a trembling hope in Jesus.

(Edward Hawes)

Ministry of Reading Scripture

I came to a little shelter tent, under which a man was lying. I bent over him and said, "You have the Christian's hope, I trust."

"Oh, yes, sir."

I saw no Testament by him and asked, "Don't you have a New Testament?"

"No, sir."

"Well, you must have one." I began opening my haversack when he told me he could not read.

"You cannot read? Then I shall read for you."

I began at the precious words: "For we know that if our earthly house of this tabernacle were dissolved, we have a building of God, an house not made with hands, eternal in the heavens." I read through the chapter and then I left him, peering up through the hole in the canvas into the deep blue beyond and longing for the country above, where his spirit must soon reside with the multitude of the redeemed.

(Edward Hawes)

Living by Faith

Reverend William M. Taylor served as Pastor of (O. S.) Presbyterian Church, Mount Jackson, Pennsylvania. As a Christian Commission delegate at Chattanooga after the Chickamauga Campaign, September 19-20, 1863, he told the story of Johnny Mitch, of the 4th Kentucky Regiment:

I met Johnny at General Hospital No. 3 in Chattanooga and became very much interested in his life story. Left fatherless and motherless at his home in Ohio before he was eight years old, he had very little direction in right living. The war broke out when he was fifteen. Too young to enlist, a captain of a cavalry unit offered him the job of caring for his horses. The two started out but, when Johnny reached Cincinnati, he saw so many very young-looking boys enlisting that he decided to join as well.

He passed safely through the fights at Rolling Fork, Hoover's Gap, and Tullahoma, but at Chickamauga he was wounded three times—in the side of his head, the right hand, and, more seriously, in the mouth. The ball lodged at the back part of his neck. For five days, he lay on the field near an old log cabin but scarcely received any food from the enemy. Afterward, the little fellow said, "For five days, they fed me nothing." After a while, he was brought back within our lines under the flag of truce. The surgeon told him he would surely die and, for four weeks, this prognosis went unchanged.

"But," he said, "I kept up good spirits. I *did* sometimes think I would die but it was no use to be disheartened about it."

Who can say that this young man's faith did not save him? Speaking of these long days of suspense, he told me, "When I awoke each morning, I would read a chapter in my New Testament and pray the Lord to help me heal. And it always seemed to me that I began to get better right away. I always felt mighty thankful."

He was a mere youth—only seventeen and he had already spent two years as a soldier. The lisp, bequeathed to him by the wound in his mouth, made his yet unchanged voice so girlish and entertaining. His eventful little history was so interesting and moving that he and I became knit together as Christian brothers. One time, I asked him what he was going to do. He responded, "I want to go home till I get well," he said, "then I want to come back and enlist again. I'm more anxious to take on the Confederates now than I ever was."

Ministry of Helps

The days after the battle at Chickamauga were the gloomiest in the history of the Army of the Cumberland. Nowhere was this sorrow felt more than in the vicinity of Chattanooga. Reverend E. P. Smith, Pastor of Congregational Church, Pepperrell, Massachusetts, wrote the following:

During the gloomy days of the siege of Chattanooga, I was riding down Waldon's Ridge on my way to Bridgeport. The day was cold and wet—everything was disheartening. It seemed highly probable that we were about to abandon Chattanooga and that this would be my last trip over the mountains. Depressed with these thoughts and chilled by the rain, I rode along until I finally overtook a solitary cavalryman, seemingly as low in spirits as myself. As I came alongside, I looked into his face and saw his eyes, filled with tears.

In our conversation, I threw in a word about my Christian experience, which caused him to turn to me and say, "Then you are a Christian. Perhaps, you can help me out of my difficulty."

I expressed my readiness to do anything I could, to which he responded, "I was just trying to repeat the first verse of a blessed old hymn I have been singing for years but somehow I can't get hold of the fourth line this morning:

> "'Sweet was the time when first I felt
> The Savior's pardoning blood
> Applied to cleanse my soul from guilt ...'

"Now there's where I'm stopped. What's the next line?"

I finished it up for him by singing,

> "'And bring me home to God.'"

"That's it! Thank you," he said. "That's it. I wonder how I could have forgotten it."

I said, "You looked troubled when I first saw you. Your tears surely couldn't have been over the loss of that fourth line."

"Oh, no," he replied, "it was the other three lines that brought the tears. I was thinking of the time of my conversion and of the many, many times when I have 'felt the Savior's pardoning blood" since that day."

Turning Misery into Opportunity

The General Field Hospital was two miles out of Chattanooga, on the opposite side of the Tennessee. Here the wounded were loaded into mule wagons for transport to Bridgeport, seventy miles away. The story of those long wagon trains of agony and death can never be written, yet even these wagons afforded a place of song and prayer. Reverend E. P. Smith, Pastor of Congregational Church, Pepperell, Massachusetts, records this incident in *Annals, U.S. Christian Commission*, 466, 467:

The road lay over precipices so steep and rocky that the wagons were often let down by ropes, from one rock to another, amid the groans and shrieks of tortured men. So excruciatingly painful was the descent of Waldon's Ridge that some of the sufferers begged for the privilege of crawling down the rocks and dragging their wounded limbs after them. During the war, no more touching scene could have occurred than what took place one morning among these wagons, freshly loaded with the wounded and about to start their perilous journey to Bridgeport.

Lying on the wagon bottoms, the men had no straw to break the jolting of the rough ride and many lacked canvas covering to protect them from sun and rain. Each man was experimenting to find a comfortable position for the journey. They were resorting to all manner of tactics to provide themselves with a canteen of water and a few hard crackers in their haversacks. All were thoughtful and anxious. Chickamauga had been an excruciating defeat and the gloom of an army strikes first and deepest upon its hospitalized.

As much as possible, the delegates were busy tending to the personal wants and needs of the men in the different wagons. While the train sat, waiting for the order to move, Mr. K. A. Burnell, of Milwaukee, stood on a driver's seat and shouted, "Would you like a prayer meeting?"

"Yes, yes. Give us a prayer meeting," was the response from a hundred voices.

The service, which followed, consisted of the hymn, *When I Can Read My Title Clear*, a few spoken words about the Savior's love and cheer, and a prayer for the sufferers—some of whom would die on the way. We also prayed for their country and their friends back home—friends and family who, perhaps, even now were praying for them. The service ended with a benediction of peace, which was met with a fervent "Amen." To not a few of the worshipers, this wagon prayer meeting would be their last earthly scene of song and prayer.

Seeker Leads Many to Salvation

After the Chickamauga Campaign of September 19-20, 1863, the Baptist Church in Chattanooga, which the Christian Commission used as a chapel, was later used as a hospital. By early November, it had been restored for use as a chapel. Reverend Edward P. Smith, Field Agent with the Christian Commission and Pastor of the Congregational Church, Pepperell, Massachusetts, gives an account of a remarkable series of nightly meetings. These incidents are contained in the *Annals, U. S. Christian Commission*. These meetings began at once:

The first half hour of the evening was devoted to prayer and the sharing of religious experiences. Then a delegate or chaplain delivered the sermon. This was followed by a special service for those who desired to become Christians. The experiences were not the repetitious accounts often given on such occasions. Nearly all of the worshipers had been on the Chickamauga field. While many of their comrades had fallen, these men had been saved from capture and death. They crowded to the chapel with thanksgivings and confessions. They exhorted their unconverted comrades to come to the Savior. Often, a half hour before the services started, the chapel was so crowded that it was difficult to go down the aisle to the pulpit. Twenty, forty—and, one night, more than one hundred men—asked for prayers.

One evening, when no room could be found to invite forward those seeking prayer, the expression of an uplifted hand was called for. All were deeply affected upon seeing a hand thrust through the open window. An anxious soul, standing outside, desired to see Jesus.

Finding Salvation

At another meeting, an Illinois soldier arose in the audience when opportunity was given for any to express their feelings. With a forceful manner and tone, he said, "My fellow soldiers, I am not excited. I am *convinced*—that's all. I feel that I ought to be a Christian—that I ought to say so—to tell you so, and to ask you to come with me. And now, if there is a call for sinners seeking Christ to come forward, I for one shall go—not on account of excitement, for I tell you my heart never beat steadier in my life—not to make a show, for I have nothing but sin to show. I do not go because I want to—I would rather keep my seat—but going forward will be telling the truth that I ought to be a Christian, that I want to be a Christian. Going forward for prayers is just telling the truth about it. Say, comrades, won't you go with me?"

And without waiting for their answer or for a formal invitation from the preacher, he strode down the aisle and knelt at the altar. More than twenty of his comrades followed and knelt around him. Needless to say, salvation came that night to that sincere seeker.
(Edward P. Smith)

Historical Context:

Prior to Missionary Ridge, General Grant's first orders were for the opening up of a better line of communication and this was accomplished in short order. In the meantime, Sherman was marching from Mississippi to re-enforce him. On November 23rd, the assault on Bragg's entrenchments began. On the next day, Hooker captured Lookout Mountain and, on the 25th, we took possession of the rest of the enemy's stronghold in the Chattanooga Valley and on Missionary Ridge. We pursued Bragg beyond Ringgold and made no further offensive movements during the winter of 1863-64.

Comforting the Wounded

Reverend Edward P. Smith served as General Field Agent with the Christian Commission and as Pastor of the Congregational Church, Pepperell, Massachusetts. He gives the following narrative of the battle of Missionary Ridge, November 25, 1863, in *Annals, U. S. Christian Commission,* 471ff.:

General Sherman now began to strike heavy blows for the railroad communication through the tunnel. Twice we saw his long blue line move over a cornfield up to the edge of the woods and fall rapidly back. The third time they marched up and held their ground. We knew that many men must have gone down under that terrible fire at short range and that the cornfield must be full of sufferers. A party of delegates started on foot to carry such relief as they could, with coffee kettles, stimulants, and bandages. As we were passing along the line of General Wood's Division, Colonel Stanley called out to us and, pointing tip the ridge, said, "There will be work enough for you right here in a few minutes."

While he was speaking, a line of blue coats went over our first line of works and, a little further on, a line of gray coats left theirs. Both lines swept up the hill. The Confederates massed their standards and rallied their forces at the point of the ridge directly in front of our climbing columns or, rather, climbing mass, as every man was stretching away for himself, focused on the single purpose of gaining the top. Under this musketry in front of them and the enfilading fire of forty cannons trained on them from either side of the ridge, they went on and up until we gained the victory. The siege of Chattanooga was ended and the Confederates had abandoned their last stronghold along the line of the Tennessee River.

Ministry of Establishing a Hospital

While General Thomas' men were scaling Missionary Ridge, the delegates began their work. The wounded began to fall back, holding a disabled arm, limping on a musket, or borne on a blanket by their comrades. Taking possession of an abandoned farmhouse at the foot of the ridge, we opened a hospital for those who were not able to make their way to town. A half dozen cotton bales, ripped open and spread upon the floors, made good beds and pillows for the wounded. (Edward P. Smith)

Ministry of Finding Owner of Heirloom

Some of the captured Confederates had corn meal in their haversacks. We made this into a large kettle of mush and, with the coffee and soup we had brought along, made an excellent dinner. The wounded prisoners especially relished the meal. One of them, a Tennessee Major, followed our movements with an inquisitive eye as he lay before the fire. He watched while we made beds, prepared the meal, tied up wounds, and cut out minie balls. At last, his curiosity and astonishment got the best of him and he said, "Pardon me, gentlemen, but I would like to know your rank?"

When told that we were delegates of the Christian Commission, he said, "I am not acquainted with your organization but I like your name." And drawing a heavy gold watch out of his pocket, he placed it in the hands of a delegate for safe-keeping. The Major had been struck in the side with a shell and we had bound up his wound. A few days later, he suddenly died. His death was so unexpected that he left no directions about his valuable belonging. After a long search, the agent found his mother's name and residence in Middle Tennessee. At the close of the war, he had the pleasure of putting her son's watch in her hand.

(Edward P. Smith)

ALMOST UP

Dying with Undying Focus

The enthusiasm of the men over their victory at Missionary Ridge, Tennessee, on November 25th, 1863, was unbounded. Soldiers would occasionally forget they were wounded while telling of the fight. While a ball was being cut out of an arm or leg with a delegate's pocket knife, they would occupy the time by telling how he came to be hit, or "pegged," as they called it. During the charge up the ridge, four soldiers were seen bearing a comrade on a blanket. His story is told by one of the delegates who met him:

The men halted when they saw us and laid down their burden. They asked if we would see whether the Color-sergeant was badly wounded. I knelt down by him and said, "Sergeant, where did they hit you?"

"Most of the way up the ridge, sir."

"I mean, Sergeant, where did the ball strike you?"

"Within twenty yards of the top. I was almost up."

"No, no, Sergeant. Think of yourself for a moment. Tell me where you are wounded." Throwing back the blanket, I found his upper arm and shoulder mashed and mangled by a shell.

Turning his eye to look upon his wound for the first time, the Sergeant said, "That is what did it. I was hugging the standard to my shirt and was making for the top. I was almost up when that ugly shell knocked me over. If they had let me alone a little longer—two minutes longer—I would have planted the colors on the top. Almost up! Almost up!"

We could not get the dying soldier's attention on himself. The fight and the flag held all his thoughts. While his ear was growing heavy in death, it was with a flushed face and look of deep regret, he kept repeating, "Almost up! Almost up!" However, the brigade to which he belonged had captured the ridge. His own regiment, rejoicing under the colors which he had dropped from his shattered arm, was shouting the victory for which the poor Sergeant had given his young life—a death which had escaped his earthly sight.
(Edward P. Smith)

Honoring God through Thanksgiving

An Ohio soldier, of Turchin's Brigade, came into the yard of the farmhouse. His blood was smeared on his face and clothes. It hung in clotted masses on his long beard. A buck shot had passed through his nose and was lodged under the skin on the other side, close to his eye. He wanted it cut out but, with great difficulty, we finally persuaded him that it was dangerous for an unskilled hand to operate with a pocket-knife so near his eye.

While we were bringing water, he sat down on the ground and pulled from his shirt a copy of *Andrews' Latin Grammar*, covered with his blood. He turned to the fifth declension and began with *res, rei*. He said that he was at an academy in Ohio, preparing for college, when the call came for recruits. He had left his Latin at this point. As his regiment was passing a house that afternoon, which some "bummer" had plundered, he found this book and had carried it under his shirt in the fight. He thought that, if he was wounded or taken prisoner, he would be able to go on with his Latin.
(Edward P. Smith)

Ministry of Feeding the Dying

By midnight, we had given a supper to the men wounded at Missionary Ridge and, joined by the stretcher-bearers, we had searched the fields and assured ourselves that nearly all the wounded at this "flying hospital" were headed for town in ambulances. We loaded up crackers, kettles of soup, and canteens of coffee, and then went to the top of the ridge. Here, we came upon one of the dreadful scenes of war. A one-story log house was filled with Union and Confederate wounded. The floors of the two rooms and the wide, open hallway and the porch across the front of the house were covered with men. They were lying so thick, as to make walking among them perilous to limb, if not to life.

The night was frosty and there had been no fire or supper. No surgeon or nurse had tended to their needs and the men were lying in clothes, stiff with blood from undressed wounds. The ambulances had ceased running for the night. The stretcher-bearers had gone to sleep on their stretchers. In the yard, the Confederate dead were lying fifty feet in every direction. They had died in the house before the ridge was captured and had been brought out by our men to make room for the living.
(Edward P. Smith)

Ministry of Feeding the Wounded

Underneath these floors, in a hastily dug cellar, were the women and children of the house. They had remained safe from the shot and shell that had surrounded them and were sitting in the door of their cellar, smoking pipes and eating snuff. They had not the slightest concern or interest in the dreadful scenes taking place around them. During all the afternoon and night, with their house and yard full of suffering men—many of them Confederates dying for their cause—the mother, her sister, and two grown daughters had not so much as offered to tie a bandage, kindle a fire upon the hearth, bring a cup of water, or speak a gentle word.

I asked if they would not assist in preparing supper for the men. The mother, taking her pipe from her mouth, said, "You'uns brought 'em all here and you'uns ought to take care on 'em." Putting her pipe back in her mouth, she swung one foot over the other and smoked away in a most listless manner.

"But, madam, these are … many of them are Confederate soldiers, dying away from home. Can't you do something for them?"

It was the same answer, this time without removing the pipe. She said, "You'uns brought 'em all here and you'uns ought to take care on 'em."

I asked for meal, she had none; for a kettle to make coffee, she had none; for an axe to cut firewood, she had none. As I left the cellar, a black child, about twelve years old, whispered, "Missus done hid the axe." I went back and asked for it again. She repeated that she had none and that the "Negro lied."

I said, "The men must have a fire and, if there is no axe, I must take your shingles." And putting action to the words, I laid hold of the roof of the porch. I had already filled my arms when she brought out her axe from between the beds.
(Edward P. Smith)

Ministry of Feeding the Wounded

We spent the night dressing wounds, feeding the men with coffee and soup, administering stimulants, and taking notes for letters to send home. For a mile along the top of the ridge, we found soldiers gathered around their fires. They discussed scenes of the previous day—telling of their missing comrades, when and how they fell—until morning light. In nearly all these groups, we found wounded men. Sometimes, outside the group, we found the corpse of a soldier who had been removed from around the fire after death had ensued. With our stimulants and hot soup, we helped these soldiers keep their comrades alive until morning.

The wounded Confederates were as hearty in their gratitude for our relief as they were unanimous in their opinion that the Yankees made their soup too salty. We were able to write many letters by using the notes we had taken from the lips of the dying and from the letters and diaries found on the dead. Ordinarily, unless the body had been robbed, the inside breast-pocket of the shirt contained a letter from friends or a photograph, a Christian Commission New Testament or hymnbook. The man's name, regiment, and home address were included. Sometimes, we found a diary without a name. Inevitably, those records of daily marches and battles and camps almost invariably gave no clue as to the identity of the writer. Keeping it merely for his own eyes, the soldier had found no occasion to mention his name or regiment.

When morning broke, we had passed twice along the ridge where the fiercest fighting occurred. We had also given a midnight supper and a breakfast to the wounded in the log cabin. The stretcher-bearers resumed their work of bringing in the wounded and the ambulances loaded up and headed for town. (Edward P. Smith)

Soldiers' Routine

At daylight, General Turchin's Brigade was directly before us and halfway down the ridge. They had gathered up their dead and placed them in the long trench. With a dirge from the band and the farewell musketry of their comrades, these men were laid to rest. The Brigade was under marching orders to raise the siege, with which Longstreet was closely pressing Burnside at Knoxville. Granger's and Howard's Corps and Sherman's army had gone before the sun was barely up. Their campground was silent.

Passing through it on our way back to town, we found no signs of occupation, except for smoldering fires and the trench of graves. They had marked the graves with pieces of cracker boxes. The names of the dead had been cut into the wood with the pocket knives of their comrades. This, we thought, is a day in a soldier's life—more crowded with events than a whole common life at home. They fight in the evening and capture the enemy's strongest position. They divide the night between sleep, stories of the day, and gathering in of their dead. In the morning, they bury their comrades and sling on their knapsacks for a march more perilous than the fight had been. (Edward P. Smith)

Day of Thanksgiving

At noon, we were startled by heavy cannon-fire from Fort Wood and other forts around Chattanooga. What could it mean? Had the enemy rallied and were attacking us again? To those who had seen the complete rout down the slope of Missionary Ridge, such a thought was absurd. But what could this heavy, rapid firing mean? The day was November 26th—the day President Lincoln had set apart nearly two months prior as a day of National Thanksgiving. Never were thanks given by firing of cannons more appropriate than by the national salute of that noon. (Edward P. Smith)

228 Triumph Amidst Bloodshed

Reading the Bible with Faithfulness

Chaplain J. C. Thomas, who served with the 83rd Illinois Regiment, visited Sheridan's Division Hospital No. 2 after the battles before Chattanooga. Here he found a rare example of faithful Bible reading, as recorded in *Annuls, U. S. Christian Commission*, 471-476:

A soldier, wounded in the leg, was sitting on his cot, reading an octavo book open before him. While approaching, I saw it was printed in German. Wondering how so large a book could be carried by a man in the ranks, I asked, "How do you manage with that on the march?"

"You see that?" he said in broken English, pointing to a crude case by his cot. "I got the leather from the quartermaster, and cutting off strips for threads, made a rough thing as you see. When we strike tents, I put my Bible in that case and throw it into one of the wagons. Sometimes it goes in with picks and spades—no matter, it don't hurt none. When we get to camp again, I go and get my Bible and have the best kind of reading. The print is large enough to read by firelight when we don't draw candles."

"How many times have you read the Bible through?"

"Twelve times, I think; twice since entering the service."

"How long have you been in the army?"

"Twenty-eight months."

He was not a Christian when he enlisted and I asked, "What led you to seek the Savior?"

"T'was the hardships—the hardships, sir."

Curious to know what he had learned from his reading, I asked, "What must a man do to be saved?"

"He must believe Christ, he must love Christ, and he must obey Christ. He is dead—he must be united with Christ and made alive." He then proceeded to give an earnest denunciation of camp vices to voice his simple, noble views of Christian character. He had been brought up a Roman Catholic and had not wholly broken with his religious system built on salvation by works.

Later, I asked a lieutenant, whose cot was near the German's, what he thought of the man. He responded, "He is the strangest person I have ever met. He rises with the dawn, kneels beside that post, and all we hear is the low murmur of the man is talking with his God. Again at night, occasionally in the daytime, and at the conclusion of hours of Bible reading, he does the same thing. Sometimes he hobbles from cot to cot and urges the men to quit their sins and come to Christ but he does it in such a way as not to offend. Everyone knows he is a Christian."

During the entire time I visited that hospital, the German tirelessly perused his Bible and labored, as was his custom, among his sick and dying comrades.

Faithless Infidel

Mr. Thomas Atkinson, shortly after the battle of Lookout Mountain, November 24, 1863, was left in temporary charge as Chaplain of Hospitals, Number 14 and 15, in Nashville. While visiting Ward No. 6 of the latter one morning, the following incidents occurred:

I spent the first fifteen minutes with an infidel, very badly wounded, just in from Lookout Mountain. He was a refined and educated man who received me with entire politeness and was glad to have a little conversation. But the moment I approached the "Great Question," he said, pleasantly, "You understand the English language, don't you, sir?"

I nodded assent with a premonition of what was coming. He added, "Then I respectfully but emphatically request you not to open your lips to me about religion. I have 'paddled my own canoe,' as they say, thus far, and I don't want any help in that direction."

I was at a loss as to what to do. As we talked, he quickly discovered my plans to come at the subject indirectly and firmly forbade my "preaching" to him.

Hope of Heaven through Christ

Within hearing range was a very sick man who had been listening intently. He beckoned to me, so I went over to him. He asked, "Will you tell me about Jesus? That man won't hear you but I will."

I was deeply touched with his earnest, entreating manner after being driven away and I promised to tell him about Jesus. His name was Jesse Doherty. He had a wife and two children at home and had been in the army for three years.

"When did you hear from home, Jesse?"

"Six weeks ago, sir. It's a long time since … won't you tell me about Jesus?"

I began answering the longing of his heart. I told him of Christ who was lifted up to draw all men unto Himself, of how he had to look—only look—upon Jesus who was crucified. Jesse put his hands together and prayed that he, too, like so many before him, might look and live. So I believe the Spirit found him and accomplished His own precious work.

As I went away at the end of a long interview, he asked me to come again and often. As I passed the cot of the infidel, his face showed no sign that he was moved by the conversation, which he must have heard.

The next Monday morning, Jesse met me with a very happy smile.

"I have such good news," he said. "I'll be going home this week, sir, on Wednesday morning. My papers are all made out. Oh, how glad I am!"

Poor fellow, I knew he never would leave his cot until carried to the last resting place.

I said, "Jesse, you can't go home on Wednesday."

"Why not, sir?" he said hastily.

"You are too feeble. The boys might carry you to the cars but you could not stand the long ride."

"But what shall I do here, sir? Look at that water—how can I drink it?" The water was a mixture of mud and water, resembling what coffee-drinkers call "grounds" He said, "How can I drink it when I think of the old well at home in Pleasant Valley? Oh, how I long for a drink from that old well! And this bed's so hard and the one at home so soft! And there are the children, too, and wife. And you don't know what nice things she'd cook for me! I could eat them but not what I get here. If I was only home, I think I could get well."

"Well, Jesse, I'll tell you what I think about it. The first pure drink of water you will get will be from the 'river of water of life, clear as crystal,' above. When you have that water, you will no longer wish for water from the home well. And, Jesse, the first time you will see your wife will be at the right hand of God with the heavenly family."

"Do you think so, sir?" and his eyes brightened up. "Well then, welcome to the will of God. How glad I am that Jesus is precious to me now!"

On Wednesday I saw him again. "You were right, sir. I am much worse. I couldn't even bear to be carried to the cars."

As I entered the ward on Sunday morning, five or six soldiers surrounded his cot. He was in the fetal position and the men were doing what little they could for him. One said, "It's no use, sir, you can't speak with him."

Going within the sad circle, I put my mouth to his ear. "Jesse, do you know me?"

He could not move his head but there was an answer, very faint, but audible—not words, only a sound. I put my hand under the cover and squeezed his. The squeeze was returned. "It's little matter whether you know me or not but do you know the Lord Jesus, Jesse?"

Gathering up his remaining energies, the soldier tried to speak. He could not articulate but we heard the same sound he had uttered before—only louder and more intensely. He never moaned or spoke again.
(Thomas Atkinson)

Hope Found in the Bible

The hospital work grew quieter and quieter until the army moved once more. Reverend Henry D. Lathrop, Rector of St. John's Protestant Episcopal Church, Lancaster, Ohio, and Christian Commission delegate arrived in December 1863. After visiting Hospital No. 4 at Murfreesboro, Tennessee, he wrote about the following incident:

I found a poor Norwegian, weak and wasting away rapidly. I tried to talk with him. He wanted me to send a little devotional book, his constant companion, to a sister in Minnesota. After repeated trials, I found intelligible conversation impossible. He had a New Testament, given to him previously by a delegate. It contained *Danish* and English translations in parallel columns. I took my pencil and marked in the Danish column, "Come unto me, all ye that labor and are heavy laden, and I will give you rest."

Never shall I forget the eagerness with which he seized the book and ran his finger along the lines and read, half audibly, in his own language the gracious invitation. A smile lit up his face, while tears ran down his cheeks. Again I took the book and marked, "I am the resurrection, and the life: he that believeth in me, though he were dead, yet shall he live." The same scene as before was repeated. Thus, I know it was not I but the Lord who spoke to him.

After searching, I finally found a countryman of his in another hospital and had the two brought together. Through this man, all the wishes of the first could be understood and met.

Substitutionary Death

The story of the year in the Cumberland Army may be an incident related by the General Field Agent of the Christian Commission, Reverend Edward P. Smith, who also served as Pastor of the Congregational Church, Pepperell, Massachusetts. He writes the following incident:

In answer to a letter from a soldier's family, I was searching for a grave in the Soldiers' Cemetery in Nashville when I noticed a man in civilian clothing kneeling by a grave. He was evidently writing upon the painted headboard. When I went over to him, he was standing in front of the board, his arms folded, his face bathed in tears. He turned out to be an Illinois farmer and this was the grave of an Illinois soldier.

"Is that your boy, sir?" I asked.

"No, he lived in our town and I've come to find his grave."

"Do you represent his father who couldn't come?"

"Well, my neighbor was glad to have me come but I came for myself. You see, I have seven children. All of them are small and my wife is sickly. I was drafted into the army and there was nobody to carry on at the farm. I couldn't hire a substitute. My thirteen dollars a month in the army wouldn't feed the family. It seemed as though I must go and they must suffer. When we were in our greatest trouble about it, the very morning I was to report at camp, my neighbor's son came over to the house and offered to go to war for me. He told me he had nobody depending on him and could go better than I. He went to war, was wounded at Chickamauga, brought to a Nashville hospital, and this is his grave."

The stranger sobbed aloud. Under the private's name, I read the words which he had traced with his pencil in large, awkward letters: "DIED FOR ME." He had come all the way from his prairie home, at a great cost to himself, to put this grateful mark upon the grave of his substitute.

CHAPTER IX
THE EASTERN ARMIES
GENERAL GRANT'S ADVANCE UPON RICHMOND
May and June 1864

Having completed his preparations, General Grant and the Army of the Potomac crossed the Rapidan River in Virginia on May 4, 1864 and pushed forward into the "Wilderness." This tract of broken tableland, stretching southward from the Rapidan nearly to Spotsylvania Court House, seamed with ravines and was densely covered with a labyrinth of dwarf timber and bushes. Fighting began early on the morning of the 5th and continued throughout that day and the next with no decisive result, even though the slaughter was terrible. On Friday evening, May 6th, the Union line was substantially the same as at the beginning of the struggle.

By early morning on the 7th, Lee had entrenched his whole front. Choosing not to attack his fortifications, Grant resumed his march out of the Wilderness, from which his advance emerged on Sunday. The whole force emerged the following day. The army was now concentrated at Spotsylvania Court House.

On the morning of the 12th, Hancock captured a strong point of the enemy's entrenched line, along with many cannons and prisoners. Lee attempted to retake it but was unable and the Union line was unable to advance, as the murderous day sorely proved. After several days of maneuvering in quest of weak points, which were not to be found, the flanking advance on Richmond was resumed on the night of the 20th. General Meade reported his losses up to this time at 39,791 men.

Spiritual Preparation for Battle

Reverend E. F. Williams, Pastor of the Congregational Church, Whitinsville, Massachusetts, writes of the last Sunday in April 1864 at Culpepper, as the Union Army waited to advance upon Richmond:

Today, the delegates preached twenty-three times to the regiments in and around the town. At every location, the men listened intently as if they were anticipating the baptism of blood which awaited them. They were anxious to prepare for the march to death, which so many were to make.

After a few days, the Christian Commission tents came down. Cooking utensils, station furniture, books, and all heavy articles were sent back to Washington. The army gave us heavy army wagons to use in this endeavor. The delegates were divided into companies and placed under the command of experienced agents. A corps was assigned to each leader and, with mingled calmness and dread, we all awaited the forward movement.

Preaching the Gospel in the Dark

Reverend Charles P. Lyford, member of Black River Conference, Methodist Episcopal Church, tells the story of one of the last services on the last Sunday of April 1864 at Culpepper before the advance through the Wilderness:

The day before the advance, I had an engagement to preach to a brigade of the Fifth Corps. Just prior to the service, they received their marching orders. As the men passed by our tent, the Colonel of a Pennsylvania regiment called out to me, saying, "Young man, you won't keep your appointment tonight."

They were a noble body of men, marching so joyfully and gladly to the grave. My heart went out to them and I silently resolved to preach to them, if possible, that very night.

I mounted a horse and quietly followed them. After nightfall, they approached Culpepper, halted, and prepared to bivouac. Supper over, I rode up to the Colonel, who had hailed me when passing our quarters, and reported myself ready to fill my appointment. With his whole heart, he entered into the minutiae of preparation. He said, "I believe you fellows would come with us to the cannon's mouth to preach the Gospel."

He had the drums beat "church call" and saw to it that a dozen good singers were selected for a choir—and yet the Colonel was not a Christian. We held the service in front of his headquarters. I had never attended one like it before. It was pitch black that night. I could not see the men's faces, nor could they see mine—but they were there, hundreds of them. The Kind Heart on high, He alone, knew where they would be the next night. My, how they crowded about me when the meeting was over to send last words home. Some of them spoke of Warrenton Junction and about the meetings at which they had found the Lord. "Tell my friends," said a Captain, "if anything happens, that I am ready to live or die—and that whether I live or die, I am the Lord's."

On May 5th, the brigade was in the thickest of the battle and my brave Colonel fell at the head of his column.

Ministry of Trying to Quench Thirst

A poor German saw the badge of the Christian Commission and called me to his side. He had stuck some bayonets into the ground and stretched a blanket upon the handles to try and ward off the sun. His side was sadly torn by a shell but his great need was for water to quench his raging thirst. I put my canteen to his lips. Never have I seen such agony and disappointment on a human countenance as I did on his when he found he could not swallow. He tried again and again, then sank back upon the ground and said, "Pray for me, pray for me. It'll all be over soon." I did pray for him. I prayed that he might have that water of which he who drinks never thirsts again.
(Charles P. Lyford)

Ministry of Preventing Imminent Death

During the night of May 6th, the second day of the Wilderness battle, our extreme right was assailed fiercely and driven back upon the field hospital. Such a scene ensued! Ambulances and wagons went tearing by, filled with wounded who had been hastily gathered in. Orderlies swept past on horseback in close proximity to the men who were fighting and yelling. Suddenly I heard a voice out of the darkness at my feet, saying, "Don't ride over me—please don't. I'm wounded and can't move."

The poor fellow explained, "They carried me to an ambulance but it was full and drove away without me. The bearers set me down by the roadside to wait for the next one that came along but nobody had time to pick me up." By now, it was too dark to see him. His head was within a few inches of the wheel track. I stood by and protected him from an almost certain death, until he was properly removed and received care.
(Charles P. Lyford)

Lincoln on Doing Our Duty

President Lincoln told the members of the Christian Commission who called on him in Washington after the Anniversary meeting in January 1865: "We have been only doing our duty, my friends, whatever we have been able to do together. You owe me no thanks for what I have done for the country, whatever that may be—and I owe none to you. We cannot repay the soldiers."

Expressions of Gratitude

And yet, we found that the poor fellows were always grateful for the smallest kindnesses and "magnified the office" of the Commission. Reverend F. P. Monfort, Member of Whitewater (O. S.) Presbytery, Indiana, preserves the testimony of a German, wounded in the Wilderness Battles of May 5-6, 1864:

In a thick German accent, he said, "Ah, this is the Christian Commission. He's the best man in the army. He saves my life. He comes 'round when we was in the Wilderness, all two days and two nights, and no eat, and no water, and no doctor, and just pick up all of 'em, and give 'em eat and water, and nurse 'em. Oh, him so many, too—plenty of 'em—and him doctor hisself, and bring 'em to White House Landing, and bring 'em up here to the hospital. Oh, he so good. He's the best man in the army. Him work just like a black man.'"

Death a Shortcut to Glory

After the first fighting at Spotsylvania Court House, Virginia, a battle which occurred May 8-21, 1864, Reverend E. F. Williams, Pastor of the Congregational Church, Whitinsville, Massachusetts, writes this account:

Going through the wards of the hospital at Laurel Hill, some members of the 14th New York Regiment caught my attention. They were weeping over a body carefully wrapped in an army blanket and laid on the ground in a corner of the tent.

"Didn't we used to see you at Culpepper?" one of them asked.

"Yes, probably."

"Well, the man who has just died used to attend the meetings there. He was a Christian. His death was glorious—so peaceful. Anyone would be willing to die if they could die like him."

The blanket was carefully turned down. We recognized the soldier's features and remembered our last conversation with him in his tent near Culpepper. He had been very happy at the prospect of soon returning home, as his regiment's term of service was nearly over. He had told us how glad he would be to see his wife and child and being able to attend church and Sunday school.

"But then, you may fall. There is death ahead," we had said.

"I know it. If I fall, the battlefield will only be a shortcut to glory."

To glory, he had gone, indeed. His comrades admired his life and saw that his body was buried with more than the usual care. They told themselves over and over of their willingness to depart, if they could die as he had died.

Christ's Presence Nearby

In another division of the hospital, my attention was directed to a group of soldiers crowding around an open tent, under which were several wounded officers. The interest of all seemed to focus upon the slight form of one of the sufferers. The star upon his shoulders revealed his rank. The day was intensely hot and sultry and the sides of the tent were raised a few feet from the ground. The General's head was toward the center and his feet pointed to the outer edge of the tent. A few pine boughs were his only comfort. One of his legs had been amputated. Members of his staff stood weeping around him or had stooped fondly down to catch his last whispered words. From his moving lips, we surmised that he wished to be turned over.

"Which way?" asked a lieutenant.

"Toward the enemy," was the indistinct response and he was carefully and lovingly turned toward the foe. The booming guns of the enemy were telling of fearful carnage along the lines.

A moment later, a delegate bent over and gently whispered, "How does Christ seem to you now, General?"

He gave his quick but faintly spoken reply. "Nearby," he said. And with these words upon his lips, the spirit of General James C. Rice passed into the better land.

All winter, the General had been greatly interested in religion. He had aided the chaplain of one of his regiments in every possible way—going into the prayer meetings regularly and taking part in them with his men—so that death did not take him by surprise. Quietly, he sent his messages of affection to his mother and then, calmly without fear and like a Christian hero, he met the King over all Terrors.
(E. F. Williams)

Ministry of Comfort

As the army moved toward the left in its attempt to flank Lee, Fredericksburg was no longer a viable point of communication with Washington. Therefore, the wounded were all sent to the old base and Port Royal became the new center of communication. Most of the Christian Commission delegates and agents returned with the wounded but quite a few continued with the advance. Before we go forward with the latter, we must retrace our steps to the city which shall ever be remembered as a place of sorrow and of death.

The correspondent, pen named "Carleton," of the *Boston Journal*, narrates the story of two scenes dissimilar outwardly—yet part of the same Gospel. Every delegate, whether ministering to the body or the soul, illustrated this same Gospel by word or deed:

Go into the hospitals and you will find armless, legless men, wounds of every description. You will also find men on the hard floor and bare church pews, lying in one position all day, unable to stir until the nurse comes to their aid. They must wait until their food comes and some must be fed with a spoon, as if they were little children.

"Oh, that we could get some straw for the brave fellows!" said Reverend James P. Kimball, Pastor of Congregational Church, Falmouth, Massachusetts, and delegate of the Christian Commission. He had wandered about town, searching for this article and concluded, "There is none to be had. We shall have to send to Washington for it."

"Straw? I remember two stacks, four miles out on the Spotsylvania road. I saw them last night, as I galloped from the front."

Four Christian Commission delegates, armed with a requisition from the Provost Marshal to seize two stacks of straw, set out with two wagons. Away we went across the battlefield of December 13, 1862, fording Hazel Run, gaining the heights and reaching the straw stacks owned by Reverend Mr. Owen.

"By what authority do you take my property?" he asked.

"The Provost Marshal's, sir."

Reverend Mr. Kimball was on the stack, pitching it down. I was pitching it into the wagon, and the young men were stowing it away when Reverend Owen asked, "Are you going to pay me for it?"

"You must see the Provost Marshal, sir. If you are a loyal man and will take the oath of allegiance, doubtless you will get your pay."

"It is pretty hard. My children are just ready to starve. I have nothing for them to eat and you come to take my property without paying for it."

"Yes, sir, war is hard. You must remember, sir, that there are thousands of wounded men—yours, as well as ours. If your children are at the point of starving, those men are at the point of dying. We must have straw for them. What we don't take tonight, we will get in the morning. Meanwhile, if anybody attempts to take it, please tell them that it is for the hospital, that they can't have it."

With wagons stuffed, we left Reverend Mr. Owen and returned to encourage the hearts of several thousand men. Oh, how they thank us!

"Did you get it for me? God bless you, sir."

Ministering to the Wounded

Evening came and thousands of soldiers had arrived from Washington and passed through the town to take their places at the front. The hills all around us are white with innumerable tents and thousands of wagons. A band is playing lively tunes to cheer the wounded in the hospitals. I have checked on the sufferers. Two or three have already gone. They will need no more attention. A surgeon is working on a ghastly wound, taking up the arteries. An attendant is pouring cold water upon a swollen limb. In the Episcopal Church, a nurse is bolstering up a wounded officer in the area behind the altar. Men are lying in the pews, on the seats, on the floor, and on boards on top of the pews. Two candles in the spacious building throw feeble rays into the dark recesses, faintly disclosing the reclining forms. A heavy, stifled breathing serves as of constant effort to suppress involuntary cries of acute pain. You find it hard to see them suffer and not be able to relieve them.

Passing into the street, you see a group of women, talking about our wounded—Confederate wounded who are receiving their special attention. The Provost Marshal's patrol is making its rounds to preserve order. ("Carlton")

Openness to Spiritual Ministry

Starting down the street, you reach the rooms of the Christian Commission. Some of the men are writing, some eating their rations, while others dispense supplies. Passing through the rooms, you enter the grounds in the rear—a beautiful garden once but not unattractive now. The air is filled with the fragrance of honeysuckle and locust blossoms. The pennifolia is unfolding its delicate milk-white petals. Roses are opening their tinted leaves.

Fifty men are gathered around a summer house—warm-hearted men, who have worked all day in the hospital. While exercising Christian charity by imitating the example of the Redeemer of men, their hearts have been wrenched by the scenes of suffering. They have given bread for the body and food for the soul. They have given cups of cold water in the name of Jesus and prayed with those departing to the silent land. The moonlight shimmers through the leaves of the locust blossoms.

The little congregation breaks into singing

"Come, Thou fount of every blessing."

After the hymn, a chaplain says, "Brethren, I had service this afternoon in the First Division Hospital of the Second Corps. Before prayer, the surgeon in charge asked all who desired to be prayed for to raise their hands. Nearly every man, who had a hand to raise, raised it. Let us remember them in our prayers tonight."

A man in the summer house—who was so far off, that I cannot distinguish him in the shadow—says, "There is manifestly a spirit of prayer among the soldiers in the Second Division of the Sixth Corps Hospital. Every man there raised his hand for prayers!"

Similar remarks are made by others and then there are earnest prayers offered that God will bless them, relieve their sufferings, give them patience, and restore them to health. They prayed that He will remember the widow and fatherless far away—that Jesus may be their Friend.

Ah! This night scene! An allusion was made, by one who prayed, to the garden scene of Gethsemane and to the blood of the Son of God. The connection was made to the blood, which was shed for our country.
("Carlton")

Ministry of a Surgeon

The report of Delegate S. J. Parker, a surgeon from Ithaca, New York, may represent the extent and value of the work offered by the Christian Commission volunteers who were of his profession:

I arrived at Belle Plain about 5:00 P.M. on May 13, 1864, and found about four hundred men in tents, ambulances and wagons. I spent about five hours aiding in the care of wounds and went back to my room at about 11 or 12 o'clock, leaving another delegate, Dr. Reed of Philadelphia, in charge. At 3:00 A.M., I returned and took charge of them and continued on duty until 10:00 A.M. when the day surgeons came. I left and went on foot with a party of other delegates to Fredericksburg.

On my arrival, I took an hour's rest and proceeded to the hospitals, which had just received newly-wounded men. I dressed wounds until midnight until all were made comfortable and then returned to rest at the Commission rooms. Next morning, I reported early to Medical Director Dalton, along with Dr. Reed, and was temporarily put in charge of Hospital D, Second Division, Sixth Corps. The two warehouses were only partially cleared when an ambulance train with 303 men arrived. It took us from 9:00 A.M. until 3:00 P.M. to unload the train and get the men comfortably arranged. At 3:00 P.M., we began dressing wounds. After a few hours, my right hand had become poisoned from fetid discharges. By 11:00 P.M., I was disabled by excessive pain in my arm. I called in an old army nurse—a good, faithful man and kept on dressing wounds until about two o'clock the next morning. Dr. Reed remained on duty.

The number of wounded I aided directly was 703, plus another hundred or two hundred more who called for aid. I dressed at least three thousand wounds. During this time, I had charge of the north tobacco and wheat warehouse and we held a daily prayer meeting in the hospital.

God Prepares a Man for Ministry

This story of George W. Miller comes from himself and from two of his Christian Commission friends. One is Reverend Nelson Whitney, Minister of the Methodist Episcopal Church, Sebec, Maine. The other is William Ballantyne, Esquire, President of the Washington Branch of the Christian Commission. His story is remarkable for its exhibition of earnest hope and faith:

Enlisting early in the war, Miller's regiment had been detailed for detached service and had not joined the Army of the Potomac until late summer of 1863. When he enlisted, he was not a Christian, even though he had entertained a strong desire to become a minister of the Gospel from early childhood. The duty of his regiment afforded him the time for abundant reflection and caused him to think about his past life and the possible dangers of the future. His youthful yearning to be a minister also came back. Except for the encouragement of a faithful Christian friend, Miller was unaided by any special religious influences but decided to become a Christian. During the winter at Brandy Station, he attended the Commission chapel and renewed his vows. He and Reverend Mr. Whitney, one of the delegates, became good friends. Miller assisted him for several months in his labors among the soldiers.

On the second day of fighting in the Wilderness battles, Miller was severely wounded. For twenty-four hours, he remained on the field. The surgeon who examined his wound refused to operate because death was *inevitable*. A sixty-hour ambulance ride took him to Fredericksburg where a surgeon examined him once again and pronounced his wound fatal.

Three or four days of intense suffering ensued in the hospital at Fredericksburg. At last, Reverend Mr. Whitney found him. Never for a moment did Miller allow himself to think that his recovery was hopeless. His memorable words reflected his firm faith: "Mr. Whitney, the surgeon says I must die but I do not feel that my work is done yet. When I gave myself to God last winter, I promised Him that I would labor for His cause in the Gospel ministry. I feel that He has a work for me to do and I believe that man is immortal until his work is done. Can't you do something for me?"

Mr. Whitney did his best. He procured straw and a blanket, half of which belonged to Mr. Cole, the Potomac Army Field Agent. Lying upon a bed of straw, the soldier seemed to think it was the softest he had ever known. After a few days, a third surgical consultation took place and the doctors pronounced, "You will recover. This is the most miraculous recovery we have ever seen."

Miller was transferred to Armory Square Hospital in Washington on May 26, 1864. Here again, the doctors declared that his wound was mortal. Mr. Ballantyne, who visited him at this time, bears testimony to his cheerful, unwavering confidence. He said, "There was no fear, no concern about his life or that he was in danger. His desire was to do His Master's will."

On June 6th, the ball was extracted but many months passed before the soldier could leave the hospital. In accordance with his early determination, he prepared himself to preach the Gospel of Peace.

Ministering to the Helpless

Mr. E. M. Heydrick, of Brooklyn, left Belle Plain for Fredericksburg on May 15, 1864, along with a party of about forty delegates. He relates an incident that took place on the road:

Our wagons fell behind and we took the occasion to eat lunch. While standing alone and eating the small portion that had been handed me, a tall, noble-looking soldier approached and said, "Friend, can you spare a little of that? I am so hungry. I have not tasted food for two days."

"Certainly," I replied. As I handed him what I had, I noticed for the first time that his arms were both disabled. He said, "I have no hands to feed myself with. Will you please put it to my mouth?"

As I did so, tears of gratitude fell on my hand. "God bless you, my friend!" he said. The way in which he spoke the words was worth a dozen dinners.

Dedication to the Union Cause

The instances of the strength of the willingness of the soldier and his friends to submit to sacrifice are without number. Reverend Mr. E. F. Williams, Pastor of the Congregational Church, Whitinsville, Massachusetts, related this incident at the Washington Anniversary of the Commission in January 1865:

An old man had come to visit his two sons in the army and found them both wounded. As he sat between his maimed boys, someone asked if he regretted the sacrifice. He raised his hands and earnestly exclaimed, "No. If I had twenty sons, I would give them all to save this Union!"

Ultimate Thoughtfulness

The instances of the strength of the willingness of the soldier and his friends to submit to sacrifice are without number. Reverend Mr. Williams, Pastor of Spruce Street Baptist Church, Philadelphia, related this incident at the Washington Anniversary of the Commission, January 1865:

In a delegate's diary, I found this entry: A private with the 11th Maine Regiment was mortally wounded a few days before. As his companions started to carry him to the rear, he looked up to his regimental commander and, in generous thoughtfulness of others, said, "Don't trouble the boys to carry me back, Colonel. It will only tire them. I can live but a few minutes and can just as well die here." (E. F. Williams)

Blind but Dedicated

Reverend Dr. J. Wheaton Smith, Pastor of Spruce Street Baptist Church, Philadelphia, tells of great exhibition of sacrifice. The incidents were related at the Washington Anniversary of the Christian Commission in January 1865:

Thinking I was a surgeon, one poor fellow said, "Sir, will you dress my wound?"

I am not a doctor but I did my best. I took off the bandage and sponged away the hard incrustation that had gathered upon the wound. I discovered that his sight was entirely gone. He had been shot through the eyes and the bridge of the nose.

"Poor fellow!" I said to him, "this is hard."

"Yes, it is hard but I would go through it again for my country."

Brain Dead but Dedicated

Fredericksburg. A strong and noble-looking man lay upon a stretcher but he was shot through the head. His eyes were closed. He knew no one, could answer to no voice, and yet he still breathed. I never shall forget how that massive chest heaved up and down. We watched him for hours, thinking every hour would be his last. All night, he laid there motionless, except for that heaving chest. In the morning, he was no better but he began to move his feet. He evidently thought he was marching and he marched until he died—tramp, tramp, tramp—brain dead but marching on! (J. Wheaton Smith)

Faith Rest in God

Reverend Herrick Johnson, Pastor of (N. S.) Presbyterian Church, Pittsburg, Pennsylvania, spoke at the Closing Exercises of the Anniversary Celebration of the Christian Commission in 1865. In his address, he tells of the aftermath of the Battle of Spotsylvania in Virginia, which occurred May 8-21, 1864. We extract the following incident:

I remember Aaron Lamb, a soldier from Maine, who had lost his left leg. The little delicacies and attentions given him had opened his heart. He had told me of his widowed mother and loving sisters and I had written his letter home for him. Back came their noble answer. It said, "We cannot as a family, both brothers and sisters, express our gratitude enough to Him who ruleth all things if, from the glorious Army of the Potomac, He give us back our darling loved one with only the loss of one leg."

And from that couch of suffering, a message to heaven was also sent up. And that, I believe, found answer—even more blessed than the message from home. For many hours and days, he had lain on the hard floor with nothing but a blanket under him. He was both restless and sleepless from the shock to his nervous system. In the dusk of evening, with his hand clasped in mine, the patient hero breathed his low prayer, saying, "O Father, God, be pitiful—be merciful—give me rest—rest of body and of soul—oh, give me rest."

And the hard floor seemed to grow woolly soft, as if Jesus had pillowed it, and rest, "of rest, God's rest the best," came to that tired heart. "He shall cover thee with His feathers, and under His wings shalt thou trust."

Patient Christian Endurance

I saw another with both legs off close to the thigh. When I spoke to him of the sacrifice he had made for his country, be answered, "My country demands it and my Savior demands it. I believe that the kingdom of Christ will be advanced by this war."

Another said, "I am ready to go home to my parents, home to Christ, or back to the war."

This is the spirit of the army—one of patient, Christian endurance. Down from the throne of the Highest, through the highest clouds that had been charged with thunderbolts of wrath, come these gleams of light, in waves of life and immortality, telling to the people that God has not forgotten to be gracious.
(Herrick Johnson)

Repentance and Reconciliation before Death

I recall a young sergeant, whose limb had been sadly shattered. He was a brave, patient boy but remarkably reticent, resolutely maintaining a cold reserve. For days, he resisted all kindness but, at last, I found the way down into his heart's secret place of tenderness and tears. The great drops wet his cheeks as he told me how he had run away from home and almost broken his mother's heart. He said his own pain was nothing compared to the trouble he had given her.

"Shall I write to your mother," I asked, "and tell her how and where you are?"

"Oh, yes," he said, "but break the news gently—break it gently. Oh, and tell her how sorry I am for having laid such a burden on her loving heart."

And then we talked of another home from which he had wandered and another heart he had grieved. I asked him if he had a penitent message to send home to God. Before long, I believe there was joy in the presence of the angels over the return of one more prodigal son.

The surgeons finally decided that his leg must be amputated and very soon it became evident that even this would not save him. We told him that soon he would die. He was ready. His weapons, haversack, canteen, and blanket—all had been lost on the battlefield. But he clung to the flag he bore and he lay there with the stars and stripes wrapped about him. Just as he was dying, his lips moved. We stooped to listen. He was making his last charge when he said, "Come on, boys! Our country and our flag forever!"

We asked him, "Is the Savior with you?"

He whispered, "Do you think He would pass by and not take me? I go, I go." And wrapped in stars, he went up among the stars.
(Herrick Johnson)

Instantaneous Answer to Prayer in Death

A young soldier was wounded unto death. I asked, "What can I do for you, my brave fellow?"

"Speak to me of Jesus" and words came to mind:

> "Jesus, lover of my soul,
> Let me to Thy bosom fly."

"Oh, won't you sing them, sir?" As I began to sing, another wounded soldier, lying nearby, joined in the words of this blessed hymn. Then the dying drummer boy repeated the words of this prayer and, even while the words are still on his lips, the prayer is answered and his soul takes its flight to the bosom of Jesus. (Herrick Johnson)

Wonderful Power in Jesus' Name

Reverend Horace C. Hovey, Pastor of the Congregational Church, Florence, Massachusetts, writes of the power of the "Precious Name" following the Battle of Spotsylvania in Virginia, which took place May 8-21, 1864:

A brave cavalry officer, dying of his wounds, was delirious when I approached him. He thought of himself on the battlefield at the head of his gallant men. He fancied that a heavy gun was just in front of them, ready to be fired, and his distress was great. After awhile, he thought the gun had been discharged and that his men, badly cut up, were retreating. Here I interrupted, saying, "There is no gun there. You are safe among friends here in Fredericksburg."

"Let me alone," he sternly replied. "I must recover my command and renew the attack."

"No," I said, "let us not talk of battle scenes. You are soon to die. Let us talk of Jesus."

The mention of His name seemed to exert the powerful influence I had often heard ascribed to it. His agitation ceased at once. His delirium passed away. A smile lit up his pallid features and he drifted into a moment of silence. In a low, sweet voice, he said, "Jesus! Jesus! It is He who said, 'Come unto Me, all ye that labor and are heavy laden, and I will give you rest.' My friend, I want rest. I am weary. Can you sing, 'There is Rest for the Weary?'"

I complied with his wishes. He tried to sing but with a failing, faltering tongue, he spoke,

> "In the Christian's home of glory
> There remains a land of rest."

We sang the hymn entirely through and, when we closed, there was not a dry eye in the entire ward. Shortly thereafter, hse entered his "home of glory" and "land of rest." The last words upon his lips were "I have no Father here but my Heavenly Father."

Finding Strength in the Rock of Ages

Reverend George Bringhurst, Rector of All Saints' Protestant Episcopal Church, Moyamensing, Philadelphia, ministered to the wounded men of the Battle of Spotsylvania, May 8-21, 1864. He tells the story of another hymn:

Passing through the woolen factory at Fredericksburg—my immense parish of wounded and dying men—I heard a low, mournful voice singing,

> "While I draw this fleeting breath;
> When mine eyelids close in death;
> When I rise to worlds unknown,
> And behold Thee on Thy throne—
> Rock of Ages, cleft for me,
> Let me hide myself in Thee."

There were some pauses in the verse, as if the singer's strength were failing. As I passed on my errand, a look told me that the soldier was dying. Next morning the last "fleeting breath" had been drawn, the eyelids were "closed in death," and the life that had gone was hid with Christ in God.

Strength for Dying in Rock of Ages

Mr. S. E. Bridgman, of Northampton, Massachusetts, relates an incident very similar to the one above that occurred at the same woolen-factory hospital:

Afar off, under the machinery of a mill, I heard the voice of singing! It reminded me of Paul and Silas singing their praises in the guarded dungeon. I walked over and leaned upon the ponderous wheel. Near me, rose a voice, sweet and clear, and the holy strains are sung,

> "While I draw this fleeting breath."

But soon the earth receded from the eyes of the soldier-boy and the lips that gave forth so sweet a strain were still—while, at that very moment, the spirit of this man walked in the light of the angels over the crystal pavement of the New Jerusalem.

Joy Following Suffering

Mr. Stuart accompanied Right Reverend Bishop McIlvaine, of Ohio, on a memorable visit to the army in a woolen factory hospital at Fredericksburg. This incident followed the battle at Spotsylvania, Virginia, May 8-21, 1864, where they found a Massachusetts soldier who seemed to be the happiest man in Fredericksburg:

I found 550 patients, suffering from every variety of wounds and injuries. As I passed one cot, a happy and contented face caught my eye. I stopped and spoke to the soldier:

"You seem happy, my friend. I trust it is because your faith in Christ is firm."

"Yes," he answered, "I took Him with me to the army."

"I trust you are not hurt badly," I continued, deceived by his pleasant face. He rolled back his covering and showed me that both legs were gone.

"You have made a noble contribution to your country."

"I have given all but my life. And I am ready to give that if she needs it."

His name was Donald Norton, of the Boston, 22nd Massachusetts Regiment. Afterward, I learned that, while being removed from the town, he died with the same peace and in the same strength in which he had suffered.

Getting Ready for the Prince of Peace

Mr. Isaac Baker, a delegate from Philadelphia, reported to Fredericksburg after the battle at Spotsylvania, Virginia, May 8-21, 1864. Upon arriving, he was told that his son, who had been engaged in the battles, was wounded. The sight of the misery he had come to relieve was too terrible to allow him to leave his post and search for his boy. Trusting that his son would find kindness and care wherever he was, he faithfully fulfilled his allotted work. From his report, we take this extract:

On the first morning, I held a little service of singing and prayer in my division, with the common consent of the men. I told them the simple and touching story of a little girl who had lost her father but did not understand the dread nature of death and the grave. Her mother explained, through tears, that God had sent for her father and that, sooner or later, He would send for them—but no telling how soon. The innocent child exclaimed, "Well, then, mother, if God is going to send for us soon, and we don't know just when, hadn't we better begin to pack up and get ready to go?"

Finding Solace in the Prince of Peace

The *packing up* incident seemed to take hold of the men—it could be applied so well to their present needs.

"Ah, Chaplain," said a young soldier afterward, "I'm glad you told us that story about *packing up*. It made the thing so plain to me. I haven't much learning and I haven't tried to understand these things much but now I see through it all. I want you to help me *pack up*. Will you pray with me, Chaplain?"

I knelt by his side. While speaking with God, his earnest heart cried out, "Oh, do, Lord, help me, help me." It was a solemn season. The Holy Spirit was in our midst. It exemplified, "This poor man cried and the Lord heard him." I was about to go to another who had beckoned to me, when the dear boy said, "Oh, I thank you, Chaplain. I am happy now. I have found Jesus!"

He was radiant with joy, so that I wondered and said, "But what of your body?" He had been shot through the right shoulder and left leg. He had an arm taken off. "Do you suffer much now?"

"Oh," he said, "my wounds are nothing now. I can bear them all because I have peace within."

At his request, I sat down with a full heart and wrote to his wife, informing her of his condition but with particular emphasis on the blessed change that had come over his soul. Indeed, it was wonderful to see the forgetfulness of bodily suffering in the new-found joy which filled this wounded soldier's heart.

(Isaac Baker)

Forgetting Pain through the Prince of Peace

We sang "Rest for the Weary" and one man, whose whole thigh had been shattered by a shell, lay there perfectly calm, patient—even happy. As I came over to him, he and said, "Oh, how that hymn cheered me! I forgot my pains while I listened to it and I know it cheered many of the boys."

(Isaac Baker)

Going to the Prince of Peace

One group of sufferers claimed my deepest sympathy. Four Indians from Wisconsin lay together, bleeding for the country that had once been the wide domain of their fathers. After lying down next to one, I spoke of Jesus and His salvation. His eye brightened. He had heard that blessed name before and, in his broken way, said, "I love Him, I love Him!"

I commended his spirit to God, and then sang him to sleep—for he died while we were singing that sweet chorus,

> "For, oh, we stand on Jordan's strand,
>   Our friends are passing over,
> And just before, the shining shore
>   We may almost discover."

The other three Indians were unable to speak. May God help them. I gave each one some refreshment and continued to the next sufferer.

(Isaac Baker)

Learning How to Pray

Following the battle at Spotsylvania, Virginia, May 8-21, 1864, a delegate describes how reading the Bible was so valuable in soothing and calming men who agonized with pain. Mr. E. M. Heydrick relates this incident:

A young soldier, John Wagner, of the 60th Ohio Regiment, was brought to the hospital. He had been shot through the stomach. So great was his agony that he filled the building with his cries. He could not lie in one position but kept two or three people busy, turning him from side to side.

Famished with hunger, he would eat all that was given him but it would come out through the bullet holes. He kept begging that we would send to the front to find his brother but this was impossible. We asked him, "Have you ever heard of that 'Friend that sticketh closer than a brother?' He alone can help you. You only have to ask Him in prayer and He will help you."

"I do not know how to pray," he answered.

I took a little card containing Scripture texts and read the motto: "Ask, and it shall be given you," and the prayer, "Heal me, O Lord, and I shall be healed; save me, and I shall be saved." Out of his agony, he exclaimed, "Please, read the prayer again." I did so.

"I can pray that," and he kept repeating it aloud, over and over again. That night the bullet holes in his stomach closed and, for the first time, he became calm enough to sleep.

One Conversion Leads to Many Conversions

Following the Battle of Spotsylvania in Virginia, May 8-21, 1864, one incident shows the influence exerted by soldiers upon their friends at home. This story is related by Mr. S. E. Bridgman, delegate of the Christian Commission: One night, after evening prayers, a man came to our tent in tears and asked the delegates to pray for him. "I have navigated every channel to perdition but now I want to lead a different life," he said.

He was pointed to Jesus. He looked at Jesus and lived. The next day, he said, "Oh, how easy it is to be a Christian! I did not suppose it was so easy. I thought it was a long and very troublesome way. I just asked with all my heart and I didn't have to wait for the answer. I just prayed to God and light came in at once. How glorious everything is! Even this Virginia mud now seems to have become beautiful."

A week later, with a bright and joyous smile, he came to our quarters with an open letter just received from his wife. She described the scene at home upon receiving the news of his conversion. She had begun to read the letter aloud but, when she found answer to her prayers, she could read no more. Her mother took the letter and tried to read but with the same result. Also present with the family were four boarders and former companions in sin of the infidel husband. One of these volunteered to read the letter and, that very night at a prayer meeting, they all rose for prayers and all were converted. They sent word to their friend in the army, saying, "We will meet you in heaven."

Life-saving Bible

Following the battle at Spotsylvania, Virginia, May 8-21, 1864, Mr. E. M. Hey-drick and Mr. Lewis Beach, both of Brooklyn, traveled from Belle Plain to Fredericksburg to minister to the wounded. On the way, they discovered an instance of a life saved by a Bible:

Mr. Beach and I came to a stream where we met a group of soldiers crossing on a log. While waiting, I noticed that one of them, Mr. Harlem T. Garnett, 20th Michigan Infantry, a man of stately form and countenance, was looking rather sad. I approached and said, "I trust you love Jesus—do you not?"

He replied, "Don't you think that I ought to love Him? See what His Word did for me."

Opening his coat and shirt, he drew a small Bible from a pocket over his heart. He explained, "In battle, two days ago, a minie ball from the enemy had entered the Bible on the front side. It came out at the edge and passed around my side, laying open the flesh to the bone." The blood was still on his shirt.

"Were you a Christian," I asked, "before entering the service?"

"Yes, sir. A few months earlier, I became a Christian. The day before I left home, my sister came to me and said, 'Harlem, will you take this and carry it near your heart for my sake?'"

Historical Setting:

General Grant's flanking advance from Spotsylvania Court House was toward the north to the Anna River, north of Richmond. He found Lee strategically positioned to deny passage of the river and, although the crossing was successfully begun, the enemy lines were so strong that Grant decided not to attack. The river was crossed again, followed by another short march to the east, and the long columns turned southward.

On May 28th, the army passed over Pamunkey River, northeast of Richmond, and they established a new base at White House Landing. Again, the Confederate Army, moving along the inside of the circle, was able to face Grant at Cold Harbor with strong fortifications. On June 1st, another engagement began. The grand assault was made on June 3rd and the Union Army was decisively repulsed. Several days of delay were spent before the hostile battle began. Finally, on June 14th and 15th, the Army of the Potomac was transferred to the south side of the James River to operate, henceforth, against the southern approaches to the Confederate capital.

Unbearable Hardship

Following the battle at Spotsylvania, May 8-21, 1864, Grant was moving into position to take Richmond. The following account of an ordinary experience, detailed by Reverend Horace C. Hovey, shows how the hardships of the journeys of this campaign weighed heavily upon men unused to the service. This is exhibited by contrasting the soldier's sufferings and endurance:

The hardships the army endured while Grant was making his famous flank movements from Spotsylvania to City Point will never be forgotten nor adequately described. (Grant was trying to get between Lee and Richmond in order to drive his army out in the open.) Our little company of seven men, unaccustomed to hardships, was selected to go with the Fifth Army Corps. For three days and three nights, we never unharnessed our horses or take what, even in army life, would be called a regular meal. Most of us, meanwhile, had been marching on foot and were thoroughly frazzled by our double duty of keeping up with the army, while also providing Bibles and preaching as we advanced.

The third night, we found ourselves on the edge of an immense forest. Of necessity, we proceeded slowly amid the sturdy trunks of giant pines. Through their branches, the night wind sighed and moaned while the warm spring rain fell in torrents. The deep darkness was reminiscent of the Egyptian plagues, found in the Book of Exodus. The road grew worse and worse.

Inadvertently, we had become separated from our wagon train. Only two delegates with strength enough to work remained with the wagon. The driver was worn out and surly. To our complete dismay, we were passing through a swamp about midnight when our wagon sank to the axles in mud, with one front wheel planted squarely against a tree. Our only source of help was the occasional mule driver who passed by now and then. But, like us, they had also lost their wagon train. With curses, all undeserved, they told us to get out as best we could. With rails, we pried the wheel from the tree but our exhausted animals refused to pull. Neither caresses nor blows would avail.

Our precious supplies, gathered by Christian love, could not be abandoned to the guerillas. So in utter darkness, the two of us unloaded the wagon of every box, barrel, and bundle. With spades, we dug away the clay that had packed itself about the wheels and then, forcefully pushing the empty vehicle against the heels of the horses, we compelled them to go forward. With the wagon once more on solid ground, we reloaded our supplies and soon emerged from the forest. Now we realized that we were alone in enemy territory. Not a sound was to be heard in the dead of night, except for the rumble of our wagon wheels. Ignorant of the lay of the land, we drove into a field and built a fire out of fence rails. We spread our blankets in the open air and lay down to a rest, never before so quiet and so sweet.

Mother's Words Lead to Son's Conversion

The following reminiscence comes from the narrative of Christian Commission delegate, E. A. Rand. It took place as Grant continued his march to take Richmond, following the battle at Spotsylvania, May 8-21, 1864:

On June 9th, while assisting in moving the wounded to the boats at White House Landing, I met my friend, Captain William Fitz Williams, of the 2nd New York Mounted Rifles. In the battle at Cold Harbor he had received a wound, from which he had partially recovered. Anxious to be at his post, he was returning to his regiment against the advice of his surgeon. I invited him to the evening meeting in our chapel where he told us the story of his conversion. With a depth of feeling which brought tears to every eye, he described the last conversation with his mother. As he parted, she threw her arms about his neck and, bursting into tears, exclaimed, "O my son, I could give you up cheerfully—if only you were a child of God."

This outburst of a devoted Christian mother's love melted his heart and he promised her that his future life would be given to God. He told us that he had striven to keep this pledge, had been greatly helped by the Commission, and had found the Lord's service to be most pleasant and easy. He said, "I expect tomorrow morning to return to the field and think it doubtful that I shall ever see my loved ones again. But I am resolved to stand firm in God and to meet them in heaven."

The meeting closed. I bade him farewell, sensing I would see his face no more. In a fight near Petersburg on June 18th, while bending over to staunch the flowing blood of a companion, I am told, he received his mortal wound and died with a shout of praise.

Work of the Holy Spirit in Conversion

A young lady came in search of her brother, wounded at Cold Harbor. She had looked for him in vain through all the Washington hospitals. With the greatest of difficulty, she procured a pass to White House Landing from the War Department. Once there, she learned that he was dead and buried. The one wish that remained was to find his grave, recover the body, and bear it with her to her distant home. But, even in this, she was doomed to disappointment. The grave could not be identified. Suddenly, amid her grief and despair, the Holy Spirit revealed to her the fact that she had been led down this pathway of trial so she might find the Lord. Her brother had been a Christian but she, herself, was not. She had failed to find her brother but, by becoming a Christian, she could find

him in Christ Jesus, in the Resurrection, in Eternal Life. Giving herself away to the Lord, she determined to wait patiently until He called her home.
(E. A. Rand)

Correct Response to Rebuke

As Grant continued his march to Richmond in the summer of 1864, Mr. John Patterson, a Christian Commission delegate, writes of an experience about his time on board a government steamer bound for White House Landing from Washington:

General Baker, with his corps of detectives, was on board. With them, they had several fine horses that were well supplied with something I wanted badly for the Commission horses on board—fodder. Since I was not allowed to buy it, I resorted to a little ruse, which I hope the circumstances will justify. I tended to the horses of the detective officers by watering them occasionally during the warm day. My hungry animals were soon munching government fodder and I, myself, was on very excellent terms with the quick-witted members of the force.

While standing on the deck after dinner, I regret to say that my attention was drawn to a young preacher aboard who was en route to Cold Harbor to recover the body of his brother. The food on the boat was not according to his taste and he railed against the boat and government in very impolite terms. This raised the ire of the detectives and, especially that of an officer with whom I had just formed a pleasant acquaintance. He swore that, if it were not for the respect he had for the man's profession, he would put him under arrest at once. He gave vent to his wrath in language shockingly profane. I confess I wrongly feared to rebuke him on account of his kindness to me, as well as his laudable zeal for the good name of the government.

Without venturing upon him directly, I tried a chance shot at mild rebuke. While I leaned upon a box of goods with my chin resting on my hands, he concluded a volley of terribly wild expletives at the offending preacher. Without looking at him, as if I were in meditation, I said, "However the breakers of this commandment may escape punishment from man, yet the Lord our God will not suffer them to escape His righteous judgment." These words were in answer to Question 56 of Westminster Assembly's *Shorter Catechism*.

A slap on the back from my profane friend brought my pious soliloquy to a sudden end.

"My man," said he, "I know that book as well as you—from beginning to end. I have the most profound respect for truly religious men but a profound contempt for raving hypocrites. I was baptized by Dr. McLeod, of New York, in my father's arms. Father and pastor, I believe, are now in heaven."

I replied, "What would you give for a picture of your father with you in his arms, your mother standing by, and the old Doctor dripping the water upon your face and saying, 'Grant, Heavenly Father, that this child's name may be written in the Lamb's Book of Life?'"

The blow struck home. The wary look of the detective faded from his face. The thick armor in which a life of cunning and danger had encased him was penetrated by that simple thought of childhood and home. The welling of tears moistened the bronzed cheeks.

The scene made a deep impression on those present. We had no more swearing that evening as our boat glided softly over the winding waters of the York and Pamunkey Rivers on its way to receive its cargo of brave wounded men.

CHAPTER X
THE WESTERN ARMIES

FROM THE BEGINNING OF 1864 TO THE FALL OF ATLANTA

January 1864–September 1864

The first four months of 1864 were relatively quiet for both armies. In March, General Grant was called to Washington and General Sherman succeeded him in the command of the Military Division of the Mississippi. This gave Sherman command of the four great departments, namely, the Ohio, the Cumberland, the Tennessee, and the Arkansas. In anticipation of simultaneous campaigns on the Rapidan and the Tennessee, the armies were prepared for the grand spring movements.

Seeker Finds Christ

In January 1864, two ministers took charge of the work at Chattanooga, where the bulk of the army quartered for winter. One was Mr. William Lawrence, previously of Union Theological Seminary and now a Congregational Minister and Secretary of the Brooklyn Children's Aid Society. The other was Reverend J. F. Loyd, a Methodist Clergyman from Xenia, Ohio. They tell of this experience:

Nightly meetings were reopened in the Baptist Church, which had formerly been used as a hospital. One night, the evening meeting was very reluctantly canceled, by the request from headquarters of the Post Commander, to allow the use of the chapel for public readings by Murdoch.

The next night, a battery man stood up in the congregation and told of his experience, as recorded in *Annals, U.S. Christian Commission*, 477-478. He said, "This is the third night I have been at these meetings. The first time I went away saying, 'Religion is a good thing. I must have it so I'll come again.' The next night I went away, saying to myself, 'You are wicked enough without being a miserable coward. Why didn't you get up and say you wanted to be a Christian?' That was night before last. I didn't sleep much.

"In the morning, I was in a hurry for night to come. I wanted to become a Christian and thought this meeting was the only place to do it. All day long, I counted the hours when I should come. To make sure of it, I got my pass from the Adjutant before dinner and came early last night to the chapel. A guard halted me at the door. He said his instructions were to admit only officers and such men as had tickets. I told him I had no ticket but I must go into the meeting, that I needed it more than any officer. He pushed me back with his bayonet and I gave up and called the Christians hard names for shutting me out because I was a private.

"Then my sins came crushing down on me again and I went back and begged the guard to let me go in but he cursed me and ordered me away. I started for camp. When I was passing the railroad track I realized, 'It is Jesus you want, not the meeting.' So I knelt down in a rut of the road and told Jesus just what I was going to say to my comrades if I had gone to the meeting. I had hardly begun to tell Him before I felt relieved. When I got up from my knees, I couldn't help but sing. I went to camp singing and kept singing, even after I turned in, until the colonel's orderly hushed me up. These are good meetings but if I could find such a meeting as that one on the railroad track, I wouldn't mind if the guard ordered me off every night."

Victorious Departure

Reverend Jonathan L. Landis, ordained minister of the (N. S.) Presbytery of Harrisburg, Pennsylvania and a delegate at Chattanooga, reminisces about the following incident, which occurred in the early part of 1864:

I was very much interested in two Confederate soldiers who lay side by side in the same ward of one of the hospitals. Private J. P. Thompson's leg had been amputated and a Lieutenant Baker had a lung wound. Thompson sent for me one day and I found dead tissue where the artery had been tied off and that his stump was bleeding. It was evident that his condition was fatal and, when told, he became hysterical. I endeavored to calm him and finally succeeded. He expressed a most earnest wish to be with Christ, preferring it to any earthly consolations or prospects of life and health. He told me about his little sister in heaven and prayed that he might be permitted to meet her there. As I leaving, Lieutenant Baker, who had been intently observing the scene, spoke to me. He talked as a little child in

Christ's Kingdom might about his wish to go and be with Jesus. I sang with him the words:

> "I'm a pilgrim and I'm a stranger"
> and
> "Let us walk in the light of God"

He was delighted, so I sang again:

> "There is rest for the weary."

He said, "That is *the* rest. I want all others to enjoy it with me. I don't want to enjoy it by myself, would you?"

The next time I came into the ward, the two beds had been drawn close together. The two, who had fought together and were wounded together, were to enter the dark valley soon. In sweet communion and conversation, they passed the short time together until one took his departure, mere hours before his companion.

Wishing for Heaven

Willie Snyder, of Cincinnati, was one of the most interesting and loveable characters I ever met. Enlisting at the age of fifteen, he had seen two years' service. At Missionary Ridge, his severe wound required the amputation of one leg. He used to love for me sit down on his cot and talk to him about Jesus. The last time I saw him, he got very close to me and, putting one arm around me, he took my left hand in his. Laying his warm face upon my hand and kissing it, he looked up at me and sweetly said, "I wish I was in heaven."

"Why, Willie?"

"Because I feel it in my heart."

He had not long to wait for the fulfillment of his desire.
(Jonathan L. Landis)

Bound for Heaven

In January 1864, a great many regiments reenlisted for three years or until war's end and then went home on veteran furlough. With soldiers coming and going, this caused crowding in the quarters in Nashville for weeks. While in the city, the men were kept under guard but the Christian Commission had free access to them at all times. Reverend E. P. Smith, Pastor of Congregational Church, Pepperell, Massachusetts writes the following story:

These homeward-bound men were more thoughtful than had been anticipated. In many instances, with the thought of home so near at hand, they recalled the promises made two years before. Their broken vows came to stare them in the face. As recorded in *Annals, U.S. Christian Commission,* 482, one young soldier who procured a furlough, declined to use it, asking, instead, that it might be postponed a month. At the end of two weeks, he came to say that he was ready for his furlough. When pressed to give a reason for his strange delay, he replied, "I promised my mother that I would become a Christian in the army. I have neglected it up to this time and I could not go home until I could answer my mother's first question."

Sacredness of a Bible

This furlough of veterans brought about a new expenditure. They return from their homes with fewer New Testaments than taken from the battlefield. All accounts run pretty much the same:

"Mother"—or sister, or my little boy, or whatever the case might be—"wanted it, because, you see, I had carried it so long, and it had been in the fight. So I left it home because I knew I could get another."

At first, I thought they had presumed upon our generosity but now I am satisfied that they have done right. That copy of God's Truth will be treasured and read in the soldier's absence. The very form of the well-thumbed, worn book will stir up and mellow the depths of the hearts at home. This makes the Word doubly sacred.

On the boat from Chattanooga, I met an Irish woman who had come from Pennsylvania to see her brother in the hospital. Unfortunately, he had been carried to the grave the day before she reached Chattanooga. She had gathered up his few effects and was taking them home. Unrolling his knapsack upon the deck, she took from it a book—the only one it contained—and began reading. Tears streamed down her cheeks as she slowly spelled out the words and, with her fingers, traced the lines on the first page. I looked over her shoulder and discovered it was an old schoolbook on Physical Geography. She was reading the introduction. I asked, "Is that an interesting book?"

In thick Irish brogue, she replied, "Indeed, sir, it's my brother's book and he used to read it. He's dead now. Do you see his name there, the darling? He was a great scholar, my brother, and I know he used to read it. Never a word did I get from the hospital and never a word could they speak to me of him—only just he died on a sick bed and was buried entirely when I came. He was a great scholar, my brother was, and I was striving to get a bit of comfort for my poor soul out of his book."

I wished it had been the book of the God of all comfort!
(E. P. Smith)

Seeking Comfort

A young man lingered one day after our daily prayer meeting. Mr. Atkinson took him aside. I stood near but did not interrupt. The young man began, "I'm afraid I offended you this morning."

"Why, no, that can't be," said Mr. Atkinson. "I never saw you before that I know of."

"Never saw me? You were looking straight at me all the time you were talking in the barracks this morning. And every time you cut me to pieces. I couldn't stand it, so I got up and went out."

"Was that you? I thought it was some careless, ungodly fellow."

"Ungodly enough, but not careless. I couldn't have stayed there any longer. You made me think of what I had done. Oh! I am an awful sinner. Can I be saved?"

"You can be saved. The blood of Jesus cleanseth from all sin."

"I think I could, if I hadn't done *that*."

"Done what?"

"I have killed my mother."

"Killed your mother! When? How?"

"Last night, I had a letter from her. She said she was almost gone and her writing was all trembling like. She is very low with consumption. She talked to me, as she always did, about being a Christian and left me her dying prayer that I would leave my wicked life and come with her to heaven. When I got that letter, I made fun of it with my comrades and sat down and wrote her that she need not worry about my soul. I told her I would take care of that and that I meant to live just as I had and I would get all this world had to offer and look after the next when I got there. O sir, you don't know how that will make my poor old mother feel! It will kill her outright. I know it will." The strong young cavalryman bent his face to the railing and made the pew shake with his agony.

"What *can* I do! What *can* I do! Is there mercy for me?"

"Yes, for *you*. Jesus saves to the uttermost."

"What can I *do*?"

"Kneel down here with me and give yourself to God. Tell Him you are a sinner and cry for mercy. Then write to your mother and ask her forgiveness."

"It is too late for that. Mother will be dead before another letter can reach her. When she reads that wicked letter of mine, she will lay it down and die. Oh! What *can* I do?"

"Kneel down and cry for mercy. God will hear you and forgive. Then when your mother, in earth or heaven, hears that God, for Christ's sake, has forgiven you, she will remember your cruelty no more."

Prayer was offered in the vestry that day but relief eluded him. For several days, the soldier seemed not far from suicide. The next mail took his letter to his dying mother. He confessed his guilt to his scoffing comrades and prayed. Prayer was made for him in our meetings but his remorse was fearful and all-absorbing. It seemed as though God's condemnation of him that curseth father or mother had already descended upon him.

At last, he seemed to find the Savior and His forgiveness. He went home with his regiment but, whether to his mother's bedside or her new grave, I never knew.

Death Brings Blessings

A sketch by Mr. J. E. Wright, of Andover Theological Seminary, Massachusetts, illustrates the delegate's relief work in Nashville hospital service in April 1864:

A brother delegate asked me to go for him to Hospital No. 3 and see a man with acute erysipelas, an infectious disease of the skin. I was to bring him an orange. I saw, at once, that the disease had a firm grasp on the soldier. His face was terribly swollen. One eye was closed entirely, the other partially. Every feature was distorted, as well as discolored by an application of bromine or iodine. His limbs were terribly emaciated.

I sat down by the cot and talked with him. I read some precious Scripture promises and, at his request, wrote to his father. In the afternoon, I saw the poor fellow again. He was worse. Mortification had set in. It was difficult for him to hear or speak and all his faculties were yielding to the disease. He asked me if I had written a letter for him in the morning and what I had written, saying with touching emphasis, as he marked with his right hand a finger's length upon his left. He said, "I can't remember so long."

I told him I had written and asked if I should send a letter to his wife. He hesitated, and then feebly answered, "Not now, I can't hear—I can't think—tomorrow, perhaps."

As I bade him good bye, the poor fellow seemed to gather up his little remaining strength. Looking at me as I left, he clearly and earnestly said, "God bless you!"

The emphasis with which the simple words were spoken shall remain with me for as long as I live. Poor boy! His "tomorrow" never came. The letter, which he was to have dictated to his wife, told the sad story of a husband's death from the hand of a stranger.

Attending Angel

Mr. Arthur Lawrence, of Boston, tells a powerful story, related to him by a soldier in Bragg's Hospital, Chattanooga, not long before the spring movements of 1864:

A soldier told me what had led him to seek and find the Savior. Sometime before, a Christian on the next cot to his had been dying. Just before he passed away, he called the nurse to bring him a cup of water.

"Bring two, nurse," he said. "I want one for my friend here because he came a long distance and must be tired."

"I don't see anybody here," said the nurse, somewhat puzzled.

"Don't you see him?" said the soldier, pointing into what, for everyone else in the room, was only tenanted by vacant air. They assured him that there was no one there but the soldier could not be convinced. "There *is* someone standing by the bedside," he said.

And so, doubtless, there was for *him.*

"I didn't see what *he* saw," said the soldier who told me the story. But the long, last look of the dying man turned toward the attendant "Friend" awed him deeply. "For," he said, "it must have been an angel."

> "Thither we hasten through these regions dim,
> But, lo, the wide wings of the Seraphim
>   Shine in the sunset! On that joyous shore
>   Our lightened hearts shall know
>   The life of long-ago:
> The sorrow-burdened past shall fade
>   Forevermore."

Saving Grace

General Sherman's mustering of his hosts for advance into Georgia gave the work a new impetus in April 1864. At Ringgold, Georgia and Cleveland, Tennessee, very remarkable revivals began among the veteran troops. Reverend E. P. Smith, Pastor of Congregational Church, Pepperell, Massachusetts, who served as General Field Agent of the Christian Commission, writes of the revival at Ringgold in *Annals, U.S. Christian Commission,* 490-491:

The crowded church every night, the full morning meetings for inquirers of the way of life, the prayer meetings established in the soldiers' huts, and even out on the picket-post—all these things testify to such magnificent grace and the power of God so rarely exhibited. A Kentucky soldier, one of the most ungodly men in his regiment, had spent the night in prayer and found no relief. In the morning, he met his chaplain on his horse and asked him to pray for him. The chaplain promised to do so but the man said, "I mean now."

"What, here in the road?"

"Yes, *here*, Chaplain, *now*."

They knelt and prayed and others who were passing came and knelt until there were more than two or three agreeing in the petition that the sinful one should be forgiven and the answer came. The soldier went down to his tent and carried the Word of Life to his comrades. When pressed upon them so earnestly and persistently by their fellow soldier, they could not resist the claims of a changed life. He told of his trials with his profane tent mates and of the agreement they had made that if they persisted in calling in their comrades for cards, then he should have the tent every other night for a prayer meeting. The result was the prayer meeting supplanted the cards altogether and all in the tent and many men in the company came with the new disciple to his Master.

Glorious Work of Grace in Revival

Mr. William Reynolds continues the telling of this account of the revival in the early months of 1864:

Words are inadequate to describe the glorious work of grace. We found about ten thousand troops encamped at Ringgold, Georgia but only three chaplains. In our labors with these chaplains, we experienced the full sweetness of the truth, "Behold, how good and how pleasant it is for brethren to dwell together in unity." We made arrangements for holding two daily meetings, at 1:00 and 7:00 P.M. At the night meeting, the church was crowded to overflowing—not a foot of standing room unoccupied. The doors and windows were filled and the crowds extended out into the street with men straining their ears to catch the words of Jesus. Sometimes hundreds of persons would go away unable to get within hearing distance. Day after day, the interest deepened and large numbers came forward nightly for prayer. Scores of men, long hardened in sin, cried out, "What shall we do?"

Following Jesus in the Ordinances

A number of the converts had never been baptized and, as they expressed a desire to remember this command of Christ, we invited all candidates for baptism to meet at the church on Sunday afternoon, April 10th. Forty-four presented themselves. In this number, several denominations were represented and were, of course, allowed to select the mode of baptism they preferred. Twenty-four chose immersion, eighteen sprinkling, and two pouring. We marched in solemn procession to the tune and hymn,

"There is a fountain filled with blood,"

down to the Chickamauga Creek. The soldiers stood on the banks, joining hands and continuing the hymn, while their comrades went down into the water. Some were immersed, some were sprinkled, and others had pouring but all came for baptism in the name of the Father, and of the Son, and of the Holy Spirit. After administering the ordinance, we returned to the church, singing,

"Jesus, I my cross have taken."

Afterward, we sat down, about four hundred in number, at the table of our common Lord. We used commissary bread, currant wine, tin plates and tin cups—these were the circumstances of the Lord's Supper in the army. But they did not keep the Master from the feast of love, nor hinder the baptism of the Spirit upon these men, whom God was making ready for four months of marching and battle. It was a blessed communion. For many soldiers, it was the first they had enjoyed for two years. For others, it would be the last, until that day when they shall "drink it new in the Father's Kingdom." The following Sunday, forty-eight were baptized—twenty-seven by immersion and twenty-one by sprinkling. The next Sunday, the ordinance was administered to fifty-seven more and four hundred new converts sat down at the communion table.

(William Reynolds)

Absence of Divisions

As I was leaving Ringgold, some of the soldiers came to me and said they had had a little discussion about my church connection. I asked the leader of the company what he thought.

"Well," he said, "I think you are a Methodist."

"Why, so?" I asked.

"Because you ask people to come to the 'anxious bench.'"

I asked another what he thought. He responded, "I think you are a Baptist, because you and Chaplain Nash are friends. I've no ticed you around with him a good deal."

When asked, the third answered, "I think you are a Presbyterian because you stand up when you pray."

I happened to be a Presbyterian. But it was a curious and striking instance of how men put off their signs of division in the presence of the great work of the Lord.

(William Reynolds)

Tangible Fruits of Revival

Reverend E. P. Smith, Pastor of Congregational Church, Pepperell, Massachusetts and General Field Agent of the Christian Commission, writes of a similar pouring forth of the Holy Spirit at Cleveland, Tennessee during the early months of 1864:

The Fourth Army Corps quartered here, waiting for marching orders. A marvelous revival began just before these orders came. At one Sunday service, Chaplain Raymond, alluding to the terrible scenes that lay before the army and for the need of a better Christian life, said, "I want to be a better Christian. All of you in this congregation, who will join me in this solemn rededication, rise."

The first man on his feet was Major General Howard, Commander of the Corps. His staff stood up around him and all in the house who loved the Savior soon followed. From that hour, the solemnity of our meetings deepened and the work grew until hundreds were converted.

Results of Revival

At the service that night, an invitation was given to all who were ready to become Christians to raise their hand. Near the pulpit, the hand of a muscular Wisconsin soldier went up so promptly—before the invitation was even finished—and so vigorously that he attracted everyone's attention. This was his last meeting at Cleveland. He was called to duty and could not attend again before the grand move began.

In the autumn, four months after the Cleveland meetings and when "Atlanta was ours and fairly won," a ward master came hastily into our quarters at Nashville. He asked for a minister to come to Hospital No. 12 at once. I followed him back and he showed me a cot on which one of his men lay dying. It was the boy from Cleveland, the one from Wisconsin. He said, "I want some Christian friend to come and take my last words of holy trust for my parents in Milwaukee. It'll be such a comfort to them, you know, sir."

It was hard to look at that face and head and sense that the boy would surely die—eighteen years of age, an only child, as fine an eye and form as you would find in a brigade of men. I turned involuntarily to the nurse to ask if there was any hope. "None at all, sir. The doctors have all given him up."

Then, I turn again to the dying man and lose all my regrets. His large hazel eyes swim in tears, as he smiles and replies, "Yes, I am ready. My papers are made out and I shall be discharged tonight."

Then he told me of his conversion and how he went out of that Cleveland meeting dedicated to God, how God had kept and blest him all through the marches and fights to Atlanta. He told me how, in the siege of that city, he was wounded and his leg amputated. Since then, he had been thinking what he could do as a one-legged Christian until he had learned, within the last few days, that he could never get well and had grown to be perfectly willing to die in that hospital. Reference to his home in Wisconsin, to his father's plans for him, and to how his mother had been counting the days until his term should expire made the tears come afresh. But he dashed them away and said, "It's all right—all right. Ever since that meeting, it's all right."

I was about to pray when he said, "Don't forget to thank God for Cleveland."

He did not die that night but, two days later, I found his cot empty and inquired of the nurse how he died. "Oh, very happy, sir," she said. "He prayed and sang and said the Bible all to himself. His last words we didn't understand. Maybe he was getting flighty in his mind."

"What were they?"

"Cleveland—Jesus. Cleveland—Jesus."
(E. P. Smith)

Dying Soldier Leads Surgeon to Conversion

Mr. Reynolds tells of a conversation with a brigade surgeon during the revival at Cleveland, Tennessee in the early months of 1864:

"Surgeons, anyhow, ought to be Christians," he said. "I never felt the necessity of being one so much as at the battle of Chickamauga. A number of men were brought into a tent where we were amputating limbs and probing wounds. Examining one poor fellow, I was obliged to tell him he could live but a few minutes. He turned and looked at me and said, 'Surgeon, are you a Christian?'

"I had to confess I was not.

"'Is there a Christian here?' he asked. No one responded.

"'I want some Christian to pray with me before I die.'

"'Are you a Christian?' I inquired.

"Oh, yes, sir. I am a Christian but I would so like to have someone pray with me before I go away to be with Jesus. O Surgeon, won't you pray?'

"The pleading of the dying man was more than I could resist. I knelt down beside him and offered up a heartfelt prayer to God. I don't know much about such things," added the surgeon musingly, "but that prayer has had a most marked influence on my life ever since. The soldier died within a few minutes after its close."

Best Soldiers Were Christians

Just on the eve of the advance to Atlanta, this incident, told by the General Field Agent of the Christian Commission, Reverend E. P. Smith, occurred at Ringgold, Georgia:

In the midst of one of our soldiers' prayer meetings, the adjutant of a Kentucky regiment came in and told the leader that he was ordered to pick eleven men and a sergeant from the regiment, to go on special and perilous duty in Nickajack Gap.

"They must be the best men in the regiment," said the adjutant, looking over the congregation. His eye finally rested upon the front seat. There he found the men he needed. All of them were Christians and were close to the "front" of the prayer meeting—they were the soldiers for special and perilous service.

Historical Context:

On May 6, 1864, General Sherman, leading an army of 100,000 men, left his winter encampments near Chattanooga. At Dalton, Georgia, he used a flank movement to force Johnston, the Confederate commander, to turn and order his troops to fall back rapidly to Resaca. After some severe fighting, this place was also evacuated on May 16th. Johnston's retreat, with a temporary halt at Cassville, continued until he reached the shelter of the Allatoona Mountain. Continual skirmishing took place until June 1st, when Sherman made another flank movement to the left. Once more, this compelled the enemy to leave their strong position, only to take up a new and formidable line along Kenesaw, Pine, and Lost Mountains. After incessant fighting, the latter two were abandoned but a direct and fierce assault upon Kenesaw on June 27th failed. The inevitable flank movement compelled its evacuation on July 2nd.

About a week later, Johnston, with his army safely within the strong entrenchments of Atlanta, was replaced by General J. B. Hood. On July 20th and 22nd, this officer's first movements were fierce attacks on the left side of our overly confident advancing forces. These attacks, though repulsed, showed that Atlanta was not to be won easily. A week later, Hood attacked our right and, again, was repelled significantly. Unable to keep accept defeat, he sent nearly all of his cavalry under Wheeler into Sherman's rear. This only gave Sherman the opportunity to push Brigadier General Kilpatrick forward to destroy the enemy's communications temporarily. Then, on August 25th and the succeeding days, Sherman was able to raise the siege and throw his entire army, except for the Twentieth Corps, into the rear of Atlanta. Hood, completely outgeneraled, abandoned his stronghold about the 1st of September. Subsequently, our army rested after their well-earned victory.

Continuous Ministry

Reverend Dr. J. P. Thompson, Pastor of Broadway Tabernacle Congregational Church, New York City, writing to the *Boston Congregationalist*, tells the story of work following the Battle of Resaca, May 13-15. 1964:

About 3:00 A.M. on Sunday, May 15, 1864, we came upon the campfires of our forces, gloomily lighting the forests. After an hour-long nap on the ground, I was awakened by the sound of cannon. In front of the tent, a soldier, smelling of death, had just been brought in. Tents, filled with wounded and dying men, were all around. Already the hospital tents of the various army corps were set up at intervals over a span of six miles.

Mounting our wagons, we drove from corps to corps, depositing supplies at each hospital, comforting the wounded, and speaking words of Christian consolation. What scenes of horror and anguish did that day reveal! Men, lying in scores upon their beds of straw, were bleeding from ghastly wounds and awaiting the surgeon's care. Others were brought in intermittently on stretchers from the field. Six corpses lay ready for burial off to the side. A heap of limbs and body parts marked the operating tent, where the knife of the surgeon was always busy.

Strange sights and scenes and labors for a Sunday. Yet, somehow, the Master seemed nearer than ever before. He truly was the Conqueror of Death, the sympathizing Savior, the everywhere-present and all-sufficient Friend. And to do some little kindness in His name meant everything to the men. To give a cup of cold water or some timely nutrition or a fragrant orange, to adjust a bandage or soothe a weary head or write a message for the loved ones back home, to speak some brief word of hope and cheer—was not this doing *His* work?

Mother's Prayers Reach the Battlefield

"How kind you Northern people are!" said a tall, stalwart Tennessean as I stooped to comfort him. "I used to have a prejudice against you but, since I have been in the army and have seen what you do for the soldiers, I think you are a wonderful people."

He had been shot through the cheek and the blood oozed from his mouth and nostrils with every effort to speak.

"You Tennesseans," I said, "deserve all we can do for you."

"As for that, I made up my mind that people who wanted protection must first protect themselves."

I spoke to him of Christ.

"Ah," he said, "I have been a wicked man, a very wicked man, but it has been hard for me to wade through my mother's prayers." And when I showed him the freeness of salvation, he pressed my hand and thanked me again and again. (J. P. Thompson)

Wounded for a Good Cause

A young Kentuckian beckoned me to his side and welcomed me with a big smile. He said, "I professed Christ before I entered the army and have tried to live near Him. I feel Him near me now."

"How badly are you wounded?"

"Seriously, in the thigh but I hope not mortally." He continued, *"But it is a good cause to be wounded in."*
(J. P. Thompson)

Raising Spirits

A young man whose arm had been amputated at the shoulder asked Reverend Jonathan M. Holmes, Pastor of sses in Virginia. "Good," they said in one accord, "that pays for all we've suffered."
(J. P. Thompson)

Practical Explanation of Faith

Brother Holmes and I ventured down to the very front where the battle was raging. We sat down near the line of battle with a group of men who were awaiting their turn to go into the fight and had some earnest, manly, faithful talk about the one needful thing:

"Boys, you believe in Sherman down here, don't you?"

"That's so!"

"You believe in Grant, too, don't you?"

"Yes, indeed, anything for Grant."

"Well, that is faith. And we want you to feel the same way toward the Lord Jesus Christ and put your whole soul into His hands and go into this battle loving and trusting Him."

"Well, now's a time for the soldier to feel pretty solemn," said one. And so we talked on to men who, in the next hour, might look death in the face.
(J. P. Thompson)

Helping a Father bury his Son

Returning, we saw a newly-dug grave. It was for a Michigan boy of eighteen who had been shot down at the side of his father who was also a private in the same company. The father sat beside the grave, carving his boy's name upon a crude headboard. The boy was his firstborn. I took him by the hand and expressed my heartfelt concern for him. I then offered a prayer and Brother Holmes followed with appropriate words. There was no coffin but a few pieces of board were laid in the bottom of the grave between the body and the bare ground.

"Wrap him in this blanket," said the father. "It is one his sister sent him. Ah, me, how will they bear it at home? What will his poor mother do? She must have a lock of his hair."

I stooped to cut the lock with my penknife when a soldier came forward with a pair of scissors from his sewing kit. My heart blessed the Sunday school child who had made that timely gift. And so, having rendered the last duties of faith and affection, we laid the brave boy in his grave as the cannon were still roaring doom on others, young and brave—ones we had just left on the field.
(J. P. Thompson)

Thinking First of Others

An incident of the fighting before the battle at Resaca, May 13-15, 1864, is told by Mr. Arthur Lawrence, of Boston. It seems worthy to take a high place in history:

Two of us picked up a man to carry him off the field. A shell had struck him in the mouth, tearing an awful wound, which was bleeding profusely. I offered the poor fellow a drink from my tin cup—a shiny, new one I had brought from Chattanooga. From looking at the man, one would not have guessed that he could have had any thoughts beyond his pain and what would help it. It is well-known that the first sensation after such a wound is one of intense thirst. Yet the soldier refused to drink. When I asked him why, he responded, "My mouth's all bloody, sir, and it might make the tin cup bad for the others."

He was "only a private," rough and dusty with the battle, but the answer was one which the Chevalier Bayard, the knight *sans peur et sans reproche* or "without fear and without reproach," or Sir Philip Sydney at Zutphen had not equaled when they gave utterance to the words which have made their names immortal.

Experiences with a Powerful Person

The army halted one Sunday in Kingston after the victory at Resaca, May 13-15, 1864. The General Field Agent, Reverend E. P. Smith gives the following narrative, taken from *Annals, U. S. Christian Commission*, 498-501:

When we found that the army was scheduled to be at rest on the Sabbath, arrangements were made in the different brigades for each preaching delegate to hold two or three services. I had an appointment in the Baptist church in the morning and another at General Howard's headquarters in the woods in the afternoon.

The church had not been cleaned since being occupied as a Confederate hospital. The sexton, who agreed to put the house in order on Saturday afternoon, had failed me. Then, only an hour before the service was to begin, I discovered that another man I had paid to clean the place on Sunday morning had served me in the same way. It was too late to look for help so I took off my ministerial coat and, for one hour with the mercury at ninety degrees, I worked with all my might. I began by sweeping out the straw, clearing the rubbish from the pulpit, and throwing the bunks out the window. After I pitched the old seats down from the loft, arranged them in order on the floor, and dusted the whole house twice, it was time for the service.

I sprang up into the belfry because the rope had been cut away. And with some pretty vigorous strokes of the clapper, I told the people around that the hour for worship had arrived. Dropping down again through the scuttle upon the vestibule floor, a treacherous nail ripped away a noticeable part of one leg of my pants. It was my only suit I had brought to the front and while I was pondering how I should present myself before the congregation, a corporal and two others with bayonets arrived from General Sherman's headquarters to assist me in my decision. Not twenty yards away, the corporal shouted, "Did you ring the bell?"

"I did."

"I am ordered to arrest you."

"For what?"

"To bring you to General Sherman's headquarters."

"But, Corporal, I can't see the General in this plight. I am an Agent of the Christian Commission and am to preach here this morning and was ringing the bell for service. If you will tell the General how it is, it will be all right."

"That's not the order, sir."

"Well, Corporal, send a guard with me to my quarters so I can wash up and pin together this tear."

"That's not the order, sir—fall in."

Without hat or coat and with a gaping hole in my wardrobe, I was led away by the Corporal and followed by the two bayonets all the way to headquarters. General Corse, the Chief of Staff, who was standing beside General Sherman, received me. Without waiting for charges or questions, I said, "General, I belong to the Christian Commission. We are to have service in the church across the way and I was ringing the bell."

As I entered the headquarters, General Sherman was drumming with his thumb and finger on the window sill. When the Corporal announced his prisoner, Sherman fixed his cold gray eye on me for a moment and motioned to his Chief to attend to the case. Without moving a muscle on his face, he resumed his drumming and his Sunday problem—how to flank Johnston out of the Allatoona Mountains.

"Is this Sunday?" General Corse replied. "Some mischievous soldiers alarmed the people by ringing the bell earlier and an order was issued against it. But we were not aware this was Sunday. There is no harm done. At what hour is the service?" With a motion of his hand, he discharged my guard.

This extra duty as sexton and obedience to the Corporal's "order," made it necessary to procure a substitute pulpiteer for the morning. The delegate who preached reported an interested congregation and, among them, representatives from headquarters.

Attending Worship with Union Generals

In the afternoon I rode over to the Fourth Corps four miles away. General Howard had notified the surrounding regiments of the service. Two of his Division commanders were present, along with Brigadier General Harker, whose promotion was so recent that the star had not yet replaced the eagle on his shoulder. This was the last Sunday service, which this manly, modest, and gallant officer ever attended.

Five weeks later, in the charge at Kenesaw Mountain, he was shot dead. Of that Sunday in the woods, I shall never forget the earnest attention of all to the theme: "The safety of those who do their duty, trusting in God." I shall never forget the hearty responses of the Christian men and the full chorus in singing the closing hymn,

"When I can read my title clear."
(E. P. Smith)

Preaching by Major General O. O. Howard

However, the most effective sermon of the day was given by Major General O. O. Howard, Commander of the Corps. He spoke from the piazza of his headquarters, surrounded by his staff, his Division commanders, and other general officers. Nothing could be more natural than the turn of the conversation upon religious topics. The General spoke of the Savior—his great love for Him and his peace in serving Him—as freely and simply as he could have spoken to his own family. He related instances of Christian trust, devotion, and triumph. Speaking of the high calling of chaplains and the importance of always being with their regiments at the front, he told us of his visit to Newton's Division Hospital the night after the battle of Resaca. There he found a smooth-faced boy who would not live until morning. He knelt down on his blanket and asked if there was anything he wanted done for him.

"Yes, I want somebody to tell me how to find the Savior."

"I never felt my ignorance so much before," said the General. "Here was a mind now ready to hear and act on the truth. What if I should give him wrong directions? How I wished I had a minister's training."

He then told us what directions he gave the boy and the prayer he offered. He described the boy's smile and peace. He appealed to me and then to his generals for reassurance that what he had said was both right and beautiful. And so, under the pressure unconsciously applied by their superior officer, his Division commanders, with lips unused to such confession, acknowledged the power and grace of God.
(E. P. Smith)

Dying Man with Undying Faith

Reverend E. P. Smith, Pastor of Congregational Church, Pepperell, Massachusetts, and General Field Agent of the Christian Commission, tells a story of hospital work in Kingston, following the May 13-15, 1864 battle at Resaca, Georgia:

Kingston was overflowing with sick and wounded. The men were in a most deplorable condition. Shelter tents were hastily erected to accommodate them. Late one afternoon, I was summoned to see Captain Burke, of the 37th Regiment, who appeared to be mortally wounded. It did not take long to discover he was a devout Christian. He asked me to telegraph his wife about his condition, imploring me to break the news to her gently and not to say that his wound was mortal. He also spoke to me freely of his past life and of the slight hope that he would survive his wound.

I asked, "Captain, how does it seem to you to be stricken down, with all your prospects and hope for the future cut short here in Georgia? Isn't it hard for you to give up life and leave your family at your age?"

"It has come upon me suddenly," was his answer "but I feel prepared for it. I have lived close to my Savior in the army and tried to keep my accounts square every night."

He did not die as soon as we at first expected but lived to travel as far as Nashville, where his wife came to nurse him. The few months, during which he lingered, confirmed my first impressions at Kingston. He had, indeed, lived close to Christ and kept his accounts square. As he grew weak, his mind sometimes wavered. He would call for his comrades and seemed determined to go to them.

His wife could always calm him by saying, "My dear, Jesus is here. That is all you want."

Sweetly and assuredly, he always replied, "You are right, wife. That is all I want—all I want."

Dying with God's Grace

Following the battle at Resaca, Georgia, May 13-15, 1864, the army eventually moved from Kingston after a general hospital had been established further on. The men who were too badly wounded to be taken to the rear remained at Kingston—many of them to die there. Reverend E. P. Smith, General Field Agent of the Christian Commission, gives an account of a day's work among them upon his return to Chattanooga in *Annals, U. S. Christian Commission*, 501-503:

Coming back from the front, I learned that the delegates had left Kingston and that there was no chaplain in either of the two hospitals. It had been two weeks since the hard fight on the right by the Fourth and Twentieth Corps and I knew it must be the time for many of the wounded to die. They must not die alone so I determined to forego business at Chattanooga and stop over.

Many of the men were mortal cases. Four or five, I was sure, would not live twenty-four hours. One was too far gone to converse. Nothing could be done but to write to his little daughter, the only surviving member of his family, according to one of his comrades. Another man could only speak by nods and the squeezing of his hand. By this means of communicating, I learned that he was waiting peacefully to die. As I prayed at his cot for his wife and children, his "amen" came often and fervently through the squeezing of my hand. He slept in the night and awakened in heaven. Another was seeking the Savior and ventured to trust in Him before he died.

Attending the Dying

Another, an Indiana soldier, sent for me in the night. He was dying—a boy of eighteen years. His leg had been cut off by a shell and amputation had removed all chances of recovery.

He was a Sunday school boy. He wanted me to take his last words home to his mother and sister: "Poor mother, how she will take on! Tell her not to cry for me. I love Jesus. I put all my trust in Him. When you prayed with me this afternoon, I felt my soul going right out to Him. Tell my sister not to fret for me. I have done the best I could for my country and, now, I want them to meet me in heaven. Tell my sister to be sure and hold out faithful."

He gave me his memorandum and pocketbook and a number of keepsakes. He asked me to pull the two rings from his hand and send them to his sister and to tell her that they were taken off after his hand was getting cold. After prayer we sang,

"There is a fountain filled with blood."

He joined in, breaking the tune now and then, saying, "Yes, yes, if he could trust Him, I can." "Yes, *when* I die." "That *will* be sweeter." "Power to save. Power to save. I used to sing that hymn at home but it was never so good as now. Power to save."

I gave him my hand for good-bye. He drew me down for a kiss and then decided Mrs. George must have one also, and finally the nurse. Incidentally, Mrs. George volunteered as a nurse to the Indiana soldiers during the war. When General Sherman reached the coast, she met "her boys" again at Wilmington, North Carolina, and there, being laid low with toil and fever, died in one of their hospitals.

Before I had passed through the ward, the nurse called me back, saying, "He wants to speak to you." When I reached the cot, he asked to see the daguerreotype pictures (an early type of photograph) in his memorandum book. I took out three and held them up, one by one. Mother came first.

DYING IN GEORGIA

"Dear mother," he said, as he took the picture in his trembling fingers, "good-bye. I wish I could see you but I am going to die in Georgia." In tears and sobbing he pressed the ambrotype to his lips—"Goodbye. Good-bye."

He takes the next: "Sister, dear sister, don't fret for me. I'll see you again. Only be faithful. Goodbye, dear sister, goodbye," and he presses the glass with his dying kiss.

He gazes upon the next one with unutterable longing. His lips quiver and his whole frame shakes. He calls no name. He kisses it over and over and holds it under his hand near his heart. I put my mouth close to his ear and whispered, "This is hard."

"Yes, it is hard. I would like to go home but I am content."

"You are dying now before you are twenty years old. Are you sorry you ever enlisted?"

He looked at me steadily. His sobbing ceased and, with a firm, deliberate tone, he said, "Not a bit. I was glad when I enlisted and I am glad now. I am willing to die for my country."

The scene that occurred at midnight cannot be described. The patients in the ward who could walk gathered around. Others, in their beds, propped themselves up on an elbow. The nurses congregated. One of them, at the head of the cot, held the single candle in the ward. We had prayer, sang a hymn, and gave the last message. We said goodbye, took leave of his family, and consecrated this soldier unto death on the altar of country. These things fill a blessed page in my memory that I cannot possibly transfer to you.
(E. P. Smith)

Setting Aside Good Works in Finding Christ by Faith Alone

Reverend H. McLeod, Pastor of Congregational Church, Brentwood, New Hampshire, recalls an incident of his work after Johnston was driven from the Allatoona Mountains in autumn of 1864:

Captain B_____, of an Ohio regiment, was brought in fatally wounded, yet he did not think so. He was a rare man and inspired peculiar respect in all who came into his presence. Everyone who approached his part of the ward stepped lightly and spoke softly. With his consent, I read the Twenty-third Psalm and offered a brief prayer. At parting, he took my hand and pressed it very warmly, which told me that he was either already a Christian or, at least, wished to lean on Christ. A surgeon told me that, in his opinion, he was not a Christian even though he was strictly correct in all his outward life.

I saw him several times until I had a reasonable assurance that the grace of God had brought him to know the Savior. He still expected to recover. One evening, the doctor called me hurriedly, saying the Captain wanted to see me at once. I was soon at his side. The surgeon had told him that he would scarcely live until morning. He wanted me to write three letters but he could already say, "Thy will be done." The first letter was to an elder brother. The Captain's burden was that, though both had neglected the Christian teachings of their revered grandfather and precious mother, still there was forgiveness to be found in Christ. He hoped that he himself had obtained that forgiveness and expected to meet his beloved teachers soon in heaven. Then we wrote a letter of counsel to a younger brother. I do not doubt that "Dear Charlie" will prize it, coming as it did from a dying brother's heart, as more precious than gold.

Then, with hesitation and sacredness, he gave me the name of her whom he loved above all others on earth. He was too weak to dictate now. The tender duty had been put off too long and I must do it for him, as best I could.

He said, "Tell her how much I miss her sweet voice and presence. Give my love to her excellent father and mother and ask her to say that it seems presumptuous of me to try to comfort such mature and earnest Christians."

I wrote the letter and read it to him. He was satisfied, adding a wish that he had known me sooner. I read to him the description of heaven in the Revelation 7.

"Yes, that is beautiful," he said. "'Washed and made white in the blood of the Lamb.' If it was God's will," he solemnly added, "I would like to live longer but His will be done."

Completeness in Christ

Reverend G. C. Noyes, Pastor of (N. S.) Presbyterian Church, Laporte, Indiana, adds this incident from Kingston, following the May 13-15, 1864 battle at Resaca, Georgia:

Passing from one cot to another, I came to a man whose hair and beard were gray. I spoke to him cheerfully, saying, "Your gray hair shows that you ought to be a soldier of Jesus, not a soldier of the government."

He landed first on the imputation in the last part of my remark. He said, "I don't think, sir, any man in my regiment has done the government more faithful service than I. I never lost a day to sickness."

"How old are you?"

"Fifty-two. And my term of three years expires September 12th.

"What is your injury?"

Turning down the covers, I saw that his right arm was amputated close to the shoulder, his right leg close to the knee. He had been shot in the leg before Atlanta on August 7th. As he was being borne from the field, another ball struck him in the arm.

"Giving an arm and a leg for the country," he said, "is no great gift for one to whom Jesus has given all things. It is a free offering. He will accept the sacrifice and will bless all the more the cause for which it was offered up."

He had walked with the Savior for many years and I have never seen such exalted patriotism in combination with such victorious faith in Jesus. Physically, he was a mutilated man, yet "complete in Christ Jesus." He was "mustered out" by the death angel on September 7th, five days before his term of service would have expired. I doubt not that, with all wounds and hurts mended, he is now resting at his heavenly home.

Thoughts Turning toward Home

The General Field Agent of the Christian Commission, Reverend E. P. Smith, reminisces about two incidents from Kingston, following the May 13-15, 1864 battle at Resaca, Georgia, a part of the record of the Atlanta campaign:

A soldier came into our rooms in Nashville to get an envelope. He said he had a letter to send home for one of his comrades. He drew a small, carefully wrapped package from his shirt. Opening it, he held up a scrap of paper from a memorandum book. It had bloody fingerprints on it and a few words hastily written with a pencil. The writer said he was the soldier's "partner." In the charge on Kenesaw Mountain, he found him staggering back from the line, blood streaming from his mouth and covering his hands and clothes. A minie ball had cut off his tongue at the root. He tried to speak but could not. Finally, by motioning, he made his partner understand his need—paper and

THE LAST LETTER

pencil. A scrap was torn from the diary. On it, the boy, while being held up by his comrade and with fingers dripping in blood and trembling in death, wrote,

"Father, meet me in heaven."

He tried to write his name but it was too late. Life had fled. Where the name should have been was a faint, irregular, vanishing line. And thus do the thoughts of our soldiers—whether waking, dreaming, or dying—turn ever homeward.

Thoughts Turning toward Mother

After we had occupied Atlanta, a nurse sent for a delegate to see a man who was about to die in one of the warehouse hospitals. The delegate found a young man of Christian upbringing but struggling with painful doubts as to the truth of the Bible and the way of salvation through Christ. He wanted to believe but could not. The delegate had frequent conversations with him but seemed to make no progress in his attempts to lead him to the Savior.

One night, the soldier called the nurse and asked him to set a candle at the foot of the bed, so that the light might strike upon a "Silent Comforter" banging on the wall. The page that had been turned for that day bore the verse: "Whoso cometh unto Me, I will in no wise cast out." Early the next morning, the soldier again sent for the delegate and asked him to feel under his pillow for a letter from his mother. It was an affectionate entreaty to her son to accept Christ. As the delegate read, he came to the words, "Whoso cometh unto Me, I will in no wise cast out."

"There," said the sick man, "that's what I want. I thought mother said that. Read it again." It was read once again.

"Mother says that, does she?"

"Yes, and it's in the Bible too?"

"Yes."

"Then it must be true. Jesus will receive me. I will come to Him. Here, Lord, I give myself up."

So far as it could be determined from the few days of his remaining earthly experience, he made a genuine surrender of the will to his Lord.
(E. P. Smith)

CHAPTER XI

THE EASTERN ARMIES

FROM THE INVESTMENT OF PETERSBURG UNTIL THE CLOSE OF THE WAR

June 1864–April 1865

The movements to get into Petersburg before the main body of Lee's army could arrive to defend it proved to be unsuccessful. The Confederates repulsed two assaults, on June 16th and 18th, with heavy Union loss. The most that could be done was to extend the flanks of the army—on the north, along the James River toward Richmond, and on the south, toward the Weldon railroad. At the end of July, Lee's withdrawal of five divisions of his army to the north of the James to counter the attacks against Fort Darling gave Union troops the opportunity to explode a mine in front of Burnside's Corps. A Confederate fort was blown up but the succeeding assault was a failure.

Two weeks later, both flanks were extended again. This time, General Warren took and held the Weldon road. At the close of September and beginning of October, Warren's lines were extended again to the south and General Butler captured Fort Harrison, an important Confederate defense, to the north of the James. This bloody campaign closed with the movement of October 27th, in which all the forces that could be spared from the trenches were thrown against the enemy lines defending Hatcher's Run and the Boydton plank-road. Our forces had the advantage in the fighting but prudence dictated against holding the long, thin line. By November 1st, the army was in about in the same position it held before the movement.

A relative quiet followed, except for a permanent extension of the flank to Hatcher's Run in February 1865 until Lee's attempt to cut our army in two by a well-planned but poorly executed assault on Fort Steelman in March. Immediately following, General Grant began his final movements, which brought about the evacuation of Petersburg and Richmond on Sunday, April 2nd. One week later, the Confederate "Army of Northern Virginia" surrendered.

Starting the Ministry

The incidents, which occurred during this period, are of such a character that they are grouped with less regard to the order of their occurrence than what we have done in previous chapters. Reverend E. F. Williams, Pastor of Congregational Church, Whitinsville, Massachusetts, presents an account of the history of the beginning of the Christian Commission's work in its new circumstances:

In early May 1864, Mr. J. R. Miller, along with a large corps of delegates, established a station at Bermuda Hundred, outside Richmond, Virginia. This group worked among General Butler's army. Their work included two hospitals here and a number of batteries without army chaplains. At Point of Rocks, four miles up the Appomattox River, a hospital was established, which remained throughout the duration of war. From Bermuda Hundred, we visited the wounded of Sheridan's Cavalry and distributed large quantities of supplies to them. When the Eighteenth Corps went to White House Landing, Mr. Miller and his corps of delegates accompanied them and established a station, which did so much to relieve the wounded.

Delegates and supplies reached City Point, Virginia on June 15, 1864. Immediately, they established a station, which existed for more than a year. As they entered the army, delegates reported here and received supplies. Supply wagons for the front were almost always waiting in front of the warehouse. In short, this was the Commission's business center and continued as such until the fall of Richmond. It was a religious centre as well. Chaplains, officers, surgeons, stewards, gunboat commandants—all gathered here to ask and to receive.

Hearts Turned toward Home

Mr. Ludlow Thomas, of New York City, writing in July from the General Hospital at City Point, Virginia, had this to say about incidents connected with physical relief in the summer of 1864:

I found the boys very anxious to write home. Some had paid the exorbitant sum of forty cents for a sheet of paper and envelope. Pens, ink, and pencils were scarce, so I cut pencils in half and distributed these. I told the boys to write their letters in pencil and I would ink the addresses for them. The first day, I directed and mailed more than eighty letters. For many of the poor fellows, too badly wounded to hold a pencil, I sat on the ground alongside of them and penned letters for them. Many of these epistles proved to be their last. At first, they wanted me to compose the letters for them but I told them it would be much better for them to dictate, that such a letter would please their families far more than a stranger's. They knew that everything said would be held in confidence and some of those messages home were most touching. Not a few of the letters were wet with the tears of the amanuensis.

When it was possible, I always had them sign their own names and often held up the poor fellows to do it. One time, I gave a pencil to a man to sign his name and, seeing that he was rather slow, I turned to talk to another soldier, so as not to embarrass him. When I came back I saw that the grateful boy's delay was caused by his adding a note himself. With a trembling hand, he wrote, "This letter was written for me by an angel of the Christian Commission."

Intense Labor in Ministry

Mr. Walter S. Carter, of Milwaukee, Wisconsin, gives this account of relief work on the extreme right, just after the taking of Fort Harrison (later renamed Fort Burnham to honor the Union General, killed in the battle) in Virginia:

On the afternoon of September 30, 1864, I was accompanied by Reverend Dr. Philip Schaff, of the German Reformed Church and Secretary of the New York Sabbath Committee, Reverend L. E. Charpiot, Pastor of Congregational Church, Stratford, Connecticut, and several others. Dr. Schaff, incidentally, authored the 8-volume set, *History of the Christian Church.* We left Point of Rocks Hospital and headed for the front of the Army of the James. A large four-horse Commission wagon, loaded down with supplies, led the way.

Emerging from the woods into an open field near the James River, we heard the rapid discharge of artillery, intermingled with the continuous crash of musketry, which alerted us to a renewal of the contest from the day before. We hurried along and arrived at Aiken's Landing about 5:00 on Wednesday evening and crossed the river on the muffled pontoon thrown over by the Eighteenth Corps. Pushing on up the Varina road, we soon came to the skirmish line held by the enemy when, suddenly, our forces advanced. A little further on, we came to another line, stronger but not yet completed.

Entering a forest of thick pine, night and rain overtook us. Ahead of us was a long line of army wagons, behind us were the ambulances. Every moment, a horseman dashed past us—some toward the front, others towards the rear. In the woods and on either side, our men were kindling fires to dry their clothes and make their coffee. Moving along, we finally turned to the right and entered the ample grounds of the Cox mansion, where we found the flying hospital already established.

The yard was full of tents, filled with wounded men—officers of all grades and privates, Union and Confederate, white and black soldiers. Hundreds had already arrived and more were constantly arriving. From every quarter, moans of agony and cries for help could be heard but there were none to answer them. Every soldier who had gone through the two days' of terrible conflict unharmed was standing that dark, rainy autumn night without food or drink. He faced the foe in the trenches a mile ahead of us. The surgeons had prepared their operating tables and were already at their awful task.

Getting permission from Dr. Richardson, Surgeon in charge, we immediately pitched our tent for work. An adjoining house was sought, a fire built, a large kettle of water heated, and coffee made by the gallon. Condensed milk and sugar were added. With filled pails, tin cups, and lanterns, our seven delegates went forth on their errand into every tent until every wounded man was abundantly supplied. Boxes were filled with fresh, soft crackers and again we made the circuit of the tents and the men helped themselves to all they needed. Then we carried more coffee around and, after that, in cases where we thought necessary, Jamaica ginger or brandy was given to the men. Then we made another visit with a supply of shirts and drawers for those who needed them.

"We never expected such treatment as this," said a wounded Confederate to a delegate.

"Give me your name so that, when the war is over, I can come to see you and thank you better than I can now," said another.

Exhausting Work of Ministry

Engaged in such a work, the hours went by unnoticed—seven, eight, nine, ten, eleven, twelve, and one were gone before we even tried to sleep. Going into the house, we wrapped our blankets about us and were hardly on the floor when word came that twenty more ambulances, loaded with wounded, had arrived. We rose immediately and again made all the rounds of distribution to the sufferers. Making a second attempt to get a little rest, we were hardly asleep when the surgeon came to inform us that the enemy would probably renew the attack at daylight and that we were within range of their shells. Immediately, we struck our tent, loaded our supplies, and, by the time the army train was about to move, our wagon was in its place in the line. (Walter S. Carter)

Shrewd and Calculating Ministry

The ways in which the men might be helped were almost without number. Reverend J. Gordon Carnachan, Pastor of (O. S.) Presbyterian Church, Troy, Bradford County, Pennsylvania, writing in October, tells of one:

Bill D_____ was a private in the 91st Pennsylvania Volunteers. He was a young lad of about seventeen, somewhat thoughtless, and, I regret to say, given to card playing. Several times, I had reasoned with him about it. One time, I even threatened to report him if I caught him at it again, as this amusement was particularly forbidden in the wards of the Fifth Corps Hospital.

One day he accosted me and asked, "Say, Chaplain, could you get this changed for me?" while handing me a hundred dollar Treasury note with coupons attached.

"Oh yes," I answered, taking it "but what do you want change for, Bill?"

"Well, you know a fellow wants something to spend and this is of no use to me as it is."

"Well, I can get it changed for you," I said. But his card playing propensities recurred to me and, hoping to have a short talk with him, I sat down on the bed close by. In a roundabout way, I got him to talk about his mother, about his younger brother and sisters, about the Sunday school he had attended, and about home affairs in general. I could see he was in a softened mood.

At last, he said, "Well, Chaplain, read that and tell me if you think there is a better mother in the world than mine." He then handed me a letter he had just received from home.

I had Bill just where I wanted him and, handing him back the letter, I said, "I tell you what, Bill, the very best thing you can do with this Treasury note" (I had held in my hand the whole time) "is to send it unchanged to this good mother of yours."

He paused a moment. Then slapping his thigh, as if it were a most wonderful, novel idea, exclaimed, "By thunder, Chaplain, it's a good thought. Send her the note."

I walked off with Bill's note in triumph, satisfied that I had made a hundred dollars for his widowed mother and, with the conviction that Bill, in spite of himself, had a streak of real goodness in him."

Excruciating Hardship in Ministry

Reverend Dr. J. M. Lowrie, Pastor of First (O. S.) Presbyterian Church, Fort Wayne, Indiana, tells the narrative of his march in December with the Fifth Corps and the First Division of the Second and Gregg's cavalry along the line of the Weldon railroad. He gives a picture of the delegates' willingness to share the soldier's hardest lot for the sake of ministering to his comfort:

Denied the privilege of taking wagons, Corps Agent Chase asked for volunteers to go on foot. Mr. E. W. Metcalf of Bangor, Maine, Mr. Lewis Morris of Brooklyn, New York, Reverend S. T. Livermore of Lowville, New York, and Reverend I. S. Schilling of Clarksburg, Virginia, and I volunteered. We had to carry our own rations and blankets, and march with the men. We were up at three o'clock on the morning of December 7, 1864 for our march through southeastern Virginia. After stowing away our five days' supply of "hard-tack," coffee and bread, were ready to start at five o'clock for the headquarters of the 3rd division of the ambulance train to which we were assigned. The march began along the Jerusalem plank-road, in the midst of a drizzling and cold rain—only a foretaste of what was to come.

Fifteen miles from camp, we reached the Nottaway River, where we were detained until dark by the laying of a pontoon bridge. We finally crossed with the First Division and went five miles further, almost to Sussex Court House, where we camped for the night. We had no tents, so all we could do was to spread some flat fence-rails in front of our fire, put our blankets on top, and try to sleep. But to the uninitiated, the soft side of fence-rails was not conducive to rest.

At two o'clock in the morning, a sudden dash of rainwater in our faces caused a hasty resurrection from our couch of rails. Before three, the bugle sounded to begin preparation for the march ahead. Before light, we joined the forward-moving columns. Passing Sussex C. H., we turned to the right and took the Weldon road at Jarrett's Station. The work of destruction here began without any serious opposition from the enemy. By the light of the burning railroad ties, we spent our second night, encamped on high ground and exposed to cold winds. We shivered through the few hours allotted for sleep.

Before light the next morning, we were moving again. The troops tore up the track, burned the ties, and bent the rails along the nearly twenty miles to the bridge at Hicksford. With three miles to go, the main army halted. The cavalry and one infantry division finished the work of destroying the railroad while repelling repeated attacks of the Confederates. We camped by the burning railroad again the third night. This time, we put pine brush under our blankets to protect ourselves from the wet ground but, soon after we lay down, it began to rain. After a while, the rain turned to sleet and freezing, so we were stiff with ice by morning. Even our fire was hardly any protection against the pitiless storm.

Daylight brought with it the order for our return march. The expedition had been a complete success and we could thoroughly appreciate the men's joy and eager willingness in preparing for the homeward march when compared to the comfort of their camps. From early morning until ten o'clock at night, we waded through the mud and wet ground, making a Sunday journey of twenty-five miles. Of our party, one gave out on the morning of the last day and another could scarcely drag himself into camp—where our brethren warmly welcomed us and tirelessly ministered to our needs.

Only a few men were wounded in the expedition, so there was little opportunity for our anticipated work. Yet, we had endless proof that our weary mission had not been in vain. It had been our privilege to drop a word of comfort to many tired and desponding men as we went along at their side. We were able to aid materially in other ways. But what affected both the officers and men the most was the sight of our sharing with them in the dangers and toils and hardship. This strengthened their confidence in the reality of our ministry and gave us credibility and authority when we spoke to them again. We had merely done our duty, yet the brave boys thought we had done much more.

Seeking Out God's People for Fellowship

It would be impossible to measure the value of little words of sympathy, which the delegate could drop as he labored. Reverend N. M. Bailey, Pastor of the Methodist Episcopal Church, Henniker, New Hampshire, wrote the following account from New Market Roads in the Army of the James in January 1865:

One day, a soldier came into our tent and sat down. He said he had come for a little talk. He was in trouble. He went through all the particulars of his case.

At the end, I said, "My dear fellow, I am very sorry but we can do nothing for you."

"I know that—I know you can't." he rejoined. "But I thought a word or two from a Christian man would help me a good deal, even if he told me he couldn't do anything."

Joy in Spite of Circumstances

Reverend H. J. Patrick, Pastor of Congregational Church, W. Newton, Massachusetts, ministered to the wounded in February 1865 after the extension of our left wing to Hatcher's Run. He tells this story of a hospital quilt:

I came to one bright countenance, that of Jonas Hefele, Company G, 94th New York. Smiling, he looked up at me from beneath a very neat bed quilt. I asked him if he had slept well.

"Oh, yes," he answered very cheerfully.

Just then, my eye caught sight of a motto on the quilt. I showed it to him and read, "'He giveth His beloved sleep.' Kennebunk, Maine, Soldiers' Aid Society." What a smile went over his happy face as he read and re-read it.

"You *must* sleep well with that motto near you," I said.

"Yes, do you know who wrote it?"

It was in a lady's hand. I told him I did not but I knew who wrote the first words. Then I spoke to him about who "the beloved" were and who it was that gave them sleep. And I could see that he was listening earnestly to every word I said.

Finding God's Truths in Harsh Circumstances

How cheerful the brave boys were—all of them. I saw one looking comically at the bullet-hole through his leg.

"Well," he said, "that's a fancy hole. Now," he continued argumentatively, "that'll get me a furlough, just what my wife wants."

Another looked up at me with tears coming out of such glad eyes. He said, "God has been very good to me. I have been thinking of His preserving care." (H. J. Patrick)

Time and Place for Humor

Mr. C. E. Bolton, a delegate in August, 1864, writes the following story:

"One day, I was attending to the needs of wounded Union and Confederate soldiers, huddled together on board the boat 'Ida.' We had stopped at City Point on the way to Fortress Monroe and I overheard a conversation between two soldiers—one Union, the other Confederate. Both had undergone amputation and the nurses were trying to place the Union soldier on a stretcher. His leg was in such a condition that they were afraid to touch it. The brave fellow himself laid hold of the stump and steadied it. He then told them to put him on the stretcher. Admiring such courage in difficulty, the Confederate said, 'Well, Yank, you're full of pluck, anyhow.' 'Yes, Johnny,' was the Union boy's answer, 'and I calculate to keep full of pluck as long as my leg is four inches longer than yours.'"

Demonstrations of Gratitude

Reverend Thos. H. Pearne, member of Portland (Oregon) Quarterly Conference, Methodist Episcopal Church, writes of the battles at Hatcher's Run, Virginia, around February 1865:

During the night and through the next day, we helped the men coming from and getting into ambulances. We gave them coffee, cereal, cordials and words of comfort and cheer. The night was bitterly cold. Some of the wounded remained in the ambulances for ten hours, scantily covered—some of them with only a single blanket. Three poor fellows, whose wounds were not necessarily fatal, died in this condition. We had about eight hundred in all to be attended to. The men were very demonstrative in gratitude.

An Irishman, whom I had assisted several times and who was shivering in the bitter cold, inquired, "Are ye a chaplain?"

"No."

"A surgeon?"

"No."

"And what be yees, then?"

"A delegate of the Christian Commission."

"I don't know much about them but I say, God bliss all the likes of yees."

Ministry of Offering Sympathy

Reverend J. H. Moore, Minister of Farm Ridge (O. S.) Presbyterian Church, Illinois, illustrates the ministry of sympathy in a letter from City Point, Virginia, in March 1865:

I have no doubt that many sick and wounded die in the hospitals from sheer lack of sympathy. One day, I called on a soldier for the first time. He had been sick for several weeks with chronic diarrhea. He did not know if he was any better, had not written to his friends and, indeed, was not able to write. He did not want anyone to write for him, nor did he even care that his friends should know he was in the hospital. He scarcely had any appetite and could not get anything he cared to eat. I drew all this information out of him by asking point blank questions, for he was too depressed even to converse. I asked him to think of something he would like to eat.

"I don't know of anything" was the despondent answer. I tempted him with the Commission's "bill of fare," dwelling in a luscious, cookery-book kind of way over several articles. A smile—very awkward it was, for the requisite muscles had been unused for so long—came into his face at last.

"I think I could eat some canned peaches, if I had them," he said. How the poor boy relished them when they were brought! Afterward, as often as I entered the tent, he always greeted me with a smile and was very ready to converse.

Caring for Families

Reverend Edward P. Smith, Pastor of Congregational Church, Pepperell, Massachusetts, served as General Field Agent for the Christian Commission. In this capacity, he had oversight of the following details:

The army was pretty generally paid toward the close of February. For the vast majority of men, access to the express offices was almost impossible. The Christian Commission undertook the task of taking what the soldiers wished to send home to the offices and returning express receipts to the men. Giving full statistics on this work would be impossible. It was very tiresome while it lasted, often keeping a "receiver" at each station busy from early morning until eight o'clock in the evening. Then all the invoices had all to be made out.

An idea of the magnitude of the transactions may be seen in the reports of several stations. At City Point Hospital, during seven weeks of March and April, $288,000 in transactions took place. From Sheridan's Cavalry, in one day at Hancock Station, $30,000 came in. In a Division of the Fifth Corps, more than $55,000 was sent home. The amounts were mostly small, usually ranging from $10 to $50, but some men sent sums far exceeding these.

In the middle of March, when marching orders were received, another service could be rendered to the men. This was expressing home the winter and extra clothing, etc., which they would not need in the prospective campaign. At City Point Hospital, during March and part of April, 3204 packages of various kinds were thus forwarded. At a station in the Fifth Corps, the value of the clothing committed to the Christian Commission was nearly $90,000. This property would have been almost certainly a complete loss to the men, if it had not been collected before their march began.

Ministry of Temporal Relief

Reverend Dr. Robert Patterson, Pastor of Reformed Presbyterian Church, Chicago, recalls an incident connected with this work:

Riding up to a prominent pine tree pole from which the stars and stripes swung, I discovered a large chapel and tent. I would have supposed I was at an express office if there had not been evidence to the contrary. Scores of soldiers had all manner of bundles, gum blankets and other gear, packed up in candle and cracker boxes, in old shirts, handkerchiefs and towels—in everything capable of containing clothing. These men were crowding around the door of a large square tent with marquee roof, bearing a flag marked "Quinnipiac Tabernacle." (This was the old Indian name for New Haven, Connecticut.) The chapel was purchased with funds from friends of the Christian Commission in that city. The seats were made of rough lumber, church-fashion, and contained several wagon loads of parcels like those which were being received outside.

Light marching orders had come and the men must leave behind overcoats, blankets, and all surplus baggage. Where should they leave them? The government made no provision for taking them to the rear. In a few hours, that camp would not have even a guard left. They knew that the Christian Commission could do almost anything, so they came and asked if we could express their clothing home to their families. General Warren was anxious to find out if this disposition of the articles might be made if possible. So from this one station, more than $40,000 worth of clothing was shipped home. I turned to one of the men waiting his turn and remarked that I didn't hear as much swearing as before.

"No, Chaplain," he said, "there ain't half the cussin' there was. But if you were down at our camp when the boys was packing up, you'd have heard a power of God blessin' for the Christian Commission doin' this here job."

Ministry of Relieving Pain

The value of the work of temporal relief was most obvious during the hot months of 1864, among the men *in the trenches*. Not only was there great possibility of being a casualty here but they also faced the extraordinary hardships brought on by sickness. The dreary sameness of the service also did much to crush the spirits of the troops assigned to it. The Commission labored hard to supply the men with a proper diet—especially fresh vegetables and we also took care of many of the wounded. The materials for letter writing were distributed extensively.

The graphic narrative of "Carleton" in a letter to the *Congregationalist*, July 29, 1864, represents a fair picture of what was to be done and how it was done at the extreme front:

The day was hot, dry, dusty and sultry. The sun shone from a brazen sky. The grass and shrubs were scorched and withered and powdered with the dust, which rose in clouds from every passing wagon. There was not air enough to stir the aspens, or shake the long, lithe spires of the pines. The birds of the forest sought the deepest shade, and lolled and panted in the heat. It was hard even for men in robust health to breathe. They picked out the coolest places and gave themselves up to the listlessness of the hour. It required an earnest effort to do anything. And yet through this blazing day, men sat crouched in the trenches from morning till night or lay in their shallow rifle pits. They watched the enemy while parched, broiled, and burned but not daring to raise their heads or lift their hands. To do so was death.

The hospital tents, though pitched in the woods, were like ovens, absorbing and holding the heat poured from a cloudless sky. Then, upon the ground lay the sick and wounded, fevered and sore, with life at ebb tide. They laid there with energies exhausted, perspiration oozing from the faces, nerves quivering and trembling with fever, and pulses faint and feeble. Their beds were boughs of pine. They lay as they came from the battlefield, wearing their soiled, torn and bloody garments of army blue. Millions of flies buzzed around.

The surgeons in charge were kind-hearted and attentive. They used every means in their power to make the patients comfortable. This was the place where the sick were to regain health or, from which, they were to be removed to the General Hospital. They were far from home and friends. There was nothing to cheer them—nothing to stimulate. Hope was dying out and despondency was setting in, with memory summoning the dear old times, and revealing, by contrast, a dark and gloomy future.

It was Sunday and there were many among the suffering hundreds who had reverenced the day at home. It was a day of rest—of cessation from toil and care. Its return recalled their former Sundays—the still hours, the pealing of church bells, the grand and solemn music of the organ, or the hum of children's voices in the Sunday school. Is it a wonder that they had longings for home or that their future was gloomy?

The day was wearing away. There was no cloud curtain in the sky to shut out the sun but the brazen dome glowed with steady heat. The Christian Commission tent had been besieged all day by parched and fevered soldiers who wanted onions or pickles, lemons or oranges—anything sour—anything to tempt the taste. There was a box of oranges, which had been brought from City Point the night before. It was suggested that they be distributed at once to the sick and wounded. "Certainly, by all means," was the unanimous voice of the Commission. I volunteered to be the distributor.

Go with me through the tents where the sufferers are. Some are lying down with closed eyes, with pale faces and sunken cheeks. The paleness underlies the bronze which the sun has cast upon them. They breathe languidly. Some are half-reclined, leaning on their elbows, bolstered by their knapsacks, looking into vacancy—seeing, perhaps, the old home, and wondering if they will ever cross its threshold again. Some are reading the papers, which the delegates of the Commission have distributed. There are some who have but one leg. There is the stump of a thigh, or an arm, with the lightest possible dressing to keep the fever down. Yesterday, those men stood in the trenches confronting the enemy, in the full tide of life. Now they are wrecks, floating out into the unknown future, with wife and children or parents dependent on them.
("Carlton")

Ministry of Meeting Practical Needs

As we enter the tent, they catch a sight of the golden fruit. There is a commotion. Those half asleep rub their eyes. Those half reclining sit up straight. Those lying with their backs toward us turn over to see what is going on. Those so feeble that they cannot turn ask what the matter is. They gaze at the apples of Paradise. How their eyes gleam! Not one of them asks for an orange! They wait. Through military discipline, through unparalleled suffering, they have learned to be patient—to wait, to endure, to remain in suspense—to stand still and be torn to pieces! They are heroes!

"Would you like an orange, sir?"

"Thank you."

It is all he can say. He is lying upon his back. A minie bullet has passed through his body and he cannot be moved. He has a noble brow—a manly countenance. Tears moisten his eyes and roll down his sunken cheeks, as he takes the orange from my hand.

"This is a gift of the Christian Commission and I accept your thanks for those who made the contribution."

"Bully for the Christian Commission!" shouted a wide-awake, jolly soldier nearby with an ugly wound in his left arm.

"Thank you," "God bless the Commission," "I say, Bill, aren't they bully?" are the expressions which I hear behind me.

In one of the wards, I came upon a soldier who had lost his leg the day before. He was lying upon his side. He was robust, healthy, strong and brave. The hours dragged heavily. He did not see me until I stood before him—and not even then. He was stabbing his knife into a block of wood with a nervous energy, as if he was imagining bayoneting a Confederate—trying to forget the pain—trying to bridge over the lonely hours and shut out the gloom of his future. I touched his elbow. He looked up.

"Would you like an orange?" I asked.

"By jingo! That is worth a hundred dollars!"

He grasped it as a drowning man clutches a floating object, as if to lose a thousandth of a second he would miss the prize.

"Where did this come from?"

"The Christian Commission had a box arrive last night."

"The Christian Commission? My wife belongs to that. She wrote to me about it last week, that they met to make shirts for soldiers."

THAT'S WORTH A HUNDRED DOLLARS

"Then you have a wife?"

"Yes, sir, and three children."

His voice faltered. Ah! The soldier never forgets his home. He dashed away a tear, took in a long breath, and was strong again.

"Where do you hail from, soldier?"

"From old Massachusetts. I had a snug little home upon the banks of the Connecticut but I told my wife that I didn't feel just right to stay there when I was needed out here and so I came and here I am. I shall write home and tell Mary about the Christian Commission. I have been wishing all day that I had an orange. I knew it was no use to wish. I didn't suppose there was one in camp. Besides, here I am, not able to move a peg. I thank you, sir, for bringing it. I shall tell my wife all about it."

It was worth a hundred dollars to see him gulp down the juice—every drop, as if it was precious as life itself. But enough. It was one of the happiest hours of my life—that passed in the distribution of those oranges—not because I was the alms giver but because of the exhibition of spontaneous, unmixed, heartfelt gratitude, not toward me but to the friends far away. ("Carlton")

Front Lines Ministry

Another narrative, from the pen of Delegate C. H. Richards, of Andover Theological Seminary, Massachusetts, continues the story of the same work, published in the *Sunday School Times*:

We pass by regiments and batteries, by sentinels who look curiously at us, by the headquarters of officers of all grades and ranks, through field and grove until we come to the covered wagon road, which leads to the outer lines. Through this passageway, which was carved out so that ammunition and supplies might be taken safely to the batteries at the front, we pass without risk of life or limb. Following the devious windings, we find ourselves suddenly in a fort or earthwork, made of gabions (rocks stacked in a cylinder) and fascines (wood bound together), strengthened and cemented by an abundance of "sacred soil," while numerous sandbags crown the parapet. If you will look out through this embrasure (opening for firing guns), you will see that we have no further to go. For lying just beyond, you will see our abattis (a barricade of felled trees) and our thin picket line. Beyond this lays the disputed territory into which no man may advance five paces without paying dearly for it.

Ministry of Giving Literature

But somebody is tugging on you by the sleeve. Looking around, you find that several soldiers have gathered around you.

"Can you spare me one of those papers?" one asks.

"Of course, I can, my good fellow. I brought them down on purpose for you."

"And I should like one too," says another. "And I." "And I," echo all the rest.

By this time, they have discovered to the right and left of you along the lines that something is going on up in the fort. They look and wonder, "What can it be?"

"I guess it's the Christian Commission man," says one and immediately they begin to gather around us. They cluster about us like bees on a honey pot. Their faces are eager and their hands are stretched out toward you like a unanimous vote of welcome.

"Do you have something good to read? Well, that's just what we want! I'll take a paper if you can spare it."

"There's the dear old *Messenger!* That looks like home. I'd like one of those."

"A *Flag* paper for me," says another.

"Can you give me a Baptist paper? I used to be a Baptist when I was at home," says a gray-headed man, looking at the *Examiner* through his iron-rimmed spectacles.

"I'll take one of those *Methodists*," says another.

"Well, I don't care what kind you give me, provided I can only get something good to read," responded still another. And so they clamor pleasantly around you and stretch out their hands so eagerly for your papers and little books that you are almost bewildered in your endeavors to satisfy all of them. The men are hungry, positively hungry, for reading. We gradually make our way to the edge of the group, sending out a word of cheer and encouragement here and there, thinking to pass further down the lines towards the Ninth Corps.

But before we are fairly out of the circle, a soldier says, "You haven't got a New Testament to give away, have you? I lost mine in the fight at Cold Harbor and I haven't had one since. I can't stand it much longer without one, for a soldier ain't more than half-equipped without a Testament."

"Of course you shall have one, my dear sir, and may God help you to live by its teachings."

"I should like one, too. Mine was lost at Spotsylvania," says another.

"One for me, too," echoes a third until half of them are crowding around again, all wanting New Testaments. Perhaps, my experience is unusual but it is noteworthy that I have hardly ever met a private in the army, whatever his character, who did not want a Testament if he did not have one. This phenomenon provides striking evidence of the strength of religious conviction, even in the hearts of those who are apparently thoughtless and careless about their most important interests. It serves as another proof that the deepest instincts of man's nature crave comfort and strength from above.
(C. H. Richards)

Ministry of Writing Letters

Once more we make an attempt to pass down the lines when we are again stopped by a voice, saying, "Chaplain, have you any letter paper and envelopes? I haven't been able to write home for a long time because I haven't had anything to write with. If you could only give me a little, they will bless you for it up there."

"Here it is and now write a good, sweet letter to the wife and little ones."

He says, "That's what I'll do," and his eyes grow misty as he takes it gratefully. Again the crowd gathers around us and everyone must have a sheet of paper and an envelope. We are linking the chain that binds the soldier to his home.

Again, we are on our way and this time with a fairly good start. We must stay low and walk cautiously now or we shall get a headache from over the way. There are not many men to be seen in the fort over yonder. Those that we see are snugly ensconced in little pits, which they have dug out for themselves and, from which, it would not be safe to venture far. A head or a hand exposed above the ramparts here is a mark for a dozen sharpshooters in the opposing line. The soldiers cannot flock to us very well but we will creep carefully to them. Here is a good-natured-looking boy beckoning for a paper. Of course he gets it. "Zip" goes a minie ball over our heads and buries itself with a "thud" in a nearby bank. (C. H. Richards)

Practical Illustration in Teaching

"Chaplain," says the soldier, "did you ever play a game of baseball when you were a boy?"

"Yes, to be sure. But why do you ask?"

"Well, you know when you catch the ball, you're in. But when you catch one of these fellows" holding up a minie ball, "you're out," and he smiled at his own grim joke. But such a joke serves as good of a purpose as a text to preach from. He readily tells us of the deaths that occur here, day after day. He speaks of the friends and messmates he has lost while he has escaped their fate and of the peril he passes through daily. He tells you, frankly, of the solemn thoughts of death and eternity that fill his mind in these scenes. He shares the need he feels of having some firm, sure hope on which he can rely, of the longing he has felt to be a Christian. And then how precious is the privilege and how easy and delightful is the task to direct him to the Savior, who is reaching out His arms of welcome to him.
(C. H. Richards)

Courage

Selecting the few incidents which must serve as representative of the soldier's courage and sacrifice during the period covered by this chapter is difficult. Reverend George Duffield, Jr., a delegate during June and July, 1864, tells the following:

W. F. Clark, a private in Kautz's Cavalry Brigade, was taken prisoner with two others on July 2, 1864. When the Confederates were scouring the woods for other prisoners, the guards who had Clark and his companions at gunpoint ordered them, without explanation, to march in front of them. They blew out the brains of the first one, then of the second, and then poured a volley into Clark, leaving him as good as dead with one bullet and nine buckshot pellets in him. He remained where he fell until about four o'clock the next morning. When he came to, his first thought was of a stream of water he had passed on the other side of the field. Crawling as best he could to the stream, he rolled into it to conceal himself, covering everything but his nostrils when he heard anyone approaching.

That night a poor old, worn-out horse came down to the stream to get a drink. Having gained a little strength by then, Clark got up and caught the horse and made a bridle for him out of a pair of suspenders. In that condition, he rode eight miles before daylight into our lines. The men put him into an ambulance and brought him to the Post Hospital at Bermuda Hundred where Dr. Spees, of Dayton, Ohio, and I saw him and heard his story from his own lips. When I last saw him, seven of the shot had been extracted. Dr. Spees did not think the three others would be much trouble to remove. Clark said he had no inclination of dying after being shot in such an inhumane way. He wasn't much in the Confederates' debt, anyhow, and once he was able to get on his horse again, he would soon wipe out old scores.

Sacrifice

On the steamboat from Detroit to Cleveland, I noticed an officer whose straps indicated he was a colonel. He turned out to be Colonel Pulford, Commander of the 5th Michigan Regiment. Evidently, he was suffering from a severe wound but I had no idea of its nature until I met him a second time on the steamer going down the Potomac. By virtue of my Christian Commission badge, he asked me to dress his wound, which he had received in one of the Wilderness battles. The ball had stricken him sideways, entered and passed through the neck and shoulder, and carried away some very large splinters of vertebrae.

At first, the shock or the ordeal was so great that he was completely paralyzed. When he received his leave, he had very little hope of ever being able to return to the field. But the shock to his nervous system proved only temporary. His vigorous constitution helped him to rally speedily. His heart began to fret at the very thought of his men not having any officer higher than second lieutenant (if memory serves) to look after them and care for their needs. He thought he could more easily bear the pain and distress of the wound on the field than to worry about his men at home. So, with a leave of absence for thirty days in his pocket and a wound that was bad enough that a surgeon gave him thirty days more, he started off to the front where the weather was scorching hot. (George Duffield, Jr.)

Leadership

Reverend E. F. Williams, Pastor of Congregational Church, Whitinsville, Massachusetts, tells an incident of the attack upon the Weldon road in October 1864:

All the officers of a company engaged in the fighting had been either killed or wounded. The sergeant, upon whom the command devolved, was frightened and the line began to waver. A corporal instantly snatched the colors, stepped to the front, and led the men to victory. A brigadier general nearby noticed the event and sent for the corporal after the fight to learn his name. The brave corporal was distressed exceedingly, for he was afraid he had somehow subjected himself to military discipline. The general then took him to the Major-General commanding the Corps and related the circumstances. All the while, the poor corporal was trying to wish himself out of his trouble. After a little private conference, the two generals came forward and pinned a captain's straps on the corporal's shoulders and sent him back to command the company. Before night there was another charge on the enemy's position. While gallantly leading his men, the newly-made captain was shot through the heart.

Assurance of Salvation before Death

Reverend J. H. Knowles, member of Genesee Conference, Methodist Episcopal Church, was just leaving the army before Petersburg in June, 1864. This incident occurred at the close of his term of service:

A soldier had been brought in on a stretcher and placed under the shade of a green tree. He was shot through the mouth. His tongue was cut and he could not speak. The surgeon pronounced his wound mortal. On a card, the soldier wrote of his desire to see a delegate of the Christian Commission and they summoned me.

As I approached him, he again made signs for pencil and paper and wrote, "I am a Christian, prepared to die." Then, after looking at the soldiers nearby, he added another line: "Rally round the flag, boys, rally round the flag."

I took the paper and, with all the composure I could command, read it aloud to his comrades. As I read, the dying man, speaking only with his animated face, raised his bloody hand over his head and waved it, just as Marmion in Sir Walter Scott's poem shook his sword with all the enthusiasm of the charge. Then quietly, while every eye brimmed with quickly-gathered tears, he went out of the midst of the company into heaven's City of Peace.

Eternal Fruit in Missionary Work

Rev. F. P. Monfort, member of Whitewater (O. S.) Presbytery, Indiana, writes from City Point Hospital in June 1864:

Daniel McKenna, an Indian chief of the Atawa tribe from Bear Creek, Michigan, and a sharpshooter with the 1st Michigan Regiment, lay in one of our wards mortally wounded. While life was ebbing away, I questioned him through an interpreter but could get no reply until I inquired if he had ever seen a missionary.

At this point, he opened his eyes and smilingly nodded assent, saying in his broken way, "Mishnare. Mishnare. Umph. Good." He seldom spoke or noticed anything but now he seemed to be pleased and roused up:

"Ask him," I said, "if he likes the missionaries?"

The interpreter did so and communicated his reply: "He says, 'Yes, he likes them first rate. They are very good men. They teach schools and preach. I am the chief and I am the man that sees to the house and makes the appointments for them.'"

"Does he know Jesus Christ is a Savior?"

"He says, 'Yes, Jesus Christ is his Savior.'"

"Does he love Christ?"

"He says, 'Yes, he loves Him with all his heart.'"

"Does he ever pray?"

"Yes, he has been praying to God through Jesus Christ ever since he was wounded."

"Ask him if he is prepared to die?"

"He says, 'Yes, if God calls him to heaven, he will go with Him over there.'"

Clinging to the Cross of Christ

"Carleton," in a letter to the Boston *Journal*, June 1864, tells the story of the last hours of Edward M. Schneider of the 57th Massachusetts Regiment.

This man was the son of Reverend Dr. Benjamin Schneider, Missionary of the American Board at Aintab, Central Turkey. He wrote of this incident:

Schneider was slightly wounded at the battle of North Anna and was sent to Port Royal for transport to Washington but, of his own accord, he returned to his regiment and joined it at Cold Harbor. While preparing for the charge upon the enemy's works on the 17th beyond the Dunn House, he said to the chaplain, "I intend to be the first one to enter their works."

The charge was made. How grandly they moved through the woods! How quickly they swept up to the Confederate line of defensive works, like an ocean billow upon a breakwater, rolling over it, engulfing all beyond! The brave young soldier tried to make good on his words. With eager feet he led the advance, breaking out from the line and keeping five to ten yards in front.

He was almost there—not quite—almost near enough to feel the hot flash of the Confederate musketry in his face—near enough to be covered with the sulphurous cloud from the cannon—when he fell, shot through the body.

He was carried to the hospital, along with six hundred and fifty of his division comrades. He lay all night with his wounds undressed, waiting his turn. There was not a murmur from his lips.

The chaplain looked at his wound and Schneider asked, "What do you think of it?"

Seeing that it was mortal, the chaplain could neither articulate a reply, nor could he restrain his tears. He remembered the last injunction of the young soldier's older sister—"I commit him to your care." The young hero interpreted the meaning of the chaplain's tears—that his wound was mortal.

"Do not weep," he said. "It is God's will. I wish you to write to my father and tell him that *I have tried to do my duty to my country and to God.*"

He disposed of his effects, giving $10 to the Christian Commission, $20 to the American Board, and trifles to his friends. Then, in the simplicity of his heart, he said, "I have a good many friends, schoolmates and companions. They will want to know where I am—how I am getting on. You can let them now I am gone and that I die content. And, Chaplain, the boys in the regiment—I want you to tell them to stand by the dear old flag! And there is my brother in the navy. Write to him and tell him to *stand by the flag and cling to the cross of Christ!*"

The surgeon came and examined the wound.

"It is my duty to tell you that you will soon go home," he said.

"Yes, Doctor, I am going home. I am not afraid to die. I don't know how the valley will be when I get to it but it is bright now." Then, gathering up his waning strength, he repeated the verse often sung by the soldiers who, amid all the whirl and excitement of the camp and battlefield, never forget those whom they have left behind. They remember mother, sister, father, and brother. Calmly, clearly, distinctly, he repeated the lines—the chorus of the song:

> "Soon with angels I'll be marching,
>   With bright laurels on my brow;
> I have for my country fallen:
>   Who will care for sister now?"

The night wore away and death came swiftly. He suffered intense pain but not a murmur escaped his lips. Sunday morning came and, with the coming of the light, he entered the eternal realm.

Abiding Love of a Mother

From a public address by Reverend Robert J. Parvin, Rector of St. Paul's Protestant Episcopal Church, Cheltenham, Pennsylvania, we take an incident illustrating the Christian loyalty and sacrifice, which could fill a mother's heart when she heard of the death of her only son:

In June 1864, while the supply stores were being opened at our base at City Point, we opened a small square box and found such a variety of very nice delicacies that I realized they were not intended for general distribution. My suspicion was confirmed when we reached the bottom and found that the box had been opened at the wrong end.

Pinned on the top of a large cake was a note, saying, "If any one opens this box, except the person it is intended for, will they please regard the wish and anxiety of a mother who greatly desires to comfort and help her dear child and close it again and send it to him if possible? She has done a great deal for others during the war. She wants also to relieve her own son. His address is Major Charles E. Pruyn, 118th New York Regiment, 2nd Brigade, 1st Division, Eighteenth Corps."

Grieved at our mistake, I undertook to remedy it as well as I could. Carefully returning the articles to the box, I wrote to Major Pruyn, telling him where to send for it.

In the course of an hour, the messenger returned with the chaplain of the 118th who on entering the tent, said, "Major Pruyn was shot dead at the head of his regiment a few days ago."

The date of his death was that of his mother's letter. The contents of the box were handed to the chaplain. I wrote to Mrs. Pruyn, stating the sad news, telling her about the box, and asking permission to retain the letter written to her son. Here are some of the words of it:

"I have always, as you know, my dear son, felt that you were in the right place and been thankful that you felt it your duty to serve your country but I confess my patriotism is sometimes scarcely equal to this long, long trial. Your danger is now quite as great from another source as from the war. O Charley dear, seek God's counsel and, if He makes you feel it your duty to remain, then He will take care of you or prepare you for His will."

Within a few days came the mother's answer to my letter, granting my wish to keep the communication found in the box and breathing throughout a spirit of noblest Christian heroism:

"A_____, July 8, 1864.

"REV. ROBERT J. PARVIN: DEAR SIR: Your kind letter is received and opens anew the floodgates of a sorrow so deep that only He who permitted it to fall can give me strength and composure to reply.

I had come, almost insensibly to myself, to feel a sort of security that God would not take my precious child from me but would permit him to return and be my staff and comfort in the later days of my weary pilgrimage. But Infinite Wisdom saw that this was not best, either for him or his mother. God had prepared some better thing for him than the comforts and luxuries and affections of our earthly home. 'Even so, Father, for thus it seemeth good in Thy sight.'

"I had sent a box previously which, owing to purely providential circumstances, was lost in the multitude. Then I thought, God will use that to comfort some other poor sufferer and has intended it as a test of my trust in Him. So I prepared and sent a second, to prove to my own heart that I *would* trust, though God did see fit to disappoint me. That second box was sent the day after my darling child passed away into eternity.

"And, now, what can I say to this? Is God untrue and is my faith vain and shall I cease to trust Him? Oh, blessed be His name. He does not permit my mind to indulge such thoughts! No, though the clouds that gather around Him be as dark as midnight—though not one ray of light can be seen, I will cling to Him still, I will trust Him yet. He is His own interpreter and, in His own time and way, will make it all plain. While He gives me the confidence that my child is safe in glory, where he shall hunger no more, nor thirst anymore, where the sun shall not light on him nor any heat, I am satisfied. I will be patient and I will now give all that earnest desire I had for the temporal and spiritual good of my own dear child to all the poor sufferers, many of whom have no mother to bleed and labor for them. I will see a son or a brother in every noble defender of my home and of my country's honor. MARY PRUYN."

And most thoroughly was that resolve carried out.

Love for Jesus

Reverend W. G. Taylor, Pastor of Mount Carmel (O. S.) Presbyterian Church, Pennsylvania, writing in July 1864, tells a story of Christ's nearness to His children:

I went into a tent at the General Hospital and there lay a handsome drummer boy, sixteen years-old, burning up with fever. I asked, "Where is your home?"

"In Massachusetts, sir."

"Aren't you lonely here, far from father and mother and friends—and so sick?"

"Oh, no," he answered. "How could I be lonely when Jesus is here?"

The smile that lit his deep blue eyes and played for a moment over his fevered lips, as he uttered the words, will never cease to be the sweetest and freshest picture in my memory.

My companion asked him, "How long is it since you loved Jesus?"

"So long that I cannot remember when I did not love Him."

CHAPTER XII
THE EASTERN ARMIES

FROM THE INVESTMENT OF PETERSBURG
UNTIL THE CLOSE OF THE WAR
(CONTINUED)
June 1864–April 1865

Trust in God

The soldier's deep trust in God is what best prepared him for sacrifice. Reverend Abel Wood, Professor in Kimball Union Academy, Meriden, New Hampshire, writes of an interview between Henry C. Smith, 8th Michigan Regiment, and his Chaplain:

The soldier's left arm had been amputated but his life still could not be saved. Toward evening on July 30, 1864, he sent for his Chaplain and asked him to pray with him once more. The Chaplain inquired about his trust in Jesus. The man answered clearly and earnestly.

The Chaplain asked, "Do you have any messages for home?"

"No, that's all done."

"You have been a brave soldier and done your duty. Now if you can trust the Great Captain of your salvation, all is well."

"All is well, Chaplain," answered the soldier. Prayer was offered, after which the two spoke their farewells.

A little after midnight, early on Sunday morning, the man began praying in a clear, strong voice. "I commit my soul to you, my Lord Jesus Christ. Lord Jesus, bless President Abraham Lincoln with strength and wisdom. In your good providence unite our great country. I pray that the sacrifice of my life may contribute to a righteous and lasting peace. In Jesus Name, Amen." When this prayer had scarcely escaped his lips, he expired.

Power of Surrendered Lives

In August 1864, Mr. C. H. Richards related an incident, which shows the power of a good, consistent, manly life before God:

An interesting boy from one of the Middle States joined the Union Army in Virginia. He soon joined up with, what I considered, the most wicked man in the regiment, who seemed to make it his chief delight to lead the youth into lower and lower depths of vice. The young soldier was fascinated by his companion. The extremes of wickedness, to which the young man sunk, would have shocked him beyond measure before he left home. Fortunately, a pious German in the regiment caught his attention. The young soldier had never spoken with the man about religion but he saw him reading his Bible constantly and with obvious pleasure. He often heard his voice in prayer. Cheerfulness was on his face and a measure of abiding joy rested in his heart. His faithfulness in every duty was apparent and he faced great danger with courage and calmness.

Somehow, the young man could not keep from watching the older man and began to grasp the reality about this man's Christianity, which made him the happiest man in the regiment. Each day, his fascination grew. After one campaign, filled with extraordinary peril, he went to the old German and asked, "How do you manage to be so consistently happy?" The old soldier replied, "I have no other source of joy than the Lord Jesus Christ. If you would give yourself to Christ, you could know the same joy I have."

The young soldier immediately deserted his vile companion and determined to follow the advice of his new friend. God gave him His promised faith and joy and he, too, began to live out his faith. So now, two lights shined in the regiment before men. Others were attracted to the Savior as the youth had been, so this influence permeated the regiment until only God can reveal the blessed result. It was not the "tongues of men or of angels" that preached Christ here but the devoted and surrendered lives of humble followers of Christ who came to do, not His own will, but the will of the Father that sent Him.

Death As Being Removed Above

The night of August 17, 1864 followed fighting with the Confederate cavalry on the left. Some of our men were surrounded and suffered severe loss when cutting their way out. Among the wounded was Sergeant W. H. Boston, of St. Albans, Vermont. Reverend Charles L. Nichols, Pastor of the Congregational Church, Princeton, Maine, ministered to him during this incident:

I went through the little "flying" tent hospital and found one man who was deeply anxious about a comrade who fell from his horse. I went to the scene as soon as I could to search for the missing soldier. I discovered that he had crawled a short distance from where he fell. He had been shot through the lungs and death was approaching. "Water" was his first word. I gave him a taste of punch but he wanted water. Finding a cup, lost by a soldier in the fray, I gave him a drink. When I had finished washing his face and wounds, He asked me to turn him and I did so. He smiled and asked me to sit down.

"Shall I first go and get you some help?"

He smiled again and answered, "Before you could come back, I would be removed up there," pointing his finger upward. He dictated a most loving letter to his wife and another to his mother. We talked for a few minutes more when he asked me to raise him up, which I did. Without a groan or struggle, he passed away almost immediately.

Hardness of Heart

In contrast to many triumphant death records, Reverend Charles Cutler, Pastor of the Congregational Church, Francistown, New Hampshire, tells of this incident:

While I was working at Cavalry Hospital, City Point, Virginia, in September 1864, I came to a young man who was shot in the neck and completely paralyzed. I spoke to him about preparation for death.

"I might as well own up," he said. "I'm not prepared. I've lived a bad life and been a great trouble to my mother. I've got no religion and I don't want any. I won't burn out my candle now and throw the snuff in God Almighty's face. I'll die as I've lived. It's honester."

I argued with him, plead the promises of God to him, entreated him—all to no avail.

"I deserve no mercy. I won't ask for any. I've never prayed and I'm not going to do so now."

Shortly afterward, he began to recover the use of his limbs and it seemed likely that he would get better. But he always turned away when I approached and was unwilling to converse. I was obliged to leave the army without seeing any impression made upon him.

Softening of a Hardened Heart

Revered Frank F. Jewell, Pastor of Methodist Episcopal Church, Adams, New York, writes in October 1864:

In one ward of the General Hospital at City Point, we saw three conversions. One of these was that of a member of the 111th New York Regiment. Before his entrance into the army, he had been a great wanderer. Disabled in the Wilderness, he was permitted to go home on a furlough for a few weeks.

When he was about to return, his seven-year old boy caught him by the knee, and said, "Pa, when will you come back?"

The father replied, "I don't know, my son, whether I shall ever come back."

"Well," said the child, "who will be my pa if you don't come back?"

The question rooted itself in the father's mind. During the excitement of battle scenes, he had not forgotten the parting words of his little boy. When I came to sit down by his side and urge him to attend to his salvation, the work seemed to have already begun. Immediately, he made up his mind to seek Christ. The next time I met him, he was writing a letter to his wife.

He wrote, "I know now how to answer little Henry's question. Tell him the Savior will be his pa if I don't come back."

Ministry to Families of the Deceased

Here is a sad little picture of disappointment from the pen of Reverend D. Hoyt Blake of Brooklyn, New York:

"George" was a distinguished looking soldier from Jersey City. Before I left, I was called to accompany him to the last resting place. Then his letters and two well-worn pictures of his wife and mother were put into my hands.

In looking over his wife's last letter to find a forwarding address, I came upon the words: "Willie and I, Mary and the baby, will be standing at the corner of _____ Street, looking for you when the cars come in. Do come soon, George. It does seem as if I could not wait."

Poor, loving, anxious one! W at if my letter with the death news should find her waiting with Willie and Mary and baby at the corner!

Ministry of Friendship

Mr. John Patterson recalls an incident of his experience during several visits to the hospital at Point of Rocks, Virginia:

"Point of Rocks" is a very appropriate name for a place on the Appomattox River, just north of Bermuda Hundred. For miles around, no "rocks" are worthy of the name but, here, two or three enormous boulders stick in the face of a precipice which rises two or three hundred feet above the river. Nearby, on the table above the rocks, is a famous oak, reported to be the very tree under which Pocahontas saved the life of Captain John Smith. Far to the southwest rise the spires of Petersburg. City Point lies to the southeast and, to the north, Richmond. Three hundred yards from the tree is the Military Hospital and, not far off, is the cheerless cemetery. A sluggish stream passes below. Spanning the river is a pontoon bridge, crowded at both ends with soldiers passing from right to left of the grand army. Enough soldiers were within sight to meditate upon—more than enough to make one sad and blot the view with gathering tears.

Here, I met my soldier friend, James Anderson, a youth of twenty years. His eyes still retained more than a memory of their once cheerful gaze but his fallen cheeks and ruddy color marked a sure decline. So much about this man was manly and noble that his condition elicited my deepest sympathy. I found him one October evening, resting on the grass by the old oak, enjoying the coolness after the heat of day. The sun was sinking into the west, bequeathing a glory as it departed to every exposed leaf of the sleepy trees, to the sails and masts and ropes of the transports that traversed the James River and cast their shadowy arms far away into the distance, where there was no day. The steamboat bells and the softened noise of the whistles came to us over the long reach of water between us, to mingle with the nearer music of the regimental bands. It would have been pleasant to have given oneself up to the scene but the spell was ever broken by the far-off booming of the Union guns, untiringly pouring their shot into the Confederate defenses of Petersburg. One shuddered as the dim outline of the cemetery and hospital still could be discerned. I turned to the soldier, and asked him if he were sick or wounded.

"I am both sick and wounded, sir."

"How badly?" I asked, taking my seat beside him.

"A ball passed through my body near my left lung. My doctor thinks I will recover."

"That's encouraging. A great mercy allowed you to escape."

"Yes," he said musingly. "The mercy of the Lord is new every morning and fresh every evening."

His manner was very reticent and he seemed a little unwilling to talk. But he was a Scotchman, and I must know something more of him.

"Then you know something of this Mercy of God?"

"Oh, yes, 'As a father pitieth his children, so the Lord pitieth them that fear Him.'"

Every word he uttered thrilled me with joy. His manner was so refined and elegant and he seemed so to know of whom he was speaking.

"You are Scotch, I presume."

"Yes," he said as he told me his name. When he heard mine, he added, "O sir, I suppose you are pretty nearly a Scotchman yourself."

"Yes, but not altogether."

We belonged to the same visible Church and the ancestors of each matron had witnessed for the truth on the same fields in the motherland .

"I would rather be born," he said smilingly, "of such parents than be the child of kings and princes."

As I was leaving, I promised to bring him some reading materials but he said his Bible and Catechism were sufficient.

The next evening, he told me something of his history. He was born near Bothwell Bridge in Scotland. Nearby was a little valley between two hills— and a tear streamed down his cheek as he told of it. It was beautiful to see how he turned his earthly grief into blessed consolation. "But there is a land where 'the Lamb shall feed them and shall lead them unto living fountains of waters; and God shall wipe away all tears from their eyes,'" he said.

Lovingly, he went into all the particulars about his old home, even to the honeysuckle and sweetbrier around the walls and the hum of the morning bees. And then again, as his half talk and half reverie moved onward, he went up from the earthly to the heavenly and told how in the "auld house" he had learned what was "sweeter also than honey and the honeycomb." And then he told of the mountain nearby and of the brook that clambered down its sides and ran near the home door, of the trees in their winter diamonds and summer green, and of the pasture valley where he watched his father's flock.

What a precious story too was his account of the training he had received! Six farmers' families, near together, used to gather their sheep on Saturday evening to the most convenient pasture, so as to have little trouble on the next day. It seemed to him the sheep knew when Sunday came because they were so much quieter. Three miles away was the new Free Church and everyone attended on the Lord's Day with only one being left behind to care for the flock—a duty which the knowing dog administered, for he knew how to gather the sheep together on that day without even a bark. The quaint, beautiful words of the old Scotch version of the Psalms told how he thought of the "House of Prayer:"

> I joyed when, to the House of God
>   Go up, they said to me;
> Jerusalem, within thy gates
>   Our feet shall standing be:

Thus the Lord's Day was, indeed, a day of blessed rest, free from all vain talk and worldly enjoyment, "a delight—the holy of the Lord honorable," not a weariness, but a deep foretaste of the Eternal Sabbath of joy. At the close of the service, everyone gathered together, remarks were made about the sermon, the elder "bairns" (sons and daughters) catechized, and then some extract from Boston, Willison or Baxter was read before all returned to their homes. His intention to study theology had been frustrated by his father's death after his graduation at a Scotch university. Coming to this country, he had found the calling of war ever so high that he enlisted.

His story made a deep impression on me—so deep that I determined to visit him upon my return to the army the following March.

I found him amid the old surroundings, trustful and quiet and beautiful in his talk as ever and very glad to see me. All the restraint which marked his manner at first had disappeared but it was sadly evident, as I looked at him, that he was nearing his end. I made him lean on my shoulder as we walked together along the river's bank.

He said, "I imagine my case is like that of one of my own countrymen—poor Michael Bruce. But he did some good to the world. His poems will never be forgotten. He intended to study for the ministry but was early called to the Church above."

He went on to repeat some stanzas from "Lochleven," one of Michael Bruce's poems:

> "Thus sung the youth, amid unfertile wilds
>   And nameless deserts' unpoetic ground:
> Far from his friends he strayed, recording thus
>   The dear remembrance of his native fields,
> To cheer the tedious night, while slow disease
>   Prey'd on his pining vitals, and the blasts
> Of dark December shook his humble cot."

"I feel like him in many ways, far from the friends I love. I need remembrance to cheer away the gloom."

Once again, and for the last time, I saw him. His old cheerfulness remained but the nearness of the end made the conversation more solemn. Again, he returned to his favorite poet and quoted from that pathetic "Elegy," which seemed to have been written for Anderson himself:

> "Now Spring returns; but not to me returns
>   The vernal joy my better years have known:
> Dim in my breast life's dying taper burns,
>   And all the joys of life with health are flown.

"Starting and shivering in the inconstant wind,
    Meagre and pale, the ghost of what I was,
Beneath some blasted tree I lie reclined,
    And count the silent moments as they pass.

"The winged moments, whose unstaying speed
    No art can stop or in their course arrest,
Whose flight shall shortly count me with the dead,
    And lay me down in peace with them that rest.

"Oft morning dreams presage approaching fate,
    And morning dreams, as poets tell, are true;
Led by pale ghosts I enter Death's dark gate,
    And bid the realms of light and life *adieu.*

"I hear the helpless wail, the shriek of woe,
    I see the muddy wave, the dreary shore,
The sluggish streams that slowly creep below,
    Which mortals visit and return no more.

"Farewell, ye blooming fields, ye cheerful plains;
    Enough for me the churchyard's lonely mound
Where Melancholy, with still Silence reigns,
    And th' rank grass waves o'er cheerless ground.

"There let me wander at the close of eve,
    When sleep sits dewy on the laborer's eyes;
The world and all its busy follies leave,
    And talk with wisdom where my Daphnis lies.

"There let me sleep, forgotten in the clay,
    When death shall shut these weary, aching eyes,
Rest in the hope of an Eternal Day,
    Till the long night is gone and the last mom arise."

Surely here was the very scene before us: the spring returning—but not for him; the old oak under which he stood; the winged moments soon to lay him with the dead; the pale ghosts on every bed of that hospital of sorrow near; the muddy, dreary, sluggish Appomattox and the waiting crowd visiting it now, perhaps to return no more; the remembered story of his home; the graves nearby; and the Hope that turned the whole to gladness—and would yet make the long night flee away.

Only a few more days of life were left in him. About the 25th of March, the weary, aching eyes were shut, and he rested in hope of eternity.

Courage in Facing Persecution

Mr. J. H. Morley relates an incident of the result of courage in facing the consequences of doing duty:

A young man, trying to lead a Christian life, was persecuted by his tent mates. When he knelt down to pray at night, they hurled boots and sticks of wood at him. With a troubled heart, he went to ask advice of his chaplain who, for some reason, counseled him to say his prayers secretly and thus escape persecution. The young man tried to do so for a short time but finally returned to the old way. Shortly afterward, his chaplain met him and inquired how he was getting along.

"Nicely," he answered.

"Did you follow my advice?"

"I did for a little while," said the soldier, "but have changed back to the old way now."

"And what is the result?"

"All my companions" (ten or twelve in number) "kneel down every night with me. Isn't it better, Chaplain, to keep the colors flying?"

Ministry of Multiplication

Mr. H. L. Porter, of Haverhill, Massachusetts, shows how a blessed work of God's grace may come from an act of kindly relief:

One evening in August 1864, I was returning to my quarters at City Point Hospital when, in the distance, I saw a soldier leaning against a tree. I went and spoke to him and found him to be very weak. Together, it took a long time for us to reach the hospital. Afterward, I visited him occasionally. He attended our meetings and became a disciple of Christ. The evening before leaving for the front, he asked for our prayers. He did not know of any other Christian man in his regiment and some officers did not like to hear anything about religion. Eventually, he returned to work and started a prayer meeting in the woods where he told his story and several were converted. In November, he wrote me a letter, giving an account of progress:

"We now have twenty-five members and, by God's assistance, we shall have a still larger increase. Now we have a tent to ourselves which our Colonel permitted us to use. Last night, being Sunday evening, it was full. He gave us a hospital tent and pretty large but I don't think it will be large enough for us in a short time. We have prayer meetings on Wednesday evenings and Sunday mornings and evenings. We hold a Bible class on Friday evenings and on Sunday afternoons. So we are not altogether idle. We have organized a society, adopted a constitution, and taken a name; 'Young Men's Christian Association of the 9th

New Jersey Regiment.' God has been with us everywhere we have been." He goes on to recall the prayer meetings at the hospital and to thank the Christian Commission. He then concludes by saying, "The more I pray, the better I love the cause of Christ. I am just beginning to realize His religion, for I am a young beginner, but trust that I may be always faithful in well-doing."

"JOHN GERRIGAN"

Choosing the Right Identity

Reverend E. F. Williams, Pastor of the Congregational Church, Whitinsville, Massachusetts, telling the history of New Market Station, Virginia in the Army of the James in December 1864, relates the following incident:

When the Confederate rebellion broke out, J_____ was a citizen of Virginia, belonging to a company of volunteer militia. He voted against secession but when this was forced upon his State and his regiment was soon to be called into the battlefield, he and his family left Virginia and secretly moved to Maryland.

During Lee's invasion, he was recognized by an old neighbor and arrested as a deserter. He was rushed to Carlisle, Pennsylvania as a prisoner and then to Gettysburg, where under guard he witnessed the terrific battle. In the confusion of retreat, he escaped to the Union camp. Being mistaken for a Confederate prisoner, he was sent to Fort Delaware, where, after many annoying delays, he was released.

Getting his family together again, he moved to Pennsylvania. In July 1864, he enlisted in the Union Army, with the stipulation that he should only be called to do duty where he would not be exposed to capture by the Confederates—an arrangement easily overlooked by his officers. He was present at the dedication of our Christian Commission chapel on the New Market Road. God met him there and convicted him of sin, giving him faith and repentance unto life eternal.

When those who desired to enroll themselves on the Lord's side came forward to turn in their names on a piece of paper, he explained, "I had to enlist under a fictitious name, fearing I would fall into Confederate hands but," he added, "I want my right name taken among the people of God."

Changed Life

During the winter, he was full of hope. It was a treat to hear his testimony of God's grace, spoken with his strong German accent: "I used to laugh at these things and find fault with the preacher. Some were too tall and some too short. Some were too big and some too little. But now they just suits me. I love them all. I love this house. I love the Word of God and I mean to serve

Him all my life. My brethren, be firm, be faithful. Stand up for Jesus and nothing will harm you. I was afraid at first, myself, but I did my duty. I read my Bible, and though my wicked friends shake their heads and laugh, I know when they see me in earnest, they will soon quit this foolishness."

Afterward, he was transferred to the Northwest to serve against the Indians. (E. F. Williams)

Finding Light to Penetrate Darkness

Reverend Edward P. Smith, Pastor of the Congregational Church, Pepperell, Massachusetts, was called from Nashville to the Central office and visited the Potomac Army in December 1864. He writes from City Point:

After a preaching service in the crowded chapel tent, those desiring more religious instruction were asked to remain. Among some thirty who accepted this invitation, I noticed a young lad, about fifteen years of age, who remained by himself in a corner of the tent. I went to him at once and asked why he had stayed.

"Because you told me to."

"Then do you want to be a Christian?"

"Yes, sir, I do."

"What is your name?"

"Tom Brown, sir."

"Are you a New York soldier?"

"Yes."

"Did you ever go to Sunday school?"

"Yes, always."

"Do you have a mother?"

"She was a Christian. She has gone to heaven a long time ago."

"Well, why aren't you a Christian, Tom?"

"That's what's the matter. That's just what I stopped for—to find out how to become one."

"Well, what did Paul say to the jailer when he wanted to know what to do to be saved?"

"I have heard that a great many times but somehow I don't do it and I don't know how to do it."

I explained to him, as well as I could, the nature of faith—what it means to give oneself to Christ and leave all with Him and accept of Him as the Savior. But Tom seemed to get no relief. I then tried a new way of illustrating my point:

"Who is your commanding officer, Tom?"

"Lieutenant _____."

"Suppose the Lieutenant should send for you to report to him tonight. What would you do?"

"I'd report, sir."

"Right off?"

"Certainly, sir. I obey orders."

"When you came to his quarters, what would you say?"

"I'd give him the salute, and say, 'Lieutenant, what's the orders?'"

"And when you got the orders—?"

"Then I would do 'em, sir."

"Well, now, Tom, the Lord Jesus has sent me to you tonight and orders you to report to Him at once."

"I'll do it. I'll do it, sir," and the little fellow looked around for his hat as if he were going.

"Wait, Tom," I said, "until I have told you everything. The Lord Jesus is here, listening to you and me. He knows your words and your thoughts and all you intend to do. Now if you get His orders, will you do them?"

"Yes, sir, right away."

I asked him of his companions. He told me of an unreligious bunk mate.

"Tom, if you are going to be a Christian, don't you think Jesus will want you to talk and pray with that bunk mate tonight?"

"Yes, if a fellow's going to serve Jesus, he must take hold of it."

"Well, that's exactly what Jesus wants you to do—that's the order. And don't you think that He wants you to write your sister in the morning and tell her how you feel and what you are going to do?"

"Certainly."

"Well, that's the order, Tom. And this is how you'll find it all along in life—just what Jesus wants you to do—that's the order. Now, are you ready for duty?"

"Yes, all ready."

"To take all the orders He'll give you as long as you live?"

"Yes."

"Well, Tom, let us kneel down here and 'report' to Jesus."

We knelt. I prayed for him and he prayed for himself, keeping up the figurative language with which he had been led to the Savior: "Here I am, Jesus. I report for duty. All You order me to do tonight and tomorrow and for as long as I live, I am going to do." And with this prayer he went away. As he was passing out at the chapel door, Brother Blake, not knowing what had transpired, stopped him and asked if he would like to become a Christian.

"Yes," said Tom, "I'm under orders."

The next morning, he came to our quarters with his face lit up with the joy of newly-found peace and hope. During the few days he remained at the hospital, his testimony for Christ was beautifully clear.

Abundant Power in Calling Someone Father

Mr. H. V. Noyes, of Western Theological Seminary, (O. S. Presbyterian), Allegheny, Pennsylvania, served at Point of Rocks. In a letter, dated January 23, 1864, he related the following story that shows the soldier's yearning for love:

As I passed along my customary rounds one morning, a dying boy reached as far as he could reach with his wasted hand and called me to his side. He put his cold arm round my neck and drew my face down to his.

"You make me think of father," he said. "Let me call you 'father.' You won't laugh at me, will you, if I call you father?"

"No, my dear boy, call me father, if it will be of any comfort to you."

"Last night," he continued with broken utterance, "last night—when—you—prayed—I—wanted—you—to—come—nearer. I was—so—sick, I couldn't—hear."

I asked him of his dying hopes.

"I can't—read—much—now—but—thank—God..." It was too much. He could say no more and the sentence remains forever unfinished. I suppose he was thinking of reading his New Testament.

Again, he spoke, "You'll—let—me—kiss—you—won't you?" And then he pressed his lips to my cheek and gave me his farewell. I put my mouth to his ear and offered a fervent petition, that God, for Christ's sake would receive him to Himself. The cold sweat was already gathering and the darkness of death was upon him.

"You'll—stay—with—me—all—night—won't you?"

I told him I would come back after I had gone on a little further up the row of cots.

Gently—oh, how gently, I removed his arm from my neck and gave him my farewell.

A few minutes later, I heard the men saying, "Thompson is dead." I hastened back. The cot was already empty. The only thing left for me to do was find him and cut two locks of hair—one for his mother in Vermont, the other to be kept in sacred remembrance of the soldier who, in his dying breath, desired to call me "Father."

Courage from Submission to God's Will

Reverend N. M. Bailey, Minister of Methodist Episcopal Church, Henniker, New Hampshire, writes from New Market Roads in January 1864:

While having a conversation with a noble old soldier from Michigan, named Peter Whitmore, he said, "I had a pleasant home, a dear family of children and grandchildren, a good farm and all that. But I wanted to do something to help put down this rebellion and destroy slavery. I believe the Lord is on our side and will soon give us the victory. I didn't suppose I could go through so much as I have—but the Lord has helped me. I have prayed to Him every day and I trust He will take me back home again safe but, if not, it is His will and it's all right."

Spiritual Life Values

To hear such faith as this, God's sending of Reverend A. L. Pratt, Minister of Methodist Episcopal Church, Bradford, Vermont, was the best ever. He writes the following incident:

I found a Maine soldier about twenty-four years of age in one of the hospitals at City Point. His good right arm would never again bear a weapon against his country's enemies. It was amputated just below the shoulder joint. He was a devoted Christian and grateful for our slightest favor.

One day, he looked up into my face with a cheerful smile and said, "It seems to me I can't be grateful enough for losing my arm. It made me thoughtful and opened the way for your delegates to visit me and ended in my finding Christ. It is better, I think, to enter into life halt or maimed than to have two hands or two feet and be cast into everlasting fire."

Spiritual Warfare

The following narrative is from the pen of Reverend J. K. McLean, Pastor of the Hollis Congregational Church, Framingham, Massachusetts. It gives such a vivid picture of a fair and open conflict with the Adversary and illustrates so many aspects of the delegate's work:

Along with Brother George W. Bigelow, a member of my own church, I was authorized to establish a Christian Commission station at the Cavalry Depot of the Army of the Potomac. Our assignment lasted from January to March 1865 and was located two miles below City Point on the same side of the James River. The camp consisted of dismounted cavalry, numbering anywhere from 350 to 2,000 men who had lost their horses in action and were waiting to be remounted, as well as wounded men and convalescents on their way back from the hospitals. The camp consisted of a corral of horses, saddle shops, and blacksmith shops. It also had an armory, a clothing depot, an equipment store, etc.

Prior to our coming, very little work of the Christian Commission had been done for the camp. An occasional Sunday service and an irregular distribution of papers, was about all. On Monday, January 16th, Brother Bigelow and I, both entirely new to the service, filled our haversacks with Commission "ammunition" and started on foot. We traveled through the two miles of mud and animal waste for our scene of operations.

Faith to Move Mountains

Our first duty was reconnaissance and we discovered a number of things. The camp contained some 500 men, with more arriving daily. They had nothing to do, were under lax discipline and had few restrictions placed on them. They were stopping here for a few days on their way to the front to take part in the spring movements of the army, which, for the cavalry, would be especially hazardous. Shortly, many of them were sure to be maimed or killed. What was to be done must be done quickly.

The makeup of the camp was peculiar. Nearly all of the old men, those who had been dismounted or wounded, had been engaged in the constant raiding of the last campaigns—stopping nowhere for more than a few hours. With few or no chaplains, they had attended no worship service for months—some for as long as two years. During the winter of 1863, some had gone to "Camp Stoneman" on the Rappahannock River, which was the last time many of them had heard anything about "religion." Large squads of raw recruits were constantly coming in—many of whom were about the worst class of men ever sent to any army anywhere. They were professional "bounty-jumpers," thieves, and, from large cities, every form of depraved humanity imaginable. They had been given the choice between entering the army or the penitentiary.

The atmosphere of that fine January morning was reeking with profanity, vile with vulgarity and obscenity. When they came to know who we were, some of the men restrained themselves a little in our presence but, as yet, we were unknown and the foul thoughts came out in the foulest of words everywhere. It was a discouraging prospect from a human perspective—two men drawn up before this stronghold of Satan. So far as we knew, not a single Christian existed in it. Sin was rampant. Blasphemy stalked, without rebuke. Our only firearms in this battle were the little tracts and books we held—light artillery, indeed, against such a wall of sin. Yet we were there to win that camp for Jesus.

It seemed like we were two men with pickaxe and wheelbarrow, marching against a huge mountain to remove it and cast it into the sea. But remembering that faith can remove mountains, we began our work. We reckoned that, with God's blessing, we could at least make some impression.
(J. K. McLean)

Overcoming Obstacles

We visited every tent and told who we were and what we had come to do. We gave out sewing needles and thread, paper and envelopes, newspapers and books. We invited every man to come to our chapel meetings when and if we should get a chapel built. In every instance, we were kindly received—even cordially.

We found some Christians and many of them said, "Oh, yes, of course we'll come to meeting—we always used to go at home!"

"But, boys, did you swear this way at home?"

"No, we didn't. That's a fact."

"Do you expect to keep this language up after your return?"

"No."

"Won't it be rather hard to break it off all at once?"

"That's so. Just the reason we swear now. We got used to it with the horses and don't even think about it."

According to a cavalryman, the horses were the cause for a great deal of swearing. Many acknowledged the foolishness of the habit and, that day, more than one pledged to give it up. Such efforts, along with a public talk on the subject on Sunday, went far to cleanse the air of the vice. Doubtless, it still existed but was far less obtrusive. Oaths were probably discharged in private but they rattled less furiously about our ears.

Our main business was to get a chapel built and to hold religious services. In this, we encountered the most vexing delays. The commanding officer promised us men to do the work and lumber from the adjoining Confederate estates for a stockade chapel, roofed with boards. (The Commission had no canvas cover to give us at this time.) Every day for a week, the officer renewed his promise. A few logs were cut but that was all.

After waiting eight days, we took off our coats, borrowed some pickaxes, and set at work to dig a trench for our stockade in freezing weather. This brought out both the Captain of the Dismounted Camp and the officer commanding the post. They immediately took the picks out of our hands, put a strong detail of men on the project, and we rejoiced at the near prospect of having a sanctuary. However, due to stormy weather, the failure in getting boards, and other causes, we abandoned hope for a roofed building. Instead, we took a large canvas from a chapel elsewhere and finally dedicated our tabernacle on February 12th.
(J. K. McLean)

Beginnings of Ministry

In the meantime, we had been holding meetings at the Convalescent Camp in a tent where we dispensed rations a half mile away. One night, we gathered four or five men who could sing and struck up some stirring soldiers' hymns. Within a half an hour, more than forty cavalrymen had joined us. We held a brief service then asked any who were Christians and not afraid to own up to it to rise. Four stood up instantly. This was our nucleus. The next night, five others asked for prayer. From that time until the meetings were moved to the large chapel, hardly a night passed without some new individuals presenting themselves for prayer or reformation. By the time our chapel was finished, we had gathered a goodly number who were ready to take hold and help with the meetings.
(J. K. McLean)

Conquering Obstacles

It really seemed as if the powers of evil had joined forces against building our chapel. We had to use bounty jumpers, who would work only if one of us stood by and watched. The building was fairly plastered and shingled with oaths and profanity. Never did a wickeder bunch of men build a House for the Lord. Then, during the dedication, the wind ripped the canvas from its mooring, causing it to flap around the long stove-pipe. It was pulled apart and almost shed its lengths down upon us. That secured, the frame of the roof itself cracked all along one side and would have collapsed had not one of the men, just in time, caught the flying canvas. He was repeatedly lifted from his feet but held on until others were able to help secure it.

That same evening, a large squad of recruits came. Very cold weather had set in and there were no quarters for them—not even shelter tents. So we cheerfully opened our chapel to them for the night. The next morning, we were deluged with a heavy rain, which continued throughout the week. No quarters could be built and more men were arriving daily. Soon, two hundred were housed in our chapel. And such a place it became! The mud was almost as deep within as without. Water continually poured through the roof. Refuse pork, coffee grounds, spit-out chewing tobacco, and all manner of filth were trodden into the miry floor.

The air reeked with tobacco smoke and was fetid with foul breath. Some of the men grew sick. Many of them became troublesome and quarrelsome. Only by our frequent threats of turning all of them out into the storm were we able to keep them under control. The Prince of Darkness had seemingly gained a final triumph. It was with the utmost difficulty that we held our meetings in the rank and noisome place. But we did hold a meeting every night, in spite of the surroundings, and with the most blessed results.

Every evening, I think without exception, some rose for prayers or spoke of a newly-found hope in Jesus. Our meetings were crowded. Sometimes, as many as fifty or sixty would rise for prayer and as many as twenty would speak. It was no fleshly battleground. The Holy Spirit and Satan contended mightily. During the daylight, card playing, profanity and ribald songs were the order of the day. At evening, these activities gave way to prayer, preaching, and praise.

One night, after one of our best meetings, the chapel had become quiet. The lights were out and, except for an occasional snore, all was silent—when, all of a sudden, we were startled by the cry of "Murder—murder." When the alarm was given, a ferocious knockdown fight ensued. The guard rushed to the spot and we joined him with our lantern, which ended the fight. The scene we saw would be hard to describe. After sorting it all out, it appeared that some evil-minded persons, whether those belonging within or without the building we never knew, had set about picking pockets. After that, we kept a lantern burning in the chapel at all times and a guard was detailed to watch the door. Through such scenes, the perennial strife between good and evil went on.

(J. K. McLean)

Converting to Christ

It was a full week before the men cleared out of the chapel. Then, it took a detail of men a whole day to clean it. By scraping the seats, sanding the floor, and trimming the rough walls with cedar boughs, the chapel looked very pleasant and really attractive. When this work was finished, our troubles ended. During the rest of our stay, we had clear sailing. A Bible class and inquiry meeting were held every afternoon and a fully-attended service took place every evening. Conversions occurred daily.

Among the converts was a man who had enlisted in a Pennsylvania village, which contained seven churches but, for fifteen years, he had never been in one of them and had no intentions of ever attending. Coming in with the recruits who were quartered in our chapel, the first night or two he went out into the storm and waited until the meetings ended. He caught a cold and resolved to stay in the next night. He did so, became interested, and finally determined to live a Christian life.
(J. K. McLean)

Earning Trust

Another soldier, named McF_____, an iron-roller from Pittsburg and a fine-looking, stalwart man of thirty-five, came to the tent door one morning. He asked if we could put a stop to the gambling going on in the chapel. He thought it was out of place and sure to provoke disturbances. I went to the chapel with him. After stopping the card playing, I had a visit with him and he told me his story. He had been accustomed to making good wages in the iron mills. With the other men, he would quit work Saturday at noon, dress up, and in the evening go to the theater or "spree it." He would come home at midnight or later and go to bed drunk. His patient wife, a Christian—a member of the Episcopal Church—would wait up for him and help him to bed. She would take his muddy boots, dry and clean and polish them. In the morning, she would beg him to go with her to church. He would refuse and she would cry. This went on for a year or two, at least forty Sundays out of the fifty-two.

He felt his degradation and the wrong he was doing to his family but did not have the moral fortitude to break away from his associations and do better. In an act of mild desperation, he enlisted—he was desperate to be free of his wife's pleadings for a better life. He arrived at City Point the day our chapel was dedicated and was one of the squad members quartered in it. He was dismayed to find himself in the midst of our preparations for a religious service! He had left home to get rid of this prospect and, here, he was suddenly in the middle of getting ready for a meeting. He rolled himself in his blanket, lay in a corner, and tried to sleep but could not. He heard little of what was said but could not shake the feelings, which his church quarters had awakened. He slept little that night, thinking of his patient and uncomplaining wife, his children, and his own past conduct. Finally, for the first time in years, he was driven to pray. A few nights later, he rose for prayers. I felt very hopeful for him but his old propensities proved very strong. One day, he was greatly provoked, got into a fight, and came close to being arrested.

After this, he avoided us and left the meetings entirely, that is, until I met him one morning in the swampy woods in back of our camp and confronted him. At first, he tried to get away but finally sat down. I told him I was sorry about the fight and that I could hardly blame him. His provocation had been so great. I still had confidence in him and expected he would do well. It seemed to do him a world of good. That night, he was at the meeting and every subsequent meeting while we remained at camp. Whether he ever became a Christian, I do not know. However, he used to say, "The Christian Commission has done more for me than all Pittsburg could."

Along these lines, it was surprising to see how soon the men came to trust us. They would tell us about their wives, children, or sweethearts and show us their pictures. One poor fellow received a letter containing news of his aged mother's death. Though he was a perfect stranger to us, he came to us in tears and, without saying a word, handed us the letter to read. He wanted sympathy and, instinctively, he felt that representatives of Christ could give it. The boys brought us their wallets to keep. One offered us five dollars for having kept his overnight. Men put money into our hands to express home. They gave us watches to carry when we returned north. With no knowledge of our personal character and with only the endorsement of the Commission, the men placed unlimited trust in us.
(J. K. McLean)

Work of the Holy Spirit

I think it was probably the second day our Commission flag had been displayed that Brother Bigelow returned from a tour of the camp and found a man waiting at the door to see us. He was a member of the mounted squad at headquarters. He was the son of pious parents and had a pious wife at home but he, himself, had resisted all religious inclinations. He had been a member of a drinking club in Jersey City, where he had been hastening to ruin. He enlisted and came to City Point. Here, apart from any external religious influences whatsoever, he became thoughtful, penitent, and finally a child of Christ.

During the two months since his conversion, he had come across only one person with whom he could converse on the subject of religion. Passing our station the day before, he saw the sign "Christian Commission" and, knowing nothing about us, was drawn to the name "Christian." He told us: "I thought that there I should find someone with whom I could talk." As soon as he was off duty, he came over to our tent and, finding no one, patiently waited for our return. Finally, Brother Bigelow found him. With moistened eye and quivering lip, he related his story. We saw him often during our stay and were convinced that he was, indeed, a changed man.

Our last service at the camp was deeply moving. The chapel was crowded. Reverend S. L. Bowler, from Orono, Maine and agent of the Commission's Washington office, preached that evening. After some parting remarks, we bade the men goodbye. Even in the short time we had been with them, we had come to love them for we had found many noble, manly hearts among them. As we left the pulpit after the benediction, they stood in two lines all the way down to the door. One after another gave us a hearty grasp of the hand and the words: "God bless you, Chaplain!" We thanked the Lord that He had placed before us such an open door.
(J. K. McLean)

Magnificent Work of Grace

I have narrated these things fully for the reason that the experiences at this station were measurably unique. It was a definite effort, made in circumstances, conducive for showing the power of God working through the Commission. We found a camp wholly given over to godlessness. The good, which existed, was buried out of sight—almost smothered by superabounding evil.

By a moderate effort and through God's blessing, this state of things was almost wholly reversed in a short period of time—such that the good became uppermost and the evil was forced into retreat. Large numbers of men, just on the eve of the bloody battles, which terminated the war, were brought under Christian influences. Many of them yielded to Christ and rode on to death, prepared to meet it.

After we left, the meetings continued under the efficient leadership of Mr. D. C. H. Whitney, of Fitchburg, Massachusetts. The station was one of the last to be taken out of service. Our stockade chapel had to be abandoned for a larger meeting area as the weather grew warm. Night after night, many souls, a veritable "multitude," heard and "received with meekness the engrafted word" of their salvation.
(J. K. McLean)

Ministry of Multiplication

The work connected with the numerous chapels, which were erected over the entire army, was one of exceeding interest. In many of them, revivals were begun. In all, deeply fervent and prayerful meetings were held. Reverend E. F. Williams, Pastor of Congregational Church, Whitinsville, Massachusetts, records this story. He writes of Henry Station Chapel in the Third Division of the Twenty-fourth Corps in *Annals, U. S. Christian Commission*, 449:

One evening, a man belonging to a battery, three-quarters of a mile from our chapel, strayed over to the meeting. He became greatly interested in the service. When he was about half-way home, he kneeled by a stump and prayed. The next night, he brought a companion and attended the meeting again. The stump saw two praying souls that night. Upon their return to camp, they began to work for Christ and, in a few weeks, forty men out of that battery alone found peace in believing.

Ministry of Life-changing Words

Reverend William A. Mandell, Pastor of Congregational Church, Lunen-burg, Massachusetts, relates two soldiers' experiences. These were told in the chapel at City Point Hospital and are contained in *Annals, U. S. Christian Commission*, 449:

Amos L. Ham, of Company B, 18th New Hampshire Regiment, told us how he was astounded by a message from his little daughter. He labored with deep emotion as he spoke. His wife had written him a letter. Before sealing it, she turned to her little daughter and asked, "What shall I write your father for you?"

"Tell him," said little Nellie, "to look to God and trust Him and then he will come home safe."

The message went to the father's heart, humbling him at the foot of the Cross, as a "little child."

Ministry of Apologetics

Corporal Matthias had become a Christian. Before the Hatcher's Run battle, he said to a comrade: "You are detailed to go to the front, while I am to remain with the baggage. Let us change places. I'll go to the front. You remain in camp."

"What for?" asked his bunkmate.

"Because I'm prepared to die, I think, but you are not."

The exchange was made. In battle, the Christian soldier was hit three times by spent balls and sustained minor injuries. The Corporal's friend rose in our meeting and related the circumstance.

He added, "I want to tell you, brother soldiers, that this brought me to Jesus and He has made me a very different man. Some of you claim to be as happy in your pleasures as Christians are. If so, then why do you strew the way with playing cards when you are going into battle? Why are you afraid to die on the field with these in your pockets? Why do you reprove each other for profane words while you are getting into line for battle?"

The narrative and the argument both made a deep impression upon all present. (William A. Mandell)

Witness of a New Christian

Reverend H. J. Patrick, Pastor of Congregational Church, West Newton, Massachusetts, shares his reminiscences at the chapel at City Point Hospital:

A messenger, just in from the front, came into the meeting and told how he had resolved the last time he was there to stand up the next night. Before that night came, he was ordered to the front.

He said, "I was very troubled. I thought my 'day of grace' was passed. I was put out on the picket and got more and more depressed. At last, I determined I would be a Christian. I didn't know how to do it. I thought I must do something or other. The only thing I could think of was to work with my companions and get them to do as I did. I went to one and asked him if he loved Jesus. He said he didn't. I talked and prayed with him—spent most of a night praying. He became a Christian. And now I have come back to tell you how precious it is to serve Christ."

Changed Life

About two hundred attended our first meeting. We had no benches for them, so they sat cross-legged. Reverend Asa Bullard, of the Massachusetts Sunday School Society, gave them a talk and discovered that about ninety-five percent of those present had been connected with Sunday schools. A soldier with the lst Maryland Regiment told how, six months prior, he had scarcely known what the Bible was. Once he had deserted. When captured, his punishment and a letter from his wife, urging him to do better, had made him think. So one day, as he was returning from carrying rations out to the pickets, he came upon a soldier's grave. Humbled and penitent, he determined to consecrate himself to Jesus. With faltering, sincere words, he told us how he was trying to stay near to Christ.

(H. J. Patrick)

Dead Man's Ministry

Lieutenant Loomis, of the 146th New York Regiment, told us of an incident that took place on August 19, 1864, the day of the Weldon railroad fight. As his men were advancing to charge, he saw a Bible, stained with blood, on the ground beside a dead Confederate soldier. Picking it up, he later found the dead soldier's name, B. F. Porter, Company B, 11th Mississippi Regiment, printed inside the cover.

"Now," said the Lieutenant, "I am using that Bible myself and doing what I never did before—I am praying. I shall keep the Bible for the owner's friends, if they can be found."

Finding Christ through Reading the New Testament

An incident is related by Reverend Lyman Bartlett, Pastor of Congregational Church, Morristown, Vermont:

In visiting a small battery directly in front of Fort Morton, I became acquainted with the captain of a heavy battery of the 8th New York Artillery. Up until a few weeks prior, he had been a thoughtless, wild young man. His wife was a Christian and she, along with her pious brother, had written often to urge him to come to Christ. One day, he found a soiled New Testament on the ground near his quarters, so he picked up and began to read. He became interested as never before and, in a few days, completely read through it.

Going through it over and over again, he found new meaning at each perusal, though he found much he could not understand. He began to pray for light. Soon, the Spirit opened his eyes and led him to the Cross where he found pardon and direction and peace. All this time, he had not conversed with a single Christian friend. Afterward, his wife sent him a small pocket Bible. Reading it produced a new revelation to him each succeeding day. His gratitude to God for having opened his eyes to behold such wondrous things out of His Law was beautiful and childlike.

Ministry of Friendship

Reverend Perkins K. Clark, Pastor of the Congregational Church, South Deerfield, Massachusetts, writes in February 1865 from Point of Rocks:

Before I left home, a little girl came to me, wishing to send something to the soldiers. Her mother said she had been saving all her pennies for a long time and had been very unwilling to part with any of them. But when she heard

I was going to the army, she wanted her mother to come with her to bring some of them to me.

Her mother asked, "Well, how many will you take, Clara?"

"Twenty-five"—this was one-fourth of the whole amount. They brought me the twenty-five pennies in a modest, but valuable, little roll. I decided to add some of the other funds that had been entrusted to me and buy a Bible, to be given in Clara's name.

As I was visiting my soldiers at Point of Rocks Hospital, a young man of the 1st New York Mounted Rifles, who had a New Testament, asked me for a Bible. He was searching for the truth and was under deep conviction of sin. I said to myself, "Here is the man for little Clara's book." So I told him all about the twenty-five cents and wrote on the flyleaf of the book, "Albert S. May, Company C, 1st New York Mounted Rifles. Bought with pennies given by little Clara Hastings, of South Deerfield, Massachusetts. Presented by Reverend P. K. Clark, U.S.C.C., Point of Rocks. February 14, 1865. 'Search the Scriptures.'" As I gave him the book, I spoke to him earnestly about the duty he owed to God. He was overcome with emotion and, hiding his face under the blanket, he sobbed like a child. The next day, I took some blackberry syrup to him. Again, I presented Christ to him.

"I haven't found Him," he said, "and it seems to me I've been trying as hard as I can."

"Well, now, suppose you stop trying and let Him try. He invites you. Believe this and trust Him. He promises, '… and him that cometh unto Me, I will in no wise cast out.'"

Sunday morning, I saw him again.

"Yesterday," he said, "I found Him. I saw that I could do nothing but just believe."

His face and countenance indicated the deep peace of God. I was to leave next morning and came to bid him good-bye.

"Jesus is my Savior," he said, with tears rolling down his cheeks. "I can leave all with Him. I'll write to you when I can sit up. Tell little Clara how I thank her for the dear book."

When my term of service in another part of the army had expired, I hastened again to the Point of Rocks Hospital. A new sickness had befallen Albert and he was dying. He was too weak for much conversation.

"Is Jesus precious to you, Albert?"

"He is all that is precious to me now."

He whispered his wish to me that the Bible should be sent to his mother. A faint smile came upon his face as I spoke of the Better Land. It rested there.

On the morning of February 28, 1865, he died, happy in Jesus.

Comforting the Dying

Reverend W. A. Mandell, Pastor of the Congregational Church, Lunenburg, Massachusetts, tells this story of the last hour:

At City Point Hospital, a young drummer boy had been wounded and was dying. He asked a delegate to read and pray with him. A number of passages were read. The sufferer kept saying, "Read some more." At last, the delegate came to the fourth verse of the Twenty-third Psalm.

"Stop," said the boy, "that's it. Read it again." It was done.

"Read it again, please." It was read the third time.

"Will you put my hand on it, please?"

He could not see, so his hand was guided to the page and verse.

"Lay it open on my chest, Chaplain."

It was done and the dying child folded his dear arms over the sacred words: "Yea, though I walk through the valley of the shadow of death, I will fear no evil; for Thou art with me; Thy rod and Thy staff they comfort me." Still pressing it to his chest, the boy gently passed from this scene of earthly conflict to the Place of Eternal Rest.

Ministry of Helps

In February 1865, a conundrum proposed by a soldier to Reverend E. P. Smith, General Field Agent of the Christian Commission, sums up much of the real difficulty of army life:

I was riding on top of a train of cars, running over what the soldiers called "General Grant's railroad," the line that stretches from City Point up to the left of the army. While we were passing through a forest cleared by soldiers' axes, a private sitting by my side called attention to the large pine trees which had been torn out by the roots in the windstorm of the preceding night. They had been left where they fell for Quartermasters' purposes after the smaller ones had been cut away for fuel.

"Chaplain," said the soldier, "do you know how those trees that have tumbled over are like a great many men in the army?" I gave up and he answered, "Because they can't stand without 'the little ones' to help 'em."

CHAPTER XIII
THE EASTERN ARMIES

FROM THE INVESTMENT OF PETERSBURG
UNTIL THE CLOSE OF THE WAR
(CONCLUDED)
June 1864–April 1865

Obedience to the Word of God

Reverend George N. Marden, Pastor of the Congregational Church, Boxborough, Massachusetts, illustrates the general truth that the soldiers place a high value on the Word of God:

At one of the City Point hospitals, a soldier told me he had been near the gates of death.

"How did you feel in view of meeting God?" I asked.

"Well," he said, "I thought it over and felt calm and ready. I never made any profession of faith but I'm convinced of the truth of religion. When I was young, I used to read Tom Paine and Voltaire and I liked to argue, for the sake of argument, with anyone who seemed sectarian or fond of discussion. Yet I did not believe a word of what I read. I always believed in my mother's religion. No man on the face of God's earth can lodge an argument between me and my mother's religion."

Power of New Testaments

Reverend Dr. Robert Patterson, Pastor of Reformed Presbyterian Church, Chicago, writes from Hatcher's Run in Virginia, March 1865. He gives an account of the opening of a fresh box of Testaments for the men who were to march within a day or two:

"Boys, I want eight men to help with this box of New Testaments."

"Here you go, Chaplain," said a boy of fourteen or fifteen as he joined with the others.

"That's an odd little fellow," says one of the men. "He is from Hagerstown, Maryland where, when the inhabitants fled, his father bushwhacked Stuart's Cavalry and got killed, so he enlisted."

He gets a New Testament and a hymnbook and said, "If you give me another, I'll distribute it."

"To whom will you distribute it, my son?"

"To my Color Sergeant, sir. He is bringing in his blanket and great coat for the Commission to send home for him."

Another said, "I wish you would give me one of those New Testaments. I had one covered with leather. Mother gave it to me and I carried it all through the campaign until I lost my knapsack. I wouldn't have taken fifty dollars for it."

"Please, Chaplain, let me have one," said another. "I have a Bible my mother gave me but the covers are worn off it and I have to tie it with a string. I think I'll send it home."

A young convert who found Christ last week must have one. A boy who wants to send home his Fifth Corps badge, a Maltese silver cross, inscribed with Antietam and a dozen other battles. We cannot refuse him one.

The box of New Testaments will scarcely last till night. A chaplain arrives with an oat sack for all the papers and New Testaments we can give him. He will shoulder it two miles. Then here comes a Christian brother with whom I have crossed the prairie and became friends during the great revival of 1858. He says the spirit among the men is the same as during that revival. His Colonel, named McCoy, conducts the meeting when he is absent and the chapel tent is filled every night.

I attended a Bible class on Sunday afternoon in the Third Brigade, Second Division, Fifth Corps. Almost all the boys had New Testaments but one of the leaders, buttoned up to the throat, went around and, upon opening his coat, poured forth the Word of God to those who needed one. Then they all began the study of the Sermon on the Mount. That night in that chapel, more than a dozen were under conviction and seeking prayer after the sermon. They will not willingly leave the meeting until the drum calls them to their quarters.

Mother's Influence Transforms Soldier

While canvassing the army to discover its need for the Word of God, Reverend W. H. Gilbert, Joint Agent of the American Bible Society and of the Christian Commission, came upon these incidents:

In one tent, two of the four men went to the meetings and became gloriously converted. Without opposition from the other two, they began reading the Bible and praying in their tent. One of the new Christians, a short, stout man, whom they called "Chubby," was accustomed to reading for them. At length, Chubby was sent to the front. When the next hour of worship came, his companion, who was not willing to give up the exercise or to conduct it by himself, asked his comrades who should read the Bible for them.

"Will you, William?"

"No," was the reply. "I can't read the Bible. I never did."

The other tent mate, who was a very profane and wicked, responded, "I will. I ought to. My mother taught me to read it and it would have been better for me if I had always obeyed her." And the tears flowed as he took the book and read a chapter. When he had finished, his pious companion knelt to pray and he also knelt. When the other had prayed, he followed and, then and there, gave himself to Christ and began a Christian life."

Love for God's Word

In one of the meetings at City Point, a soldier said he had been trying to serve Christ for about six months. He had been seeking to encourage all in his company to come to the meeting and seek Jesus and he had succeeded in persuading eleven to attend. He drew his Bible from his pocket and said he had read it through three times since he began to serve Christ. He mentioned he would not exchange it for all other books that could be collected.
(W. H. Gilbert)

Experiences of Spiritual Renewal

Reverend John B. Perry, Pastor of the Congregational Church, Swanton, Vermont, writes in March 1865 from the chapel at Warren Station of the influence these "tabernacles in the wilderness" exerted on the soldiers:

Two boys from a regiment, not noted for their piety, began to attend the services at Warren Station chapel. Becoming interested in the meetings, they persevered and soon gave evidence that they were born of God. Going back to their own camp, they started worship gatherings in their tents. The little meetings continued nightly and the number in attendance increased. Soon, thirty men from that regiment had placed their hope in Christ.

In another regiment, only one professing Christian could be found a few months earlier. He had been alone for a year. He was an unassuming, quiet, conscientious boy of about nineteen years of age. His life was so spotless and his efforts were so faithful that interest among his comrades finally awakened. On April 1, 1865, eighteen men in the regiment cherished a substantial trust in Christ as the Divine Savior.

Dying with Faith in Jesus

The fruit of these awakenings that shone on the battlefield was what might have been expected—soldiers "strong in the Lord." On the evening of March 22, 1865, a soldier who had recently found peace with God was baptized and received into the Army Christian Association. In the severe fighting of March 25th, he was mortally wounded. When brought off the field, he was happy in spirit even though he was suffering intensely. He asked for messages to be delivered to his friends at home and to his companions in arms, urging them to seek Christ. As his breath ebbed away amidst the outward signs of extreme bodily anguish, we asked, "Where are you going?"

He replied, "I am going home. Yes, I am going home to be with Jesus." (John B. Perry)

Spiritual Influence of Soldier's Chapel

Reverend W. Howell Buchanan, of Elverston, Illinois, writes of the way in which the soldiers became attached to the chapels:

I attended one meeting in the chapel at Meade Station where the men's passion for deep, quiet, religious earnestness I had never seen. The service was literally baptized in tears and it was certainly baptized by the Holy Spirit. One young man, whose emotions continually choked his words, told me, "I helped to build this chapel and I shall never forget the place. I didn't know when I was working here what good it would do for me but I was converted here. I've been home since then and united with the old church, Dr. Plummer's, in Allegheny City, Pennsylvania, but I can never, never forget this chapel. It's been the gate of heaven to me."

Lives Transformed by the Gospel

Just before the order came for an advance along the whole line, the chapel meetings were at the peak of their interest and power. This narrative will illustrate this. It proceeds from the pen of Reverend Dr. Patterson, Pastor of Reformed Presbyterian Church in Chicago. He writes from "Quinnipiac Chapel" near Hatcher's Run on March 20, 1865:

Yesterday afternoon and evening, two crowded meetings were held at General Gwyn's headquarters in the chapel tent where the men have held meetings every evening for weeks and without any chaplain. When I went in, a soldier with a sergeant's chevrons was preaching Christ—"His name shall be called Wonderful." It was a noble gospel sermon. I thought of Cromwell's preaching and praying "Ironsides" and took courage for our future.

At night, I preached to a crowded house. The officers and men, instead of sitting on benches, sat on round poles with pins stuck in for legs. What our velvet-cushioned pew-holders would say to meetings, which lasted for three hours on such a "roost," I can't say. However, General Gwyn with his colonels and officers seemed satisfied to obtain room a midst the crowd. After the sermon, we held a prayer meeting. The faces and utterances of the men denoted the deepest feelings. I had not been accustomed to so much excitement in my meetings at home and expressed my thoughts to an officer present.

He replied, "You should have heard them express their feelings," he said, "when they took the enemy's works at Dabney's Mills with their skirmish line. It did seem as if they were wrestling in mortal combat with sin. Of the men who were praying, the colonel said, 'They are the best men in my regiment. In the fight, there's no 'hold back' about them.' That little drummer boy over yonder was a terrible fellow once but we have no trouble with him now."

Powerful Revival

The chapel meetings were at the peak of their interest and power just before the order came for an advance along the whole line in March 1865. This narrative illustrates the meetings in the Sixth Corps, conducted by the Corps Agent, Reverend George A. Hall, member of Troy Conference, Methodist Episcopal Church, in the station chapel:

The crowded nightly meetings in the chapel witnessed such scenes as have never been known outside of army lines. The night before a fight on the left, a question was put to a most solemn assembly. The speaker asked, "How many of you who are seeking Christ are ready to surrender to Him now?"

In answer to the question, some twelve to fifteen men came forward and knelt by the front seat—among them was an interesting youth. Upon seeing him, an old man darted from his seat, pressed through the crowded aisle, and threw his arms about the young soldier, sobbing, "My son, my son. He was lost and now is found."

Just then, the Adjutant from Division headquarters entered, apologizing for his intrusion, and called out, "All men belonging to the _____ Division, fall in."

They were to march in the darkness of night to secure a position for the attack at daylight. The men on the front seat arose, fell on each other's necks, and wept. Some of them were to go. The aforementioned father was not in the division ordered out but his boy was. The parting was tender and cheerful. He kissed him and said, "Go now, my boy, since the Lord is going with you."

There were hurried pledges to be faithful and then they all took hold of hands around the altar and sang,

> "Say, brothers, will you meet us
> On Canaan's happy shore?"

Then they hurried to their quarters to make ready to fall in. Some did not return from that fight. Two were brought into City Point Hospital badly wounded. They told us of the meeting, of their consecration, of their fearlessness in the fight, and of their readiness to meet death if it was God's will. Others came back and participated in a few more meetings in the chapel and joined with us in our closing Communion service—the last meeting in the chapel and the last meeting in the Corps before the final movement on Richmond.

Ordinance of the Lord's Supper

It was a wonderful service, the ordinance of the Lord's Supper under marching orders. Officers, soldiers and delegates—all united hearts and said parting words. Some of them, without doubt, would next drink of the fruit of the vine anew in the Father's Kingdom. None expected to commune together again in this world but, in this, they were happily disappointed.

When the Sixth Corps had finished its noble record of marching and fighting and came back to rendezvous near Alexandria, Mr. Hall, with his station in working order and his chapel flag flying, called in his boys once more. The blessed meetings were resumed and on the last Sunday before mustering out, one more Communion service was held in memorial of Christ's love. It was a fitting time and place for testimony to Christ's love by men who had come into the service as His disciples and who had been kept true and were returning as veterans in His service. It was also a fitting time for testimony by men who had fallen under army temptations and had been rescued, as well as those who were going home after a three years of service to testify to their families and neighbors of the power of the Christian life for the first time.

(George A. Hall)

Historical Context:

Before closing the story of the armies operating against Richmond, reference must be made to the special work undertaken by the Christian Commission in behalf of the black troops who made up the Twenty-fifth Corps in the Army of the James. A Conference of Chaplains met early in the winter 1865 at Butler Station and was immediately followed by an appeal from the Executive Committee at Philadelphia for fifty teachers for black soldiers. General Butler gave *carte blanche* approval for all the needed lumber. Primers, spelling books, and Bible readers were forwarded in very large numbers.

Soon, thirty neat buildings attested to the eagerness of the men to learn to read and write. Schools were in progress in nearly every regiment of the Corps. Two large Commission stations, "Birney" and "Wild," one mile apart, were established to facilitate the general work. Long before this, however, the attention of the Commission had been called to the necessity of doing something toward the instruction of this part of the army.

Ministry of Teaching People to Read

Reverend J. W. Harding, Pastor of Congregational Church, Longmeadow, Massachusetts, was part of this effort. Writing from Bermuda Hundred in September 1864, he tells of these men:

These black soldiers have strong arms and warm hearts. They salute us respectfully, their demeanor is soldierly, and the highest favor we can give them is a Primer, a First or Second Reader, or a Testament. They are bent on learning to read. It would please you to see me in the capacity of a primary school teacher to some brawny cavalry six-footer. He stands by my side, cap in hand, booted and spurred, his bright saber clanking at his heels. He eagerly spells out the words which shall unseal for him the fountains of knowledge. I could devote my whole time in giving them spelling and reading lessons.

And then you should see them on their well-groomed horses, bringing in a squad of Confederate prisoners. They say nothing but they look all around—and so do their more than crest-fallen captives. We found some men in the guardhouse yesterday who were actually in mortal dread of their black guard. Remembering Fort Pillow, they feared their guards might lay violent hands on them. We have no doubt that a proper fear of our black soldiers pervades

QUESTIONING GENERAL GRANT

the prison camps. And then you should see these black troopers escorting their wives and little ones and sweethearts into camp. Each of these loved ones carries a load on their head and in both hands, as if carrying the spoils of the Egyptians. The laughing children who cannot march, nestle in the left arms of their protective mothers.

Encouraging the Faint-hearted

It would be impossible, within reasonable limits, to give anything close to an adequate idea of the characteristics of the black soldier. Yet, an incident or two may help to form a partial picture. Reverend E. F. Williams, Pastor of the Congregational Church, Whitinsville, Massachusetts, provides a story that took place at the City Point General Hospital:

On one of the hottest days in August 1864, Lieutenant-General Grant rode up to the Christian Commission headquarters and asked for a drink of water. A cup of lemonade, sweetened with black-brown sugar, was handed him with the apology that we had no water and the lemonade was what we gave the men in the hospitals. The General obviously relished every drop, thanked us for it, declared it could not be better, and shook hands with the delegates who crowded around him. Asking for the accustomed "light," he was just about to mount his horse when one of our black employees, without hat, coat or vest, elbowed his way through the crowd. He reached out an enormous hand and said, "How do you do, General Grant?"

The words were spoken with gentlemanly deference, and the man's whole appearance indicated that he had been attracted not by mere curiosity. The General shook the extended hand warmly. The man then disclosed his purpose when he asked, "How are things going, general?"

To appreciate the question, it must be remembered that it was at a time of great depression among the black people. This incident occurred not long after the fatal mine explosion near Petersburg. The General's simple answer quieted the man's fears at once: "Everything is going right, sir."

Politely bowing in a gesture of respect and with eyes beaming with gratitude, the black man backed out of the circle and returned to his work. On his way back, I met him and asked where he had been. He responded, "Been to see General Grant, sir."

"What did he say to you?"

"Said everything was going right, sir."

Before long, the General's authoritative statement was known by all the black people near City Point. Everyone was astonished to observe the effect which the simple words had in reviving the spirits of those who, a few hours earlier, had been so depressed and disheartened.

Perspective on the Cause of the Civil War

Reverend George N. Marden, Pastor of Congregational Church, Boxborough, Massachusetts, gives a black soldier's idea of the cause of the war:

Joseph Upcheer, of a black regiment, was sick at City Point Post Hospital. He was full of Christian faith and patriotic fervor. He said, "Some say there's no God in this war. But I put my trust in the Lord, and minie balls don't scare me. The hand of the Lord is in the war."

"What do you think is the cause of it, Joseph?"

He mulled over the question for a moment and then earnestly said, "So much unfair work is the cause of the war. My old uncle, who died twenty years ago, put his hand on my head once, and says he, 'Young dog, make haste and grow. By-and-bye you'll have a gun and fight.' We've been expecting this war, sir. There's been so much unfair work."

Diligence in Learning

Mr. Edwin Ferris, of New York City, gives his experience of the eagerness of the men to learn:

The black soldiers had no reservations, no cold formality. The greetings I received made me feel at home at once. Young and old alike were anxious for instruction and applied themselves so diligently that their progress was very rapid. One day, I was teaching one of them his letters. He found it difficult to keep them straight—his eyes were so unaccustomed to letters. I shall never forget the way in which he lifted his sleeve and drew it across his face, dripping with perspiration, and said, "Master, this does make me sweat."

One noble old Christian soldier said, "I bless the good Lord for what He's helped me to learn. I'm going to keep on. I've got to work sharper than these young men, because I haven't so much time left to study in."

Incredible Desire for Learning

Mr. Herbert C. Clapp, of Cambridge, Mass., writing from Wild's Station in February 1865, gives a remarkable instance of diligent work by a black soldier:

"One night, I taught a man the alphabet and a few elementary principles. The next evening, he came to me, prepared to recite *one half of the spelling book* I had given him. He had studied the whole day, with occasional assistance from a friend."

Ministry to Runaway Slaves

One incident of eagerness to learn is related by Reverend George Marden, Pastor of Congregational Church, Boxborough, Massachusetts:

On February 14, 1865, I discovered a nest of huts on the edge of a little ravine within two stones' throw of our chapel at City Point. These huts housed runaway slaves and the men were laborers in the railroad department. The huts were of the cheapest construction. The dwellings consisted of two or three boxes and the same number of old barrels, a few nails and an old bootleg, a few sticks and stones, and the all-pervading Virginia mud. An old cut up bootleg served as hinges on which swing the window and door, bits of board that had been painfully dovetailed.

My advent seemed to signal a resurrection of sorts. Just as the capsules of certain flowers yield little black seeds when the cell is broken, so from the patchwork huts the dwellers now poured forth. Each one wanted a book. One eleven year-old boy read so well that I gave him a New Testament, which made his face burst forth with the "countless laughter" of Aeschylus' (an ancient Greek playwright) sea. Mothers came begging for a primer for their children. All were eager, curious, and delighted.

Upon receiving a book, one black man gave vent to a guffaw, the likes of which I had never dreamed the human throat capable of producing. The women, unselfish as ever, seemed more anxious to get the primers for their children than for themselves.

Attachment to the Bible

Mr. C. E. Bolton, a student of Amherst College, Massachusetts, was accompanied to the army by Professors Seelye and Hitchcock. As a delegate to the army in July and August 1864, he tells a striking story of the attachment of the black soldier to the Bible:

William and Thomas Freeman were brothers living in Connecticut at the outbreak of the war. They enlisted in the 30th Regiment U. S. C. T. and were transferred later to the 31st. At the close of the first day's battle in the Wilderness, they entered a large house, once the property of an extensive slaveholder. Several slave women in the dwelling were nearly famished with hunger. The soldiers kindly emptied their haversacks of all their rations and gave everything to the women. The only way the women could return the favor was to present William Freeman with a large, finely-bound and beautifully clasped quarto Bible, weighing about nine pounds. Thomas and William were both Christians and valued the gift most highly. This Bible took the place of blankets in William's knapsack. He carried it through all the marches to the entrenchments of Petersburg.

On July 30, 1864, he went into the fatal charge after the mine explosion and was wounded in the chest. The great Bible went with him into the battle in his knapsack. He would never allow it to go beyond his reach. His brother Thomas, who was a black Sergeant, was wounded in the same engagement. He was among the few who struggled beyond the chasm made by the mine blast and was carried back to find his brother dead. As the men were bearing him further toward the rear, he begged that his brother's knapsack might be placed upon the stretcher under his head. With the task completed, the precious book reached the hospital of the 4th Division of the Ninth Corps, where I was working in the Commission service.

William was buried between the picket lines under a flag of truce. Poor Thomas' wounds were discovered to be mortal as well. Weak and worn out, he was taken to the General Hospital at City Point a few days later. Sergeant Edward P. Gilbert, of Bath, New York, was a wardmaster of our hospital. When Thomas left for City Point, he sold the cherished volume to Sergeant Gilbert.

A few days later, I purchased this Bible, which represented so much faith and heroism, from the Sergeant. Afterward, I gave it to Amherst College. In receiving it on behalf of the Trustees, President Stearns remarked, "I consider it one of the most valuable reminiscences of the war, presented to the College." The book now has a prominent place in the showcase of the "Appleton Cabinet" at Amherst.

Ministry of Bringing Comfort

Taking another page from Reverend Mr. George Marden's experience, we can learn a lesson in trust. This Pastor of the Congregational Church in Boxborough, Massachusetts shows us how, in the last hour, the black man could exercise great trust in his white brother:

I met Thomas Jackson Yager in one of the City Point wards. He looked up at me with a smile when he saw my badge and gave me his hand, thin and hard worn with years of unrequited toil.

I asked, "Do you love the Lord, Thomas?"

He responded, "I do love Him. He is all to me. I am happy lying here—full of joy and praise. I pray the Lord, bless you in your work."

"Where are you from, Thomas?"

"I'm from La Grange, in old Kentucky. I come into the army to fight for freedom. Left my wife and the child behind me and I don't know how they treat her. But the Lord's been good to me and I don't feel like nothing but thanks."

A fortnight later, I met him again. His cheeks are sunken and his eyes were dimmer than before. I take his hand again and he begins to talk, saying, "My time won't be long here. All my trust is in the Lord. I believe the Lord is waiting for me. I'm weak but I'm ready to go. Wish I could get a letter from my wife. I'd like to know how she's getting along. She wasn't a Christian when I left but it looked mighty like as if she wanted to be one. I'll never be of much more account here *but I hate to give up before the Lord gives up. When He says I can live no more, then I'm ready to give up.*"

A little later, this Christian soldier had gone away to his everlasting rest.

Christ-like Worldview

The story of a conversation between a black Sergeant and Reverend E. P. Smith, the General Field Agent of the Western Army, may give a little insight into the depth of the motives which animated the black soldiers. This took place while Reverend Smith was on a visit in the East:

On the steamer from City Point to Fortress Monroe, I came upon a group of black soldiers in friendly conversation and banter with several white artillerymen. They were all on a furlough and, consequently, were good natured. The black men were going to Norfolk. They had been selected on their merits, as being entitled to a furlough. One was a sergeant in the 36th U. S. C. Infantry—a fine, honest, muscular man of about twenty-eight years of age, wearing his belt and sword.

He quietly listened to the conversation on fighting men, high bounties, and all that until a batteryman turned to him and asked, "What bounty did you get?"

"No bounty. I wouldn't enlist for bounty. I have twenty-three more months to put in. I don't say I will go in again when that's over. I can't say until the time comes but, if I do, it won't be for bounty. I wouldn't fight for money. My wages are enough."

"How much pay do you get?"

"Seven dollars a month, until they raise it to sixteen. That keeps me along right smart. Those big-bounty men don't make good soldiers."

"What's the matter with them?"

"They come in for money. There's no Country about it and they have no stomach for fighting and digging and knocking around like soldiers have to."

"What's money got to do with that? Why can't a man fight just as well if he leaves a thousand dollars in the bank to have when he comes back—maybe sick or wounded?"

"Well, he might but, you see, it's the greenbacks that fetches him in and he keeps studying how he can jump for another bounty and those sort of soldiers ain't no count for fighting."

"Sergeant, didn't you enlist because you had run away from master and had no place to go?"

"No, sir," he said with spirit. "I had a place and good wages—heap more than a soldier gets—driving a team for a quartermaster. And when I told him I was going in and wanted my back pay, he cussed me and said I shouldn't enlist. I told him I had a right and I would, and all I asked of him was to pay what was coming to me—more than two hundred dollars. He swore and took on about arresting me, and the next day when I had enlisted, he saw me on the street and called a guard, and put me in irons for ten hours. That's my bounty, two hundred dollars—wages—given up, and ten hours in irons by a copper head quartermaster."

The soldiers had gathered around, highly interested in the Sergeant's straightforward, earnest story.

"I'd a split his copper head open with the irons," said one of them.

"That's not me," said the Sergeant. "I don't take vengeance—that's God's business and He'll work it to suit Himself."

The men drew back a little and were silent all-round the ring. I stepped forward and said, "Sergeant, how long have you been a Christian?"

He looked at me with a full, quick eye, as if he had found a brother and said, "Ten years, sir."

"How old are you?"

"Twenty-eight, sir."

"Then you were converted when you were eighteen years old. Where did you live?"

"Near Richmond."

"Do you have a wife?"

"Yes, I left my wife and son when McClellan came close up to Richmond and everybody reckoned he was going to walk in."

"How old is your son?"

"Not quite a year old when I got away."

"Do you hear from them?"

"Yes, I seen a lady from there in Norfolk and she said master done and sold Nancy and the boy."

"You will hardly see them again, will you?"

"When they get done fighting, I reckon I can find her."

"But you won't know where to look."

"Then I'll keep looking and I reckon I'll find them. Anyhow, I trust in Providence about it."

"What do you mean by that?"

"I mean the Lord God Almighty. He knows all about it and He will do what's right."

"Yes, Sergeant, the Lord may do what's right but the man who has bought Nancy and your baby and carried them off may not do what's right about it. What then?"

"Why, then, I reckon that's for Him to settle about. I've nothing to do with that."

"You are pretty near your master. He might be looking for you one of these days."

"Yes, he might and then, you see, I might be looking for him. Chance is the same on both sides now. They say my master was 'scripted' and had to go in."

"Perhaps, you will have a chance yet to pay him back," said the batteryman.

"I never pay back. The Lord Almighty takes the vengeance. That's His and I don't have nothing to do with it."

"There's his doctrine again. Don't he stick to his text?" says a Pittsburg soldier. "He's right too, all the time," says another.

"Don't know about the right," called a voice across the ring, "but he's bully on consistence."

"Well, Sergeant, have you really made much by running away?"

"Made much? I made two hundred dollars in Norfolk but didn't get it."

"I mean you are not much better off soldiering, lying out in the wet, digging in the trenches, and going in where the minie balls hum. That's not much better than to be at home on the old plantation with wife and baby."

"Soldiering is hard work but there's a heap of difference."

"What's the difference?"

"Freedom, sir, freedom! I say 'Liberty' in 'Dutch Gap.' I wake up in the night and say 'Liberty.' Yes, there's a heap of difference. I can say 'Liberty' all the time."

"You said you enlisted for your Country. What has your Country done for you except to give you a chance to make tobacco and cotton for your master and have your wife and baby sold down in Georgia?"

"*God* has done a heap for me. He has given me my life. I never had no sickness and now He's made me free and I'm willing to fight for the rest of them."

"Sergeant," said a white soldier, "do you know that you are just like Jeff Davis on the war question?"

"Not much, I reckon."

"Exactly alike—you are both fighting for the black man.'"

"That may be but it makes a heap of odds to which whips."

"Do you think Jeff will put the black men in?" he asked.

"He is doing it now. It will not be long before a corps of those black fellows will be down on the 'right' to drive you Twenty-fifth Corps men into the river. What will you do then?"

"If I should see my father in the 'Confederate' Army, I should shoot him. He's got no business there. There's some black people got no sense. Confederates have talked foolishness to them so much, you can't beat sense into them. I've no use for that sort black folks. I fight for the black man when he's right."

"Bully for him!" came the cry from a dozen lips of soldiers gathered round. My thankful heart said, "God be praised for such piety and patriotism!"

At Fortress Monroe, on parting from the Sergeant who was going to the Norfolk boat, I offered a prayer for the mother and baby far away. I prayed that a Country, saved by such devotion, may learn, at last, to deal justly by all her children.

Patriot's Last Letter Home

Reverend C. D. Herbert, Pastor of Congregational Church, West Newbury, Massachusetts, writing in September 1864 from the Base Hospital of the Eighteenth Army Corps, preserves this memorial of a black soldier's sacrifice:

In the knapsack of a dead black soldier, I found a letter written a few days earlier, along with a postscript added on the day of his death. It seems that when he was first brought into the hospital, before he knew of the nature of his wounds and while expecting to recover, he wrote, "When this cruel war is over, I hope to meet with the dear friends I love so much. Fond memory brings back days gone by and I hope to return to a blessed joyfulness in my once happy home. I feel anxious to serve you, O my dear country, but I am weak with infirmities. May God heal me is my prayer in this army and make me a soldier of the Cross and clean my heart of all its sins in the world. For Christ's sake. Amen.

JOHN C. WHITEN."

When he learned how badly he was wounded and that he would die, he took the letter from beneath his pillow and added this touching postscript:

"Most sincerely yours—departed. John C. W. — *Volunteered to die.*"

In my letter to his home, I broke the sad news as gently as I knew how. I also enclosed the patriot's last letter to his wife and children with its postscript.

Victory Brings Comfort in Death

Reverend A. Fuller, Pastor of the Congregational Church, Hallowell, Maine, records two incidents of the memorable Sunday on which our army broke through the Confederate lines around Petersburg. They are a type of the triumph of the cause:

The fighting just in front of us, around three or four forts, had been desperate and both sides had suffered severely. Among our own and the Confederate wounded, we had all that we could handle until late at night. Near evening, the boom of the cannon, which had been almost constantly rending the air since the previous midnight, had ceased. Even the scattering shots of scouts and skirmishers had gradually died away. The troops had stacked their arms and were eagerly talking over their coffee of the day's events or planning campaigns for the future. The bands, gathered about the flags of their respective regiments or brigades, were filling the air with music. The warm April sun was breaking through the clouds, which lay heavily along the west. The glory of its beams was adding the crowning touch to the glory of the day.

The effect was marvelous. The quiet, solemn stillness of the hour, which the melody of the bands seemed only to render rhythmical and deeper, was in such strange contrast with the strife and carnage of the day that it would be hard to describe the attending emotions. It was a time neither of war nor yet of peace. It was the hour of precious, hallowed but costly victory. Many a weary head was turned feebly, but eagerly, on its bloody pillow of turf to look upon the scene and listen to the softened notes of triumph. This they did until earthly sights and sounds were lost in the beauty and melody of the Other Land.

As I was resting for a moment in my work, a band at army headquarters near us suddenly struck up one of our most spirited national tunes. A Union soldier, whom I had supposed was past all earthly waking, was lying near me. At the first note of the music, he was startled and gazed wildly about him, as if trying to understand where he was. With a great effort, he raised himself on his elbow and looked eagerly at me. Half fiercely and half pleadingly, he asked, "Is that a Confederate band, sir?"

"No, that's Union all through. Don't you hear the tune? Confederates are a long way from here. We have carried their whole line of works."

He looked somewhat incredulously at me as if it was almost too much to believe. Then, as he gradually drank in all the truth and saw and heard more distinctly for himself, his whole countenance was kindled with enthusiasm. Looking reverently toward heaven, with a voice of the deepest solemnity and fervor, he said, "Glory to God! It's all I ask. You may do what you like with me now," and without another earthly word, he sank back and died.

Suffering for a Greater Cause

Long after dark, we were groping about with the aid of lanterns to find any who still might be left without proper care when, suddenly, I almost stumbled over a man lying by himself in great agony. His leg had been shattered between the knee and hip joint by a piece of shell. I had him carried to a surgeon's table, where his leg was amputated.

In the morning, when he had somewhat recovered from the severe operation he had undergone, I carried him some food and drink. He was very grateful for the little attention. He had been a slave of a gentleman near

Norfolk, where his wife, mother and children were still living. Escaping from his master, he made it to the Union lines where he was one of the first to enlist in our army. He was a Christian and had become a soldier from a deep sense of duty to his race. Wounded the day before the general engagement, he had lain on the field, uncared for, with wounds undressed, and in great bodily agony.

"Well," I said, "you did not expect this when you enlisted, did you? If you were at home and well, would you come back again?"

He seemed moved at the thought of home but, in with deep emphasis, he quickly replied, "Yes, sir. Yes, I would. I expected all this when I 'listed. I expect to suffer. I expect now I'll die. But bless the Lord, I'm free and Susy and the children are free and I'm ready to die if the Lord wills."

I offered a brief prayer and left him, never to see him again, and yet ever to remember the black hero, so worthy to be an American citizen.
(A. Fuller)

Experiencing Fellowship

The Christian Commission made full preparations for the emergencies, which might arise during the pursuit of General Lee. Happily, not all of the anticipated needs arose. The August 1865 edition of *The Christian Banner* relates a story told by General Edwards of the battle of Sailor's Creek in Virginia, fought on April 7, 1865:

In the very thickest of the fight, C. F. Drake, of Company B, 37th Massachusetts Regiment, ordered a Confederate Colonel to surrender. He replied that he would never surrender. Drake then shot him, inflicting a mortal wound. The Colonel fell, exclaiming that he was dying. Drake said, "I am a Christian and will pray for you." The Colonel thanked him and Drake knelt by his side and prayed with him—while hand to hand combat raged around them. After prayer, the Colonel pressed Drake's hand, called him "brother," told him that he also was a Christian, and thanked him. Then Drake removed his gun from his holster and went on fighting.

Spiritual Impact of Christian's Life

After the surrender, the main body of the army took up its line of march to Washington. Christian Commission stations were retained and work continued among the troops in the vicinity of the recent events. Reverend J. H. Moore, Minister of Farm Ridge (O. S.) Presbyterian Church, Illinois, provides a narrative illustrating this as we now close the memorial incidents of the active operations of the Army of the Potomac:

It might be supposed that these great events, so exciting in their nature, would destroy the religious interest of the men, which was so remarkably manifest in the army previous to the advance. But such was not the case. True, for a few days, nearly all the troops around City Point were away in the battles and our chapel services for the time being were almost deserted. Then Richmond fell and the regiments, which had been encamped here, came back and soon filled up the chapel again.

A soldier, whom I had often seen at our services, came forward one evening and told me that his closest companion, who used always to attend the meetings with him, had fallen in the fighting before Petersburg.

"He was my dearest friend in the army," the soldier said. "He was the instrument God used in my conversion. I remember how mad I used to get when he knelt down and prayed in our tent before going to bed. I used to turn over and try to go to sleep and forget all about him. I held out a good while but had to give in at last. So I began to pray too. We prayed together afterward and came here together. The last thing he did before going to the front was to kneel down and commit himself to God in our old tent. He fell dead at my side on the field and now I have to come to chapel alone."

CHAPTER XIV

THE EASTERN ARMIES

OPERATING NEAR WASHINGTON AND HARPER'S FERRY

June 1864–June 1865

The advance of General Grant's army gave an immense increase to the delegates' work in the Washington hospitals. When the hospitals at Fredericksburg were closed, the wounded of earlier battles in the great campaign were moved there. Camp Distribution, the point of departure for the convalescents of these hospitals was filled with men. Here, the blessed work of grace began, long before the victorious armies returned, and continued until the close of the Commission's operations.

Conversion through Reading Baxter's *Call to the Unconverted*

In June 1864, Reverend J. W. Hough, Pastor of the Congregational Church, Williston, Vermont, writes fro m Camp Distribution in Virginia:

One of our candidates for baptism had been, to use his own words, "a very hard boy."

Some months prior, he had been confined in the guardhouse for a misdemeanor. Upon being released, he was ashamed to mingle with his comrades, fearing they would taunt him with his disgrace. So he decided to find something to read. Entering the barracks, he picked up a volume placed there by the Christian Commission—Baxter's *Call to the Unconverted*.

"I was mad," he said, "when I found it was a religious book and threw it across the barracks. But afterward, when I could not find anything else, I picked it up again and lay down to read. It interested me and impressed me from the beginning. The question 'What right do I have to treat God as I do?' came to me. He has never injured me. I was greatly troubled for a long period of time but, when I began to think less of myself and more of Jesus, His love came into my heart."

On the day he was discharged from the camp, this man publicly entered into covenant with Christ.

Expressing Christ's Love

Reverend Milton L. Severance, Pastor of the Congregational Church, Boscawen, New Hampshire, has preserved a soldier's straightforward way of expressing his thoughts. From Camp Distribution in Virginia, he tells of this incident that took place in June 1864:

The apostle says, "By this shall ye know that ye have passed from death unto life, because ye love the brethren," and I have never seen a more vivid test of this than what a black soldier gave at the close of one of our evening meetings. The simplicity of his expression and manner touched all of our hearts when he said, "I love my Savior. I love the Church of Christ. I love the world. I love everybody. I love them that don't love me."

I felt that this poor son of Africa had reached the pinnacle of Christian experience. Like the martyred Stephen and his Savior before him, he could pray for those who had despitefully used him.

Barriers to Understanding the Gospel

Reverend Dr. C. W. Wallace, Pastor of First Congregational Church, Manchester, New Hampshire, writes from Camp Distribution in Virginia in December 1864:

One Sunday morning at the camp, I met a boy at my door, waiting to see a delegate. Poor little fellow, what a life he had had! His parents died when he was quite young in New York City. He fell to the care of a brother who had abandoned him. No one remained to care for his welfare. The only faint bond between him and anything higher was the faint remembrance of a good mother. F or years, he lived on city streets, sleeping at night in boxes and doorways—anywhere to escape summer heat and winter cold. For food, he learned various, indiscriminate skills to sustain himself. In his fifteenth year, he entered the army. I found him to be a sincere inquirer of the truth.

"What shall I do?" he asked. "Since I was a boy, I've done nothing but swear and steal and everything else that's bad. And now, to try to be good—it's very hard."

In his lost condition, the poor fellow would weep and put his hands out gropingly for the better way but I found it difficult to direct him to Christ in a manner he could understand. The few times I saw him, he would come to the place of prayer and bow himself very humbly among the others. Soon, he was ordered to the front and I saw him no more. His strange, pitiful face and earnest cry for the truth deeply impressed me. Surely, he must have found an answer.

Wife's Conquering Love

The permanent Agent in charge of the Christian Commission's work at Camp Distribution was Reverend James P. Fisher of Westfield, New York. After his death, his wife prepared the final report, containing the following incident:

A soldier rose one evening and said, "My friends, I left home an infidel but I left a praying wife. A week ago, I received a letter from her in which she expressed anxiety for the welfare of my soul and desired to know if I still held to my old views. I wrote an answer and defended my old position in bitter words. As I was about to seal the letter, I could not bring myself to send it. I wrote another, softened it down considerably from the first but could not send it either. I began a third letter but the power of the Spirit upon my heart was such that I fell upon my knees and begged for God's forgiveness. I could not finish the letter until I could say to my dear wife that Christ had forgiven my sins. I have been permitted to write to her that I am rejoicing tonight in her Savior. I feel that I am now prepared for the battlefield and, if I am ever permitted to return home, I trust I shall go back prepared for that also—a better man than when I came into the army."

Powerful Grace

At a meeting, a soldier rose to tell of God's preserving care. In broken English, he communicated, "Oh, yes! I think it is not right when my God I forget to thank. He cares for me. The bullets go through my clothes and hurt me not. I must mend my sleeve and my shirt in the side and in the front. Oh, yes! I must love my God and keep fast to the Christian life. And my heart pulls me so heavy sometimes. When the priest says we shall get up in the meeting and say something and I cannot speak good English."

The one leading the meeting then asked, "So you can say you love Jesus."

"Oh, yes. I have said that and keep saying that all the time."
(James P. Fisher)

Witnessing in Season and Out of Season

Mrs. Fisher, wife of Reverend James P. Fisher of Westfield, New York and Agent in charge of the work at Camp Distribution, had this experience—a peculiarly rich one. The story takes place at the hospital connected with the camp:

On one of my visits, I was rushing out after staying over my time to speak to nearly all in the ward. But the sad, despairing look from a cot I was passing so impressed me that I returned. When I inquired about the soldier's health, he answered, "Yes. I'm sick but I don't care."

"Do you love Jesus?"

"I don't know as I do."

"Do you have a wife?"

"No, she died on the way to …" and his voice trailed off.

"Children?"

"They died. The only two I had."

"Parents?"

"No, they died in … and as for me, I don't care what becomes of me."

"Poor soldier," I said, "how sorry I am for you! No friends on earth and no Friend in heaven! You are, indeed, to be pitied. But hear what the Savior says to you. He said, 'Ye believe in God; believe also in Me. In My Father's house are many mansions.'" I repeated this passage in John 14 through the sixth verse.

Gradually, the look of despair gave way and slowly, in low tones, he uttered, "That is beautiful. That is very beautiful. Where is it?"

I told him the book and chapter. He reached under his pillow for his New Testament, found the place and asked me to mark it. We read it over together and he followed every word in his Testament with wonderful eagerness and interest.

"Now, my boy, doesn't the Savior love and care for you?"

"Yes. I had forgotten Him in my trouble."

"Don't you want to come to Him and trust Him now?"

"I'll try."

Dying Because of Sacrifice in Ministry

Mrs. Fisher, wife of Reverend James P. Fisher of Westfield, New York and Agent in charge of the work at Camp Distribution, tells of her husband's passing:

In June 1865, worn out with incessant toil, Mr. Fisher left his work at the camp. He reached the home of his brother-in-law in Newburg, New York and, unable to go any further, sank and died. Some of the scenes of his last days were touchingly beautiful. Like so many other Christian Commission delegates who have died in the service, all his wandering thoughts were on his work for the soldiers. He was preaching, praying and exhorting. In his lucid moments, his mind turned at once to Jesus and heaven, alternating and combining the Christian's work and faith in a beautiful way. The change from delirium was marked by a desire to get on his knees and offer prayer. He loved to be on his knees. His supplications had little reference to himself, except for purification from sin.

"Last night," in troubled sleep, he said "was the great night of the feast. Jesus stood and cried, 'If any man thirst, let him come unto Me.'"

In a conscious state, he spoke to his son and said, "My son, there is one passage of Scripture I wish to impress on your mind. I adopted it many years ago to die upon: 'The blood of Jesus Christ, His Son, cleanseth from all sin.'"

On the last day of his sickness, he called in his sleep, "Frank, ring the bell. It is time for meeting. I am to preach tonight. Is everything ready—ready for the celebration of His dying love?"

And so he passed on, not to the preaching in a crude chapel at Camp Distribution but to the praise where God is the temple. Everything was ready and our dear brother celebrates the dying love.

Girl's Gift Leads Soldier to Hear Gospel

In July 1864, Confederate General Jubal Early made a raid into Maryland and Pennsylvania from the Shenandoah Valley. He thoroughly succeeded in alarming Washington and Baltimore but accomplished little else. Mr. H. M. Whitney, of Northampton, Massachusetts, tells of an incident occurring shortly thereafter:

Before leaving home for my work as a delegate of the Christian Commission, a little girl had given me ten cents, the first money she had ever earned. She wanted me to use it for the soldiers. I bought a New Testament and determined to give it to the manliest and most deserving soldier I met. For a long while, it lay in my valise because I felt that I had not yet found the right owner for it. At last, after General Early had been beaten back from Fort Stevens by the Sixth Corps, I found a new and bright face in one of my hospital tents.

"How are you, my friend?" I began.

"First rate."

"Lightly wounded, then, I suppose?"

He drew back the sheet and showed me that his right arm was gone, cut off close to the shoulder.

"Is that first rate?" I asked.

"Why, it might have been ever so much worse, you know."

Day after day, I found him as cheery and uncomplaining. At first, he was overflowing with fun all the time but the terrible heat and the strain upon his system finally reduced his strength. When I visited, only a merry twinkle in his eye and a word of cordial greeting was all that remained.

Little by little, I learned his history. The action, in which he had received his first wound, was his thirteenth battle. When he dropped his musket and reached around to take his useless arm tenderly in his left hand and walk off the field under a shower of minie balls, it was his first time to be off duty since he entered the service.

He was only nineteen years old but his patriotism was so ardent and his courage so magnificent that I felt he had become my teacher. As soon as he could sit up, he was busy with pencil and paper, training the muscles of his left hand to replace those of the right. His face had grown pale and thin, his eye dull, his manner languid, and his voice broken. But his heart was still as strong and manly as ever. Low spirits or complaints seemed impossible for him.

I thought I should have to look long and far to find a soldier more worthy of the little New Testament. He was eager to get one, having lost everything in that last charge against the enemy. So I wrote his name, company and regiment on the flyleaf of the little book. I added how it had come from a little girl in the Connecticut Valley who had given her first money to comfort the soldier. As I read it, the tears began flowing from his eyes.

"I wish," he said, "I had that arm so that I could thank her myself."

He told me afterward that, since he had been lying there, he had been thinking a great deal and was going to try and lead a better life. I tried to show him where the best and highest Life was to be found but I know not whether he found it or not.

Living with Humility

Mr. H. M. Whitney of Northampton, Massachusetts tells about meeting a Union soldier, following Confederate General Jubal Early's raid into Maryland and Pennsylvania. He alarmed Washington and Baltimore but accomplished little else. This incident occurred in the summer of 1864:

I discovered in one of the wards of Mount Pleasant Hospital, Washington, a young Swede, who had earned his first degree from the University at Lund. He could converse fluently in five languages and was familiar with Greek and Latin. He was a private in a Maine regiment, a member of the Lutheran Church at home, and a sincere Christian. He wanted a New Testament. I asked him what language he wanted. He said he did not care but, on being pressed, he chose English because he was not so familiar with our language.

I asked, "With your fine education, comfortable circumstances and excellent prospects, what brought you to this country and to enlist?"

"Why, I heard there was a war over here and I came."

The simplicity and candor of this blue-eyed, flaxen-haired son of the North, plus his complete freedom from bloodthirstiness, puzzled me profoundly. So I asked, "Did you find the realities of the war anything like what you expected?"

"Yes, but better. I have looked into these things a great deal at home and in Germany and I think no government and no people ever took such good care of their soldiers."

The patient contentment with which he bore his severe wound, his existence in poverty, his absence from home and friends, and all the little things, which would have grated on most men of his education, was an unceasing marvel to me.

Sharing the Fruits of Christian Labor

In September 1864, the writer with the pen name "Carleton" visited one Sunday evening with delegates who shared their experiences at a meeting in Washington. He wrote an account of it for the *Congregationalist*:

The Carver Hospital delegate reported that he found one-third of the men in his wards to be professing Christians. They were glad to see him—very glad to get religious reading material. A few days prior, he gave an old man a little book, entitled *The Blood of Jesus*. He had seen him again today and the old man greeted him with a smile, saying, "I have found Jesus, and oh, He is so precious!"

Witnessing Tactic

Another from the same hospital said, "Among the patients, I found a minister who had enlisted as a private. He has been in the hospital for sixteen months and has maintained his Christian character through all the trials of camp and hospital life. I also found some convalescents playing cards and asked, 'My boys, you don't play cards on Sunday, do you?'"

"It isn't Sunday, is it? Why hang it all, Chaplain, we can't keep track of the days in the army."

I talked to them of home and of their mothers and the tears rolled down their cheeks. They put up their cards and decided to read the papers I gave them. ("Carlton")

Complete Openness to the Gospel

The Emory Hospital delegate continued, "I never saw men so ready to receive religious instruction or who were so easily impressed with the truth. I am satisfied that this is a golden opportunity for the Christian Church. I found a young man today, who said, "I want you, Chaplain, to tell me just what I have to do to be a Christian. I will do just what you say. I want to be a Christian."

"It was a sincere desire. I find that the Catholics are just as eager to have religious instruction as the others."
("Carlton")

Witnessing While Approaching Death

Another Emory Hospital delegate reported, "I found Sergeant _____ of Massachusetts very low but he met me with a smile. He said, 'It is all right. I am happy and I will die content. Tell my friends so.'"
("Carlton")

Non-Christians Want Relatives to be Saved

Another delegate said, "I have been over the river to see some detached regiments, men who are not in hospital. I asked one noble-looking soldier if he loved Jesus. He replied, 'No, I don't.'

"'Are you married?'

"'No, but I have a sister. She isn't a Christian but she wrote to me that she wanted me to become one and I wrote to her that I wanted her to be one. Chaplain, I guess that everybody who believes the Bible feels this way. If they ain't good themselves, they want their friends to be.'
("Carlton")

Courage for the Cause of Christ

"I found another soldier, writing a letter on a little piece of paper. I gave him a full sheet and an envelope and he asked, "'Are you a Christian Commission man?'

"'Yes.'

"'You are a d—d good set of fellows.'

"'Hold on, soldier, not quite so hard.'

"'I beg your pardon, Chaplain. I didn't mean to swear but, darn it all, I have got into the habit out here in the army and it comes out before I think.'

"'Won't you try to curtail it?'

"'Yes, Chaplain, I will.'"
("Carlton")

Gospel is Better Than Gold

Another delegate related, "As I went among the men, they eagerly gathered about me. They were a little disappointed, however, when they found out that I was a delegate of the Christian Commission because they mistook me for the paymaster. 'But I have something that is better than gold.'

"'Give me some of it,' said one, the son of a Baptist minister, a tender-hearted Christian."
("Carlton")

Boldness in Ministry Reaps Eternal Results

Reverend E. F. Williams, Pastor of The Congregational Church, Whitinsville, Massachusetts, gives some reminiscences of work in the Soldiers' Rest at Washington D.C. in March 1865:

In the opinion of recruits fresh from home, it was a rough kind of "Rest" but to the "veteran," it was "home." The tight roofs, hard floors, and neatly-spread tables were vastly preferable to canvas tents and mud floors, hard tack and salt pork. The principal barrack was about three hundred feet long with several smaller ones near it. Our visits were usually begun by distributing papers, books and stationery, giving notice of a meeting as we passed along. Sometimes we were obliged to modify our course.

In one instance, the barracks were nearly vacant throughout the day. So our work had to be done just after breakfast or supper. Coming around rather late one morning, I found a regiment drawn up in marching order. Approaching the officer in command, I inquired, "How long has it been since these men have had the gospel preached to them?"

"Some three months," was the reply.

"Can I preach to them now?"

"Yes, if you can do it in five minutes."

Instantly, I stated the case to the men, taking my text from Proverbs 9:12, which says, "If thou be wise, thou shalt be wise for thyself; but if thou scornest, thou alone shalt bear it." My subject was "Individual Responsibility." Any Christian would have impressed to see how the men eagerly drank in the only sermon they had heard in three months. But the five minutes were quickly gone, a hasty benediction pronounced, and my audience moved down the street to the music of fife and drum.

Boldness Leads to Opportunity to Preach

On another occasion, the whole barracks resounded with the noise made by a body of men whom an orderly sergeant was drilling. With some hesitation, I asked permission to distribute my papers to the men as they passed. Permission was readily granted. This work accomplished, I was turning to go when the orderly politely asked if wanted to preach.

"Certainly," I said, "that was what I came for but your men are busy drilling, so I suppose we shall have to let it go."

"By no means," he replied, "a little drilling for Jesus is needful now and then to make us good soldiers of the Cross."

The music ceased, the men stacked their arms, and sat down in lines on the floor. Then we had a most meaningful meeting, in which the pious officer played a most cordial role. As I left the barrack, the tramp and ring of the military drills resumed.
(E. F. Williams)

Boldness Leads to Prayer Meeting

Another evening, we found nearly all the men gathered around a comic who was making a speech for their amusement. The moment seemed inopportune for a meeting, so we went on to another barrack.

Coming back in an hour, we found the same men had become spectators of some obscene dancing. Father Noble and I held a brief "council of war," the result of which was that he stepped into the ring by the side of the dancers and called out in his booming voice, "I want to know if you are new recruits or veterans."

"Four years in service," was the general answer.

"I thought so," he said. "Now, we Christian Commission delegates don't want to interfere with your wishes, only to give you an option. You have had fun here now for over an hour. Those who, by way of change, want a prayer meeting, show your hands."

Nearly every right hand went up. Only two or three seemed offended and muttered as they stalked off. The rest seated themselves in an orderly manner and enjoyed the meeting greatly.

As we were leaving, a fine-looking young man grasped my hand and said, "We are ordered to the front tomorrow and can't tell what awaits us. Will you pray that I may be a faithful Christian?"

After I had reached the door, one who had followed me called to me. With broken sobs, he told that he was a guilty sinner in deepest need of Christ. I was honored to show him the Way.
(E. F. Williams)

Historical Setting:

General Philip H. Sheridan was placed in command in the Shenandoah Valley in Virginia in August 1864. At Opequan and Fisher's Hill in September, he so thoroughly defeated General Early, the Confederate commander, that he was driven from the Valley into the mountains. Returning after the chase, the Union Army rested at Cedar Creek. During Sheridan's absence,

General Early ordered a surprise attack on the camp on October 19th and drove the Union forces back. However, before nightfall, "Sheridan's Ride" from Winchester turned a stunning defeat into a spectacular victory. After this, hardly any fighting took place in the Shenandoah Valley.

Ministry of Feeding Wounded Soldiers

Mr. J. R. Miller, formerly Field Agent of the Eighteenth Corps in the armies operating against Richmond, became the General Field Agent in the Shenandoah Valley about the time of the battle of Opequan, September 19, 1864. He writes of the scene after the battle:

Winchester was literally one vast hospital. The churches and public buildings were filled while nearly every private house had its quota. External relief was greatly needed because nothing was left in this area. Government supplies were all at the rear and the nearest base, Harper's Ferry, was more than thirty miles away. The intervening countryside was overrun with guerrillas.

As soon as the railroad was restored, Martinsburg became a place of great importance to the work of the Christian Commission. Almost every wagon train from the front brought in 200-300 men, sometimes as many as 500 hundred. They had been transported, jolted and wounded, in hard army wagons over rough roads the entire twenty-two miles from Winchester. They arrived with no beds, no straw on which to lie, no rest, and with nothing to eat.

We were always apprised of their coming an hour or more before they began to arrive and we quickly made all our preparations. With tea and coffee, crackers and jellies, bread and meats, cheese and fruits, the delegates hurried around until all were fed. We then did the bathing, washing, and dressing of wounds. Usually, all was completed in the early morning hours. When the morning dawned, the same routine was renewed. At noon, the brave fellows were as comfortable as we could make them for their tedious trip to Harper's Ferry by train.

Power of Kindness

Reverend P. B. Thayer, Pastor of the Congregational Church, Garland, Maine, writes in October 1864 of his ministry to the Confederate wounded, brought to Martinsburg, Virginia in the same wagons with our own men:

As we ministered to their wants and addressed them with words of kindness, tears flowed from eyes unaccustomed to weeping. They overwhelmed us with their generous expressions of thankfulness. "This is what I call living Christianity," one would say. "This is the religion for me," another would add. "I can't stand this," said a rough, hard-looking fellow who was badly wounded in the foot but able to hobble along on crutches. "I can't stand this, boys. It overcomes me. I give in." As he came toward us, his whole body shook with emotion while big tears fell from his sunburned face—tears which he awkwardly and vainly tried to hide from his comrades and us.

"You know," he continued, "I am no coward. I can face the enemy and not blink but this kindness kills me. It breaks me all to pieces. I tell you, boys, this is no hoax. It's a big thing. It's the Gospel for body and soul—just what we all need."

And so he proceeded with great eloquence for some minutes. He closed with the ever-recurring soldier's benediction, "God bless you!"

Historical Setting:

In the winter of 1864-65, a deep and pervading religious work began in Winchester, Virginia. The larger part of the army lay near Winchester and most of the chapels were erected in that vicinity. Of the thirty built, four of them were large marquee tents, while the others were stockades, roofed with canvas. A few incidents from delegates' reports illustrate the general character of the work.

Right Praying

Reverend Sewall Brown, Pastor of Baptist Church, East Winthrop, Maine, writes in March 1865 of service at Maryland Heights and Camp Remount in Maryland:

John Sangden, a Swede, made a fine specimen of what a Christian should be. One day, he came to our store, wanting something to read in Swedish. I had nothing at the time but hunted up *Baxter's Saint's Rest* in Danish, which he could read. He expressed deep gratitude, but not knowing how to speak in English, he could only grasp our hands and shake them again and again without speaking.

At an evening meeting a short time afterwards, a delegate noticed a tear in Sangden's eye and a glow in his face. He was invited to rise and speak:

He said, "Yag kan ecke saga," meaning "I cannot speak it," Then in English, he added, "You say, 'My Lord Jesus,' and I feels it in my heart."

He then offered prayer in Swedish. The only words we could understand were, "Fader," "Jesus," and "Christian Commission" but the prayer was so intensely fervent that scarcely a dry eye remained in the congregation. He seemed to be praying earth up to heaven.

Hardened Sinner Becomes Seeker

George N_____, a New York soldier, had come out of the lowest levels of society in that city. His temper had become remarkably violent through years of practice. When provoked, he lost all control of himself and even became oblivious of what he was doing. Liquor always made him "mad." Once, I remember seeing three men struggling with him while he was in the midst of one of these tempestuous episodes brought on by whisky. He foamed at the mouth and was, indeed, a fearful sight.

For this offense he was sentenced to thirty days' hard labor, a sad spectacle to watch. At the end of the fifth day, his sentence was commuted. I went to him to try and show him what kindness I could. He remembered some encouraging words of mine, spoken while he served his sentence, and his heart was touched. In a day or two, he came to the chapel and asked for a Bible. He received it, along with a hymnbook and other good books. He then set himself to study them diligently. Afterward, he never missed a meeting and, when my term of service ended, he was a humble, sincere seeker of truth.

(Sewall Brown)

Physical Healing follows Spiritual Healing

Mr. J. H. Earle, of South Abington, Massachusetts, the Agent at Stephenson's Station, writes of the following incident:

One evening, after our usual meeting at the chapel, a lieutenant asked us to go with him to the hospital to see a soldier in his company who was reported to be dying. Passing through the dimly-lighted ward with its sleeping patients and yawning nurses, we came to the cot of a fine-looking boy in great distress about his soul's salvation. After a frank talk with him, a delegate prayed and the boy joined audibly in the petition. In humble submission, he exclaimed again and again, "Here, Lord, I give myself to Thee." We felt that such a yielding up would be blest of God. And so, indeed, it was.

"Oh, I'm so happy! I'm happy all over," he exclaimed in a moment.

The surgeon who was standing nearby and watching the scene said it was just the needed medicine for his body also. Amazingly, from that hour onward, the soldier began to recover.

Turned to Christ by Love

Reverend W. H. Kelton served as Pastor of the Baptist Church, West Waterville, Maine. He relates this incident prior to being rendered incapacitated from doing ministerial work due to disease he contracted in the service of the Christian Commission at Winchester, Virginia in May 1865:

I found a Frenchman in the hospital sick with rheumatism. He was intelligent and pretty well educated but he was quite derisive about the idea of reading the New Testament. However, he eagerly accepted my offer to bring him a French book, so in a day or two I handed him Monod's *Lucille*—from our Loan Library. The next time I visited him, he greeted me very cordially and, drawing the little book from under his pillow, he said, "It is good. I like it. I read it through. I want a Bible for myself."

He opened the book and showed me the words he had written on the fly leaf, which read, "I like this book. I will read the Bible. Give me one. Jules Bernard, Bugler, Company F, 5th New York Cavalry."

His joy in receiving the Bible assured me that he would peruse it with profit.

Finding Christ

A soldier from Company A, 1st U. S. V. V., of Hancock's Corps had been cast upon the world early in life to earn a livelihood. He became skeptical, profane, and very intemperate. One day, while he was giving expression to his religious and irreligious notions, he made the following points: "There is no law but what men make. There is no such thing as inspiration, only in that sense in which any man is inspired when he can impress and move men." To him, Christ was the greatest man who ever lived, simply because, to this late date, His words exert such a powerful influence on the world—but He was only human! His teachings have no Divine authority."

He told me afterward that, while he was uttering the words, a comrade known for his wickedness, was looking at him very strangely. The look troubled him somehow. Silence ensued for a brief moment when, suddenly, his comrade spoke out, "If I believed all that, Captain Kidd would be nowhere to me." (Captain William Kidd was a legendary pirate hunter turned pirate in the 1600s.)

The remark struck him like a thunderbolt.

Later he said, "If, indeed, no Divine Law exists and no power existed to execute it," I thought, "what is there to restrain my passions? What man can make, I, or any man, can break. At last, I resolved to read the Bible with an open mind. I was utterly amazed at its revelations. Each perusal gave me something new to think about. Somehow, it was different from every other book. Gradually I became fully persuaded of its Divine authority."

While he was in this state of mind, his regiment encamped at Winchester, close to the village cemetery. The seclusion and shadow of the "city of the dead" were in harmony with the man's troubled spirit. He frequently retired to wander and meditate in this "city." One day, he sat down by a small grave with a plain marble headstone, inscribed, "Her name was Mary." Carved above these words was a hand with a pointing finger aimed upward. The whole meaning of this arrested his attention at once. He expressed, "This was my sermon book. I came to it often. It always had a lesson for me."

Finally, he was led to the Christian Commission prayer meetings where the truth came home to him with power. In the presence of a crowded audience one Sunday evening, he rose to his feet and clearly and decisively stated, "Fellow soldiers, I am not a Christian but I want to be one." God heard and answered his earnest plea and prayer.
(W. H. Kelton)

Occurrence of Spontaneous Revivals

In May 1865, the victorious armies of Grant and Sherman began to gather near Washington for the "grand review." This was the Christian Commission's last opportunity and its forces were mustered accordingly. General Field Agents, Field Agents, and delegates, sixty in all, combined all their strength and zeal for this last work. Chapel tents and Commission stations were opened throughout all the camps of the veterans surrounding Washington. The narrative of Reverend E. P. Goodwin, Pastor of Congregational Church, Columbus, Ohio, illustrates the character of the extensive operations during May and June of that year:

My first work was in the heart of Provisional Camp, some two and a half miles from Alexandria, Virginia where a Christian Commission station was opening. Tents were barely up and the chapel was without pulpit and benches. Our gifts to the men were scattered about in hundreds of unopened boxes. Evidently, our party of delegates faced an afternoon of hard work while chaos reigned around us. Crowds of soldiers, eager to find out "what them fellers had got in their new shebang," as they phrased it, thronged us from every side. They were covetously eyeing and banging about every box of our treasures, as if, by instinct of their need, they caught the odor of new shirts, drawers and socks.

With lunch finished, we began our work in earnest. Six of us joined in opening boxes and distributing gifts. So great was the mass of humanity upon us that we were unable to meet the need. After toiling continuously until dark, we had to dismiss scores of others with the pledge—better than nothing, to be sure, but not particularly comforting to shirtless men—that we would resume the distribution early the next morning.

I never saw such an intensely eager bunch. Every single article we offered, from a shirt to a newspaper, was in constant demand—often by a dozen voices at once. And there was good reason for the eagerness. Around ten thousand men were in the camp. Most were from Sherman's army. Not a man among them, from what I heard, had a dime of money and all had been without pay for many months. Their condition verified their stories. I had never dreamed it was possible for our soldiers to become so ragged and beggarly. Scores of men, if not hundreds, came to us and requested shirts—often with beautiful and touching modesty. Meanwhile, their uniform jackets, on this hot day, were close buttoned about the neck to hide their condition. Shirts and pants hung in shreds. Some wore drawers only, the pants being past all usefulness. The shoeless and sockless were innumerable. Our hearts certainly lacked no lack of motivation in the blessed work of relief.

Yet, all this time, my heart was growing heavy over the prospect of the work on the spiritual level. I doubt if our camp was often overmatched in terms of vileness. Its makeup will furnish a significant reason for this. Ostensibly, this camp was occupied by men, who had been disabled by long marches, and by convalescents, still unfit for active service. They were sent here, chiefly, by boat from Newbern—in advance of their comrades who were to come by land. But in addition to these, a large number of stragglers and "shirks" had contrived to pass themselves off as invalids and, as such, had managed to dodge such a fatiguing march. The camp was also comprised of a generous sprinkling of "bounty jumpers" and conscripts. Inevitably, the morals of the camp were of the worst sort. On that first afternoon, our ears were so incessantly assailed with profanity and vulgarity that the very thought of trying to preach the Gospel to so corrupt a group almost filled me with dismay.

However, one circumstance occurred to check my despondency and to inspire hope. Just as we were ready for our lunch of crackers and bacon, a pleasant-looking soldier came to me and drew me aside to ask if preaching in our chapel was planned for that evening. Upon hearing my affirmative reply, his eyes filled with tears and an expression of sincere thanks broke from his lips. His personal experience was a very remarkable one. A sailor for nine years, he had been a very wicked man. Nothing had arrested him in his course until a few evenings ago when, upon passing a tent, he heard some Christian soldier singing a hymn. He was struck by the melody, so much so that the music constantly kept ringing in his ears. He unburdened himself to his comrade and, together, they went to find the tent but could not. However, their consciences were now thoroughly awake and they agreed between themselves that they ought to be better men.

Finally, Wright—this was the soldier's name, Charles Wright, of the 32nd Massachusetts Regiment—told his comrade that talking would not make them any better. The other suggested prayer but neither of them knew anything about praying. After considerable hesitation, they got down on their knees, confessed their common sins as best they could, and asked forgiveness. They found that prayer helped them very much. So they continued a day or two, working without encouragement from any around them. Suddenly, it occurred to them that they were being selfish about the matter and agreed to try to get some of their comrades involved. After that, they successfully organized an evening prayer meeting at their tent and ten men attended. Wright was a member of the Fifth Corps, scheduled to arrive within the hour. He was distressed over this because he feared that, when his Corps came, he would have to join it immediately before our meetings began. Regardless, he went away with a happy face when he found that we were to have a meeting that evening.

I had no idea that such a considerable number of the men would turn out. To our surprise, the tent was crowded full and, when we rolled up the sides of the chapel tent, probably another one hundred and fifty men lay down on the grass within hearing distance. Near the front of this crowd sat Charles Wright. A squad of soldiers sitting near him had evidently formed the nucleus of his remarkable prayer meeting. Our doubts of the day, however, were still hanging about us. Even though we had grand singing and everyone gave us their fullest attention, we had a little meeting among ourselves to decide what to do next.

We proposed, not very courageously, a meeting to follow for the purpose of sharing testimonies and prayer. To our great embarrassment, not a man stood to leave. Supposing they had not understood, I repeated the announcement that those who wanted to share their Christian experience might remain. But nobody moved, so we had a whole tent full. The soldiers were invited to speak. Wright promptly rose and told the story, which he had related to me in the afternoon. After that, we had no lack of men wanting to speak. The Lord seemed to be present, indeed.

With that service, revival began. A remarkable fact emerged in these meetings—that a succession of revivals had occurred in the army all around Chattanooga and beyond. Various places were mentioned, which had been the scenes of deep interest—Dalton, Goldsboro, and Raleigh, to name a few. Some of the men had agreed to hold meetings every night during the long and perilous march to Provisional Camp, outside Alexandria. For instance, in the 3rd Brigade, 2nd Division, of the Twentieth Corps, prayer meetings were held every night, all the way from Tennessee to Washington.

These were often held under peculiar difficulties, as many time the soldiers gathered in the dark, where they did not dare to light fires. I never heard men speak more ably or with deeper conviction than these. In those solemn, quiet meetings of the "great march," held under such dangers, they seemed to have entered into the meaning of the Psalmist's song: "Whoso dwelleth under the defense of the Most High shall abide under the shadow of the Almighty. He shall defend thee under His wings, and thou shalt be safe under His feathers. His faithfulness and truth shall be thy shield and buckler." And so, when they came into the country of safety, their song became, "Oh, what great troubles and adversities hast Thou showed me! and yet didst Thou turn and refresh me; yea, and broughtest me from the deep of the earth again. My praise shall be always of Thee."

Every night, three to fifteen men came forward for prayers. Our chapel tent was filled to capacity at every meeting until we broke camp. One night, I remember we had a tremendous thunderstorm. My impression was that it would be useless to hold a service. I wrapped myself up to keep out of the drenching rain and stepped over to the chapel. It was two-thirds full. The rain was dripping through the canvas. The water chased itself across the ground like a mill race and the men had to keep their feet out of it as best they could. The candles spluttered and died out as soon as they were lit. With the exception of the one or two we managed to keep burning at the pulpit, we were in utter darkness. Yet, we not only had the regular service but also a prayer meeting afterward. Two new recruits for Christ came forward to ask our special petitions.

The men told of many precious incidents of Christian spirit they encountered during the long march. Once after a skirmish, a soldier told me, they held one of their usual night prayer meetings. The wounded were being brought in and cared for as the soldiers were singing a hymn. A poor lad, fatally wounded, was among the number. As they came up, they said to him, "You are pretty badly wounded, ain't you?"

"Yes," he said, "almost gone but didn't I hear some singing?"

"Yes, we had a little prayer meeting."

"Tain't any use carrying me to the hospital. If you'll just carry me up to the tent near the prayer meeting, that'll do. I would like to die up there."

The soldiers carried him tenderly to the place. He lay there listening to the singing and the prayers until he died.

Across the river, the Fourteenth Corps was encamped. After the grand review in Washington, we established ourselves among them. We had many cases of interest. I remember one rather remarkable incident of a soldier named John H. Shay, Company F, 104th Illinois Regiment. He had saved up five hundred dollars from his army pay, which he proposed using to educate himself for missionary work after his discharge. As he told his story at one of our meetings, he awakened a deep interest as he told it—omitting any reference to the money he had saved—in a peculiarly simple and artless way. He spoke so gently of his having no earthly home and then, with faith and trust shining in his eyes, he said he had One Friend who, he knew, would never forsake him or go away from him. His parents had been Roman Catholics.

Emanuel A_____, Company F, 31st Ohio Infantry, had the reputation of being the most accomplished gambler in his regiment. He was a fearfully intemperate man also and just as profane as he was intemperate. To our great astonishment, he rose for prayer one evening. Afterward, he told me something of his experience. He had heard about the meetings and so one night, out of curiosity, he came to hear the singing. He sat down on the grass outside of the tent to listen.

After awhile, something was said, which struck him as a personal affront. He got very angry and rose to stalk away. A comrade followed him out and told him that was not the way to leave, that he was acting "like a coward." The man prevailed on him to go back. Again something sharp in the address cut him to the quick and, again, he started off in anger. His friend, who himself was not a Christian, stuck to him and shamed him into going back again. This time, something riveted his deepest attention. He began to feel trouble within. He went away at the close of the meeting, feeling all crushed down. He carried his load for a day or two and felt as if he must return to the meetings to confess his sins. He soon found out the way of peace. Coming into the meeting, he asked earnestly for prayers in behalf of the friend who had urged him to go back to the chapel when he was going away angry.

The success of our revival work was due, more than anything else, to the religious element among the men. I attribute it to the Christian spirit of those who had held to their prayer meetings during the march from Atlanta.

Last Words

A story, involving the men who conquered with Sherman and Grant, occurred near the close of the work in Washington hospitals. Reverend Mr. E. P. Goodwin, Pastor of Congregational Church, Columbus, Ohio, relates this incident:

In Ward 75 of Carver Hospital, Washington, I found John Gillespie, a Pennsylvania soldier who had lost a leg in one of the recent engagements before Richmond. His father was present and sat at his side, holding his hand. The soldier was in a deep stupor. Various attempts had been unsuccessful in rousing him. When the Chaplain and I came in, we continued these efforts but he seemed too far gone to heed us. In the meantime, a little circle of comrades had gathered around the cot. I offered a short prayer and then we all stood awhile, watching for any change which might occur. We expected him to expire at any moment.

Suddenly, one of his friends blurted out that he thought he was going to speak. Evidently, a kindling up of the little life, which was left in him sprang up. After trying to clear his throat and mouth a little, he faintly articulated at first. At last, he broke out with "Forward," as though he were again at the head of his company. "Double-quick" and then "March" came out short and quick and clear.

The effort had exhausted his last remaining strength and his dull weight fell back upon the pillow. He was dead.

Regret for Lost Ministry Opportunities

An incident occurred near the close of the work in Washington hospitals. It involved the men who had conquered with Sherman and Grant and is related by Edward P. Smith, Pastor of Congregational Church, Pepperell, Massachusetts:

Lieutenant Wood, of a Maine regiment in the Army of the Potomac, was on his way to the "grand review." He had gone through the war with neither a wound nor a hospital experience. At the last halt his division made before reaching Washington, he was standing in his tent door when he was struck, mortally wounded, by the accidental discharge of a gun. He was brought into Campbell Hospital. When I found him, he was apparently peaceful with the immediate prospect of death. He had enlisted as a Christian but, while he had kept an unsullied reputation for uprightness and integrity, he was not known distinctively in the regiment as a Christian. This was now his bitter grief. He wanted to live to see his family again but—more, far more—he said he wanted to recover those lost opportunities. He sent for his fellow officers, told them his mistake, and asked their forgiveness, while he himself trusted in the Savior for his own forgiveness.

"I die as a Christian," he said to me, "and I die contented but, oh, if I could have died as a Christian worker!"

"I am peaceful and assured in view of death," he continued, "but I am not joyful and glad about those three lost years that keep coming back upon me." Then, lying quietly for a moment with closed eyes, he added, "Chaplain, do you suppose we shall be able to forget anything in heaven? *I would like to forget those three years.*"

CHAPTER XV

THE PRISONERS IN THE SOUTH

WITH NOTICES OF THOSE WHO RETURNED TO ANNAPOLIS

One purpose throughout this volume has been to give a representative but not an exhaustive collection of incidents. This chapter will continue in that vein, not by entering into the history of the Southern prisons but by grouping a few narratives together to show the religious life of the men who suffered in them. The method of presentation throughout the previous chapters and repeated here is the general one—the chronological.

Depressing News Turns to Joy

Reverend C. C. McCabe, Member of Ohio Conference, Methodist Episcopal Church, relates this incident. After the war, Chaplain McCabe served as a collecting agent for the Christian Commission, principally in the West. He helped in collecting written material for the writing of this book and *Annals, United States Christian Commission*. As Chaplain, he worked with the 121st Ohio Regiment and was taken prisoner, along with the Regimental Surgeon in June 1863, after General Milroy's abandonment of Winchester. The next month, news of Gettysburg was brought to Libby Prison in Richmond, Virginia where the Chaplain was confined. He tells how the prisoners received it:

I had a relative in Richmond, a staunch Confederate. The day they received the first news from Gettysburg, he came to see me, his face wreathed in smiles.

"Have you heard the news?" he asked.

"What news?"

"Forty thousand Yankee prisoners in the Valley are on their way to Richmond!"

I was astounded. In dumb amazement, I listened to the Confederate officers speculating where the new prisoners should be stowed away and how they were to be fed. I went upstairs and told the news. Despondency settled into every heart. That night, we assembled for "family prayers" and the singing, as was our custom, of the long-meter Doxology. It trembled forth out of quivering lips to Him who has said, "Glorify ye Me in the fires." We felt we were doing so that night, like never before.

That night, I slept not a wink but listened wearily to the watchman calling out the hours and singing out "All's well," as he did so. When the day broke, I waited for the footsteps of Old Ben, a character well-known to every inmate of Libby. He was an old slave, a Union black man who was the prison news agent and sold papers for twenty-five cents apiece. At last, his footsteps came. He pushed the door ajar, looked around for a moment upon the sleepers, and then raised up his arms, and shouted, "Great news in de papers!"

Did you ever see a resurrection? I never did but once. Oh, how those men sprang to their feet—and what was the news? The telegraph operator at Martinsburg, when putting those zeros to the four, had clicked his key once too often. His

NEWS IN LIBBY PRISON

made a mistake of only thirty-six thousand men! But more was yet to come. Lee was driven back! The Potomac was swollen and the pontoons were washed away! I have stood and watched when long-parted friends meet again with tears raining down and a fond embrace. But never have I witnessed such joy as what swept into these strong men's faces where the deepest sorrow resided only a moment before.

Joy Brings Forth Singing

Well, what did we do? Why, we sang. We sang as saved men do. We sang until Captains Flynn and Sawyer, isolated in the lowest dungeon below and doomed to die within ten days, heard us and wondered what was happening. We sang until the very walls of Libby quivered in the melody as five hundred of us joined in the chorus of Mrs. Julia Ward Howe's "Battle Hymn of the Republic." We sang,

> "Mine eyes have seen the Glory of the coming of the Lord;
> He is trampling out the vintage where the grapes of wrath are stored;
> He hath loosed the fateful lightning of His terrible, swift sword:
> His Truth is marching on.
>
> "I have seen Him in the watch-fires of a hundred circling camps;
> They have builded Him an altar in the evening dews and damps;
> I have read His righteous sentence by the dim and flaring lamps:
> His day is marching on.
>
> "I have read a fiery Gospel writ in burnished rows of steel,
> 'As ye deal with My contemners, so with you My Grace shall deal,'
> Let the Hero, born of woman, crush the serpent with His heel,
> Since God is marching on.
>
> "He has sounded forth the trumpet that shall never call retreat;
> He is sifting out the hearts of men before His judgment seat:
> O! be swift, my soul, to answer Him! be jubilant, my feet!
> Our God is marching on.
>
> "In the beauty of the lilies, Christ was born across the sea,
> With a glory in His bosom that transfigures you and me;
> As He died to make men holy, let us die to make men free,
> While God is marching on.
>
> Glory, Glory, Hallelujah!"

It was early. I am not sure but, with that song, I suspect we woke up the President of the Confederacy himself.
(C. C. McCabe)

Celebrating in Captivity

Adding to our joy was the date and we had already determined to celebrate the Fourth of July. Our program was arranged—speeches, toasts and songs. But where could we get a flag? In the prison office below, several were turned ingloriously upside-down underneath the Confederate banner.

We might make a flag but where could we get the material? A happy thought occurred to us. We found one man who wore a red shirt. Another had a blue one. White shirts, rather, formerly white shirts, were aplenty. From a combination of these emerged, at last, the emblem of liberty with all thirty-four stars. One of Grant's men was chosen to hang the flag from the rafters—no easy task. Once he successfully and safely accomplished the job, I never saw men gaze for so long and so earnestly at a flag before or since. What memories it brought back!

Colonel Streight, President of the Day, made an opening speech in which he warned us not to make too much noise or else the guards would interrupt. Just as he ended, a Confederate officer made his appearance and addressed the Colonel, saying, "Colonel Streight, by order of the commanding captain, this fuss must stop."

"'Fuss,'" said the Colonel, "do you call this a 'fuss'? Do I understand you to mean that we can't celebrate the Fourth of July here?"

"Yes, sir, you can, but…" and just then, looking up, he spotted the flag. Evidently, it astonished him. He looked at it intently and for a long while. Finally, the power of speech returned and he ordered, "Somebody take that flag down."

A man, back in the rear, rose. In a trembling voice, he said, "Let any Union boy here touch that flag that dares!"

None moved. The officer's command was repeated. No one stirred. He realized he must execute his own order, so he began the perilous ascent. He was not as acrobatic as the man who had put it up and looked, once or twice, as if he would surely crash without his prize—but he finally succeeded.
(C. C. McCabe)

Light Shines in Darkness

Such was our humiliation. Little did we think of our compensation if he had fallen. Little did we know about the full import of the victory at Gettysburg. We knew even less of the other flag that came down that very day at Vicksburg—"the Gibraltar of the Rebellion!" The witnesses that day were not a few half-starved and half-clad captives but a vanquished Confederate Army. So God "commanded light to shine out of darkness!"
(C. C. McCabe)

Faithfulness in the Midst of Captivity

In the midst of the long weariness of captivity, no inner help and consolation equaled that which was afforded us by the Gospel of Christ. Reverend Benjamin Parsons, a delegate in August 1863, stationed to the right of Rosecrans' army, recalls this incident:

Sergeant Thomas A. Cord, of the 19th U. S. Infantry, was a member of an association of Christians in the division to which his regiment belonged. Because of the pressure of military duty and the cold indifference of superior officers, he and his four or five companions were obliged to engage in the privilege of prayer through stealth. When off duty, they took it on themselves to secure a secluded spot in the woods where they poured out their hearts in prayer and praise. At Chickamauga, the Sergeant was taken prisoner. Through some of his escaped comrades, we heard that his fellow prisoners appointed him to conduct a prayer meeting at night in a subterranean room within the notorious stockade at Andersonville. Faithful to his country, to his comrades, and to Christ in the quiet camp, he was found foremost among the faithful in the land of captivity.

Profound Impact of Conversion

The Christian Commission held meetings at Chattanooga in January and February 1864. Mr. Thomas J. Sheppard attended and later became a delegate of the Commission in the summer of 1865. He aided in finishing the Western work. At the time, he was a soldier of an Ohio regiment and, afterward, was a prisoner at Andersonville Prison. He writes of this incident:

One evening at the Chattanooga meetings, a man rose and told us he was a "sutler," someone who sold food, liquor, and other illegal items to the soldiers. He desired to confess his wrongdoing and, under a sense of his sinfulness, he asked for the prayers of God's people that he might become a Christian. He said that he was on his way home to become a better man, and then added, "If ever I come into the army again, it will be with a gun on my shoulder."

His confession made a profound impression upon the soldiers. They marveled at the radical nature of the change, which the Grace of God had effected.

"There's no use doubting God's power in converting men," they said, "when He makes a soldier out of a sutler."

And most honorably did the renewed man fulfill his vows.

Months afterward at Andersonville Prison, a soldier voluntarily remained to care for the sick when he was supposed to go to the lines for a prisoner exchange. Known throughout all the prison as a dedicated disciple of Christ, he turned to me one time and asked, "Do you remember how a sutler asked for the prayers of the Christians in a meeting at Chattanooga and promised that if he came to the army again he would come as a Christian and a soldier?"

"Certainly, I do."

"I am that sutler," was his reply.

Amid rags and filth and sickness, faithful and patient, no Christian Commission delegate ever illustrated the Gospel of temporal and spiritual relief more beautifully than did Sergeant Frank W. S_____, of the 124th Ohio Regiment.

Hardship Makes One Heaven Bound

Reverend J. W. Hough, a delegate at Camp Distribution near Washington in June 1864, furnishes the following narrative:

In the autumn of 1861, a volunteer cavalry company of home guards was formed in Williston, Vermont—half in sport and half for the sake of drill. A faculty member of Williams College, who was vacationing in the village, was chosen as chaplain of the company. A gentleman from New York, connected with the Bible Society, sent him a bundle of New Testaments to distribute among the members. One Sunday afternoon, the chaplain presented these, along with an address about the "Christian soldier."

One of these Testaments has come back to Williston and lies before me as I write. On the flyleaf, an inscription in the chaplain's handwriting, reads, "Williston Cavalry Company, September 1861" and beneath it, the name "Charles B. Chapin" is penciled.

He enlisted in the summer of 1862 in the 1st Vermont Cavalry and the little New Testament was carried to the war. It traveled through Virginia from Harper's Ferry to Petersburg and rode with its owner under Kilpatrick's lead within the defenses of Richmond. On May 5th, the day of the first fighting in the Wilderness, Chapin became a prisoner and it went with him. Its owner had been learning the value of the little book. During the busy campaigns, in which he had proved himself a cool, courageous soldier, new life had sprung up in his heart. He could never trace its history or fix its dates.

"I could not go into action without committing myself to God in silent prayer," he wrote "and presently I came to feel that my prayers were answered."

He had learned the secret of faith in God, so the little Testament became a priceless treasure during the long days at Andersonville.

When captured, his watch, his money, and a pocketknife were taken from him but he was permitted to keep a memorandum book and the New Testament. Together, these volumes tell the tale of his life in prison life. They give hints and brief suggestions of sufferings, which could never be told, and of joys, which even that life of horror, could not wholly darken. The diary paints the dark side of the picture, a sentence here and there, vividly bringing out the indescribable filth and wretchedness of the prison. It tells of the intolerable heat, the ever-increasing insufficiency of rations, the progress of disease, and the sinking of the heart. As hope almost gives way to despair, it wrings the groan out of him: *"O God! Will there never be an exchange?"*

But the well-worn Testament goes into the inner life and tells a history of the heart in its marked passages. Many of these were evidently brought to life by the surroundings of prison life, such as, Christ's discourse upon the "Living Bread" in St. John's sixth chapter, St. Paul's many allusions to his imprisonment, and St. Stephen's martyrdom. Others struck a deeper chord, like Christ's prayer for His disciples after his words of assurance: "In this world ye shall have tribulation." He underlined the close of the eighth chapter of the Romans, beginning with: "Who shall separate us from the love of Christ? Shall tribulation, or distress, or persecution, or famine, or nakedness, or peril, or sword?"

He marked St. Peter's injunction: "I think it not strange, concerning the fiery trial which is to try you." He also underlined St. Paul's triumphant message to Timothy from out the old Roman Mamertine dungeon: "I am now ready to be offered, and the time of my departure is at hand. I have fought a good fight; I have finished my course; I have kept the faith; henceforth there is laid up for me a crown of righteousness." With deep interest, I read the soldier's markings in Philippians 1:12: "But I would that ye should understand, brethren, that the things which happened unto me have fallen out rather unto the furtherance of the Gospel." The thought continues in Philippians 1:21: "For I know that this shall turn to my salvation through your prayers."

Entries in his journal declare, "Cannot get half enough to eat;" "Very, very hot;" "Do not hardly draw half rations;" "Had no blanket so lay in the dirt;" "Water poor;" "Washed a pair of drawers for the first time in two months." These entries lend something inexpressibly touching when finding his mark upon such passages as: "These are they which came out of great tribulation and have washed their robes and made them white in the blood of the Lamb. They shall hunger no more, neither thirst anymore; neither shall the sun light on them, nor any heat. For the Lamb which is in the midst of the throne shall feed them and shall lead them unto living fountains of waters: and God shall wipe away all tears from their eyes."

Not only was the New Testament read and reread during his seven months of imprisonment but he also lent it to others. The day of prisoner exchange, so earnestly bathed in prayer, came at last. But when the wasted form dragged itself out of the stockade, the little volume could not be found. He had gladly left it in the hands of some fellow prisoner so it might continue to comfort him.

Chapin reached Annapolis and sent a cheerful letter home. His father went down to bring him back, he hoped, to the old fireside but it was not meant to be. Starvation and cruelty had done their work. He had "fought a good fight, the time of his departure was at hand."

Under the hardships of prison life, into which was crowded the discipline of a score of common years, he had ripened for heaven. When his father arrived, he said, "Father, sit down by me. I want to tell you how I feel. I don't know as it's just right. I feel so perfectly satisfied with all God has done. I wouldn't have changed one thing. I would be glad to go home and see mother again but if God arranges otherwise, it's all right. I would have it just as He pleases. Tell Eddie and Allie and Millie to meet me in heaven and tell Mr. Hough to say to all my young friends in Williston to meet me there too."

The last entry in his journal reads, "Mustered for pay." He was being "mustered for pay," indeed. The Captain of his salvation was saying even then: "Behold I come quickly, and My reward is with Me." Peacefully, even gladly, he entered into rest. We can only imagine the contrast between Andersonville and heaven.

During the weeks in which he lingered, business called his father to Washington for a brief time. In the depot, he spotted a group of soldiers. Upon approaching them, he found that one was a released prisoner from Andersonville.

"Did you know Charley Chapin?" he inquired.

"Charley Chapin? I surely did," was the quick rejoinder.

Explanations followed and the soldier expressed his surprise that he was still alive. Suddenly opening his knapsack, he added, "Here, I've got a New Testament that belongs to him. He lent it to me and I couldn't find him to return it. I've read it through four times. I wish you would give it to him."

So the precious little book came back to him who had fed upon it when starving and, in whose eyes and the eyes of his friends, it was a priceless treasure. It lies on my table this afternoon, where the "chaplain" wrote in it more than four years ago. It bears the scars of service. Its sides and edges are worn. Its back cover, having fallen off, has been replaced by a piece of rough leather, once apparently part of a bootleg, carefully stitched on. Its pages are wonderfully clean, testifying to the care with which it was used and reminding us of one of old, who in the depths of an experience, not wholly dissimilar, exclaimed, "I have esteemed the words of His mouth more than my necessary food."

Brokenness Leads to Humility

During October and November 1864, Reverend J. M. Clark, Pastor of the Methodist Episcopal Church, Ashburnham, Massachusetts, labored among the returned prisoners at Annapolis. From his report, we take these extracts:

One of the men, who asked for prayer, awakened uncommon interest in our evening meetings. After a season of prayer, a converted soldier rose and said, "I am glad to see this brother soldier here for prayers. We were in Richmond prison together and I have often prayed for him."

After a brief moment, the penitent rose to add a few words himself:

"I have been a backslider from God. Before I entered the army I enjoyed Christ but, since then, I have not lived as I ought. I've been home on furlough and if anyone had heard the babbling of my little boy, he would have been struck with it. How do you think it made me—his father—feel when he asked his mother, 'When papa comes to dinner, will he talk to God like he used to?' Oh, I tell you, it cut me to the heart. I am determined, if God be pleased, to live a Christian life."

Two other men came forward for prayers at the same time. Both had been wounded and in captivity. They came limping along together and bent their crippled limbs in earnest humility and petition before God.

Wounded Returning Home

One of the saddest sights we had to witness were the men leaving camp for home on furlough and promising to return. Twelve horse drawn ambulances from the city came to transport those unable to walk. About fifty others hobbled along on crutches—a pitiful sight! God help and bless them! Poor, brave fellows, they are cripples for life, a short life for many. It was mournful to watch this band of more than one-hundred men as they turned their faces homeward. It was even more mournful to think of the aching eyes that would fill with tears again when these maimed heroes arrived back to the old hometown.
(J. M. Clark)

Proclaiming Love for Jesus

Reverend William DeLoss Love, Pastor of Spring Street Congregational Church, Milwaukee, Wisconsin and Editor of the *Wisconsin Puritan*, was a delegate at Annap olis in December 1864. He adds a few sketches from his pen:

When the steamers, bearing the paroled prisoners of the Union Army, reached the wharf at Annapolis, it was customary for the delegates of the Christian Commission and others to go down and greet those grateful, dedicated men, as they stepped onto the shore of what they often termed "God's country." The hospital band also met them on the dock and poured forth the sweetest strains of music.

One day, I was delayed in meeting a steamer and, when I reached the wharf, some were bearing the feeble, freed prisoners on stretchers to the Naval Hospital. Others were placing some of their suffering companions on a platform car, which was to be rolled over to St. John's College Hospital.

As I came near the steamer, my attention was drawn to an emaciated, feeble man, lying on one corner of the car platform. The welcoming sun, with its gentle and soothing rays, fell upon him He feebly touched my hand and exclaimed, "Oh, that pretty hand!" My associate delegate of the Commission had taken his name and was trying to learn his regiment and his father's name and residence. It was evident the young man could not survive for long. Unless we obtained these particulars, the poor soldier would have that sad word "Unknown" placed on his little headboard in the cemetery. No relative would ever know where or when he died and where was buried.

The soldier was not so far gone as to forget his own name but he was obliged to take a little time for thought to recall his regiment. When the delegate asked for his father's name and place of residence, he could not tell us at first but, in his great effort at recollection, he said, "Wait a little and I'll get it." Soon, he did get it and the attention of most of the bystanders was then turned to others.

But in my heart, I felt a longing to know whether this soldier so near to his end was a friend of the Savior. I came close and, putting my lips near his ear, I asked, "Do you love the Lord Jesus Christ?"

He immediately sprang into animation not seen before and turned his feeble and glassy eyes straight and lovingly upon me. He put a rare but intense energy into his voice and replied, "My friend, I do."

It was enough. I never saw the soldier again. Doubtless, before the day wore away, he was carried by angels into Rest.

Skeptic Recommends Christ

Some months before, a skeptic had come to Annapolis to see his severely wounded and feeble son who had recently arrived from the Richmond prison. Now that the son had exchanged quarters in Libby for those at Annapolis, the father tarried, hoping to witness his son's improvement. But the change he had anticipated was of a different character. Gangrene had set in and the flesh of the young man's limb was gradually rotting away.

The surgeons abandoned nearly all hope of his recovery and the benevolent chaplain told the father that his son would probably die soon. He told him that he should inform him and advise him to make all necessary arrangements before leaving the world.

The father replied that he could not bear the task and asked the chaplain to do it for him.

"And," he said, "speak to him in regard to all his interests, those of the future also." Then he added with great seriousness, "I have been an unbeliever, a wicked man, but my son's mother is a Christian and he had better follow her."

The chaplain gladly went to the son and told the father's message and asked what reply he should take to his father.

"Tell my father," he said, "that I have not deferred preparation for the future to this late time. Long, long ago, and prior to going into battle, I gave myself up to Jesus and now I am ready to go and meet Him when He calls me. Tell him also that I hope he will prepare to meet Him too."

This message, tenderly given by the chaplain, made a deep impression on the loving but skeptical father.
(William DeLoss)

Lost Son Found

One evening, as I sat writing letters for soldiers in Chaplain Henries' office at the Annapolis Hospital, Division No. 1, a very aged and feeble man from Cambridge, Illinois came into the room. With trembling and sadness, he inquired if we could tell him anything about his son, N. H. Tilson. We replied that we did not recollect having seen him. He said that he had received a letter from someone at this hospital, informing him that his son, a paroled Union prisoner from Savannah, had reached this hospital.

He also mentioned that, before receiving the letter, he had not heard from his son for about a year and had learned that he was probably slain in a battle near Knoxville. He and his family had given him up for dead. But when they received the news of his arrival and sickness at Annapolis, they all sat down and wept with joy. They decided that he and his daughter—both of them feeble in ill-health—must set out to find him. They had traveled a thousand miles or more. He had left his daughter at the hotel, telling her that she must be prepared for the worst.

Chaplain Henries told him that he would go through the wards and inquire about his son. After he had gone, I endeavored to comfort the dear old man—a tender-hearted Christian—by saying that we found that many of the prisoners from Andersonville had either been converted there or soon after their arrival at Annapolis. In tears, he replied that his chief prayer for his son all along had been that, if still living, he might become a Christian.

While conversing, I turned the pages of my Christian Commission notebook to see if I could find any trace of this aged man's son. At last, I discovered his name but did not mention my discovery at first, for fear that I would find a record of his death. Glancing rapidly along the lines, I found this: "N. Holmes Tilson, Cambridge, Henry County, Illinois. Been in prison a year; taken prisoner at Knoxville, Tennessee, November 18, 1863; *became a Christian last of June or first of July at Andersonville.* Not heard from home for about eleven months."

I read my sketch to the father. He was so overcome with joy that he could hardly speak. Soon the Chaplain returned with the glad news that he had found him. He said that, as he went into the room where the boy lay, he recognized him as one he had visited several times, both alone and with me. In the multitude of faces, his name had been forgotten. The young man said, "Chaplain, you have not been to see me in a great while. Have you gotten a letter from my father?"

"No, I have no letter from him. What would you give to see your father right now?"

"I will give twenty-five dollars this minute!"

"Well, I'll go and bring him."

Chaplain Henries had uttered this last sentence so playfully that the boy hardly knew what he meant and presumed it must be someone other than his father.

But soon, the Chaplain escorted the old man to the room where the boy lay. The father hurried over to the low cot in the corner, knelt down, put his arms about his son, and the son threw his arms around his father's neck. They kissed each other's cheeks and wept joyfully.

The lost son was found—in more than one sense, the father thought. Not only had the Lord found him at Andersonville but, in a few days, it was evident that he would never recover. This earthly loss would be a heavenly finding.

(William DeLoss)

Gospel Services in Andersonville Prison

Perhaps, one of the most remarkable episodes of the history of the war, if it could be fully written, would be the narrative of the preaching of the Gospel in Andersonville stockade. However, little remains except for a mere, shredded outline of an account. The Pastor of Methodist Episcopal Church, Ashburnham, Massachusetts, Reverend J. M. Clark became the Christian Commission's permanent agent at Annapolis after his first experience as a delegate. He preserves a few disconnected reflections of soldiers concerning this phase of the prison story:

Among the thousands of unfortunate men imprisoned at Andersonville, some Christians and Christian ministers were willing to preach the Word in season and out of season. They were called "chaplains" but I suppose few, if any, of them held commissions.

Within the bounds of the camp, the men were accustomed to three locations where they could hold preaching and other services in the evenings. When the smaller area was too small for the congregation, notice was given to move to the next larger space. The location most frequently used was on the south side of the stream in the place used for the execution of the six criminals or "raiders" as they were called. Those in attendance numbered as high as four, five, or six hundred at a time. Unfortunately, the soldiers reported that they were often disturbed by wicked fellow-prisoners on the outskirts of the congregation. However, the meetings were attended and sustained by sincere, dedicated men whose labors were not in vain.

Many of the men tell me that, during their time in captivity, they "began to call upon the name of the Lord." Some of them told touching stories of their weakness and consequent inability to get to the prison prayer meetings.

One said, "I was too weak to walk. Yet I wanted to go to the meeting, so I crawled on my hands and knees and got halfway to where I could hear. I stopped there, thinking I could pray. Afterward, I crept back to my old place."

One poor fellow, who had been very wicked, became too sick to leave his place. He had a desire to go to the meeting, so two of his comrades picked him up and carried him. Lying on the ground amidst the congregation, he listened and was deeply convicted of sin. A number of devout soldiers gathered around and prayed for him. He was converted and, afterward, began to recover.

Converted to Christ in Confederate Prison

In one of our wards at Annapolis lay a brave soldier who had escaped with life and no more. He had recurring thoughts of the old prison meetings. The first evening I met him, he was suffering from a severe cough, which continued for more than two hours. His agony was intense and great drops of sweat trickled from his brow. Meanwhile, his heroic wife stood at his side, grave and composed, as she had been through many anxious days. During the intervals of coughing, he would offer short prayers like this: "O Lord, bless those men whose cruel treatment has caused all this suffering. Have mercy upon them and show them the right way. Give them life—eternal life."

As we stood by him on another occasion, he said. "The blessed Lord has been very good to me. Oh, yes, He has brought me out of that horrible prison. Yes, He heard my prayer. He can make me well. They did treat me badly, wife. May the Lord have mercy on them! Oh, I think of the poor prisoners left behind. They are wicked—many of them. I have heard them swear and curse and mock those who prayed. Then, after a few days, I have seen them go to the meetings and fall down upon their knees to pray. Some of them came away with new hopes. Oh, yes, the Lord heard prayer for sinners there. He hears prayer always. How good He has been to me!"
(J. M. Clark)

Prisoner Asks for Prayer

In the same room lay another poor boy whose severe sufferings moved all to pity. He had been a prisoner for fifteen months and had endured even more than the usual privations. Both his feet were frozen, discolored, swollen and intensely painful. So acute were his sufferings that the tears forced themselves from his eyes in spite of his efforts to restrain them. I tried to soothe him and asked, "Is there anything more I can do for you?"

He looked earnestly up in my face and answered, "Give me a prayer, if you please."

So kneeling by his side, I besought the Lord for him. During the night, the nurse told me he was much engaged in prayer. Early the next morning, he died.
(J. M. Clark)

Speaking Out for Christ

Reverend Dr. Robert Patterson, Pastor of the Reformed Presbyterian Church, Chicago, puts into a few words his experience of the prayer meetings at Annapolis, attended by the returned prisoners in March 1865:

If one wants to know what prayer and thanksgiving mean, he must hear our returned prisoners pour out their hearts before God for their redemption from Southern bondage. He must hear their supplication for their brethren still in the prison house. Choirs, organs, *Te Deums*, and doxologies are poor, dumb things compared to the tears streaming down the smoke-dyed cheeks of these veterans. As the manly trumpet voice quivers and grows husky and breaks down in sobs at the throne of grace, one begins to understand what is meant by "intercession with groanings which cannot be uttered."

There is a lad of nineteen who stands up and says, "I promised the Lord that, if I ever got out of prison, I would stand up for Him at the very first chance. And now I want to serve Him and I ask for your prayers."

Another man can only hang his head and weep and stand up also when the invitation is given. Just behind him, a manly-looking fellow gets up and says, "Ain't there some more here who promised God that, if He would get them out, they would be Christians? Now, soldiers, don't be afraid of men. We weren't afraid of men in Salisbury. We can't put down God with a lie, no how. Just speak out and don't be ashamed of Christ. He was not afraid to be ridiculed. He was put to the most ridiculous kind of usage and death for us. Now, stand up for Him." In this way, the meeting goes on.

Yielding to Christ

Mr. Charles Harris, City Missionary of Peoria, Illinois, a delegate at Camp Parole in April 1865, recalls a few interesting incidents of the meetings and hospital work:

An Irish soldier, who formerly served in the navy, was led to Christ at our meetings. He was a tall, noble-looking man and his change seemed to be thorough and deep. He thought highly of a certain corner of the chapel in which he had been accustomed to sitting about the time when the Savior was seeking him. He used to speak of it as his "sweet little corner" and was under the impression that the Spirit was somehow especially present there. When anyone from that section rose to ask for the prayers of those present, the Irishman's heart used to go out to them with special sympathy and a strong faith in their salvation.

When we asked him how he came to think about coming to Christ after so many years of careless trifling, he said, "The Lord got His grapnel-irons ahold of me. He pulled on the starboard side and then He pulled on the port side until I could not hold out any longer. So I surrendered the ship."

Prisoner Faces Death

These poor fellows! Only God knows how utterly devastating their trials had been. One of the soldiers in the hospital asked the nurse to bear a message for him—the tragedy and hopelessness of which is beyond all comprehension: "Ask the Christian Commission man to write a letter to my sister and to tell her that I am dead and to come for my body." (Charles Harris)

Testimonial to Man's Depravity

In the original book, *Incidents of the United States Christian Commission*, published in 1869, the writer/compiler makes this point: So much had been written upon the subject and so few villages throughout the North lacked stories—always told with horror and tears—of their own un-returning men. So many of these soldiers had been carried away into the hopeless country that he thought it was not necessary to enter into the harrowing details and misery of imprisonment. But Reverend J. M. Clark, Pastor of the Methodist Episcopal Church, Ashburnham, Massachusetts, gave an account of the arrival of 2739 paroled men at Annapolis on March 9, 1865, which persuaded the author to the contrary. These final prisoner of war stories will bring this subject to a close.

It has always been my custom to meet the transports at the wharf and to render all the assistance in my power, especially to the sick and disabled. Stimulants—cherry cordial and brandy—given under the supervision and approval of the surgeons were most valuable in reviving the men and in prolonging or saving lives.

The scene on one of the boats was beyond description. After the relatively healthy men had passed to the wharf, I went below to the lower deck. Seventy-five poor fellows, unable to help themselves, lay in that dark, closed part of the vessel. The place was filthy, ragged, and infested with vermin. These sufferers were without shirts, many of them barefoot, and some were absolutely naked. Others had their fleshless limbs exposed and were too feeble to gather what shreds and rags that laid about them. One man, a naked skeleton with only a blanket thrown over his shoulders, was helped along toward the hatchway. Another lay utterly nude and so demented as not to notice his exposure. I covered him with a bit of matting that lay nearby and gave him some cordial. Another lay on his right side, stark naked and dead, the same position of contortion and agony in which he had died.

By the dim light of a lantern, I went to every man and offered him a cordial. Many were too weak to drink, except with the greatest difficulty. Two dead bodies lay on deck, covered with coarse bagging. I lifted the cover to look at the face of one. It was a countenance of complete emaciation and agony. A thoughtless prisoner looking on, laughingly said, "Give him a drink."

Deliverance from Man's Depravity

One man on a stretcher on the way up to the hospital seemed very weak and faint. The bearers paused and I lifted up his head to give him the cup with cordial. His thin, trembling hand carried it to his lips. Then holding it out from him, he said, "Here's bad luck to the Confederacy. May I never fall into

their hands again." Something about his words and actions, in his condition, thrilled the bystanders.
(J. M. Clark)

Joy Follows Release from Man's Depravity

A man tottered down the plank from the transport, pale and haggard, but with a smile upon his face. As he neared the wharf, he raised his fragment of a hat, swung it in the air and tried to cheer but his voice was too weak to make a sound. All spectators took the man's will for the deed and cheered for him while the nurses conducted him to the hospital.
(J. M. Clark)

Speechlessness after Release from Man's Depravity

Another prisoner told me of his feelings when he came onto the Union ship to embark: "I thought I should shout lustily but, when the moment came, I felt only as if I would like to go down and kiss the deck of the transport, over which floated the dear old stripes and stars."
(J. M. Clark)

CHAPTER XVI

THE WESTERN ARMIES

FROM THE FALL OF ATLANTA TO THE
CLOSE OF COMMISSION WORK;
WITH SOME NOTICES OF HOSPITAL
AND OTHER WORK BEFORE ATLANTA FELL

June 1864–September 1865

Heaven Bound

The great hospitals in the rear were soon overflowing with patients from the front, both sick and wounded. In June 1864, Mr. A. E. Chamberlain, Chairman of the Cincinnati Branch of the Christian Commission, writes from Cincinnati:

A friend telegraphed me from Northern Michigan to go and see his soldier-son, William Van Tine, in Marine Hospital. I did so and, afterward, continued to attend to him in his sickness. He had been married only a few months before coming into the army and now, the surgeon told me, he would surely die. William was very cheerful about it and continued to be so during all his sufferings. Very near his end, I received a dispatch from his father, saying that he would be at the hospital next morning.

When I told him, Van Tine looked up at me with a pleasant smile on his face and said, "That will be good but he won't find me here. I shall be gone before that."

The soldier's words were evidently true. I asked him for any last message for his father. He was silent for a moment, while the smile still clung about his lips and eyes, and then said, "Tell him I have gone home."

"Have you any message for your wife?"

"Tell her I have gone home."

"Is there nothing more you want to say, William—no other message I can pass along for you?"

"No, that is enough. They will all understand it. I will have gone home."

If we could have sung a hymn by that couch, what one song would have been more appropriate than Dr. Bonar's?

> "Beyond the parting and the meeting,
>   I shall be soon;
> Beyond the farewell and the greeting,
> Beyond the pulse's fever beating,
>   I shall be soon.
> Love, Rest and Home!
>   Sweet Home!
> Lord, tarry not, but come."

Within half an hour he was resting at home.

God's Everlasting Arms

Mrs. E. I. Ford, the wife of Post-Surgeon Ford of Nashville, a faithful friend of the Christian Commission, relates an experience in July of 1864. It describes the work in the wards of a newly opened hospital at Nashville for the men from the front:

Most of the boys, even those whose limbs had been amputated, were doing well when the hot weather brought the dreaded scourge of gangrene, which, in spite of every precaution, attacked a good many of the patients. With most of them, it was arrested but, still, the constant vacillation and suspense of their condition caused them to need more than the usual sympathy and encouragement. The Commission delegates were always gladly welcomed.

Soldiers do not force their sorrows upon others. Only when you stoop down to them and ask them of the homes they have left and the toils they have encountered do you catch a glimpse, if even then, of the sacrifices they make for their country. A boy of eighteen with an athletic frame and cheerful countenance had suffered amputation of a right arm and was doing well when he was attacked by gangrene. From this time forward, he became an object of my special interest and attention.

Many little luxuries were procured but, soon, they proved to be of no real usefulness. The disease, once arrested, reappeared with renewed vengeance. The inroads this disease made upon his constitution could not be repaired. A friend from his western home came to cheer him with the kindest conversation and sympathy day by day.

One day before an operation, the soldier said, "Sometimes I feel like giving up but when I think of home and friends, I try to live for their sakes."

"But, my boy, you were brave in the face of the enemy. Can't you meet this foe with the same courage? You may have an Almighty Arm to lean upon."

"Oh, how much I need it! How I long to find it!"

"But you may find it at once. Jesus says so. He said, 'Come unto Me, all ye that labor and are heavy-laden, and I will give you rest.'"

"Ah, yes, but I've been such a sinner, so wicked, such a hard life—and all the while I had a praying mother at home."

"But the blood of Jesus Christ cleanseth from all sin. Only receive Him now, and your mother's prayers will be answered."

The Holy Spirit soon enabled him to accept the Savior. He drooped gradually and cared less about the comforts brought to him but he never wearied of listening to the "sweet story of old."

He looked at me thoughtfully one day and said, "I have made up my mind that I can't live and I'm ready to die but, oh, if only I could die at home with my mother and little sister beside me, I would be satisfied! That's all I want now."

With an imploring look, he added, "Will you ask my doctor if I may be carried home? This is my last request," and then the tears came. I went away heart-sick to entreat my husband for what I knew could not be granted. He assured me it would be an impossible task, so I carried back my reluctant response. The young man was calmer by then.

When I told him, he said, "I could hardly have expected it."

"Shall we send for your mother?"

"No," he said. After a long pause, he added, "She is feeble and must not come here."

No more earthly complaints were uttered. No more wishes for what might not be were made. The "Everlasting Arms" were underneath and around him until he was "present with the Lord."

Dramatic Experience of Conversion

The two following letters from a Tennessee cavalryman are remarkably similar in their sincerity and their frank, blunt, unmistakable way of putting things. In the upper right corner of the first, it read:

Tullahoma, N. & C. R. R., Tennessee, July 18, 1864.

GEORGE H. STUART—Dear Sir:

Will you be so kind as to send me the two-volume set of the book, entitled *A Pastor's Sketches*? In looking over the contents I see a few pieces, the headings of which fit my case so well that I want to see the reasoning. Paul said that he was the "chief of sinners" but I think, if he were here, I could drill him for two or three years in that well-known science of the devil—wickedness.

I have taken it into my head that if there is grace for the devil's "right bower" (referring to the jack in a deck of cards), I will, through Christ, try and obtain it. I have no faith that I shall ever be saved but it is perhaps worth an effort in that direction. I was brought to that conclusion yesterday, by reading *The Young Irishman*, published in tract form from *A Pastor's Sketches*. His case and mine are not parallel, by any means, but I hope some of the other sketches are.

If I thought God would forgive me at all, *I would go about praying with a light heart, even though the blessing was deferred until the last moment of my existence. But I have been so wicked that I know He ought not to pardon* and I fully believe He *will* not. So I do not feel like praying. Another thing, *I Can't Repent; I am Waiting for Conviction;* I think I may have committed *The Unpardonable Sin;* I have *No Escape; I Can't Pray; I Can't Feel; What Can I do?*

I do not have the money equal to the price of the two books or I would cheerfully send it. Like the prodigal son, I have spent my money in "riotous living." I merely ask for the books as a favor—not that they will benefit me but they may be the means of *Driving the Arrow Deeper into my Divided Mind.* [Note to reader: These capitalized phrases serve as titles of several of the sections of Dr. Ichabod Spencer's classic book, *A Pastor's Sketches: Conversations with Anxious Souls Concerning the Way of Salvation.*] If the books do any good, you shall hear from me.

Yours respectfully,
Amos L. Griffith, Co. F, 5th Tennessee Cavalry.

The aforementioned books, along with one or two others, were procured and sent to him. In due time, the following letter came to Dr. George Stuart, Chairman of the Christian Commission:

Tullahoma, August 12, 1864

DEAR BROTHER:

The books came safely to my hand and they have more than met my expectations in removing the obstacles in my way. I trust, under God, through the merits of Christ, that every prop of unbelief and sin will be knocked from under me and that I shall be compelled by the holy influences of the Divine Spirit to flee the wrath to come and embrace the truths of Christ crucified.

I do not know in what terms to express my gratitude to you for your kindness. I shall study the precepts of the books in as prayerful a manner as my wicked nature will permit and I pray to God that, if you hear from me again, you will find I have fully embraced Christ.

I have been desperately wicked but I believe Christ died to save sinners and I know I am one of them, so he certainly died to save me. Brother, will you pray that His dying will not be in vain so far as my individual case is concerned? I know you will and, after this life shall have been spent, I hope to make your acquaintance in that region where there is no sin to corrupt, no doubts to blind our vision, but where we shall see as we are seen and be forever under the shadow of that love which fills the soul with eternal bliss. May God forever bless you and yours is the sincere prayer of your unworthy brother,

Amos L. Griffith, 5th Tennessee Calvary.

We have only one other trace of this dedicated Tennesseean's life. After the war, he located in a town of southern Tennessee. We find him laboring to establish a school for the neglected children of the neighborhood, sending for books for them, as he had once done for himself. God grant him full entrance into the privileges of the children of God!

Most Sincere Appreciation

The Pittsburg Branch of the Christian Commission had sent a large invoice to the office at Nashville for the purchase of crutches, an unusual request. In a letter dated August 12, 1864, Reverend E. P. Smith addressed his concerns about this bill to Mr. William P. Weyman, Receiver of the Pittsburg Committee:

I have sent you a package of crutches by express mail, a slight return for the fifteen hundred your Commission office has given to enable this office to assist the maimed who come hopping and hobbling in from the fights. And, yet, I think you will agree with me that my package of a dozen represents a heavier outlay than your boxes of a thousand and a half. Each one of the sticks I send has been cut and shaped by a man who lost a limb or its use in the service. They are the representatives of battlefields all the way from Lookout Mountain to the hills overlooking Atlanta. We have hailed the boys trying to make their way along the streets with them and brought them into our office for a trade. I find it delightfully refreshing to hear their remarks and to see their satisfaction as they go hopping off, trying the new pair.

One said, "That's a bad trade for you."

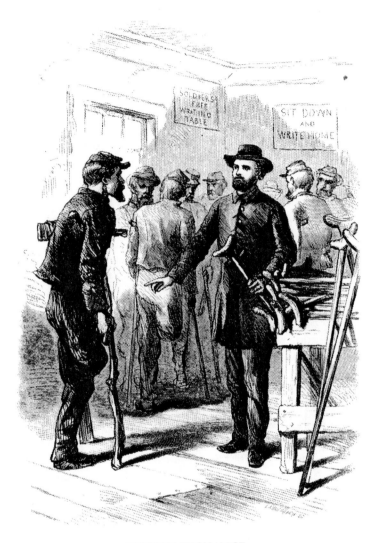

CRUTCH EXCHANGE

"No, I think not," I said, "if you can give that much of your leg"—it was off above the knee—"we can give you the crutches and have the best of the arrangement."

He thoughtfully looked down at the vacant space where his leg once was and answered, "I never saw it that way before but that's so."

"That was a mistake of yours," I said to another who came in, leaning on the oddest pair of crutches I had ever seen. One was fashioned from a paneled board, the head wrapped with cloth and a bit of suspender. The other was an oak stick, pulled up by the roots with one of the roots left branching out to form the head of the crutch.

"What's a mistake?" he asked.

"Why, losing that leg."

"Don't see how I could help it."

"Easily enough," I replied, "suppose you had stayed at home, as others did?"

"I can't see it in that light," he said. And then with flushed face and flashing eye, while stamping the sticks on the floor, he added, "I would rather be here on crutches than at home a cowardly Copperhead."

He thanked me for the new ones—they all do that, most touchingly. When I said it was he that was giving and not I, he said, "It was not that much for me to give. I would like to give it over again—and the other leg also—if it would help with the work of the Commission.

Absence of Bitterness

The following story of prison work at Nashville in August 1864 is told by the General Field Agent of the Christian Commission, Reverend E. P. Smith:

Mr. Walter Tearne, from Covington, Kentucky, was a visitor to the military prisons. Of the number of men confined, some are not only innocent but are also Christians. Through some misapprehension or carelessness, these Union soldiers have found their way to captivity. Of course, based on the prisoners' own statements, very few would be found guilty. But after investigation, we did find men who ought to be released—and this is not infrequent. Sometimes, we are able to help them out or, at least, we are able to comfort them in their trouble by giving them our personal attention and sympathy.

Mr. Tearne found one young man who was very eager to receive a Bible. He had read his New Testament "all up," he said. When he received a Bible the next day, he could not conceal the glow of satisfaction, which lighted his face. He sat down to read aloud to a group of prisoners in the yard, some of them coming over with "ball and chain." He once had read his New Testament as a student but now he read as a teacher.

The, next day the delegate found his Bible student with paper and pencil, collating and comparing passages. In other words, he was making his Bible, with its ordinary text, into a reference Bible and so he continues now, "searching the Scriptures." When he finds a passage, which matches or throws light upon one in question, he is as glad as the woman who found a piece of silver with her candle. He comes to Mr. Tearne as the neighbor to rejoice with him.

The boy has a history. According to his account, he had been brought up by "the best father and mother in the world," trained from youth in the Christian life. He was converted before joining the army and had joined the army three years ago with a mother's blessing upon him and God's love in his heart. In his regiment, he was known as a true soldier and faithful Christian.

Last winter after the Chattanooga battles, his division was sent to relieve Burnside and raise the siege at Knoxville. For three days and nights, his regiment had been on duty, marching and fighting. He had scarcely an hour's sleep. Prisoners were captured and he was assigned to guard one who, it seems, was as tired and worn out as himself. He told the lieutenant who ordered him to guard the man that he could not keep awake and could not even keep his eyelids open while receiving instructions. But he was assigned anyway.

Afterward, he remembered nothing except the snoring of the prisoner lying at his feet, until he himself was aroused by a guard and put in irons. His sentence was six months' imprisonment. We would have interceded on his behalf but his sentence would expire before official relief could be obtained, plus his three years' service was set to end about the same time.

He speaks of "these dreadful six months" with horror. Only through the utmost vigilance, by day and by night, had he kept himself clear from vermin. The single cotton shirt he wore was actually hanging in shreds and his pants and uniform jacket were patched and tattered, even though they were neatly washed and most elaborately darned. At what cost such vigilant neatness must have cost him, anyone who has not seen military prison-quarters and life could never know.

Then, the soldier says that six months in contact with such a crowd of wretches, so thoroughly abandoned and impure, has horrors unimaginable. In it all, the faithful boy has been cheerful and without a word of murmuring against the government. He says it is an awful crime for a guard to sleep at his post and has no doubt the military court sentenced him with deep regret. They had to do so for the sake of making him an example.

When congratulated upon his double deliverance by the expiration of his army service as well as of his prison term, he said, "Oh, no. I am coming in again. I shall run up and see my mother and be back in the ranks in a month. I couldn't stay out while this thing is going on. I think too much of the old flag to bang around home while others are still fighting."

We suggested, "With your three years' duty and the last six months' treatment, don't you think you have done your part?"

He rejected the idea, saying, "Nobody had done his part until he had done all he could do."

The boy goes home to his mother next week and in good clothes. If I could get a furlough, I would give half of it to follow him to his father's cabin on the Illinois prairie just to see the greeting.

Conquering Malice

Reverend Victor Miller, Pastor of the Lutheran Church, New Wilmington, Pennsylvania, gives an account of two items of work in Murfreesboro and Nashville during October 1864:

We had a daily prayer meeting at our rooms in Murfreesboro. A Scotchman who had been a miner in the "old country" told me his experience with these back home:

"They did me a wonderful amount of good. I was a wicked man when I came to the army. I cared for nothing and once I was to be shot for sleepin' at my post after I'd been drinkin'. I had a 'bairn' [son] at the Deaf and Dumb Asylum in Columbus, Ohio. He wrote me when I was in prison and told me of some who had found a freeing in Jesus. I couldn't help thinkin' of it but then there was my hate for the officers and as long as I kept hold of that, I couldn't find Him. I couldn't read a chapter, nor pray. Since I came to the meetin's, I let all the spite go. When I have to stand guard, I change with someone else at the meetin' times."

As the humbled man talked, the warm tears rained down bronzed cheeks.

Words of Profound Appreciation

As I went down the steps after a preaching service in the Zollicoffer Barracks, I was passing between the two guards.

"Let the Christian Commission man pass," said one—and a tremor came into his voice when he added, "Wherever you find that bunch, you find home." (Victor Miller)

God's Miraculous Provision

Mr. A. E. Chamberlain, writing from Cincinnati, gives a glimpse into the meaning of faith in Christian planning and work:

Our treasury in Cincinnati ran dry in October and we scarcely knew where to look for more money. Just then, word came from Nashville that our men wanted onions immediately. I looked at Mr. Marley, the Secretary of the

Cincinnati Branch of the Christian Commission and a member of Cincinnati Conference, Methodist Episcopal Church, and he looked at me.

"You haven't got a dollar in the treasury," he said.

"That's a fact," was all I could say in reply. But I thought I would start out and see what I could do. At Seventh and Western Row, I found fifty barrels of very nice onions.

I asked, "How much are you asking for them, Mr. Buck?"

"Seven dollars a barrel, sir. Cost me six."

"Send them down to the boat at six dollars," and Mr. Buck, for the soldiers' sake, obeyed.

When I returned to the office, I told Mr. Marley what I had done.

"But where on earth is the money going to come from?"

"I'm sure I don't know, unless the Lord sends it."

Of course, under the circumstances of the purchase, the bill must be paid on presentation. Soon a clerk brought it in and, while he was laying it on the desk, a little boy entered the room. He brought two checks from gentlemen I had not known to be even remotely interested in our work. One was for $200, the other for $100, and both were made out to the Christian Commission. Did not the money come from the Lord?

God's Instantaneous Provision

A month or two later, our Field Agent sent word that the men were dying of scurvy—that he must have a supply of sauerkraut and cabbage for immediate distribution. For months, we had been spending all we received as fast as it came into our hands. We had no funds to make any new purchases.

The remembrance of how God had helped us earlier returned to encourage us. Yet, we did not know just what to do. While musing on the matter, I stepped to the window and saw the carts, used in my own business, unloading casks on the sidewalk. I called to the driver and asked what they were. He didn't know but told me he had left a letter on my desk. I opened it. It was an invoice from the town of Lebanon, Ohio, for thirty-four barrels of sauerkraut and pickled cabbage.

I could not help crying out on the spot, "Thank God for Lebanon! Thank God for the sauerkraut and cabbage."

That very day, these barrels were sent down to the army as a first installment. A grateful surgeon sent word to me that if barrels of gold dust had been sent instead, they would not have compared in value with that sauerkraut and cabbage. (A. E. Chamberlain)

Historical Setting:

Confederate Lieutenant General J. B. Hood, after the fall of Atlanta, made several abortive movements to draw Sherman from Georgia. But after unsuccessfully attempting to lay his hand upon the nimble-footed Confederate general, Sherman committed the defense of Tennessee to Major General Thomas. Then he gathered up all his garrisons and, breaking off all lines of communications, he began his memorable march to the sea on November 11, 1864 through Georgia and the Carolinas.

Two Christian Commission delegates, Mr. William A. Lawrence and Mr. Arthur Lawrence, accompanied the army to Savannah. There they received and distributed the large invoice of supplies with which the New York Committee of the Commission welcomed their arrival. The opportunities for Commission work were so restricted by the character of the march and the losses to the army of life and limb were so limited, that we shall not need to delay upon the incidents of the movement. (A few incidents of the movement were related at the prayer meetings about the time of the "grand review" in Washington and can be found *Annals, U.S. Christian Commission*, 391-392.)

While the Federal General lingered before beginning his hazardous march, Hood encamped along the Tennessee River around Florence, Alabama. The moment the news of Sherman's movement reached him, he immediately moved his army toward Nashville. On the last day of November 1864, the bloody battle of Franklin was fought, resulting in Hood's temporary repulse and the continued falling back of the Union forces. On December 2nd, Hood appeared before Nashville and sat down to his impotent and impudent siege of a city defended by a force twice as large as his own.

On December 15th, Thomas moved out of his entrenchments against the besiegers. On the evening of the next day, heaven witnessed the complete defeat and disorderly rout of the Confederate Army. From this time forward, it essentially ceased to be an army. In the following spring, Forrest's cavalry, the special pride of the Western Confederates, could manage but a poor resistance to Wilson's raid through Alabama.

Brilliant Insight

As a side note, while all in the city were held in no slight suspense by the siege and apparent inaction of General Thomas, an interesting conversation took place the night before Thomas' movement against Hood. Mr. Edward P. Smith, General Field Agent of the Christian Commission, was returning from doing reconnaissance along the lines when he overtook a gray-headed black man hobbling into town.

Mr. Smith asked, "Well, uncle, how are the times?"

"I was just studying that, Colonel."

"What about General Hood?"

"That's it, Colonel. I was just studying on him."

"Is he coming into Nashville?"

"That's it, Colonel. That's it exactly. I was studying that very particular."

"Well, is he coming in?"

"No, sir, General Hood won't come in."

"Why not?"

"He couldn't do justice to hisself in here, sir."

Others Considered More Important

Mr. B. F. Jacobs, faithful and devoted Secretary of the Chicago Army Committee and of the Northwestern Branch of the Christian Commission, preserves this incident from the battle of Nashville, December 15-16, 1864:

General Steedman's Corps of black troops made a reconnaissance, in force, on the eve of the battle of Nashville. Mr. John A. Dutcher, Esquire, of Milwaukee and I made every preparation to receive the wounded. Soon they began to come in on stretchers. Suddenly, we saw a bare-headed soldier staggering toward us. His hand was on his forehead, blood was pouring down his face, and tears were washing away the blood almost as fast as it came. I supposed he must be very badly wounded and went to meet him.

I asked, "My boy, are you hit?"

"Yes," he answered in a dazed way. Taking his hand from his forehead and seeing the blood, he said, "I believe so."

"Doesn't it hurt you?"

"Oh, no, I don't mind it much."

"Well, what are you crying for?"

Turning around with a scared look, he pointed to the woods from which four men had just emerged, bearing a stretcher with an officer's body on it.

"Oh," said the poor fellow, "look there! My Captain's wounded! My Captain's wounded!"

This was the hero's sorrow. All the time we were caring for him, it seemed to be his uppermost and only grief.

Unlikely Place for Worship Service

This incident, following the battle at Nashville on December 15-16, 1864, comes from the pen of Mr. B. F. Jacobs, faithful and devoted Secretary of the Chicago Army Committee and of the Northwestern Branch of the Christian Commission:

During the cannonading on the Sunday before the raising of the siege, I was in front of the headquarters of the Fourth Corps, at Acklin Place. General Wood was in temporary command. Major Bridge's Battery held the summit of the hill just beyond. After distributing some things among the men, I suggested to the major that we might have a meeting in spite of the cannonading. After all, it was Sunday morning. He immediately said that I might take all the men who were not absolutely needed to work the guns.

Two infantry regiments were supporting the battery and, after the singing of several hymns, a pretty large audience had gathered. Officers rode up and all were on the *qui vive* of expectation. I mounted a cracker-box for a pulpit, read a chapter and then talked for fifteen minutes, while the battery near us was sending its constant response to the Confederate shells. By this time, Generals Wood and Schofield, the Chief of Artillery, and their staffs were a part of the audience. I reminded all present of the peril of the hour and asked them to unite with me in prayer. The Chief of Artillery shouted to his orderly to have every gun cease firing. The soldiers knelt upon the ground and the officers took off their caps and bowed their heads. During the silence of the guns, we invoked the Divine blessing.

The Chief came to me when it was over and, with great sincerity, said, "In the name of these soldiers, I want to thank you for this."

Comforting Family Member

The General Field Agent, Reverend E. P. Smith, gives the narrative of the service of relief during the night of the first day's battle, contained in *Annals, U.S. Christian Commission*, 508-509:

The work for the night was to go over the field in search of men who had been missed by the stretcher-bearers. We gathered up the dead, identified them through their comrades, when possible, and marked them with a card. We also gave out coffee and hot soup at the flying hospital and befriended men who were dreadfully wounded—many of them dying.

Coming upon a stack of straw in our search for the dead, we found two bodies side by side, as if laid together by some friendly hand. As we were lifting them onto the stretcher, one of them sprang out of our hands.

Pointing to his comrade, he said, "It's my brother, sir. It's my brother that's dead. We two were all that were left. We enlisted together and I am alone now."

Missing him in the fight, he had hunted over the field and found him dead by the stack. Lying down to watch over him until morning, he had fallen into "the image of death," from which we had awakened him. When we took the body to lay in line with the others, the brother followed, bringing straw to make a bed for himself and his dead. We gave him room in that long row of silent sleepers and, nestling close to the corpse, he laid down for his last night's rest with his brother.

Hospital Ministry

The scene at the house, converted into the flying hospital, baffles description. While General Hood was falling back, the citizens who still believed in the Confederacy had taken their movable property, including bedding and their best furniture, to the rear for protection within Confederate lines. This house had been made into a storage area for neighbors' furniture and, as a result, we were able to put a first-class mattress under every wounded man.

All the rooms below and the porch on three sides of the house were laid thick with officers and privates. Some were sleeping under the relief of opiates; some were already sleeping in death, while still others were writhing in mortal agony. Some were calling for the surgeon, some for water, and some for mercy. Others were offering a prayer of trust and the joyous hope of heaven, at hand. And some were waiting in silent, anxious suspense for the surgeon's decision as to the nature of their wounds. (E. P. Smith)

Ministry to the Mortally Wounded

Mr. B.F. Jacobs writes of a soldier to whom he ministered at this hospital:

Our improvised hospital was at the foot of the hill, which our boys won by storm on the first day's fight. Shortly after it was established, I met four men bringing in a soldier from an Indiana regiment, named Jackson. I saw that he was shot through the lungs and was near death. Indeed, I thought he would live but a few minutes.

I stooped down to him as the men walked along and asked, "Are you badly wounded?"

"Yes."

I asked his name, his regiment and home. He told me about his family. I inquired if he was a Christian.

"Yes, but why do you ask that question?"

"Why, my brother, you are going to die."

"Oh! Am I?"

"Yes."

"Soon?"

"Yes, very soon."

He was in much pain. We laid him down on the porch and arranged as soft a place as we could. His groans were dreadful. He told me what to write to his wife and gave me her photograph and his watch to send home. After taking care of many others, I went back to him about eleven o'clock that night. Kneeling at his side, I strove to comfort him in his pain. I told him he would not suffer long and asked how he felt.

He replied, "It would be so sweet if I could hear somebody pray once more."

While I offered a short prayer, he held my hand in both of his and sobbed out responsively to the petitions. At the close, he added, "Oh! I do so love to hear you pray. Ain't you going to stay with me?" he said as I turned to leave. "Ain't you going to stay with me until I die?'"

"I can't, Jackson, while all these men here have so many needs."

Amidst the sudden attacks of pain, he labored until his last breath. He frequently exclaimed, "Blessed Jesus, come and take me out of my pain!"

Ministry to Those Suffering Painful Death

Mr. Smith's attention fell upon this soldier later in the night. He writes of him:

At one o'clock and after having given personal attention and arranged a watch relief for every man, we rolled up in our blankets for a little rest. But, from among the wounded, rose one voice above all the others—either in a shriek of torture or in a tender appeal to the Savior. It was from an Indiana soldier, wounded in the bowels.

One of the delegates, bending over him, whispered, "Jackson, do you love Jesus?"

"How I love Him!" was the instant reply.

His wound was mortal, beyond any human relief. We were obliged to leave him and go back to our blankets. Long after midnight, that voice from the porch was distinct among the dreadful chorus of groans, making sleep impossible. It pierced its way through the chilly night air like the voice of a flute floating above a chorus of trumpets.

He cried, "Dear Jesus, You know I love You. Come, Jesus, dear Jesus. I am all ready now. Come, Jesus. You love me and You know I love You, dear Jesus."

Fainter and less frequent came that sweet, divine appeal until it ceased and we slept. In the morning, we found a smile in the eye and on the lips of the dead patriot who still seemed to be repeating, "Dear Jesus, You love me and You know I love You." (Story taken from *Annals, U. S. Christian Commission*, 509.)
(B. F. Jacobs)

Funeral Service in Unlikely Place

Mr. Jacobs continues the account of the second day's conflict:

About four o'clock in the morning, we began supplying the men with whatever we had to comfort them and we especially attended to the removal of the wounded from the immediate front. This work continued throughout the day while our men were lying down, awaiting orders for the final charge. The monotony of the position, along with the accrued weariness of the previous day's fighting, put one poor fellow to sleep. A shot rang out as he lay unconscious, piercing his head and killing him instantly. His whole appearance and physique made him a magnificent-looking soldier. No change came upon his face as his comrades bore him back. Even the smile of rest was undisturbed.

In a little while, the charge would be ordered. But I was anxious to give him a Christian burial. The boys said, "Aye, aye," with strong conviction. So with such crude things as we had, pieces of boxes and boards, we dug a grave. Before he was wrapped up in his blanket, I looked to find some little token to send home to his family. Not finding anything of special interest, I cut a lock of hair, still warm with his life's blood, and put it in my memorandum book to be sent to his mother. No dying word would accompany it. We buried him hastily but decently. On the end of an old ammunition box, I inscribed his name, his only headstone.

When the grave was filled, I said, "Let us have a moment of prayer, boys."

Just as we had all bowed around the grave, the hastening hoofs of the aids' horses called the men to the charge. The prayer was brief but, before it was over, the bullets had begun to sing, the men were back in their places, and the line was sweeping on in triumph toward the doomed works of the enemy.
(B. F. Jacobs)

Ministry in Midst of Danger

Just before this scene and while I was moving about among the men, General A. J. Smith, commanding the Sixteenth Corps, came by with his staff. He jumped off his horse near where I stood and looked at me curiously. I imagine I was a rather strange-looking figure with two large haversacks, protruding with crackers and tea, dried toast and whisky, bandages and brandy and sponges, thrown over my shoulders. I held a three-gallon coffeepot in one hand, a big twelve-quart pail with fresh water in the other, and had slung a bundle of tin cups over my back and shoulders and arms. I suppose I looked like Robinson Crusoe or somebody stashing supplies for an indefinite siege or life on a desert island. The General demanded to know who I was. I told him I was a Christian Commission delegate.

He asked, "What have you got in that big pot?

"Coffee, General, for these wounded men. It is very good for some of them, you know. Won't you have a cup?"

"Thank you. I don't mind if I do. I haven't had a mouthful today and I've been in the saddle since four this morning."

An orderly rode up just then and, seeing the General drinking, said, "I'll take some, if you please."

"Haven't you had your breakfast?" asked the General, sharply. When the orderly replied in the affirmative, General Smith barked, "Don't give him any. Keep it for the men. I don't think I ought to have taken any myself."

When the fighting was over, General Smith was in a tent with General McArthur and a number of delegates. After recounting the incident above, he said, "I must say that since Jesus Christ left this world, there has never been a more heavenly institution than the Christian Commission. When I passed your folks going out, I thought that their place was about six miles in the rear but now I have now come to a different conclusion. Many a man owes his life to you."

It was the unequivocal testimony of an officer who made no pretense of being a Christian.
(B. F. Jacobs)

Meeting Needs after Battle

When the charge was ordered, the troops to whom I had been ministering overtook the enemy's works and captured eighteen hundred prisoners. In the charge, they suffered heavy losses. A Minnesota regiment had one hundred killed or disabled. While following the troops, I pressed onward through a cornfield and came to a large house about a mile beyond. It had served as the headquarters of a Confederate General and its occupants had all run away during the battle.

No one was on hand to organize a hospital, so I undertook the task myself. I directed stragglers—and all other available people I could find—to clear the rooms and bring in the wounded. Then I went out to the place where the fighting had ceased and turned the streams of wounded toward the house. It had been supplied with magnificent furniture, which we had to put out into the yard to make room for the wounded. Every floor in the house, the great halls, the porches in front and rear, were soon covered with suffering soldiers. About this time, a Surgeon Kennedy with a Minnesota regiment arrived. He asked who was in charge of the hospital. I introduced myself as a Christian Commission delegate who had taken the direction of matters until the proper parties should arrive and that I was very glad to surrender my task to him.

"By no means," he replied. "Retain your command and I'll serve you to the best of my ability."

Two assistant surgeons came in shortly and we all went to work feverishly. With the beef jerky in my haversack, we soon made twenty quarts of soup. We added what crackers and crusts of bread we had and I was able to give every wounded man in the house a light supper. Poor fellows! They were almost starved—with only a few having had anything since their early morning rations. I succeeded in confiscating a horse and sent a soldier back through the mud at midnight to our office in Nashville with an order for supplies. He returned about two o'clock with supplies packed into two grain bags and otherwise filling every pocket. By three, we had made coffee and soup and the men had another meal.

About seven the next morning, our Christian Commission wagon made its appearance, loaded down with supplies. With that wagonload, the men were fed morning, noon and night, on both Saturday and Sunday. Not an ounce of government supplies reached the hospital in answer to the Surgeon Kennedy's requisition until late Sunday afternoon. When they did come, the Surgeon had some potent words for the Assistant Medical Director who accompanied the supplies. He said, "If it hadn't been for the Christian Commission, these wounded men would have starved to death before this."
(B. F. Jacobs)

Wounded Join in Worship

We wanted someone to take charge and manage our supplies, so on Sunday I found an able-bodied Englishman of fine personal appearance whom I "detailed" as Hospital Steward. He did a most efficient service.

SONGS FOR SIGHING

In clearing out the house on the evening of the battle, only three things remained in the house—a piano, a family portrait, and a large mirror with a six-pound shot through it. After the men had been cared for on Sunday morning, we arranged to hold service. Thinking it would be pleasant to have singing, I made the remark that if only we had someone to play the piano, it would be everything we could want. The surgeons were still at work in the amputating room, so they could not help us even if any of them had been able to play the instrument.

To my surprise, my English Steward stepped forward and modestly said, "Colonel, I used to play the piano a little in England. Maybe I could draw down a tune for you."

He had on a red flannel shirt, picturesque but unfashionable, and his sleeves were rolled up above his elbows, even more unfashionable. Without stopping for any preparations, he took his seat on a cracker box to give us a preliminary trial run. The practice was highly satisfactory. He then accompanied us in excellent fashion while we sung our songs of Zion and "My country, 'tis of thee" to the melody of "God save the Queen," familiar to every Englishman. And never did the boys enjoy music as did our wounded in that morning meeting.

(B. F. Jacobs)

Dying with Dignity

Surgeon Ford, of Nashville, a constant and valuable friend of the Christian Commission, furnishes the narrative of Henry Cutler, a young Illinois soldier wounded in the Nashville battles and brought in the night to a hospital:

I examined his wound—in the right lung and liver—and gave the nurses directions about the dressing. As I was about to leave, Cutler asked what I thought of his case. I replied, "You have a very serious wound."

"Do you think it is mortal? You need not be afraid to tell me the truth, for I am not afraid to die."

"Such wounds," I said, "are necessarily fatal and I fear you have not long to live."

"Well," he said, "it's all right, though it seems hard to die so young. I had high hopes but God has so ordered it and I am willing to go."

"Do you feel that you are a Christian and ready to die?"

"Well, I don't know. I have tried to be a Christian but the army is a hard place."

"True. But if you put your trust in Christ now, He will not forsake you."

He spoke of his mother and asked if I thought she would have time to reach him before he died. I had to tell him that I thought it impossible but would telegraph her if he so desired. He thought for a moment and then said that, perhaps, it would be best not to request her presence.

I asked him for any message he might have for her. He said, "Tell her I would like to die near her but that I die happy. I am thankful I can die among friends and that I did not fall into the hands of the enemy. I had a premonition when

I left home that I would never see mother again and, when I leaped the breast-works to make the charge, I was sure I would be wounded or killed."

"Do you regret now having enlisted in the service?"

Immediately his eye brightened and a smile of profound satisfaction shone on his face, as he answered with the greatest emphasis, saying, "*Oh, no, by no means.*"

It was painful for him to speak, so I bade him goodbye. He lingered until the morning in great agony, yet without a murmur, until death eased him of his pains. (Added note: In the post-battle chaos of caring for the wounded, Surgeon Ford unfortunately lost the address for Mrs. Cutler. But it should be noted that, during the four or five days after the Nashville battles, an average of 35,000 sheets of letter paper and envelopes were distributed daily by the Christian Commission delegates.)

Meeting Physical and Spiritual Needs

Mr. Charles Harris, City Missionary of Peoria, Illinois, writes from Nashville in December 1864:

A Mission Sunday school in Peoria had sent me the means of supplying many little needed luxuries for the soldiers. Purchasing some oranges once, I handed one to a sick young man in the Post Hospital. He took it with a calm exclamation of delight, held it up, then turned it round and round, and at last broke forth, saying, "My little daughter wrote me two days ago. She said, 'Papa, I would like to send you some oranges but I can't do it.' And now, here the Lord has sent me one. My little girl couldn't send any to me but God puts it into some other child's heart who could."

Conversion of a Surgeon

After the benediction in our prayer meeting the other day, a surgeon rose and said, "I have been at this meeting twice and perhaps some of you think I am a Christian but I am not. I have risen to ask for your prayers. I want to be a Christian."

We had a few moments of silent prayer on his behalf and I am sure the petitions were offered fervently. The next day, he rose again and testified of the power of Jesus to save. Our thanksgivings now were as fervent as our prayers had been before. He was the second surgeon converted at our daily meetings while I attended them.
(Charles Harris)

Mention of Jesus Revives Comatose

Laboring in the hospitals at Paducah, Kentucky in January 1865, Reverend H. McLeod, Pastor of the Congregational Church, Brentwood, New Hampshire, tells the following story of his experience:

I was called one night to see a soldier who was thought to be dying. Two days earlier, he had been put ashore from one of the transports traveling up the river. He was unconscious and no one could tell me anything about him, except that he belonged to a Michigan regiment. Remembering that the mere utterance of the name of Jesus had often revived the wandering senses of the dying Christian, I sat down by him and, opening the little New Testament on the stand, I read, "For we know that if our earthly house of this tabernacle were dissolved, we have a building of God, an house not made with hands, eternal in the heavens."

I then read Jesus' words to Martha: "I am the Resurrection and the Life: he that believeth in me, though he were dead, yet shall he live; and whosoever believeth in me shall never die."

The dying man opened his eyes and looked at me. I asked, "Does it pain you to hear me read?"

"Oh, no. When I was well, I used to love to read the New Testament. There's one in my knapsack."

"Are you afraid to die?"

"No," and the face grew bright. "I long to go to heaven."

"Is Jesus with you?"

"Yes, He is with me."

I asked for his father's name and home and he gave me the particulars, then added, "Write to mother. She is a Christian. Father is not," and he again passed into the state of unconsciousness. I began writing a letter to his mother. After a little while, he opened his eyes and asked for me. The nurse pointed me out and he said, "Oh, yes, you are writing to mother. Tell father to become a Christian."

Calmly he gave directions about the division of certain property between his two younger brothers and very soon he was resting with Christ.

Decision to Do the Right Thing

Mr. A. E. Chamberlain, Chairman of the Cincinnati Branch of the Christian Commission, writes of a visit that he, along with Judge Bellamy Storer and Reverend B. W. Chidlaw of Cincinnati, made to a Nashville hospital:

We came to a soldier who looked very despondent.

"My good fellow, you look sad," I said.

"I feel so," was his reply. His left foot was removed at the ankle from a wound received on the last day of the battle of Nashville. His father and mother were living at home in Missouri and his wife lived on Empire Prairie in the same state.

"Have you written to your wife since the battle?"

"No, sir, I got one of the boys to write for me."

"But you told everyone about your wound?"

"Well, I told him to write that I was slightly wounded. I didn't want to let her bear all the worst at once."

"Did you tell her about your amputation?"

"No, sir. That would have broken her heart."

I told him how I thought he was doing wrong in concealing his condition.

"Now I am going to write her and tell her about how you are. Is she a Christian?"

"Yes."

"Are you?"

"No."

"You need your wife's prayers, my brave fellow."

"Yes, and I have them."

"But you know she can't pray for you intelligently unless she understands all about your case."

I wrote all the particulars, so far as I could get them, and then told the soldier that I wanted him to add one more paragraph at the bottom of the letter.

"Your wife has been praying alone long enough. I want you to add that, from this very moment, you are going to pray for yourself. And then, hereafter, if you never meet her again on earth, your prayers will go up from here in Nashville while hers go up from Empire Prairie, both meeting at the throne. It will be an arch of prayer with God at the keystone. Will you leave the arch incomplete? Will you authorize me to tell your wife that you will so pray?"

The poor fellow went through a deep struggle. His whole frame shook with emotion. But after a minute, he threw up his arm and said, "God helping me, I'll do it. Put it down."

I knelt and prayed with him. Then reading over the letter with the added clause, I asked if that was all right—if he was willing to stand by it.

"Yes," he said, "that's all right."

The next morning, I went in to see him again. One of the most pleasant countenances I ever met was that of the poor soldier. It seemed as if the invisible arch of prayer had been already established.

Surgeon's Baptism of Fire Ministry

Mr. G. W. R. Scott, of Pittsburg, Pennsylvania, a student of Andover Theological Seminary, Massachusetts, went to the Army of the Cumberland as a delegate in March 1865. On the road to Nashville, he played a role in the following incident:

As the train was passing through a gorge in the woods about six miles southwest of Cave City, Kentucky, it was attacked by guerrillas. They had previously torn up about one hundred yards of the track and now they fired volley after volley into the cars. All the while, they shouted non-stop like demons. The train guards returned fire but, seeing the robbers were protected by a high bank, no injury befell them.

Soon the train was surrendered by the military conductor and the bandits began their work of pillage. Each passenger and soldier was thoroughly searched. Money, watches, and even finger rings were taken. The amount of property, which so unceremoniously changed owners, was estimated at fifty thousand dollars. Their work completed, the train was set ablaze and seven cars were consumed. Remounting their horses, the guerrillas rode off with their booty.

The wounded were now to be looked after. There was no surgeon on board, so Mr. Scott found it necessary to begin his Christian Commission work before all expectations. He began to dress wounds and, wholly without bandages, he was obliged to tear up his own shirts. Two soldiers volunteered to assist. Five balls were extracted, dislocated members set, and the wounds of sixteen men were dressed. Mr. Scott remained with the wounded until the next afternoon when surgeons came. He had the gratification of hearing from the surgeons that the disabled men had all been properly cared for and that their wounds were doing well.

Dying Soldier Sees His Mother

From Mr. Scott's work at Tullahoma, the post to which he was assigned, come these incidents:

I stopped at the bedside of a young man and asked if he was getting better.

"No, I am going to die."

"Are you prepared?"

"Oh, yes," he said with a glad smile. "I gave myself to Christ long ago."

"Shall I write home?"

"Yes, sir, do. It would please mother so much. Tell mother—tell—father" and his voice faltered. Soon his mind began to wander. Afterward, he lay unconscious for a little while. Then waking from his stupor, he said something I can never forget. He said, "Wait, Chaplain, you needn't mind. Mother's here."

He lay quiet for a moment, filled, perhaps, with the invisible communion, and then "fell asleep."
(G. W. R. Scott)

Death Came While Singing a Hymn

An incident in one of the wards impressed me with its deep solemnity. Three convalescing soldiers were gathered around an old, gray-haired "veteran." They had just finished singing a familiar and beautiful hymn. Evidently, the old man's heart was deeply touched by the song of Zion. His face was lit up with something of the brightness, which must have radiated from St. Stephen's face. He scarcely seemed to be a creature of earth.

The convalescents began singing another hymn. The old man's lips quivered but no words were sounding forth. By and bye, the smile and the brightness on his face became fixed. I looked closer. He was dead! The soldiers sang on, not noticing the change. The hymn would not open the dull ear of death but who can say that the freed spirit did not partake of the upward, floating melody?
(G. W. R. Scott)

War Seen As Preparation for Heaven

In the summer of 1865, General Clinton B. Fisk, who earlier worked in the operations of the

Western Army, was now heading up the Freedmen's Bureau in the State of Tennessee, with headquarters at Nashville. In February, Reverend Edward P. Smith had been called from work in the Western Army and relocated to the Potomac field. In March, he was transferred to the post of Field Secretary at the Central Office in Philadelphia. He relates an incident told by the General at the close of a Sunday service in Cumberland Hospital at Nashville during July:

One of my brave boys, very young, and a Christian, was brought into the hospital, stricken down with malaria. He had grown weary with the tedium of camp life and, as he lay on his cot through the "lazy, leaden-stepping hours," he longed for the active fray. He envisioned that the ideal life for a soldier was "at the front." Learning of his sickness and that he would soon die, I hastened to his side.

After talking with him about his life in the military, his home and his approaching death, I asked, "Now, my boy, when I get back to St. Louis, I shall go to see your mother and the first question she will ask me will be, 'How did Charley die?' Can you tell me in a few words exactly how you feel about dying?"

"Yes, General," he said, fastening his deep, blue eyes upon me. "I think I can. It seems as if I am just *going to the front.*"

And so, indeed, he was. For does not the real campaign, for which this life is only the drill camp, lie beyond?

Leadership of a Determined Woman

Reverend Jeremiah Porter, Pastor of the Edwards Congregational Church at the outbreak of war and now serving at Seventh Presbyterian in Chicago, was laboring in August 1865 among the troops of General Logan's Corps in and around Louisville, Kentucky. He writes about a devoted, energetic lady, whose care and kindness had won for her the title of "Mother of Sherman's Army." She is the subject of this incident:

Several regiments had been ordered to Texas. All indications pointed to scurvy within their ranks. The situation called for leadership and promptness in providing the men with potatoes, a major anti-scorbutic (scurvy cure), because the men were to embark that very day. Mrs. Bickerdyke determined that they should have them. This meant the potatoes must be removed from the sanitary supply rooms and shipped that day—or the men would suffer greatly. An ambulance was ordered for Mrs. Bickerdyke and my wife but it was raining in torrents that Sunday, causing major delays. So they went to the Quartermaster's for the teams, which had been promised the day before. They also arranged for the captain of one of the steamers to transport the potatoes.

The ladies waited in the storm until the army wagons were loaded with all fifty barrels of the needed vegetables. Then, hastening in advance of the wagons to the river bank, they were astounded to find that the boats had already moved from their moorings.

The spectators volunteered their comfort by remarking, "You're too late. The boats have gone."

"Gone! They shall come back," announced Mrs. Bickerdyke decisively.

Assuming an attitude of command worthy of Joan of Arc, she waved her sunbonnet and gesticulated with her hands to make known her orders. The steamer obediently returned to the dock and took the supplies on board.

CHAPTER XVII
THE WESTERN ARMIES

WORK ALONG AND NEAR THE MISSISSIPPI RIVER
July 1863–December 1865

The fall of Vicksburg, under siege from May 25th to July 4, 1863, was the last mention of our work on the Mississippi River. After that event, General Grant sent Sherman after Johnston who hovered at the edge of the Union Army and waited for any opportunity that might compel the raising of the siege. Sherman drove his adversary out of Jackson after a painfully fatiguing march from Vicksburg.

Ministry of Multiplication

Mr. A. E. Chamberlain, Chairman of the Cincinnati Branch of the Christian Commission, narrates an incident connected with this movement:

The 57th Pennsylvania Infantry was one of the regiments, which went with Sherman. The intense heat and rapid pace of the journey compelled the exhausted men to throw away their baggage. A soldier named Wilmarth carried a Bible—a mother's last gift. When he had thrown away his knapsack, he carried the book in his hand for a long distance, until the question of keeping it became one of life itself. At last, to keep up with the rest of the men, he was obliged to leave it behind on the road. He put it where he could see it for a long time as he marched away. When it had faded from view, he could not say that his burden was any lighter than before.

When the expedition was ended, several factions of regiments, which had suffered greatly, passed through Cincinnati. Among these was Wilmarth's. On their arrival, I went over to see them at the Regimental Hospital. For six weeks, the men had had no changes of clothes and were fearfully dirty and neglected looking. Wilmarth lay on the first cot. He pulled up the blanket to hide his squalor and wretchedness. I had brought some portions of Scripture for distribution but, the moment I entered, I saw it was not the time for tracts in that room. The seventeen men needed another phase of Christ's Gospel.

"Boys, you want clean clothes first of all," I said. Then I began taking an account of all missing stock that needed to be supplied. Coming to Wilmarth, I asked what could be done to make him more comfortable.

"I was never a beggar in my life," he replied.

"My dear boy, this isn't begging. All I want to do is to pay a little installment on what we owe you and your fellow soldiers."

The surgeon sent his ambulance to the Commission rooms for the goods and, within three hours, I called on them again.

The three hours had certainly developed into a revolution. One would not have known the place or the men's faces. Now was the time for Testaments. Coming to Wilmarth, I asked him if he had one. He answered by telling me about the incident on the march to Jackson. I put a copy of St. John's Gospel at his side, marked a few passages, and spoke of God's great love for him, just as I did with all of them. After a short service, I bade them good-bye, never expecting to see them again.

Two weeks later, Reverend Mr. Chidlaw and I held Sunday service at Licking Hospital. I noticed a soldier leaning against a post. Going over to him, I asked if he was a Christian.

"I don't know, sir. I'm trying to be one," he replied

"How long have you been trying?"

"Ever since," and he held up a little portion of Scripture as he spoke, "ever since you gave me this book, sir."

I remembered him at once. Seeing that his was already worn with use, I took out a bright, new copy and asked, "Suppose you give me that one and take this."

"You could not get this book, sir, in exchange for the whole State of Kentucky. I*t brought me to Jesus.*"

Not long afterward, I went back over to the hospital with a supply of reading material and Wilmarth met me at the gate. He said, "Mr. Chamberlain, I want to ask a favor of you. Would you mind giving me the reading papers you send over here to the hospital? I could talk to the men about Christ if I had it to distribute."

I gladly assented to the arrangement and, until he was sent back to his regiment several weeks later, he did a faithful chaplain's duty in that hospital.

Amazing Conversion

The work along the Mississippi River was mainly in the field of the St. Louis Committee of the Christian Commission. Mr. K. A. Burnell and Mr. F. G. Ensign were Agents with their headquarters at Memphis. The following incidents are some of Mr. Ensign's reminiscences:

In the Gayoso Hospital at Memphis, I found a soldier who had lost an arm and leg in the first grand assault on Vicksburg. I gave him some cordial and made him as comfortable as I could. Being surprised, he asked, "Who are you? Where did you get these things?"

I told him how they came from Northern homes.

"Who sent them?" he asked again in a kind of bewilderment.

"The people at home who love you sent them."

Tears came into his eyes as he lay quietly for a moment.

"Why?" he asked. "I haven't done anything to be remembered so."

"You have given your leg and arm."

But this fact did not strike him as important at all. He only reiterated, "I haven't done anything." I told him I had a nice little New Testament for him.

"My eyes are weak, sir. I'm afraid the print's too small," and he looked longingly at the book.

So I gave him one of the beautifully-printed Scripture portions of the British and Foreign Bible Society. When he found that his eyes rested on the page without pain, he said, "Well, this is the best of all. I have been here for weeks and I have wanted to read the Bible so much. This is just what I want. Who sent it?"

"Those at home and across the sea who love you and pray for you."

Again the unselfish heart found utterance, saying, "Why, I haven't done anything."

Afterward, I spoke to him of Jesus and visited him often. He gave his heart to the Master.

Unexpected Gifts Lead to Conversion

About the beginning of November, a soldier of the 7th Indiana Cavalry came into our rooms with soiled clothes and a generally worn appearance. Cut off from his comrades while scouting, he had straggled back to Memphis with much difficulty. His first request was for envelopes and paper to write home.

Bringing his letter to me, he asked, "Could you lend me a stamp? I have no money."

"I'll mail the letter for you."

"Well, but," he said argumentatively, "I want to pay for it."

"We don't take any pay here."

"But how do you get these things to run this concern?"

"Friends at home send them."

"Whose friends? You don't mean mine."

"Yes," I replied, "friends who are Christians sent them."

"Why," he said musingly, "my wife's a Christian."

"Very probably then, she helps to send such things."

I showed him an envelope on which was printed, "This is a gift of Christian love to you, soldier."

His eyes filled, as he read it and said, "I never knew religion meant this before."

In the afternoon, we began our daily prayer meeting with the hymn, "All hail the power of Jesus' name."

During the first prayer, I heard someone sobbing aloud. When the meeting was over, I found it was my soldier-friend I met that morning. He told me that, while passing the door, something urged him to enter. It seemed to him that he would be lost if he passed on and that salvation would be his if he obeyed the inward voice. We prayed for him and, with the confidence of a little child, the man there gave himself up to Jesus.

He came in the next morning. Another letter must be written, it seemed, to tell of a life turned, at last, into its right course and to gladden the heart of a waiting, praying wife.
(F. G. Ensign)

Mother's Prayers Lead to Son's Conversion

At the beginning of 1864, a soldier of the 89th Indiana Infantry Regiment came in one morning, sat down at my desk, and opened a letter. He sobbed aloud as he read it. I asked what I could do for him. He gave me the letter to read. His sister's letter contained the sad news of his mother's death.

The poor, bereaved man said, "My mother's been praying for me all my life and especially since I came to the army. I've felt her following me. Those prayers have been a great protection and, now she is dead, and she won't pray for me anymore. What shall I do? I don't feel safe without mother's prayers."

"Why," I said, "Jesus loves you and you must pray for yourself. Your mother's prayers cannot save."

"But, can I pray?"

"Certainly you can."

"Won't you teach me how to pray?"

"I will try," I answered. "Don't you want to give your heart to Jesus and love Him for giving you such a mother? Now, I'll pray first and I want you to follow me."

I prayed with the burden of the poor, chastised heart on mine and I shall never forget his childlike petition: "Dear Jesus, my mother is gone home to Thee. Teach me to pray as You taught her." This was his deep and earnest longing, something to fill the void which he had made in his life. Soon he gave himself entirely to Jesus and shined forth as a bright and devoted Christian.

Often I heard him say, "I want to live as my mother prayed." For as long as I knew him, his life was consistent with his desire.
(F. G. Ensign)

Women's Ministry

The St. Louis Committee succeeded in enlisting quite a number of dedicated, self-denying ladies in its work. Some of these dedicated themselves to laboring in the barracks and hospitals in and near the city. A sample of their service and method of dealing with the men may be gathered from the following extracts from the journal of Miss Sue McBeth:

"No. 1, Schofield Barracks" is a transportation depot for men going south or returning home on furlough. It goes from being crowded one day, to almost empty the next. All classes of men pass through here.

"We have about the hardest men in our hospital that you can find anywhere," said the commanding officer, one November afternoon. Mrs. M. and I had gone for a visit to see if he would not appropriate a room for us to use in conjunction with the Christian Commission. We needed a place to store our library, stationery, etc.

"We've been upstairs all afternoon and haven't yet found any 'hard cases,'" we told him.

"Of course, they wouldn't behave badly before you."

He was very kind and promised us the room. Afterward, he allowed the men to go across the street to prayer meeting—and very precious hours were some of these.

"Can you raise yourself up so as to look out?" I asked a sick boy. The wind, that day, bore the voice of singing from the yard below. As he looked out, I asked, "Isn't that a pleasant sight?"

"Yes, indeed, it is," was his answer.

The setting sun was glancing off a hundred or more new uniforms, as their wearers sat in rows on the narrow piazza or stood facing the delegate who spoke to them the words of life.

(Sue McBeth)

Women's Ministry

As I was talking to this same soldier the day before, I noticed two strangers coming into the ward. One of them belonged to the 176th Illinois, a regiment just discharged and going home, but this man was too sick to proceed and had asked a comrade to stay with him.

When I spoke to this sick soldier, he said, "I've wanted so much to see you again."

"Why, did you ever see me before?"

"Yes, in Ward 1, Benton Barracks. Don't you remember? I was the one you said who was taking jaundice."

I could not remember him but he went on.

"I've been thinking so much of what you said then and I wanted to see you again to tell you. You remember I said something about 'getting ready to die' and you said you didn't believe in that—it wasn't the right thing to do. You told me I ought to 'get ready to live,' that I owed my life to God and it was not right to keep it back from Him. You said I ought to present my body as a living sacrifice to God, which was my reasonable service, instead of turning to Him at the last moment so as to get into heaven."

"And did you do so?"

"Yes, I think I did," he said sincerely.

He had many of the characteristics of one belonging to the Christian family and expressed his strong desire, in life or in death, to be only the Lord's.

"You remember you wanted me to promise to begin praying that night," he said after a little while, "and I told you I was afraid to make the promise for fear I would break it."

"But you did pray?"

"Oh, yes, that night and many times since."

(Sue McBeth)

Tract on Substitution Leads to Conversion

His friend came up and I offered him some of my little tracts.

"You gave me that one before," he said as he handed back *The Substitute*.

"When did I give it to you?"

"I was in the hospital in Benton Barracks where I was sick. Don't you remember? I have all the little books you gave me in my knapsack here and I'm taking them home to the children."

"You have a 'Substitute,' have you, brother?" I said as I returned the tract to my satchel. You see, the last, great 'Draft' is coming, for which every man on earth is 'enrolled.' I was in Ohio a few weeks ago and some who didn't want to go to war tried very hard to get 'exempted.' If they could not, they went to great trouble to find a 'substitute,' even paying large sums to get others to take their 'chance,' as they called death. Now, against that last grand 'Draft,' a 'Substitute' has been provided—a 'Substitute' who has already taken our place, even unto death. He has offered himself 'without money and without price.' Have you accepted Him as your 'Substitute'?"

"I hope so," he said earnestly. "I have never made a profession of religion but..."

"You think you possess it," I said, as he hesitated.

"Yes, I do hope so."

We had a little talk about the duties of a new life. He said, "My wife wrote me that she had been thinking about these things too. In her last letter, she said she was going to join the church and wanted me to do the same. I was so glad to hear it but told her to wait until I came home and we would take each other's hand and go together."

The "supper call" sounded. So I wrote their names in their New Testaments. Their goodbye to me was "God bless you," and mine the prayer, "Send them forth into Thy Kingdom, dear Savior."
(Sue McBeth)

Wife's Prayers Lead to Conversion

One Sabbath toward the year's end, while talking to a little fourteen year-old drummer-boy in Ward P, Jefferson Barracks, I noticed a soldier, writing busily, at a little distance with his back toward me. Going to him, I asked, "Writing home, are you?" When he looked up, I saw he was one whose wife had been visiting him lately.

"No, I wasn't writing a letter. I was only copying a prayer my wife sent me. You see, when she was here, I told her how I felt and, when she went home, she wrote down two prayers. I'm copying them in this," showing me his notebook. "I might lose the letter and I'm learning them by heart. My wife's a Christian but I never cared anything about these things until I came into the army. I had no father or mother or anybody to teach me anything good when I was a boy and I just worked my own way the best I could. I didn't know how to pray right and, oh, I've been so wicked."

"Then you feel how much you have sinned against God?"

"Yes, oh, so much."

"Did you tell God how you felt?"

"Yes, but you see, I used to pray so little that I hardly knew how."

I told him that

> "Prayer is the soul's sincere desire,
> Unutter'd or expressed,"

so I urged him to give himself to the Savior now.

"I have tried to do that," he said humbly.

"Do you think He has pardoned you?"

"I don't know. Sometimes I think He has. Then again, I'm afraid to believe it for you don't know how great a sinner I've been." While saying this, the soldier's lips quivered.

"'But this is a faithful saying, and worthy of all acceptance, that Christ Jesus came into the world to save sinners—not the righteous.' Don't you find some love for Him in your heart?"

"Oh, yes, a great deal."

"Even more than your wife? Could you give up her and the little ones, rather than Him?"

He hesitated a moment, then looking up with tear-filled eyes, he slowly said, "Yes, I think I could give up everything in this world rather than give up on Him."

I spoke a few words of cautious encouragement, for evidently the Spirit was teaching him. It didn't take long until he bore witness of this. While he remained in Ward P, his life was quiet, consistent, and upright. Back to the battlefield, he carried the sure trust that Christ would be with him "even to the end."

(Sue McBeth)

Revival Meetings and a Revived Heart

The veterans of General A. J. Smith's Corps, after cooperating in the ill-fated Red River Expedition, were brought back to Vicksburg. Reverend R. Brown, Pastor of First Congregational Church, Oswego, Illinois, served as a delegate during June and July 1864. He describes work among these infantrymen:

Worn out and discouraged, they lay on the sands by the Mississippi River near Vicksburg. The tents for the troops did not average more than one to a company, so they spent most of the day under their blankets stretched out on sticks to shelter them from the intense heat of the sun. Meetings among them were impossible in the daytime. As we distributed papers from company to company, they kept asking if we could have a night meeting for them. The men were more than willing.

Chaplains Smith and Bardwell cooperated, the band was procured to play, and the soldiers began gathering about us in the darkness. Night served the double purpose of sheltering from the heat and of hiding the nakedness of many who lay under their blankets during the day for lack of clothes. A solemn glory descended upon the scene. It shown in the sparkle of stars stretched far above our heads and the dark, broad, and silent river with the fleet of transports on its breast. It made itself known in the unseen presence of the distant city, in the flickering lights of the circling campfires, and, closer to us, in the shadowy forms of the brave men upon whom rested the dust of battle.

We spoke of friends and loved ones at home and then of the "Friend that sticketh closer than a brother." Half-suppressed sighs and sobs began to reach us out of the midst of the great company. When, at last, we asked who would pledge themselves to become the friends of Christ, we knew that many were standing up in solemn dedication, even though we could not see them in the darkness. Our hearts went out in earnest prayer that their consecration might be unto life eternal.

Black Woman's Prayer Leads to Revival

During our two weeks' stay with these brave men, the night meetings continued with great success—with sundown as the "gun," which signaled the time for gathering. These meetings also had a great effect upon our daily prayer meeting in the city. The best-dressed men came in large numbers from the camp and the testimony borne by some of them was remarkable.

One young soldier rose the day before my departure and, with deep emotion, said, "Early this morning before sunrise, I heard the sound of a human voice coming up from a sheltered ravine. I followed in the direction of the sound and found it was the voice of an old black woman in prayer. She was thanking God for His mercies to her, praying for the soldiers who were fighting for her liberties, and for the masters who had enslaved her, her children, and her race. She committed the yet undecided contest, along with all her personal interests, into His hands. She did so with such implicit, childlike trust that I turned away utterly condemned. Since then, the broken vows and pledges of numerous troops have come to mind. My own broken vows and pledges are so many and have filled me with such confusion that I have come here today to renew them before all of you. I want to pledge again my whole heart and life to the Savior."

The soldier's intensely sincere manner thrilled every listener.
(R. Brown)

Ultimate Motivation for Learning to Read

In the fall of 1864, the chaplain of a large black regiment, encamped near Vicksburg, wrote to Mr. A. E. Chamberlain, Chairman of the Cincinnati branch of the Christian Commission, asking for primers. Mr. Chamberlain sent them and adds a subsequent history:

Soon after, another request came for five hundred New Testaments, followed by another for five hundred more. In his last letter, the chaplain told me that he had one thousand men who could read the Testament. Shortly afterward, I had a visit from him. He asked me especially for a large-print Bible or New Testament to be used by an old soldier named "Uncle Sam," whose story is worth preserving.

"The day before I came away," said the chaplain, "we were organizing regimental writing schools. Even though 'Uncle Sam' was an industrious student of reading, he seemed to lack enthusiasm in the new enterprise.

"'Uncle,' I said last, 'you want to learn to write, don't you?'

"'No, no. Uncle cares nothin' 'bout the writin'.'

"'What made you so anxious to learn to read then?'

"'Wanted to read God's own Word.'

"'Can you read it yet, uncle?'

"He took his Bible and opened it to St. John's third chapter, 'God so loved the world that He gave His Only Begotten Son, that whosoever believeth in Him should not perish, but have everlasting life.'

"He began spelling the words. When he was halfway through the sentence, his feelings overcame him.

"Looking up, he asked, 'Is this real? Is this the sure-'nuff Word of the Lord?'

"'No doubt about it, uncle.'

"'And uncle readin' it for hisself!'

"He took the book and spelled through the rest of the sentence.

"'Now,' he said, 'if ole uncle dies, he can go up thar, and tell the good Lord Jesus that he read in His Own Book, "Whomsumever believes on him shan't perish, but have everlastin' life," and the Lord knows that Uncle Sam believes on him—an' he read it for hisself in His own book.'"

Uncle Sam's indifference to his opportunity to learn to write was fully explained and fully understood. His mind was occupied with the direct revelation from God.

Christians Make Better Soldiers

An interesting letter, written in October of 1864, by an officer of the army in Louisiana to Mr. J. H. Parsons, the Corresponding Secretary of the St. Louis Committee of the Christian Commission, gives an observant soldier's opinion upon the comparative mortality rate among Christians and others in the army:

H. Q. Provisional Brigade, Morganzia, La., Oct. 19, 1864.

"… We have suffered severe losses in men and officers this summer and fall. Some regiments have buried nearly one-half of their men. From the beginning, I had taken special pains to have religious services held often in my regiment when I commanded it. Often I heard irreligious officers say that this was one of the causes of great mortality, as 'religion tends to depress the spirits of the men.' They thought that if these exercises were banished, the health of my men would improve, so I determined to find out the truth about this. Upon a careful examination, I was *disappointed, I must acknowledge,* when I found that *two-fifths* of my regiment had died since entering the service. But *only one in eight* of those who died were Christians, showing a great disparity in favor of the latter. By the same examination, I also learned that those who were most zealous in learning were least given to sickness and, when sick, they generally recovered the soonest.

"These facts, at first, impressed me as strange but I have no reason to doubt them as they were obtained by careful officers.…

"A. J. EDGERTON,
"Colonel Commanding Brigade."

Profound Effects of Letter Writing

By an arrangement between the Western Branches near the close of 1864, the care of the important station of Cairo, Illinois, the "gate" of the Western Army, was transferred to the special superintendence of the Peoria Committee of the Christian Commission. Cairo was located strategically at the confluence of the Mississippi and Ohio Rivers. From reports of their Agent,

Reverend J. D. Wyckoff, Pastor of Congregational Church, Elmwood, Illinois, we select the following incidents:

No part of the delegate's ministry was more filled with consolation and blessing than the duty of writing letters home for the men. I remember a noble-looking, reticent Indian of the 16th Wisconsin Regiment named Peter Powels. He had not heard from his wife or mother for six months and was too shy to ask anyone to write for him. By degrees, I found out something about his friends and family and was able to write a letter for him which pleased him mightily. I shall not soon forget how his brown face flushed when he found that, in his delight, he had let go and said, "Tell her I would be glad to see her," as if that was too much for an Indian to confess.

Encouragement of Christians

Passing along the street, I once greeted a stalwart soldier who warmly grasped my extended hand. Without further introduction, he said, "I have no 'abiding city' here."

"May I ask if you seek one to come?"

"Yes, thank God, I do. I don't have any time to myself but I try to keep the lamp burning."

On inquiring, I found his to be a most remarkable case. Away from home and all Christian associations, with no Sunday worship, with inadequate rest, with no time for even a prayer meeting, he pursued his laborious duty as wagon master in the wicked city of Cairo. Yet, he could keep the inward light burning such that, when I first met him, it seemed to shine out from his eyes into mine.

(J. D. Wyckoff)

Ministry of Grace

The Receiving Ship at Cairo held six or seven hundred sailors but, from all I could discern, only a single Christian was among them. Accidentally, I discovered another when he asked me for a Bible.

"Haven't you got one?" I asked.

"Yes, sir, I want it for a mate, though."

I gave him one, along with a word of encouragement, and left him to go watch for the tugboat, which would carry me to Mound City. Presently, he returned and asked me for a New York *Observer*. Some further conversation ensued. I found that he had no father or mother, that Jesus was his only friend, and then I bade him goodbye once again. The tug still had not appeared when the sailor came up a third time.

Extending his right hand, partly closed and inverted, he said, "I want to do something for Christ. Won't you take this for the Commission?"

Out of his poverty, he had handed me five dollars and would not be denied the privilege of giving it. I asked his name and reluctantly he gave it—a rare one, I believe—John Jones. I shall not soon forget his quiet, subdued, half-tearful manner on that brisk day in November.
(J. D. Wyckoff)

Joy in Ministry

Two months later, I started out from Cairo to visit the Mississippi gunboat fleet. After boarding several vessels, I was transferred to the *St. Clair*, commanded by Captain J. S. French. I had been so disheartened at not meeting with any Christians on some of the other boats that this visit boosted my spirits exceedingly. This boat had three Christian officers. The commander was a generous, courteous "old salt." The first evening, he called the men on deck and introduced me to them with some crisp, telling words. He showed me a well-worn copy of the little book called *Daily Food*. He told me it was just as natural for him to read it in the morning as it was to eat his breakfast.

I also found four Christian sailors on board. After a meeting on Friday evening, a man came up on the quarter-deck and I overheard him say he would like to "see the Reverend." I turned to see him and he handed me a five dollar bill, saying, "Put that where it'll do some good."

I squinted to look at him, and, lo, my old friend, John Jones of last November had reappeared. A visit home could not have been better. I was so delighted to meet him again and find him still holding to the blessed way.
(J. D. Wyckoff)

Seeking Forgiveness

The terrible "*Eclipse* disaster" of January 27, 1865 changed all my plans of visitation. The Mississippi steamboat blew up while returning members of the 9th Indiana Artillery to the North. May God grant that I never have such work to do ever again. The severely burned were in such dreadful condition that they required our immediate attention. The men with broken limbs had to wait a whole day before receiving attention. The frightful burns and the excruciating pain made the scene one of living death. One poor fellow recognized my voice. He had been at our Cairo meetings a few times. He was fearfully scalded all over the body and could scarcely see. He moaned that he wanted "to see the Christian Commission man."

I came to him and said, "I am the Christian Commission man, my dear fellow. What can I do for you?"

"I was in your meetings there. I was ashamed to ask you to pray for me then. I've been a great sinner but I'm seeking repentance and forgiveness. I'm not ashamed to ask Christians to pray for me now. I've been in battle since I saw you but, oh, that was nothing compared to this!"

I told him about the Healer of pains—the ever-waiting Savior of the world.

The day was a solemn and oppressive, one that left me feeling dazed. It made me wish for the end of the misery of war and long for the coming of the day of Eternal Peace.

Poor fellows! They had taken passage on their way home from the war, many of them just having finished their terms of enlistment or headed home on furlough. They had had bright anticipation of pleasant greetings hidden by the hills and the long stretches of prairie between them and home—greetings which, to so many, never came.
(J. D. Wyckoff)

Women's Ministry

Miss Katharine M. Bissell, of Hartford, Wisconsin, was a delegate in the Christian Commission supply stores at Vicksburg toward the close of 1864 and the beginning of 1865. She tells of an incident that illustrates the value of the work, which could be done by ladies in the army:

A brigade of soldiers was quartered close to Vicksburg that December. For various reasons, they were in a demoralized condition and were almost unmanageable. Only one of the officers seemed to have any means of maintaining control over them and he never left them for a moment. He continually exerted himself to restore reason and authority in the chaos.

Sergeant Fuller, from one of these regiments, came into our stores one morning and leaned against the reading rack. The expression on his face was one of homesickness and indifference—or, perhaps, something worse. I taxed my brain to find some way of approaching the Sergeant without giving offense when, suddenly, I thought of a beautiful bouquet of flowers, which I had received that morning.

Holding them out to him, I said, "Don't you think they are pretty, Sergeant?"

His response was condescending. With a peculiar, masculine glance, he bowed and smiled carelessly, then turned back to his reading. I was a little nonplussed at first but soon saw that he wanted to talk with me. Whether it was their fragrance, which reached him, or possibly some memories from home, which the flowers had quickened, I don't know. I watched him awhile until I was sure he wanted to talk and then told him I would be with him in a moment. We began a general conversation.

As soon as I could, I introduced the great question, saying, "Are you a Christian, Sergeant?"

"I am not a Christian now. Awhile back, I hoped that I was but there seemed to be so little about it, which I could claim as a Christian experience, that I came to doubt it altogether. Now I'm as reckless as any of the others."

I talked with him seriously and earnestly. He seemed deeply impressed but would make no promise concerning the future. After that, he came often to our stores and always renewed the conversation about the Christian life until one day, after an unusually long talk, he stated his determination to become a Christian. From that time forward, he was one of the brightest examples I ever met. His comrades noticed the change and often asked, "What makes you so still?" He told them be had found something to keep him quiet all the days of his life.

Gift Honors the Dead

In May 1865, Reverend Ewing O. Tade, Pastor of the Congregational Church, Washington, Iowa and the Local Agent at Memphis, sent a watch to the Chairman of the Christian Commission. The watch had been handed to him by a big-hearted, Christian soldier of the 113th Illinois Infantry. The following note, which accompanied the gift, explained its beautiful meaning and purpose:

"A soldier's earthly light went out when his little boys—Paul and Frankie— died last March. He thought that decent gravestones should mark the spot where they lie, listening for the trumpet call, which shall call them forth to immortality.

"But now, he thinks he sees a more excellent way. Their precious dust needs no costly memorial, seeing that He who redeems shall watch it carefully. Let the price of the marble be expended in sending forth the Living Word, so that they, being dead, shall yet speak. Whatever the accompanying watch may bring monetarily shall be devoted to the American Bible Society, as the gift of two little lambs, Paul and Frankie, who are walking in the green and pleasant pastures by the side of river of life. This is the wish of their father,

"S. L. URMSTON."

The watch, with a narrative of the particulars, was sent to the American Bible Society. The reading of the soldier's letter at a meeting of the Board of Managers excited deep interest and sympathy. Urmston was made a Life Member of the Society and presented with a handsomely bound copy of the Bible.

Honoring Christ in Throes of Death

The work among the troops in Arkansas was much the same as elsewhere. A few incidents from the reports of agents and delegates will follow. Mr. C. C. Thayer, Field Agent in Arkansas, formerly of Chicago [Congregational] Theological Seminary, and now a missionary of the American Board in Central Turkey, narrates an incident at Little Rock:

A very devoted Christian soldier, whose love for his country and family surpassed any I had ever seen, lay dying. He was dreaming and, as he approached the River of Death, a vision of his home came back to him vividly. He seemed to be leaving it, once more, for the war and to be passing along the old road. A bend would soon hide from view all whom he loved. In the dream, he turned for one last look.

In his agony, he cried out, "O, my wife, my darling wife, who made my home so happy, must we separate? My dear, only son—our joy and pride—must I leave you?"

He was silent a moment. Perhaps, in the meantime, a new and brighter vision—the verity from which the earthly one had ever drawn its brightness and beauty—was revealed. Beyond another bend in the road were kinder arms than behind. He uttered, "Yes, wife, I can give you up and darling Henry too—country, friends, all—*all*. But, Jesus, I cannot give *You* up."

The eyes that were looking upon the "Elder Brother" shone brightly. Doubtless, before this, he had found that pure human ties never break but they can be weak, here on earth, because our perception of Christ's unseen presence was also weak. He had discovered that when Christ's presence grows into a continual knowledge, human ties will become infinitely more real and beautiful.

Choosing Christ

A sketch by Miss Katherine M. Bissell, of Hartford, Wisconsin, about the work at Little Rock in June gives the result of an effort to bring a soldier to a decision for Christ:

Joseph Adams was a small, slender boy belonging to the 25th Ohio Battery—a wild set of men as far as any religious influences were concerned. They also had the reputation of being rather aristocratic.

Delegates used to say they were the most difficult men to reach with the gospel on the whole station. They prided themselves on their fine appearance, were always well-dressed, and never left their camp without polishing their boots. They were impeccable at cleaning their teeth, arranging their hair, and sprucing themselves up. Adams was nineteen years of age and had already contracted many of his comrades' bad habits. He was also one of the best gamblers in the battery. His habit was to save his wages and use his gambling gains for other expenses.

The first time I saw him, he was bringing back a book to our library. He said, "I'm tired of these religious books. I'll take a history."

I found the desired history book for him and began a conversation. He was very communicative but his use of tobacco was excessive to the point of impeding our little chat. Several times, he begged my pardon while he awkwardly hurried to the door to discharge his overflowing mouth. It began to dawn upon him that chewing in a lady's presence was hardly in good taste. So mortified was he that he not only apologized but also declared that he would never chew again. In our visit, he expressed his utter unbelief in Christianity and spoke lightly about conversion.

When he was through, I asked, "Mr. Adams, do you really know what we mean by conversion?"

"Well, no," he said. "I don't know that I do—exactly."

I gave him the best idea of it I could—how it was our duty to put ourselves in harmony with God and consecrate our lives to Him. Disregarding his sneers against Christianity, I urged him to make this consecration at once. He was unwilling. I told him how much less willing he would be in three or four years into the future.

He looked up in a sharp way and asked, "I suppose you would have said the same thing three or four years ago."

"Very possibly," I replied, "and can you say that it would not have been true?"

As he went away, I gave him *God's Way of Peace, A Book for the Anxious* by Horatius Bonar. He promised to read and return it. When he came back, I found that he was trying to evade the matter but I held him to the point of present decision.

Finally, he could elude the issue no longer, so he said, "I won't decide the matter here. I want to think it over more."

He looked at the clock. It was just a quarter to eleven. I asked, "Can you decide within twenty-four hours?"

"Yes," he said. "I can and will."

The next day at a quarter before eleven, a note came, stating that, last evening, he had been assigned to duty and could not get off. His note mentioned that he had been thinking about the matter while walking his beat and had decided to become a Christian "with God's help." He added, "I mean to be one truly."

He kept his word nobly and, for the months during which he remained at the post, he gave the clearest evidence of a change of heart. Of course, he was subjected to no small measure of ridicule but he endured it bravely for the sake of the Master.

Conversion of a Self-righteous Man

The lieutenant of his battery was an exceedingly upright and moral man and, because of this, the boys nicknamed him "Abe Lincoln." He was not a Christian, even though he had given serious thought to the subject. One day, Adams went to him to ask for permission to come to the prayer meeting at our stores. The lieutenant was struck with the request, hesitated, and looked at him for some time before granting it. From that day forward, a change came over him. The impression made by this young soldier's request did not lose its hold upon the officer until he became a humble, sincere Christian.
(Katherine M. Bissell)

Helping the Helpless

In the fall and early winter of 1865, Reverend R. Brown, Pastor of First Congregational Church of Oswego, Illinois and delegate among the troops at Fort Leavenworth, describes an episode from his work there:

About one hundred men of the 17th Illinois Cavalry were charged with mutiny and confined in the Military Prison at Fort Leavenworth. While investigating the matter, I became satisfied that, while they had done wrong, many extenuating circumstances deserved consideration. They certainly needed all the help we could render. Many of them were without shoes, shirts, or socks. Some were very sick and all were sad and anxious. I petitioned earnestly for their release and, at last, Governor Oglesby of Illinois procured an order from the War Department. They were to be sent to Springfield before their discharge.

Just as they were preparing to carry out this order, I visited them again to hold a parting meeting. Never did praise and prayer seem so delightful. Never was a temple of worship more truly filled with the Divine presence than was that forlorn prison house.

True Religion

A lady of fashion and culture from the East reluctantly accompanied us to our last prison meeting with them. A box, the only movable thing that would serve as a seat, was placed in the center of the cell for her. She wept as she saw the gratitude glowing in every face, in every grasp of the hand, and in every utterance of the lips. She was a church member but this scene of praise and prayer gave her an entirely new view of life itself.

Afterward, she was silent about the meeting. Before her return to the East, I asked for the reason. She replied, "When I think of my reluctance to accompany you and of the evident presence of God in that meeting, I began to fear that my own hope is false and my religion is empty."

It was the occasion of a new consecration and a determination to do some of Christ's work among the poor.
(R. Brown)

Prison Revival Leads to City Revival

Interaction between the citizens of Leavenworth and the imprisoned soldiers had been quite frequent and rewarding. In fact, a wonderful revival visited the city soon afterward. It brought an additional one-third to the membership of Protestant churches there. In the opinion of many observers, the revival was due in no small measure to the quickening granted to many during their visits to the Commission meetings in the prison and elsewhere.
(R. Brown)

Opportunity Lost through Being Too Busy

Miss Sue McBeth of the St. Louis Committee provides this sketch of St. Louis hospital work in the latter stages of the War:

"Why, who is this?" I asked. "How did you get here, little brother?"

After the lamps were lit, I had slipped into the wards to see some of the new patients who had reached us from the South that day. Just as I opened the door, my eye fell on the strangest sight of all. The bed nearest me had been freshly filled with straw and lying upon it was the oddest, oldest-looking boy I had ever seen. A pair of bright, black eyes, looked up at me out of a little, thin, withered face. His little limbs scarcely reached more than half its length.

"I came up on the boat," he answered. "I belong to the … Regiment—I have forgotten the number." If only the face were so easily forgotten!

"A drummer boy?"

"No, a soldier!" And what pride there was in that shrill, childish voice as he called out the names of the battles in which he had fought. He was a waif from one of our great cities, such as only large cities can produce. He had never known either of his parents or home but "just growed up," Topsy-like. He struggled up and out into the world the best way he could until a recruiting officer, seeking one more name to complete his quota, added this name to his list and the boy became a soldier.

As I came out of the ward that night, a nurse asked, "Have you seen 'our baby' yet?" And thus all had christened him from the first. I never knew another name for him. They moved him to a cot near the stove. Attendants and convalescents patted and nursed him and, for a time, he grew better under their care. Our hospitals were very full at the time and death was busy in every ward. I gave my energy to those I knew would die soon and gave "our baby" only a few passing words, hoping and waiting until I could have more time with him. He was getting much better, I thought, and needed careful instruction.

He could neither read nor write. He knew little more of God than a heathen child and had scarcely heard Christ's name, except as an oath. I knew I must begin with the very rudiments of the Gospel. And so I waited for a more convenient season, giving him my brightest-covered little tracts for his comrades to read to him. When I came home at night, I rested by putting all the old engravings I could find into picture books for his amusement. At last, a day came when I thought I could give him an hour but, when I stood beside his cot, he had gone beyond my reach! At first, I thought he was asleep—but no, he was dying! I bent close to his ear and tried to make him hear me but not a muscle of that still face moved. Neither light nor sound of earth could reach him thereafter.

Self-Condemnation Leads to Eternal Condemnation

During a brief visit to St. Louis, Reverend E. P. Smith, General Field Agent in the Western Army, was invited by Miss Sue McBeth of the St. Louis Committee to see a Michigan soldier in Jefferson Barracks. She had taken a particular interest in his case. Mr. Smith reports this exchange:

At a glance, I saw that he had not long to live. In his pale, thin face, flushed with the last sign of flickering life, I could see a beseeching—a piteous longing, such as I had rarely seen in all my hospital experience. At first, he gave me little heed but, as I laid the back of my hand upon his burning cheek and stroked the hair from his forehead, he turned his eyes full upon me in a look that spoke things unutterable.

"How are you today, my soldier friend?"

"Poorly, sir. Very poorly. A few days more—only a few."

"You are all ready, I trust?"

"I am going—there is no help for it. If you call that 'ready,' then I am ready."

"But I mean are you prepared to die? Is this exchange of worlds going to be pleasant to you?"

"Pleasant! It is awful, sir. Horrible beyond all account! But I have got to come to it!"

"No, my brother, there is no such thing as 'got to' about it. You are in this world yet and we live in a world of mercy. This is the world where Christ died. Let me tell you what He says, my friend: 'Whoso cometh unto Me, I will in no wise cast out.'"

I CANNOT COME NOW I WILL NOT

"I know it, I know it all. I have heard it a thousand times."

"Well, isn't it true?"

"It may be—but not for me now."

"But He says, 'If you will come to him.' He does not say, 'If you had come,' or 'If you would have come,' but 'if you will come'— 'whoso cometh'— comes today— He will not cast out.' It's a great pity you haven't come already, but…."

"Pity! It's my ruin, sir. I cannot come now. I will not. See there, stranger, do you think I am going to give that withered, dried-up hand to God after I have given all its strength to the devil? Do you think I'm going to drink the devil's wine all my life up to this last day in hospital and then offer the settlings to Jesus?"

"It was wrong. It was self-serving for you to refuse to give the best to your God but see what you are doing now. Jesus has followed you through all your yesterdays and, today, He asks for this remnant of your life, 'these settlings,' as you call it. He really desires your affection and trust in Him for the little while you will lie on this bed."

"Is it honorable or decent to give it now?"

"If He can ask it, is it honorable or decent for you to refuse it now? You have refused everything but Jesus makes a last request. Will you refuse that?"

"I see it—that's so—but—I am afraid I shall. You come a little too late! It's getting dark now."

I prayed at his bedside but he was only partially conscious. As I sat watching him, he said something scarcely audible. He whispered, "If I could get back again—back again."

Supposing he was thinking of his friends, I asked about his home in Michigan. Rousing slightly and with a shake of his head, he said, "No, no—a boy again—a boy again."

Thinking he might have fallen into sleep from exhaustion, I left him for a while. But it was the sleep of death. The grip of sin held him tightly through his course. He could not break it. He thought he must begin anew, if at all, with the beginning of life. But, alas! The boyhood with its thousand invitations would come back no more!

Historical Comment:

The work of the Western Army Committees did not close as soon as the field labors in the East. The St. Louis Branch kept its office at Memphis open until October 1865. The work upon the Plains, directed from Fort Leavenworth by Reverend W. J. Gladwin as Field Agent, continued into 1866.

CHAPTER XVIII

ALONG THE COAST

1861–1865

From the beginning, the New York Branch of the Christian Commission took charge of the work among sailors and soldiers operating along our extended coast line from Virginia to Texas. This service was found to be quieter than in any other field of the war. Because of the distance from New York, delegates were chosen for longer periods of labor. However, so much of their experience was common to that of the army that we shall not repeat ourselves by attempting to give even a representative series of incidents of this coast work. We begin with incidents recorded off the coast of North Carolina.

Finishing Well

Reverend Dr. A. L. Stone, who was previously Chaplain of the 45th Massachusetts Regiment, wrote a letter from Newbern, North Carolina to the people of Park Street Church, Boston—his home parish. He gives a narrative of the illness and death of a soldier of his regiment, a younger brother of the Reverend Phillips Brooks of Philadelphia:

George Brooks, one of our own Boston boys and a member of Company A, was recruited by Major Russell Sturgis when he was still a Captain. Brooks had taken ill with typhoid fever about a week prior. From the first, be expressed his whole-hearted resignation to the Divine will and enjoyed the constant presence of Jesus at his side. Daily, I asked, "Is the Savior near you today?" The look upon his face would shine with a radiant answer before his lips could even speak and, throughout his sickness, that faithful Presence sustained and encouraged him.

He was never dejected, nor did he ever murmur. As his lungs became congested, he would say very little. One day, he drew my face close to his so that he could make me hear his faintest words. Through gasps and whispers, he explained that he had never had a full assurance of his pardon from sin and acceptance into the kingdom until he became a soldier. He said, "We were under terrible enemy fire at the battle of Kingston. Then and there, my Savior came to me as never before. He declared His presence, revealed His love, and held my soul in His hand."

As the hour of death drew ever closer, he seemed to have three burdens of prayer. The first was quickly disposed of as he prayed, "O Lord, keep me, hold me fast, leave me not, never let me go!" Then all thoughts of self seemed to end. Moments later, his lips moved audibly and his second burden was laid at the Divine feet when he uttered, "My God, spare my country. Oh, save my dear native land!" After a brief silence, the voice of prayer was again heard again—his tongue's last articulated thoughts on earth. He spoke the words of the old familiar petition: "Thy kingdom come. Thy will be done, on earth as it is in heaven."

His own soul, his country, the Israel of God—he commended these three interests in his last utterances to the faithful One who promises. How could a Christian life close more appropriately, more triumphantly?

Heroic Self-sacrifice and Courage

The following incident occurred during the Confederate siege of Washington, North Carolina in March and April 1863. A soldier of Company G, 46th Massachusetts Regiment relates this stunning instance of heroic self-sacrifice and courage:

Outnumbered ten to one, a brave band of soldiers were set for the defense of Rodman's Point. The enemy pressed heavily upon them to drive them from the Point or destroy them. Overpowered, they fell back to the Tar River, where only a scow remained in which they could escape. They hurried into her but the Confederates were close on their heels. The minie balls flew thick and fast. The boat had to be pushed from shore with poles but now loaded she was stuck in the mud. The sides afforded some shelter to the soldiers while lying down but who would leap overboard and push her out into the stream? Who would deliberately lay down his life for the possible salvation of his fellow soldiers?

When several soldiers were about to do it, a large black man said, "You keep still and save your life. I can't fight but I can push off the boat. If they kill me, it's nothing. You are soldiers and they need you to fight."

Leaping overboard, he pushed the boat out into the stream, then sprang back—pierced by seven bullets. Two days later, he died. Does Greece or Rome offer a higher degree of patriotism?

Soldier's Conversion

In 1863, Reverend A. P. Johnson, Pastor of First Congregational Church, Charlemont, Massachusetts, served as a delegate in the vicinity of Hilton Head, South Carolina. He recalls several incidents from his experience:

Aboard one of the gunboats, I found a number of very sick men. From our supplies, I gave them what was needed to make them comfortable and I also talked and prayed with them. I found one of them, evidently a foreigner, to be quite interesting.

I asked him, "Are you a Christian?"

"Yes," he said, "but there are few Christians in my country."

"What country is that?"

"Turkey."

I asked him how he became a Christian in Turkey. His answer was very interesting as well. He told me the story about a missionary, named Reverend Dr. Dwight, and about how he had placed his trust in Jesus because of this man's labors. Now, far from home and family, he had fought for his adopted land and was now dying in perfect peace.

He told me he was waiting for the fulfillment of St. John's vision of the one song in one language, which reads, "After this I beheld, and lo, a great multitude, which no man could number, of all nations and kindreds and people and tongues, stood before the Throne and before the Lamb, clothed with white robes and palms in their hands; and cried with a loud voice saying, Salvation to our God which sitteth upon the Throne, and unto the Lamb."

Child's Wisdom

Large numbers of blacks lived at Hilton Head and I had interesting conversations with many of them. One day, a number of children came asking for books. One wanted a New Testament. Plainly, this boy was as bright in mind and spirit as were his teeth and eyes. His only name was mythological—Neptune, or as he called himself, "Nep." He informed me that "Nep, only eleven years old, sir."

He could read well. I asked him why he wanted with the New Testament. He replied, "To learn 'bout heaven."

"Why do you want to learn about heaven?"

"So I can go there when I die."

Playing devil's advocate to test his convictions, I asked, "Why do you suppose you can go to heaven? You are only a little slave boy. You don't imagine there are any slave boys there, do you?"

"Yes, I do."

"But, you see, white children go there. And black and white children don't love each other much—can't play together. How can you get along together in heaven?"

"Don't know, but I 'specs they will."

I kept on raising objections, until finally I asked, "Now, do you really believe that there are any black children in heaven?"

He reflected a moment and then answered, "No, I expect they isn't."

"Well, then, you can't go there, can you?"

"Reckon I can."

"But how can you go there when there are no black children in heaven?"

"Cause they is all white."

"But how's that?"

"Oh, they is all 'washed white in the blood of the Lamb.'"

This was a "child's" perfect faith, true to fact, that I prodded out of him. (A. P. Johnson)

Bible Scholar Assumes Leadership

A correspondent of the *Sunday School Times*, writing from Bentley, New York in June 1863, gives an account of a Bible class scholar from that town. He enlisted on board the gunboat *Daylight*, one of the squadron of ships blockading Charleston:

In a crew of two hundred men, he found only one Christian. One Saturday, it occurred to him that he would like to hold a prayer meeting the next day. His friend suggested the propriety of asking the captain about it. To their great astonishment, he replied, "Yes, you may have the free use of the ship and I am proud to think I have young men on board that do pray."

About ten o'clock the next day, he got his hymnbook and Bible and took charge of the "right wing" of the ship to begin his meeting. It was a very solemn service, ending with an invitation to all those who felt their need of receiving Christ. Twelve men came forward and knelt. They asked the two leaders to pray for them and several of these found the "pearl of great price."

Subsequently, the Bible class scholar found another field of usefulness, far away from his own beloved Sunday school.

Example for Prayer

Throughout the war, more than a few of our naval officers were faithful in their efforts to bring the Gospel, along with its holy influence, to the sailors' hearts. A correspondent writes of Admiral Samuel F. DuPont:

Before going into the "ironclad" fight off Charleston in April 1863, the Admiral had prayers offered on his flagship, the *New Ironsides*. From the Admiral to the powder boys, all humbly knelt and sought strength for the coming trial by joining in a short, touching prayer read by Commodore Turner. The recollection of seeing those four hundred determined, battle-eager men, bowing before their Maker in picturesque groups amidst the grim implements of war will forever be etched upon my memory.

Epilogue: On April 7, 1863, nine Federal ironclads entered Charleston harbor and conducted a prolonged bombardment of Fort Sumter. *New Ironsides* took considerable enemy fire but, in contrast to several other ships in the squadron, she was not seriously damaged. In a later battle, she was struck by a torpedo but remained afloat.

Ship Captain Leads Prayer Meetings

Captain Winslow of the *Kearsarge*, destroyer of the *Alabama*, made an address to the Port Society of New York in December 1864. This speech, coincidentally, revealed a strong Christian influence over his men:

He stated that, with the exception of two Sundays during the long cruise of the *Kearsarge,* religious services took place every Sunday on board the ship. His custom was to have the bell tolled to signal the call to prayer in his cabin, which was often filled with sailors. In addition to the prayers, he commonly took a portion of Scripture, expounded on it, and endeavored to illustrate it. When the ship was in the vicinity of lands where Bible history and prophecy took place, he would call attention to the fulfillment of God's Word and set his crew to thinking about the reality of Divine truth.

God's Grace in Midst of Dying

The following incident about the assault upon Fort Wagner in July 1863 was related by the relatives of the soldier who had enlisted in Colonel Shaw's Massachusetts Regiment:

Toward the close of the battle, this black soldier, shockingly torn with wounds—wounded unto death, was carried back to the rear. Someone came to him, washed the grime from his face and attended to him while he was unconscious. After a while, he began to talk as if he were in a dream. He thought that his wife Chloe was near him and giving him all the kind attention he was receiving.

He told Chloe of his joy and assurance in the approaching freedom of his whole race. He said, "The Lord kep' us patient all along, Chloe, then His Kingdom come."

As he continued, he may have been recalling his last conscious sight of the repulse and of his falling and flying comrades when he said, "It don't look as if He thought we was ready for it yet but then, Chloe, *it am gwine to come.*"

He murmured for a while about Jesus, Chloe, and the children and then fell asleep.

Battlefield Conversion

In the New York *Parish Visitor* of October 1863, the following narrative describes an incident about a delegate on the South Carolina coast:

On returning to quarters, I found a soldier of the 7th New Hampshire Regiment who begged for some reading material. He said, "I am a poor sinner and want something to guide me. The night of the assault on Fort Wagner, when the balls were so swift and thick around, I heard men swearing dreadfully and it seemed so awful that I could not bear it. It made me afraid and I promised my God that I would swear no more but would serve Him from that hour. He is my witness that I have tried faithfully and now I want to read something beside my New Testament to help me along. This religion has a wonderful effect over me—even in my dreams. When I got into temptation the other night in a dream, I turned away from it."

He spoke with the deepest convictions of his early religious training, his pious parents, and of all the mercies of God. In all, he said it seemed as if the very marrow of the man was penetrated by this new fear of God and love of His Son, which had come to him in the hour of peril.

I gave him the little book, *Come to Jesus*, and turned to the *Soldier's Series* to find a tract entitled *Past Sins*. While holding it in my hand as we talked, I saw that the title caught his attention. In a moment, he eagerly asked me for it. Mr. B_____ said something to him about being a missionary in camp now.

"Yes," he said, "I try to be. You may depend on my doing what I can."

At parting, his "God bless you" was fervent and heartfelt.

Some time afterward, I was walking along the beach in a crowd of men when the salute of a guard caught my eye. I looked up just in time to catch the pleasant smile of my Christian soldier friend. It told of a heart completely happy in the Savior's love.

Wife's Testimonial to Her Godly Husband

In February 1864, Reverend Robert J. Parvin, Rector of St. Paul's Protestant Episcopal Church, Cheltenham, Pennsylvania, furnishes a sketch connected with the battle of Olustee, Florida:

Recruiting for the 31st U. S. Colored Regiment took place at Camp William, Pennsylvania, not very far from St. Paul's Church in Cheltenham, Pennsylvania, where I served as pastor. Its commander was Colonel Fribley, who had formerly been a Captain in the 8th Pennsylvania Regiment. At the camp, he became deeply interested in his own spiritual condition, as well as that of his men. About two weeks before leaving for Beaufort, he and his young and devoted wife were confirmed at St. Paul's by Bishop Potter, now deceased. Soon after reaching Beaufort, the regiment was ordered to Florida. On February 20th, the Colonel was killed at the head of his men by the withering fire of rifle and cannon at Olustee in Florida. His body was left upon the field.

When his regiment started from Camp William Penn, I gave him a Christian Commission New Testament. Under his name, I wrote, "Be thou faithful unto death." He carried the precious volume with him to the fatal field.

News of his loss struck a very severe blow to his wife. For a time, it was almost too great for her to bear but it eventually brought forth a beautiful purification. After many unsuccessful attempts to recover her husband's body, she returned to the north. Afterward, she sent a letter, which revealed her feelings.

She wrote, "I have been ill both in body and mind and could do nothing or think of nothing. This great grief has darkened my whole life. God alone knows how much I have suffered. I fear I have rebelled against Him for my heart constantly questions why it must be so. I question why my dear husband—so good, so noble, so brave—must lay down his life in the bright promise of his youth, why the great work in which he was so earnestly engaged was cut short. My happiness was so bound up in him and my life was so complete in his love. And now, what is it? A blank. A wreck.

"Yes, I do think of him often. My heart softens when I think of that Sunday morning in December when we knelt together in your little church and made an open profession of our faith in Christ. My dear husband was led there by a deep sense of his duty and love for God. I fear I did so out of my love and duty to him. I hesitated for a long time for I feared my heart was not right. But I knew that he greatly desired that I should unite with him and I felt it my duty to do so. With him to lead and advise me, to assist and encourage me, I hoped to be able to live a Christian life. But now, my pillar of strength is gone and I am left alone in the darkness.

"Many beautiful things were in my husband's past life that I should love to tell you but I cannot at present. But I will say that the last words I heard from his lips were those of prayer. He left me in the night. The adjutant came for him in great haste, as the ship was weighing anchor. Even then, he did not forget to pray for us before we parted. And this what he always did in our many meetings and partings. Prayer was always his first and last thought."

After recovering from the first sadness of her loss, Mrs. Fribley resolved to devote her strength to care for the race of people in whose behalf her husband had been so especially interested. For a time, her home was the Christian Commission headquarters in Memphis where she was a teacher under the direction of the Freedmen's Bureau. She was one of the earliest of these and still continues in the work, which serves as both a memorial labor and a joy.

Personification of Bravery

A story of the battle of Galveston on January 1, 1863 serves as a good example of the bravery and determination of our sailors. The New Orleans correspondent of the Boston *Traveler* has preserved it for posterity:

William Reid, an old sailor and man-of-war's man, who was on board the *Owasco*, was one of the heroes of the fight. During the hottest moments of the battle between his ship and the Confederate batteries, this man who is forty-eight years of age received a severe wound while loading his rifle. Two fingers of his left hand were shot away and the surgeon ordered him below but he refused to go. Tying his handkerchief around his fingers, he remained on deck and continued firing his rifle. Thirty minutes later, another shot struck him on the right shoulder and the blood came out through his shirt. Master's Mate Arbana then ordered him below to the surgeon.

The brave old fellow said, "No, sir. As long as there's any fighting to be done, I stay on deck."

When the engagement was over, he had his wounds dressed. He remains on board the *Owasco* and whenever they beat "to general quarters," William Reid stands at his post, ready for orders. One day, the Captain told him to go below, as he was on the sick list and his place was in the hospital. Displeased with the remark, he replied, "No, Captain, my eyes are good and I can pull a cannon lockstring as well as any of 'em."

Struggling to Reach Location for Ministry

Reverend Jeremiah Porter, Pastor of the Edwards Congregational Church (now Seventh Presbyterian), Chicago, and his wife were appointed by the Christian Commission in the fall of 1865. Their ministry was to labor among the troops in Texas. Extracts from Mr. Porter's narrative of that work—the last field work of the Commission, which continued into the first months of 1866. It may fitly close the coast record of incidents:

Just before we started from Chicago, Mrs. Porter informed Mr. E. W. Blatchford, Treasurer of the Northwest Sanitary Commission, of our destination. With accustomed liberality, he placed at our disposal four thousand dollars' worth of choicest supplies. With supplies in our possession, we started on October 20th, accompanied by Miss Lizzie S. Gary of Galesburg, Illinois. A month later, while attempting to go from Brazos Santiago to Brownsville, our headquarters, we encountered a terrific "Norther." It so crippled the steamer and exhausted all our fuel that, unable to cross the bar, the commander ran the boat ashore on the beach near Bagdad in Mexico. In the yawl, we went as close to *terra firma* as we could and were eventually carried safely ashore in the sailors' arms.

On the beach, we unexpectedly and joyfully met Mr. William Kirkby, of Brooklyn, New York, another Christian Commission Agent. That morning, he had ridden from Brazos to learn how we had withstood the storm. The next morning, a Sunday, we witnessed the genuflections of Maximilian's soldiers at the mass. Afterward, I crossed over into Texas and, upon finding some black soldiers assembled for worship, we joined them. An appointment to preach filled up the day. Mr. Kirkby had happily prepared the way for us at Brownsville. We were most cordially welcomed by Mr. and Mrs. Edward Downey, "faithful among the faithless" during the rebellion, by Reverend Hugh McLeod, and by Mr. James A. Martin, of Brooklyn, New York.

Multi-cultural Ministry

We placed our supplies for Indianola in the hands of Mr. Town and gave supplies for Brownsville and the Upper Rio Grande to Mr. Martin. Reverend Mr. McLeod labored with a brigade of white soldiers three miles from town. In his Commission tent, he preached every Sunday, with myself and others assisting. Mrs. Porter and Miss Gary made their home in a tent pitched for us at Orange Grove Hospital. Here Mrs. Porter distributed her supplies and Miss Gary taught the black soldiers in a tent, prepared as a dining hall and place of worship.

On the night of November 29th, we had our first social meeting in the Commission Rooms in town. Thirty-five attended and the Holy Spirit was evidently present. Professor Shephard of Yale College had recently returned from a geological expedition to the Mexican mines. He and Mr. Lyon, an American merchant from Monterey, encouraged us by their presence and remarks. Three Christian army officers spoke and we prayed for many.

Among the black soldiers, we found many strange notions and convoluted physical ways of looking at spiritual realities. However, in no way did this distract from their precious and beautiful simplicity of trusting in Christ. (Jeremiah Porter)

Ministry to the Dying

A soldier named Emanuel Rickets had entered the army in New York, about ten months prior. When I first met him in the hospital, he told me his history and spoke with confidence of his knowledge of Christ as the Savior, with whom no earthly pleasures or hopes could compare. The next time I passed his cot, I found him sinking rapidly. Thinking an orange would comfort him, I gave him one.

As I offered it to him, he was thoroughly engaged in heartfelt prayer: "Do take me to Thyself, dear Father. I want to go."

After prayer, he exclaimed, "I see my Father. I see Him. Don't you see Him? All around Him, they are singing and dancing. Why shouldn't they dance? Well, I'll dance soon."

He tried to thank me for the orange but could express himself only with the simple words: "My Father has oranges enough." As I moved to the next soldier, He continued, "Tell my mother that I die happy. I didn't want to stay here anymore. It ain't a good place."

Shortly after the first day of the New Year, he went home where he could sing and dance in his Father's presence.
(Jeremiah Porter)

School for Both Protestants and Catholics

In Brownsville, we were grieved to find no Protestant school of any kind, so we planned one for our soldiers and the Southern children of the town. Aided by government officials, we secured a building and transformed it into a school. On March 1, 1866, we took possession of the seminary for our own dwelling.

Our school began with only six scholars, all from one family. But in a few days, some Mexican children enrolled and prejudice began to give way. One anxious father approached Mrs. Porter and asked, "Do you teach any 'religion' here?"

"Oh, yes," came the answer, "we teach the children to love one another, to love and obey their parents, to be kind and gentle, to obey God, and to love the Lord Jesus. And we teach the Ten Commandments."

With considerable relief, he said, "Oh, that's good."

At the end of four months, sixty scholars attended the school with more than half of them coming from Spanish Catholic families. In April, the Christian Commission closed its work and all its delegates and agents, except for ourselves, left the field and returned home. By the middle of June 1866, with our work accomplished, we left Brownsville—the last of the Christian Commission delegates.

(Jeremiah Porter)

CHAPTER XIX
THE HOME SIDE

The experiences and sacrifices that Christian Commission workers beheld—in hospitals, in camps, on the march, and on the field—were both beautiful and wonderful. But in many ways, other sacrifices and experiences occurred in the homes of saddened, anxious, and loyal family members of brave military personnel. The "mites" of poor men and women swelled into the millions, which the nation gave. Mothers and children considered it a privilege to forego many luxuries and comforts in order that the boys at the war might be helped and cheered. The purpose of this chapter is to preserve a few of the many incidents of the home side of the war.

Penniless Man Gives

Mr. Charles Demond, one of the original members of the Christian Commission, provided oversight of Commission work in New England, which brought him in close contact with those who prayed and gave. He furnishes the following account:

At a meeting in a small town in New Hampshire, Professor E. T. Quimby of Dartmouth College, who had been a delegate in the Army of the Cumberland, told his experience. When the boxes were passed at a meeting, an old man of eighty put in a small, red cotton handkerchief. The collector, thinking be had made a mistake, was about to return it. But the old man motioned to retain it.

When the meeting was over, the clergyman at the church approached the speaker and said, "Captain Weston has given to you the last thing he owned that he could give. A few years ago, only one of his sons was available to care for his elderly parents and they looked to him for support in their declining years. When war broke out, the son felt it was his duty to enlist and his father gave him his blessing. The son now fills a soldier's grave in the South. Since his death, the old man has supported himself and his aged wife by his own labor. He is utterly penniless. He recently told me that he would be glad to do something benevolent but, 'for six months,' he said, "I have had but three cents of my own.'"

Giving Out of a Pure Heart

Reverend E. G. Parsons, of Derry, New Hampshire, served as a delegate in the Potomac Army. In a letter to me, dated July 28, 1864, he wrote, "I told my little story to my congregation last Sunday afternoon and took up a collection. Afterward, a good lady, who has a son in the Union Army, sent in a silver dollar. With it, she sent this message: 'Twenty years ago, my dying mother gave me this dollar, which I have cherished to the utmost. That mother, if now living, would have five grandsons in the army. One has fallen on the battlefield and another has barely escaped death, suffering with a malignant disease. I think she would have given this dollar for the soldiers!' Acting on the convictions of her mother's wishes, she sends the precious coin to your treasury."
(Charles Demond)

Giving Out of Pure Motives

One of the most touching incidents I remember was that of a widow who sent me her wedding ring. First, she gave her only son to die for the country and then she did not withhold this dear pledge of love, made sacred by the death of him who gave it. Such benevolence gives patriotism a purer luster. It even makes the smoke and carnage of battle radiant with the reflected brightness of heaven.
(Charles Demond)

Power of a Changed Life

Mr. B. F. Jacobs, Secretary of the Chicago Branch of the Christian Commission, tells two incidents from scenes while on his collection tours through the Northwest:

Speaking at Mineral Point, Wisconsin after the addresses were over, we were raising a contribution and men were announcing their pledges. A soldier in the far gallery rose and said, "Maloney, five dollars."

Three or four gentlemen who stood near me immediately remarked, "He can't afford to give a cent. He ought not to do it. He has a wife and four children and they are very, very poor. He has hardly been able to support them with his soldier's pay."

At the close of the meeting, I asked for him and he came forward to the desk. "Mr. Maloney," I said, "they say you ought not to give five dollars to this cause."

"They don't know anything about it," he said very emphatically.

"Well, do you think you ought to?"

"Let me tell you," he said, "Seven years ago when you were a clerk in Chicago, I used to buy goods from you. I failed in business and became depressed until I was nothing but a miserable, wretched, drunken sinner. My wife and children were well-nigh beggars—and almost worse than that before I entered the army. In Virginia, I was led to the Christian Commission meetings where I gave my heart to the Lord Jesus Christ. After that, I saved every dollar of my pay to send home. Before that, I never sent home a cent. All that I have, all that my family has, and all that I hope to receive in eternity under the blessing of God, I owe to the Commission. Don't you think I ought to give five dollars?"

Gratitude for Fruitful Ministry

Early in 1864, a Commission meeting was held in Milwaukee. After the audience had departed, I discovered that a lady was waiting to speak with me. She was standing near the doorway dressed as one in deep mourning.

When I went to meet her, she extended her hands with great sincerity and said, "I could not go away without thanking you and telling you how grateful I am."

I replied, "You must be mistaken, as I do not remember having met you before."

"Oh, no! I'm not mistaken. It makes no difference. Any delegate of the Christian Commission would be the same."

"What has the Commission done for you, madam?"

"My only son died in the hospital at Memphis. I was too poor to go and see my boy after the letter came telling me that he was sick. But a lady delegate of the Commission visited him daily, ministered to his wants, and comforted him in his loneliness. Above all, she led him to Jesus. When he was dead, the same lady cut off a lock of his hair and sent it to me in a letter with his dying words. *She was a mother to my boy*. And as long as I live while the Christian Commission lasts, I want to pray for God's blessing upon all who love it and work for it." (B. F. Jacobs)

Earning Trust

Mr. B. F. Jacobs, Secretary of the Chicago branch of the Christian Commission, illustrates both the confidence placed in those connected with the Commission and the "stuff" of which many a soldier was made:

A man came into my office in Chicago about the first of May 1864. He was an Irishman. He said, "I want to see Mr. Jacobs, the Secretary of the Christian Commission."

I told him I was the man and he replied, "I have come to ask a favor of you. I've been in the service since April 1861. I was rather wild before that. After I enlisted, I saw how men went straight to ruin and I made up my mind I would try and save myself and my money. I have saved up $700. Before the war, I lived in Chicago and at the end of my second enlistment, I have returned with that amount of money. I have bought a house and lot on the west side of the city and paid the $700 down payment and mortgaged the balance, payable after one year. I have reenlisted and am going back to Virginia. I have no relatives in this country except a brother in New York, who is quite well off. I want to put my property in trust with someone—and I want you to take it. Here are the papers which I have drawn up myself. I have been protected so far but I may fall in the next battle, so I have brought my will also. Will you take charge of the matter for me?"

I told him I was a perfect stranger to him and hesitated about assuming the trust. I asked, "Who recommended me to you?"

"Nobody," he answered, "but I have been in the army and have seen the delegates of the Commission and how faithful they have been. I am sure they won't steal. That's the reason I have hunted you up. Won't you take charge of all this until I come back, if ever I do?"

I opened the will and read it. In case of his death, if unmarried, he had arranged that his property should go to the Commission with a proviso remunerating me for my services. This latter directive was changed on the spot. I then asked, "Why did you will your money to the Commission?

"I know of no men to whom I would so soon give my money as to the soldiers of the army. And even though I have never needed the services of Commission Chaplains in a hospital, I have seen what they have done for others. They have given me little books at times. I know if I leave my money to them, the soldiers will get every cent of it."

I humbly accepted the trust. As the soldier went away to war, I spoke to him of the duty he owed to God.

The man lived to return from the war. He paid off the mortgage on his house, took back the deed and will, and is now a member of the Young Men's Christian Association of Chicago.

God's Enablement in Fundraising

Mr. William Reynolds, the President of the Peoria Committee, compiled numerous narratives out of his wide-ranging and successful experience as a volunteer fundraiser. He furnishes the following incidents:

Chaplain McCabe, who ministered at the infamous Libby Prison in Richmond, Virginia, came to Peoria. Here we determined to canvass Central Illinois for the purpose of raising fifty thousand dollars. Our first meeting was held in Galesburg where $1800 was collected. We then traveled to Peoria and Bloomington, where $1500 from each city was raised. We then went to Jacksonville and held a meeting at "Strawn's Hall," where $2000 was contributed.

I knew that Mr. Jacob Strawn, owner of the largest farm in the State of Illinois, lived two miles outside of Jacksonville. The next morning, we went out to his house to solicit a contribution. He was away but we understood that he was going to Springfield the following day. Meeting him on the train, we presented the cause. He said he knew nothing about the Christian Commission but was on his way to call on Governor Yates. If Yates said it was all right, he would make a contribution and he appointed an hour to meet us at the hotel.

We met him at the prescribed hour. He informed us he had seen the Governor, who had told him the Commission was "all right—a good institution." He then wrote a check for $500 and handed it to me, saying, "If you raise $10,000 from the farmers of Morgan County, I'll make it $10,000 instead of $500." We thought the sum was too large to acquire, especially since Mr. Strawn refused to let us count the $2000 just raised in Jacksonville. Our efforts to have the sum reduced to $5000 were unsuccessful. We had no alternative but to work for the $10,000, trusting in God to open up the hearts of the people.

Mr. M. P. Ayres, a Jacksonville banker, encouraged us to accept the proposition. He promised the aid of his extensive network of acquaintances, throughout the county, in setting up meetings and in arranging for full attendance by the people. He saw to it that we had eleven meetings in various parts of the county—in school houses, small churches, and groves. We entered into this "boxing match" and, within nine days, held eleven meetings and raised $11,400. A noteworthy item is that the meetings occurred in July, the farmers' busiest season. Many came from their fields to the meeting places and immediately returned to their work after hearing us.

Wealthy Man's Gift

When we came back to Mr. Strawn with proof of our success in hand, he immediately gave us his check, remarking, "Pretty smart fellows. I didn't think you would do it."

After dinner he took us to the top of his house to show us his splendid farms lying in every direction, as far as the eye could see. I asked, "How many acres do you own?"

"Forty thousand—all under cultivation."

"How much is the land worth by the acre?"

"Not less than $50, sir."

"Then you are worth $2,000,000. Am I correct?"

"Yes. I made it all myself. When I started, I didn't have fifty cents."

A look of pride flushed his face while his eyes swept the country in every direction. I turned to him and asked, "Mr. Strawn, you have asked me to look north and south, east and west, and view your possessions. You say I cannot see the end. Now may I ask you to look up yonder. How much do you own up there?"

"Ah," he said, the tears filling his eyes, "I'm afraid I am poor up there."

At this point, I tried to point him to the treasures and the mansions above.

This was the largest single donation ever received by the U. S. Christian Commission. Mr. Strawn died very suddenly about one year later.

(William Reynolds)

God's Intervention in Fundraising

I went to Sparta, a little town in Monroe County, Wisconsin, where I was a complete stranger. This visit took place shortly after the Wilderness battles. To the large crowd of people who had gathered, I set forth the objectives and labors of the Commission but felt, somehow, that they might be unwilling to believe a stranger's words about so great a work. I longed for a familiar face, someone in the audience to whom I could appeal for an endorsement. But everyone was unknown to me. While speaking, I had noticed a one-armed soldier sitting immediately in front of me. I watched his face with great interest to see what impression my story was making upon him.

When I had concluded and was calling for contributions, this soldier rose and said, "I would like to say a word, citizens, before the collection is taken up. You all know me, who I am, and where I came from. I have lived here a long time in your neighborhood. I enlisted in the first regiment that went from this district and fought through the battles of the Wilderness. Near the end of one day's fight, I fell wounded. I dragged myself under a bush to conceal myself from the enemy and lay there. Night came on.

"I was thinking I would die before morning if I don't get help. It grew very late and, still, no one came. At last, I heard a sound as if there might be help in the distance. I tried to call out but my voice was too weak. It went but a short way. Finally, a light came near me. I summoned all my energies and raised my voice to its loudest. Soon I saw a lantern approaching. A man's voice asked, "What is the matter?" I told him I was dreadfully wounded. He set his lantern down and started off to get assistance. Soon I heard the sound of wheels and an ambulance had come for me. He put me into it. From that time until I was well enough to come home on furlough—no, until I reached Chicago—I was never outside of the care of the delegates of the Christian Commission. Citizens, I owe my life to them."

Unbounded enthusiasm generated by this testimony found practical expression in an excellent collection. From that time forward, we were reminded often of the soldier's testimony by the contributions, which regularly found their way to us from that little town.
(William Reynolds)

Mother's Contribution to War Effort

The story of Mrs. Ellet of Philadelphia recalls the memory of some of the deeds of the mothers of Civil War soldiers:

Mr. Stuart, the Chairman of the Commission, and Reverend Dr. Robert Patterson of Chicago, called upon Mrs. Ellet in early 1863. She brought out two valuable and beautiful shawls, the proceeds of which she wished to have distributed among the widows and orphans of soldiers who had fallen in battle.

The dead body of her grandson had just arrived and Dr. Patterson expressed the hope that God would sustain her through her bereavement. She stated that she had given her two sons—Commodore Charles Ellet of the Ram Fleet and Brigadier General A. W. Ellet of the Marine Brigade, as well as four grandsons—to the war effort.

She then added, *"I do not regret the gift to my country. If I had twenty sons, I would give them all, for the country must be preserved. And if I was twenty years younger, I would go myself and fight to the last."*

Lincoln Addresses Mother's Grief

Few men in the country could so appreciate the motherly sacrifice, which was being made all over the land as did President Lincoln. His letter to a pious widow living in Boston deserves a place in history, along with his speech at Gettysburg and his second inaugural address:

EXECUTIVE MANSION, WASHINGTON, *Nov. 21, 1864.*

DEAR MADAM: I have been shown in the files of the War Department a statement of the Adjutant General of Massachusetts that you are the mother of five sons who have died gloriously on the field of battle.

I feel how weak and fruitless must be any words of mine which should attempt to beguile you from the grief of a loss so overwhelming; but I cannot refrain from tendering to you the consolation that may be found in the thanks of the Republic they died to save.

I pray that Our Heavenly Father may assuage the anguish of your bereavement and leave only the cherished memory of the loved and lost, and the solemn pride that must be yours to have laid so costly a sacrifice upon the altar of Freedom.

Yours, very sincerely and respectfully,
A. LINCOLN.

To Mrs. BIXBY, Boston, Massachusetts:

To receive such a letter, written by him who, within a few months, was to realize the sacrifice about which he here writes, seems almost a compensation for the loss.

Father's Caring Words

The following soldier's letter needs no introduction. Its reading moistened every eye at the meeting, which organized the Central New York Branch of the Christian Commission in Utica:

FORT BAKER, *Oct. 20, 1864.*

DEAR LOTTIE: I found a small white envelope among the others that you put into my box before I came away from home and I knew that you put it there because you wanted me to write to you. Well, it always does us good to please those that love us and I am glad to think that my little girl would be pleased to have me write to her. It is a pleasant task for me and the thought of good, loving children at home who think of me every day who, for my sake, are trying to be good to their mother and make her happy is a source of comfort and encouragement and consolation that I cannot describe with my pen nor tell with my tongue.

How far this thought goes or how much it contributes to reconcile me to the separation that, for their sakes, I have voluntarily endured, you can never realize. I know that you do not realize that I am here because I love you and that you do not appreciate the necessity of my being here. But by and bye, when you grow up, you will understand things better and, when you read in history of this war and of its causes and objects, you will be glad that your father left home when you were a little girl and went forth to contend for the right. You will love me all the more then and so will all the rest of my children.

This is the thought that encourages and consoles me. And then, besides this, the consciousness of none other than good and pure motives and, above all, the consolation from day to day that religion affords me, all these things contribute to make me happy, even while the constant longing, lingering anxiety about my home and family keeps them in my thoughts every moment.

Try and be good, Lottie, if you love me and want to do what you can to make me happy. Be good to your mother and grandmother and brothers and sisters. Try and be good to the Lord, and then you will be happy yourself and everybody will love you. And if I should never see you again on earth, we shall meet in heaven.

I pray for you many times every day and I want you to pray for yourself and me. Try to learn in your books. Always go to school and Sunday school when you can. Save this letter until you get old.

Tell Harry I will write to him before long and let Freddy know that I mean to send him some pretty stones I have picked up for him. Kiss all the family for me, from grandma to the baby, and love them all. God bless you!

FATHER.

Epilogue: The father who penned this letter received his mortal wound the next day.

Caring Project Reaps Fruit

Occasionally throughout these chapters, the story of a "comfort bag" or "housewife" (sewing kit) has been told. These were mainly the gifts of little children and often contained letters to soldiers, which, in turn, brought replies from the camps and hospitals. This caused many a pleasant and profitable correspondence to spring up. Reverend E. P. Smith, while a delegate early in 1863 near Belle Plain, Iowa, wrote back to his Sunday school at Pepperell, Massachusetts concerning these bags:

It seems that the Sunday school children in Albany united to send "comfort bags" to the soldiers. On a particular Sunday, each scholar brought a bag to her class. The superintendents collected them and on Monday, when they came to count them, they found five thousand bags ready to go. They came in boxes to the Christian Commission office at Washington and have been given out, one by one, to the soldiers in this army.

If you could see their faces when I hand out a bag and say, "Boys, do you want any needles, pins, thread and buttons? Some little Sunday school girl made this for you and sent it to me to give to you."

They would say, "*To give to us?* Bully for you! A *new kind of sutler*, boys!" (That's a fellow who follows the regiments to sell them things.) "See here, Jim, if a fellow goes ragged after this, he's a *bummer*." (That's a soldier's name for loafer.) "Sunday school girls, eh? Those are great little girls. They don't forget the boys gone a-soldiering." "I used to go to Sunday school." "That's where I belong." "I have got a little girl in Sunday school. Wonder if she had a hand in one of these bags."

This is how they talk until I am out of sight. Some of them pull out the tract and some find a letter in the bag and read it aloud. The news that Vicksburg was taken by Union troops would not awaken more lively and pleasant feelings among the men than a quantity of these bags you have freely given.

I read some of the letters. Here is one as nearly as I can remember it:

"DEAR SOLDIER: It must be hard for you to keep your clothes nice, so far away that your mother cannot come to mend them. So I send you this bag of needles and thread and you can mend for yourself. I would send you a thimble but mother says you could not use it. Now I hope you will keep your clothes very nice, so that when the ragged Confederates see you, they will be ashamed of themselves.

"We talk about you and pray about you in the Sunday school concert and, every night, I pray, 'God bless the soldier!' Good-bye, soldier!

> From your young friend,
> HATTIE"

I suspect the soldier will put that letter in his New Testament and, if he lives to go home, it will go with him.

Sunday School's Project of Caring

Some children in Lewistown, Pennsylvania sent a box of seventy-three "housewives" (sewing kits) to the army in February 1864. Each child enclosed a note with the little writer's name and address. After awhile, the answers came back. The one man who read them all, writes of them:

One of the letters spoke of verses contained in his little "housewife." The soldier said he had never felt the great importance of the words before then. Another spoke of the "housewife's" usefulness and said he would always carry it with him and, if he fell, it would fall with him. Another said that, on his return home, he would go quite a distance out of his way to see and thank his "little friend Hallie." Another wrote that he called himself a Christian but "somehow he did not get along as he would like" but promised to renew his efforts in "walking the narrow way."

Another had made a profession of faith five years ago but, sadly, had gone astray. Now he had renewed afresh his "covenant with God" and he prayed for strength to endure unto the end. Another was one of six who, on the previous Sunday, had been baptized. He was from Maine and had been away from home for four years. He could apply the beautiful verses contained in his gift. They had touched a tender chord in his heart.

Another brave fellow's acknowledgment reads this way:

"I have received your kind gift, for which I return my most grateful thanks. I have been in the army two years—have been in all the battles my regiment has engaged in and have escaped unhurt. I thank the Almighty.

Our good chaplain preaches for us every evening. When I first joined the army I was wicked and would laugh at good men. But I had no parents. My father and mother died when I was young. I was taken by an uncle, who was a wicked man and let me run wild. I went to sea and enlisted after that. *This is the first time I have written a letter since I have been in the army* and it makes me feel *so happy* to have a chance to write to a friend."

The letters brought out the charm of the child authors. Their simple, hearty, confiding words caused the soldier to envision bright, sincere eyes following little hands that guided unsteady pens across the paper. This vision brought back all the remembrances and sweetness of home.

(E. P. Smith)

Child's Letter Witnesses through Caring

Mr. J. N. Stearns, the Editor of *Merry's Museum*, a Delegate at City Point, Virginia in July 1864, transcribes two of these children's epistles:

"BOSTON, MASSCHUSETTS

"I am but a very little girl, six years old. But I thought I would like to make a comfort bag for you as well as the big ones.

"I go to the Shawmut Infant School. I know lots of verses in God's Holy Book. I have got a mother but do not have a dear father. I hope he is living in heaven with Jesus Christ.

"TENY."

Child's Letter of Caring

"NEW IPSWICH, NEW HAMPSHIRE.

"MY DEAR SOLDIER: I wonder whether you are a well or a wounded soldier. I hope you are not sick. I am a little boy, nine years old. I hope you love Jesus Christ. I hope you will love Him, if you do not. I shall pray for you. I hope you will write me a letter if you have time. From

"JOHN W. CUMMINGS."

(J. N. Stearns)

Witness from Child's Letter

The following, written by a very little girl whose brother had fallen on the battlefield, is from the *Sunday School Times*, dated January 7, 1865:

"DEAR SOLDIER: It is Sunday afternoon and I thought it would be so nice to print you a little letter to put in the bags I finished yesterday. Mamma gives my brother Charlie and me twenty-five cents a week each for giving up sugar. We have earned a good deal of money already to give to the soldiers, so we both bought some of the things to put in the six bags. I hope you will take as much comfort as I did in making them for you. I hope this cruel war will be over soon and let you come home to your children and friends. Won't we all be happy then! I pray to God every day to bless you and bring you home. I hope you love Jesus. If you do not live to get home, I hope you will go home to Him, where I hope to meet you. Good-bye.

"From your little friend,
MINNIE OLIVE C."

(J. N. Stearns)

Expression of Appreciation

Reverend Luther Keene, Pastor of the Congregational Church, North Brookfield, Massachusetts, was a delegate during October and November 1863. He gives the following account of an interesting letter a soldier sent to two little children of his parish:

As I was going away to serve as a Christian Commission delegate, little Charlie Huntingdon and Katie Walker gave me a little money for the soldiers. With the money, I bought a Bible and intended to hand it to some soldier. But illness so hastened my return home that I left it with Reverend Mr. Bowler, the Agent at Washington. The address of the two children was written on the flyleaf, along with this request:

"Will the soldier who receives this book, when he is converted, please write a letter to these children to tell them about it?"

About six months after my return, they received the following reply:

"To Katie Walker and Charlie Huntingdon,

North Brookfield, Massachusetts:

"Reverend Mr. Bowler gave me the Bible you wanted to give to a soldier. It gives me great pleasure to acknowledge its receipt. I have a great many things to tell you but you know a poor soldier does not have a great many advantages. If you were here with me, wouldn't we have a nice time? I would take you to the 'front' and show you the big guns and the soldiers on dress parade. I would tell you how they fight when they are in the line of battle. I would tell you about the fourteen regular engagements I have been in and how I was wounded five times. I would also tell you about how the Confederates took me prisoner for three months and gave me very little to eat—and how God delivered me safely back again.

"And then I would tell you how I used to drink a great amount of alcohol and what a bad man I once was. But now, I don't drink at all and, oh, how I love to read the little Bible you sent me. I would share my rations with you and give you my cot. We would say a little prayer together and I would kiss your foreheads. Then God would watch over you and me until we awoke again to enjoy His love, His sunlight, His flowers in their spring bloom and their glorious fragrance—and then we would praise Him again.

"I dearly love little children because I see God in their ways. So let your little hands be busy at all times and bend your tender hearts to the service of God. Never waste one moment because life is very short. In Southern climes, the firefly shines beautifully when it flies at dusk but it looks ugly the very moment it rests. So it is with us. We are beautiful while we are working in the vineyard of God but seem to grow ugly when we turn toward worldly things.

"Now, my little friends, you will continue to be good, will you not? And you will say a little prayer for me now and then—asking the good Lord to forgive me for what wrongs I have done and to make me good in the future.

"I sincerely thank you for the Bible and your loving concern. If you would like to hear from me again, it would be my pleasure to write you. If you have little pictures, kindly send them to me. And now, 'may God bless you and keep your hearts full of the Holy Spirit' is the prayer of,

"Yours very affectionately,

"E. H. Uniac
"Camp Distribution, Virginia
"Care of U. S. C. C."

Epilogue: Following the war, Mr. Uniac worked as a successful Temperance Lecturer.

Honoring through Practicality

Chaplain J. C. Thomas, who served with the 83rd Illinois Regiment, tells how a little Chicago girl made herself useful to sick soldiers in the Western Army:

Jennie D_____ wanted to do something for the sick soldiers. She remembered how they were deprived of the delicacies and comforts of life and her heart yearned for their relief. Not discouraged, as so many are because they cannot do everything, she resolved to "do what she could." She decided to save her lumps of sugar. When she had accumulated more than a pound of sugar in the spring of 1863, she asked our Brigade Quartermaster to deliver it to the Army of the Cumberland.

Upon his return, he handed me a package, labeled: "Lump sugar saved by Jennie D_____, a little girl six-years old, to give to some sick soldiers."

"Do you know any sick soldiers, Chaplain," asked the Quartermaster, "who need that?"

"Yes, sir, a good many of them," I replied.

At a prayer meeting in my tent, I held up the package and told the men present what the little girls at home thought of the soldiers. They were not accustomed to tears but, if I am not mistaken, an unusual glistening of the eyes took place as they looked at the package. Afterward, I carried it to the four Regimental Hospitals in our Brigade and gave a lump of sugar to every sick man, telling him who sent it.

How happy the poor boys were at this child's practical remembrance! They made all sorts of grateful and thoughtful remarks.

Child Gives Honor

One more incident of the children's interest in the soldiers is told by Reverend Robert J. Parvin, Rector of St. Paul's Protestant Episcopal Church, Cheltenham, Pennsylvania:

I had been addressing a meeting in Rochester, New York toward the close of 1864. A little girl was greatly interested in my story and wrote to me after my return to Philadelphia. She enclosed a small contribution:

ROCHESTER, *December 23rd,* 1864.

DEAR MR. PARVIN: What you said about the Soldiers has made me think of them very often every day and when I kneel down at night. It makes me very happy to send some of my Christmas money to buy some little comfort for a Soldier. (Mamma says I should use a little "s" for Soldiers, *but I think they deserve capital letters.*)

I mean to do all that a little girl can to help you.

Your affectionate friend,
JENNIE LEE.

Measure of Christian Commission's Success

These illustrative sketches of purposes, saved lives, and deeds begotten of the war will find an appropriate closing page in the words of Reverend Herrick Johnson, Pastor of (N. S.) Presbyterian Church, Pittsburg, Pennsylvania, and delegate about the time of the Wilderness battles. These remarks brought to a close his address at the last Anniversary of the Christian Commission in the Capitol at Washington:

"Once I was privileged to stand upon the summit of Mount Righi in Switzerland and, from its queenly perch, witness an autumn sunset. Far away to the west, the monarch of day wrapped the drapery of his couch about him and lay down as if he were a god revealed. He flung his splendors on that unequaled landscape with royal magnificence. He kissed the waters that lay embosomed among the hills until they all blushed. The bald peaks to the right and the left of us bared their storm-beaten brows and bathed in the sunlight. Higher up and farther away, the snowcapped monarchs of the Alps tossed back the sun's last rays from their icy sides in cold and proud disdain.

"But, more beautiful than all, the gem of that most wondrous picture was the bridge of golden sheen that stretched over hills and valleys, the lakes and dells from the far distant horizon to our very feet. It seemed as if heaven's gates had been left open and glory had stolen through. It was cast up by the hand of God, a path of gold on which angels might have trodden.

"So I have stood beside the dying soldier when it seemed as if a bridge of golden sheen were let down from heaven, a highway for the ransomed of the Lord. And that way, cast up of God, has glowed with the steps of the angels, which come to bear the soldier—who has made his last charge and fought his last battle—*home.* And up that shining path with angel convoy, the spirit has gone—away from the clang of arms and the din of strife and the groans of the wounded—away, away to the very gates of pearl, to the Peace like a river and to the Eternal Rest of God.

"Oh, *there* are the undying tokens and proof of the success of the Commission. The Nation may point to its States won back from treason! The army may point to its battle flags wrung from the foe by vigor and valor and victory! Generals may point to their starred shoulders as proofs of undaunted heroism! Sanitary Agencies may roll up their peerless record of sublime beneficence!

But *there*, up *there*, are the souls that are marching on—marching on! *There* are the trophies immortal that have been snatched from death! *There* are the unfading stars that have been set in Christ's diadem through the agency of this Christian Commission."

THE MESSAGE OF THE U.S. CHRISTIAN COMMISSION TO SOLDIERS

Amidst the bloodshed of Civil War battles, it became critical to quickly identify the needs of wounded soldiers. After assessing the physical needs of the soldier many delegates asked, "Is Jesus precious to you?" Apparently, experience had revealed this question as the quickest way to discover the spiritual needs of the casualties. If the answer was affirmative, fellowship and prayer followed. If the answer was in the negative, a brief invitation to faith in Christ followed. The delegates came from denominational churches of the period. There was general theological unity related to the Gospel message. Its core was based on Paul the Apostle's definition in 1 Corinthians 15:1-8:

> Moreover, brethren, I declare unto you the gospel which I preached unto you, which also you have received, and wherein you stand; By which also you are saved, if you keep in memory what I preached unto you, unless you have believed in vain. For I delivered unto you first of all that which I also received, how that Christ died for our sins according to the scriptures; And that he was buried, and that he rose again the third day according to the scriptures: And that he was seen of Peter, then of the twelve: After that, he was seen of above five hundred brethren at once; of whom the greater part remain unto this present, but some are fallen asleep. After that, he was seen of James; then of all the apostles. And last of all he was seen of me also, as of one born out of due time.[1]

In simple form, the Gospel message presentation would likely have followed the Apostle's message:

For all have sinned, and come short of the glory of God. (Romans 3:23)

But God commendeth his love toward us, in that, while we were yet sinners, Christ died for us. (Romans 5:8)

For the wages of sin is death; but the gift of God is eternal life through Jesus Christ our Lord. (Romans 6:23)

But what saith it? The word is nigh thee, even in thy mouth, and in thy

---

[1] The Holy Bible: King James Version.

heart: that is, the word of faith, which we preach; That if thou shalt confess with thy mouth the Lord Jesus, and shalt believe in thine heart that God hath raised him from the dead, thou shalt be saved. For with the heart man believeth unto righteousness; and with the mouth confession is made unto salvation. (Romans 10:8-10)

Is Jesus precious to you?

For more insight or to leave comments about *Triumph*, visit:
www.CivilWarStories.org